*This publication has been made
possible by a grant from the
Pepsi-Cola Alton Bottling Company
(Alton, Illinois) through
the generosity of its
President, Mr. Nick Maggos.*

KOSTER
An Artifact Analysis of Two Archaic Phases in Westcentral Illinois

by Thomas Genn Cook

Prehistoric Records, No. 1
Koster Research Reports, No. 3

NORTHWESTERN UNIVERSITY ARCHEOLOGICAL PROGRAM • 1976 • EVANSTON, ILLINOIS

The Northwestern Archeological Program, Stuart Struever

Goals of the Program

THE NORTHWESTERN University Archeological Program was begun in 1964 and has four objectives.

1. *To excavate and interpret the archeological record of the American Midwest.* It is believed that this record is at least 12,000 years long. All cultures in the Midwest prior to the 17th century were nonliterate. This means that written documentation is absent for more than 98% of the cultural history of the Great Lakes and prairie areas to the south. Archeological sites are the only remaining record of this prehistory.

The Northwestern Archeological Program has focused its field activities on sections of the Illinois and Mississippi valleys, where complex cultural developments occurred in prehistory. In many ways, it is believed, these valleys were the center of cultural development during most prehistoric periods. Yet these valleys are the scene today of urban and industrial expansion that has resulted in extensive destruction of archeological sites.

It is imperative that research effort be focused on these valleys while they can still yield important archeological information.

2. *To develop and refine new archeological methods.* In the past 20 years American archeology has gone through more rapid change than in perhaps any comparable period before that time. Significant new goals - focusing on an understanding of cultural process and biological interactions - have been defined for archeology.

Achieving these goals is dependent on new approaches to archeological research. These range from developing more effective institutional structures to support large-scale, programmatic research, to innovation in every phase of research performance from initial project design through excavation and laboratory analysis.

The Northwestern Archeological Program is exploring a variety of field and laboratory methods that appear to have significant potential for increasing the archeologist's capacity for reading the prehistoric record. Through its Kampsville Archeological Center, it is attempting to develop more effective strategies for integrating 15 or more natural and social science disciplines into truly interdisciplinary research. These disciplines range from cultural and biological anthropology to statistics, from nutrition to zoology.

3. *To provide a complete clinical training program geared to the needs of students becoming archeologists at a time when this science is undergoing rapid change.* Traditional graduate programs in universities generally have not incorporated many of the new techniques and methods of archeology into their curricula. The Northwestern Archeological Program is making these curriculum changes in an attempt to

stimulate similar changes in other university archeological programs.

A variety of clinical training courses have been developed in archeology, bioanthropology, and collaborating disciplines. More than a dozen of these courses are now taught each year at the Kampsville Archeological Center during the Summer and Fall quarters.

4. *To develop an organized program for training scientists in the interfaces between archeology, bioanthropology, and various natural sciences (zoology, pollen analysis, geology, etc.).* These specialists, working with the archeologist, are able to develop models for environments on local and regional levels during thousands of years of midwestern prehistory. Without them, the study of man-land relationships in prehistory is not possible. It is in this relationship that archeologists hope in part to discover general principles of cultural change.

Geographic Focus of the Field Program

The focus of the Northwestern Archeological Program is a 40- by 70-mile area immediately north of the confluence of the Illinois and Mississippi rivers. This area continued as a major center of prehistoric cultural development for thousands of years, a fact that probably relates to the incredibly rich and stable resources of the river floodplains.

Aside from its long and complex culture history, there are practical reasons why the lower Illinois Valley is an ideal field laboratory for the development of new methods and approaches in archeology: (1) Today this region is sparsely populated farmland, its southern limits separated from the St. Louis metropolitan area by the Mississippi River which has acted as an effective barrier to the northward spread of the city. Thus the lower Illinois Valley has escaped the widespread site destruction that has greatly reduced the archeological research potential of many comparable river valleys throughout the U.S. (2) The cost of performing research in the lower Illinois is as low as can be expected anywhere in the world. (3) Extensive information on climate, landforms, soils, water resources, flora and fauna is available on this region. These data provide an essential baseline for the cultural-ecological studies which are a major focus of NAP research.

The *cost* of doing archeological research has been too long overlooked as a significant factor affecting both the limitations archeologists impose on the goals of their research and the outcome of that research.

As long as archeological dollars are scarce, "cost" and "accessibility" are key factors when selecting an area for performing archeological fieldwork and experimenting with new methods. The cost of transportation between the university and the field, the cost of maintaining and operating a field headquarters, accessibility to cooperating natural scientists, accessibility to supplies and equipment, cost of transporting and maintaining students in the field, ability to maintain continuity in the field program in terms of political and economic factors, the prior availability of information on the natural environment (past and present), and the ease of transporting artifacts to the home institution and technical specialists to the field: All are factors which give the lower Illinois Valley a significant advantage as a testing ground for new archeological strategies and methods.

Educational Program

Research aside, the lower Illinois Valley provides an ideal environment for developing new educational programs in archeology. The 34 buildings of the Kampsville Archeological Center, 270 miles from the Evanston campus, present a retreat-like situation that enhances interaction among researchers and between researchers and students. Its dorm houses, dining hall, library, and other support facilities now enable the NAP to provide initial archeological field experience to an increasing number of students each year.

The Kampsville Center also provides an excellent context for the multidisciplinary training of professional archeologists. The summer and fall Kampsville programs combine training in excavation technique with laboratory experience in a number of disciplines relating specifically to archeology, e.g., bioanthropology, botany, geology, and zoology. Resident instructors, each with his own teaching laboratory, train students in the rationale and techniques of their special disciplines. Some students excavate artifacts from a prehistoric village while others process the recovered materials through a diverse series of operations which range from the conventional analysis of artifacts to the study of plant and animal remains reflective of prehistoric subsistence and the study of snails and soils that disclose the environmental setting to which early cultures adapted.

Over several Summer or Fall quarters the student has the opportunity to participate in a variety of field and laboratory operations, thus providing him with a sense of the various disciplines and how they achieve integration within the total research program.

Research Program

A major focus of the Northwestern Archeological Program has been the delineation of economic (particularly subsistence) activities, settlement patterns, population changes and interdependent human biological changes that characterize the various phases of the Archaic, Woodland, and Mississippian periods ranging from 8000 B.C. to A.D. 1600. Efforts have been made to identify adaptive junctures, periods of significant change in the adaptations of lower Illinois Valley cultures. This work has led to the generation and testing of models that explain the observed shifts.

By 1975, more than nine separate but related research projects were underway in the lower Illinois Valley. All of these, each headed by one or more members of the NAP faculty, are conducted as separately defined projects, projects which have grown out of a series of closely reasoned questions stemming from earlier observations on the cultural and biological history of the lower Illinois region. Therefore, in a very real sense, the individual projects are mutually dependent and supportive; together they form a comprehensive approach to the culture history of a single world area.

The intensity of focus that the NAP has given lower Illinois Valley prehistory is unusual in archeology. There are both practical and philosophical reasons for the general lack of intensive research by archeologists into the prehistory of a single geographic area. Nonetheless, it is believed that such an intense focus, supported by an appropriate research design and a panoply of new methods and techniques, can produce a degree of detail in the prehistoric data that will enhance observation of relationships between cultural variables, and between cultural variables and environmental and human biological variables, making possible the generation of significant explanatory models that might otherwise elude the archeologist. Only time will tell whether this geographically focused research effort will produce a significantly higher level of interpretation for archeology.

Publication of Research Results

Between 1969 and 1973, the Northwestern Archeological Program published eight research monographs in cooperation with the Illinois State Museum. These eight studies comprise the *Research Papers* series of the NAP; these volumes were also listed as numbers in the State Museum's *Reports of Investigations* series. While this cooperation between institutions worked well, the growth of the archeological programs at both Northwestern University and the Illinois State Museum has made continuation of this publication arrangement impractical.

Therefore the Northwestern Archeological Program has begun the publication of research under its own imprint. Two volumes, by David L. Asch and Jane E. Buikstra, have been published in a series entitled *Scientific Papers*. These volumes explore questions of demography and human biology and their interactions with cultural variables during the Middle Woodland period.

The present study, by Thomas Genn Cook inaugurates a second NAP series, *Prehistoric Records*. It is also the third in a continuing series of research reports on the Koster site. The *Koster Research Reports* include:

No. 1. Koster: A Stratified Archaic Site in the Lower Illinois Valley, Report of the 1969 Field Season, by Gail L. Houart. *Ill. Valley Archaeol. Program, Res. Pap.*, No. *4*. 1971

No. 2. Paleoethnobotany of the Koster Site: The Archaic Horizons, by Nancy B. Asch, Richard I. Ford, and David L. Asch. *Ill. Valley Archaeol. Program, Res. Pap.*, No. 6. 1972

No. 3. Koster: An Artifact Analysis of Two Archaic Phases in Westcentral Illinois, by Thomas Genn Cook. *Northwestern Archeol. Program, Prehis. Rec.*, Vol. 1. 1976

A fourth progress report consisting of 12 papers on various aspects of Koster research is forthcoming.

Stuart Struever
Evanston, Illinois

May, 1976

Contents

Illustrations

Tables

Acknowledgments

THIS STUDY reflects the combined intellectual influence of many scholars I have had the pleasure of knowing during the last several years at the University of Chicago, the University of Michigan, and Northwestern University. Foremost among these are the members of my doctoral dissertation committee at the University of Chicago: Robert McC. Adams, James A. Brown, Leslie G. Freeman, the late Paul S. Martin, and my chairman Stuart Struever. In addition, James B. Griffin and Edwin N. Wilmsen provided excellent training in North American archeology and lithic analysis during a semester I spent as a CIC Traveling Scholar at the University of Michigan.

I would like to thank the various researchers in the Koster research group for their aid, assistance, and encouragement: David Asch, Nancy Asch, Jane E. Buikstra, Karl Butzer, Della C. Cook, Frederick C. Hill, Gail Houart, Manfred E. Jaehnig, and James Schoenwetter to name a few. I would also like to thank Michael Daily for the artifact photographs, Ray E. Druhot for computer assistance, and Ronald R. Royce and Kenneth Brown for drafting.

In addition, the vast quantities of material analyzed here could not have been sorted, measured, weighed, and catalogued without the help of four excellent research assistants: Alice Berksen, Rose Duffield, Susan Hauser, and Renata B. Wolynec.

Finally, the research presented here was supported by a National Science Foundation Predoctoral Dissertation Improvement Grant (GS-30153) and by the Northwestern University Archeological Program. This generous support is gratefully acknowledged.

Thomas Genn Cook
Department of Anthropology
Indiana University

December 1975

1

Goals and Methods

GOALS

THE GOALS of the research presented here are --

1. To develop a multidimensional definition of the phase as a framework for hypothesis testing.
2. To develop and test an explicit model concerning tool-using tasks within specific phases.
3. To document adaptational shifts in the lower Illinois River valley region during the third millennium B.C.* using the results of the first two goals.

The archeological evidence used to achieve these three goals includes materials excavated from the Koster site in westcentral Illinois during 1969 and 1970, surface survey materials from the lower Illinois Valley region (through the 1974 survey season), and published materials.

PHASE DEFINITION

Neither the definition of the basic concept *phase* nor the definition of new phases have been adequately dealt with by the New Archeology. For example, Willey and Phillips (1958:22) define the phase as "an archaeological unit possessing traits sufficiently characteristic to distinguish it from all other units similarly conceived." But Binford's new systematics (1965:205) claims that culture should not be defined in terms of trait lists because a cultural system is multivariate and "its operation is to be understood in terms of many causally relevant variables which may function independently or in varying combinations." Dunnell's *Systematics in Prehistory* (1971) does not resolve the conflict between trait lists and causally related variables. Brown (1971a) recognizes the distinction between trait lists and understanding the cultural behavior which produced the archeological record, but does not make recommendations for redefining basic archeological units such as the phase.

The practical problem for phase definition is twofold. First, it is necessary to follow Binford's suggestions about the definition of culture so that we will be dealing with specific examples of multivariant systems when we speak of phases in terms of the New Archeology. Second, it is necessary to identify examples of these specific cultural systems in the archeological record. Willey and Phillips are using traits to separate segments of the archeological record. Binford is defining these separate segments in a systemic sense; they can be dealt with as prehistoric cultures. Therefore, the typological and systemic definitions of phases are actually different aspects of the phenomenon called the archeological record and serve somewhat different but complementary purposes.

The Eastern Archaic is a 7000-year period subdivided into three temporal periods (Early, Middle, and Late) by Griffin (1968:130-134) or into two successive adaptational stances (Formative and Exploitative) in Caldwell's *Trend and Tradition* (1958). Only rarely have

---

* The time scale and dates presented in this study are based on the uncorrected Libby half-life for radiocarbon.

finer subdivisions been defined for the Archaic (Coe 1964; Ritchie 1968; Winters 1969). For westcentral Illinois, one must deal either with *foci* such as the Titterington focus and the Kampsville focus or with major blocks of time defined from excavations at Graham Cave (Logan 1950; Klippel 1971) and Modoc Rock Shelter (Fowler and Winters 1956; Fowler 1959a). Because the excellent stratigraphy of the Koster site has left us with a succession of discrete, relatively short-term samples of the archeological record, it was decided to deal with each temporally distinct occupation as a phase. Such short-term phases would produce both a fine-grained control over systemic changes during the Archaic period and analytical units comparable to the later Woodland and Mississippian phases. However, because we wish to satisfy Willey and Phillips' typological approach to phases as well as Binford's systemic definition of culture, a new definition of phase is developed here. This new definition of phase, based upon dimensional analysis, is applied to the two occupations at Koster discussed in Chapters 3 and 4.

Clarke (1968:101-128) presents a model for the sociocultural system which is a composite of a number of subsystems: economy, social pattern, material culture, and religious pattern. These subsystems are always present although the manifestation of each subsystem and the interrelationships between each subsystem and the environment are changing at various rates through time. Therefore, we must consider these four subsystems plus the environment when we define archeological units such as the phase. In addition, there are situations in which some of the subsystems changed markedly, while others were relatively stable. For example, burial in earthen mounds begins before 3000 B.C., continues past A.D. 1000 in the Midwest, and hence is a custom of more than 4000 years' duration (although the particulars of burial changed during this period), while the economic basis of these same prehistoric periods changed radically (Yarnell 1964; Struever 1968a; Asch, Ford, and Asch 1972; Ford 1974:Fig. 2) from selective hunting and gathering, to intensive harvest collecting, and finally to maize agriculture.

Because these different subsystems are changing at different rates, the new definition of phase must take this into account. Clarke's subsystems are very difficult to work with directly. (One locality such as Koster site provides only a single example of each subsection.) I have developed a somewhat less abstract formulation: *dimensional analysis* (Huntley 1967; Brown 1971b). Dimensional analysis is merely an analytical technique to set systemic variables at comparable levels of abstraction. Instead of comparing pots, for example, one compares a more general class such as containers.

The dimensions chosen here represent major categories of data which reflect the workings of Clarke's model but which make provision for classifying prehistoric data. These dimensions include --

1. Stylistic dimensions
   a. Stylistic definition of certain key artifact forms
   b. Manufacturing trajectories as traditions
   c. Time-space distribution of dimensions 1a and 1b
2. Technological dimensions
   a. Manufacturing trajectories
   b. Tool types
   c. Tasks
3. Adaptational dimensions
   a. Classes of sites defined by maintenance and extractive tasks
   b. Subsistence-settlement systems
   c. Structure of segmentation of the society
4. Trade dimensions
   a. Exotic raw materials and styles
   b. Exported raw materials and styles
5. Mortuary dimensions
   a. Burial program
   b. Classes of mortuary sites
6. Human biology dimensions
7. Sociocultural dimensions

This brief listing is adequate for the Helton and Titterington phases. As more data become available, new dimensions can be added. For example, Brown (1971b:95) includes eight social dimensions for mortuary practices at Spiro, whereas only two are listed above.

Because the fundamental unit of analysis in processual archeology is a discrete episode of human behavior, or task as used here (Dimension 2c), the basic data set is not *artifactual* but can include any number of things such as artifacts, features, burial programs, trade systems, temple complexes, aspects of human biology and demography, climatic studies, ecofacts, and resource availability. Unfortunately, the time-space framework for North American archeology is based upon either trait lists such as the Midwestern Taxonomic System (see Dunnell [1971] for a discussion of this outdated system) or certain key artifact styles and stages of systemic complexity as conceived by Willey and Phillips (1958). Neither of these organizational schemes is adequate. The former leads to an endless description of traits rather than an analysis of how these traits go together. The latter defines whole cultures in terms of their diagnostic materials and on a priori assumptions assigns each phase to one of five levels of technical-adaptational-social complexity (Lithic, Archaic, Formative, Classic, and Post-Classic).

Another consideration of phase definition is that *horizon* and *tradition*, as defined by Willey and Phillips, are based upon artifacts rather than systemic variables. As a consequence, the study of systemic change in the past is greatly hampered by an organizational scheme which (1) deals with pseudovariables and (2) does not deal in directly comparable units.

Instead of accepting Willey and Phillips' definition of the phase, a more encompassing definition is developed here to exploit the expanded data set used in task analysis and the systemic definition of culture. This new definition of the archeological phase involves a multidimensional framework. Such a definition requires that we see culture as a complex system. To understand how these systems function and change, it is necessary to monitor systemic variables rather than artifacts or items.

For example, the relationship of rabbits and rainfall in one prehistoric adaptational system may have little to do with the relationships of hares and snowfall in some other system. Yet in both systems one is dealing with the problem of availability of biomass to prehistoric hunters. To get around this comparability problem, the technique of dimensional analysis is borrowed from formal analysis, especially as it is applied in the physical sciences (Huntley 1967). In the example given above, the dimensions might be climate, biomass, seasonal availability, hunting techniques, and the like, rather than rabbit bones, reconstructed rainfall, and net weights versus hare bones, reconstructed snowfall, and snare loops. Brown (1971b) presents a worked example using the social dimensions of mortuary practices rather than tabulations of mortuary furniture.

This dimensional phase meets two essential requirements: (1) that the definition of each phase be in terms of a number of dimensions such as style, technology, structure of segmentation, adaptation, trade, mortuary practices, and human biology rather than in terms of several distinctive artifact types or a stage name; (2) that the various dimensions of each phase be directly comparable, so that analogous parts of hunting and gathering, horticultural, and agricultural societies can be directly compared. Because change can be monitored within each dimension, the dimensional phase permits the development and testing of complex models explaining the interaction of such variables as diet, disease experience, land use, social organization, population density, style zones, and technology for a succession of temporal periods.

Therefore, we have a framework which makes possible the development of specific multidimensional definitions of prehistoric cultural systems. Obviously much archeological research will have to be done before we have reasonable models of these prehistoric systems. This then leads us back to Willey and Phillips. It is still necessary to "define an archaeological unit possessing sufficiently characteristic traits to distinguish it from all other units similarly conceived" (1956:22). Characteristics used to define prehistoric systems may have little or no value in differentiating these various systems. In fact, one would anticipate just the opposite. Therefore one becomes a taxonomist to determine which trait or traits just happen to distinguish one phase from all other phases. By analogy, the color of an automobile may have little or nothing to do with the fact that it has an internal combustion engine, is part of a highway transportation system, and is a status symbol. But the color may conveniently distinguish your car from someone else's.

Stylistic dimensions must be used first to separate phases from one another; otherwise it would not be possible to assign components of sites to their proper chronological/cultural position. It is best to start with materials which are as little mixed as possible, e.g., well stratified sites. Stylistic dimensions have a number of advantages in determining the time and space extent of single phases: single sites may have enough materials to define a phase's *characteristic* style; styles change relatively rapidly in the region under analysis and no other dimension provides a potentially finer grained control over time.

However, stylistic dimensions have a number of limitations. Stylistic change may reflect a number of factors. Style zones may be larger or smaller than the culture under analysis. Styles made from less plastic media (e.g., chert versus clay) are difficult to analyze. Stylistic elements on tools are to a certain extent under functional and material constraints. Stylistic materials at mortuary sites may be very different fron analogous objects found at habitation sites. At the same time, while stylistic elements permit us to define temporal blocks in the historic record, it must never be forgotten that we are studying cultural systems and not art objects. There must be constant feedback between systemic concepts and stylistic necessities. The definitions given here for the Helton and Titterington phases are merely the first, not the last, step in unfolding the Archaic period and new data will certainly modify these definitions.

METHODS: TOOL-USING TASKS

The fundamental unit of analysis in processual archeology is neither the artifact nor the site. Instead it is a discrete episode of human behavior called a *task* relating to maintenance, extractive, or social behavior (Binford and Binford 1966). An explicit model is developed (Chapter 2) to answer the basic question "What were the maintenance, extractive, and social tasks performed at a specific locality?" This model includes a series of 17 tasks, the tools used in these tasks, and the resultant debris and trash formed as a *direct* consequence of task performance. Tasks at a specific site are determined by the variety of tools present at that site. Then, if the explicit model is accurate, it will predict the trash and debris present at that site. Independent tests of the model and suggestions concerning the typology of the tasks and the typologies of the tool and debris classes are presented in Chapters 3 and 4.

Because the behavioral model involves tool usage and manufacture, Chapter 2 develops two different typologies of Koster site artifacts. The first typology assigns artifacts to manufacturing trajectories so that maintenance tasks can be recognized at Koster, while the second typology assigns artifacts to functional categories so that extractive tasks and tools-to-make-tools will also be recognized. Stylistic variability is largely ignored in these two typologies, except for projectile point types which are defined in App. A. The two typologies of Koster artifacts include objects made of chert, ground stone, antler, bone and teeth, and shell.

The typologies developed in Chapter 2 utilize the model for studying tool-using tasks. The categories chosen probably have little to do with the prehistoric desires of the manufacturers, despite Spaulding's beliefs (1953: 305), and they reflect only a small portion of the known variability in stone tools. Like Ford's ceramic typologies (1962) designed to maximize chronological information, the typologies developed here reflect function and manufacture, rather than a broad spectrum of variability (cf. Mellars 1970).

METHODS: ADAPTATIONAL SHIFTS

One of the major shifts in human adaptational strategies is the Neolithic Revolution (Childe 1936). This change from a subsistence base of collecting to growing one's food has been a primary focus of archeological research in both the Old and New worlds. In terms of current theory (Flannery 1973), Flannery's cybernetic model (1968) of increased use of genetically unstable maize plants in Mesoamerica (or similar models used elsewhere) provides a strong argument for in situ development of domestic foods and their cultivation.

Flannery's feedback model has obvious implications for the other aspects of prehistoric systems: social organization, population density, environmental fluctuations, and the like. These exogenous variables are very important in understanding why and when a deviation-amplification loop would form in the subsistence system. For example, Boserup (1965) developed an hypothesis relating technology, change, and population growth in terms of shifts of intensity of agriculture rather than concentrating upon a lock-step assumption that a single variable such as technology would explain systemic growth. One major reason that archeologists have not often included these exogenous variables in their models for the earliest stages of the Neolithic Revolution is simply the lack of knowledge concerning these variables. (See Smith and Young [1972:Fig. 1.4] for the Near East; MacNeish [1973] for portions of Mesoamerica, etc.) For the American Midwest, Prufer (1964), Struever (1968c), Farnsworth (1973), and Roper (1974) among others have examined subsistence strategies, settlement patterns, and social complexity of societies (mostly Middle Woodland) in the early stages of plant manipulation in an attempt to understand the interrelationship of the exogenous variables to the rise of agricultural systems.

Turning to the earlier Archaic period which is generally not involved in the use of cultigens, we can detect a wider variation of social complexity, material culture, technology, etc., than is usually conceded for this stage. For example, Gibson (1974) sees the first North American chiefdoms, ca. 1500 B.C., at the Archaic earthwork called Poverty Point; Lewis and Kneberg (1959) define two major Archaic traditions in the Middle South; Winters (1969) reconstructs a localized Archaic Riverton culture in the Wabash Valley; and Fogel (1963) discusses trade systems dealing in copper artifacts during the Late Archaic. Such variability in hunting and gathering societies is documented in ethnographic studies of North American groups, with the Calusa and the Kwakiutl at one end of the scale and the Naskapi and Gosiute at the other.

Obviously, to understand the transition from this state of predomestication to occasional use and eventual reliance on cultigens requires a broad-based approach. One must consider that culture-bearing organisms adapt not just to one but simultaneously to three environments: the natural, the human-biological, and the social. Furthermore, these three environments are interrelated and as changes occur in one, compensatory changes occur in the strategy of adaptation to all three. Rather than using Childe's concept of *revolution*, it seems better to consider a long series of small adaptational shifts which required several millennia

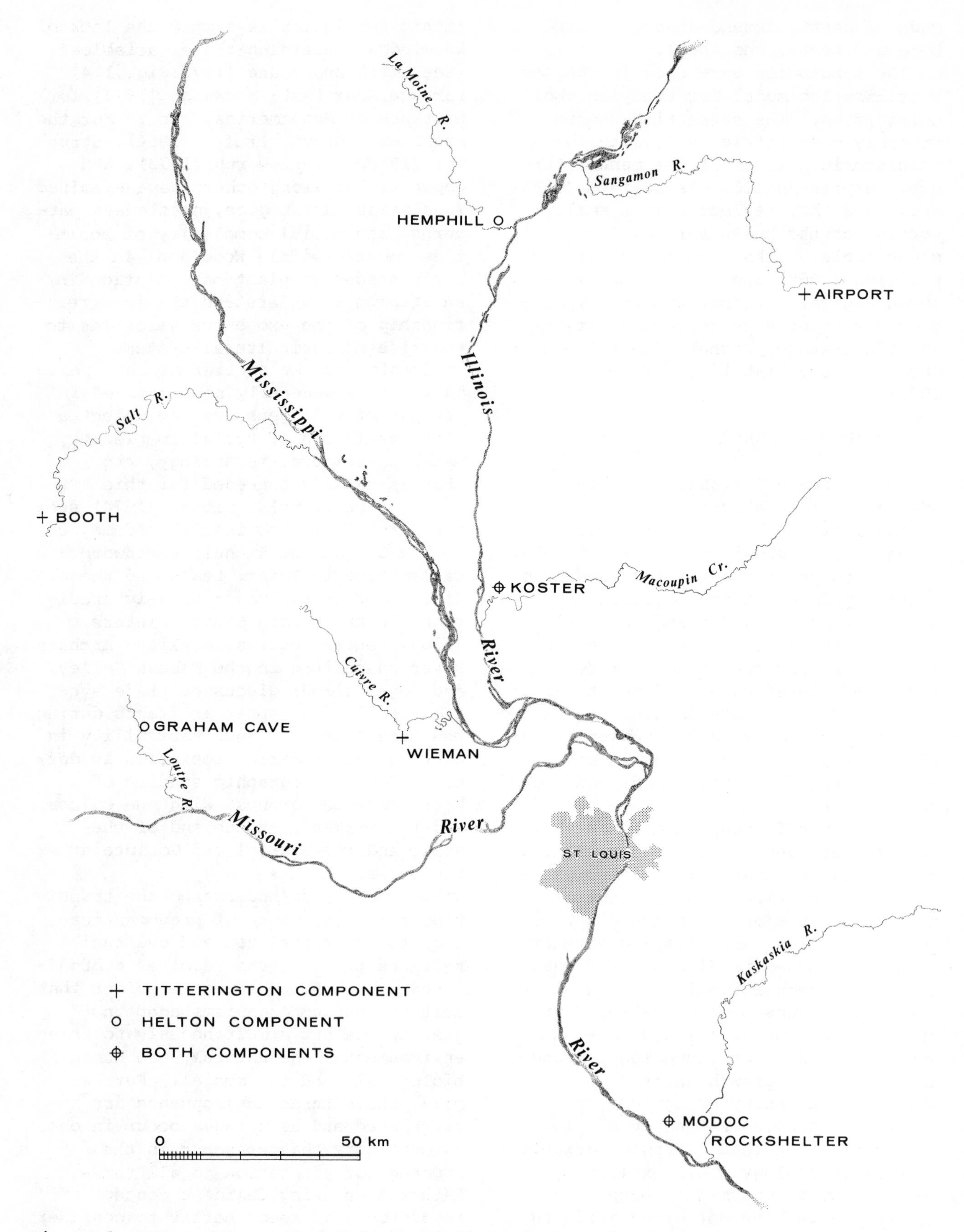

Figure 1. Map of excavated Helton and Titterington phase sites.

to accomplish. Studies of such shifts should (1) attempt to generate and test models relating the various aspects of hunting and gathering phases, (2) determine some of the specific conditions under which Flannery's deviation-amplification model for domestication will come into play, and (3) discover other situations in which one portion of a system grows at the expense of the other components of the system, e.g., status, trade, and mortuary practices.

The following research has been done to deal with shifts in adaptation. Chapter 5 presents surface survey data from the Illinois River valley region for the Helton and Titterington phases. An analysis of site location in three major resource (topographic) zones suggests that an adaptational shift occurred between 3000 and 2000 B.C. However, the surface survey data do not indicate if the shift in adaptation is a result of environmental, human-biological, or social changes.

While the problem of environmental change rests in other data sets (cf. Asch, Ford, and Asch [1972] concerning carbonized plant remains), the model for tool-using tasks does permit observations of which maintenance and extractive tasks occur in certain environmental zones for each of the two phases under study. Chapters 3 and 4 document seven excavated components of habitation sites in two of the three resource zones exploited by the Helton and Titterington phases. By extrapolation to the surface survey data, this information potentially gives us two Archaic systems of land use, although not enough excavated materials are presently available to define these two systems. Information about social organization can be gleaned from several mortuary sites for the two phases, although useful human remains are preserved only for the Helton phase sample (Jane Buikstra, personal communication).

Chapter 6 summarizes the research of this study on the multidimensional definition of the phase, the development of explicit models concerning tool-using tasks, and the identification of small adaptational shifts.

KOSTER SITE

The basic data set for this study was excavated from the Koster site during the 1970 field season. The Koster site is located in westcentral Illinois (Figs. 1-2) in Greene County, sec. 21,

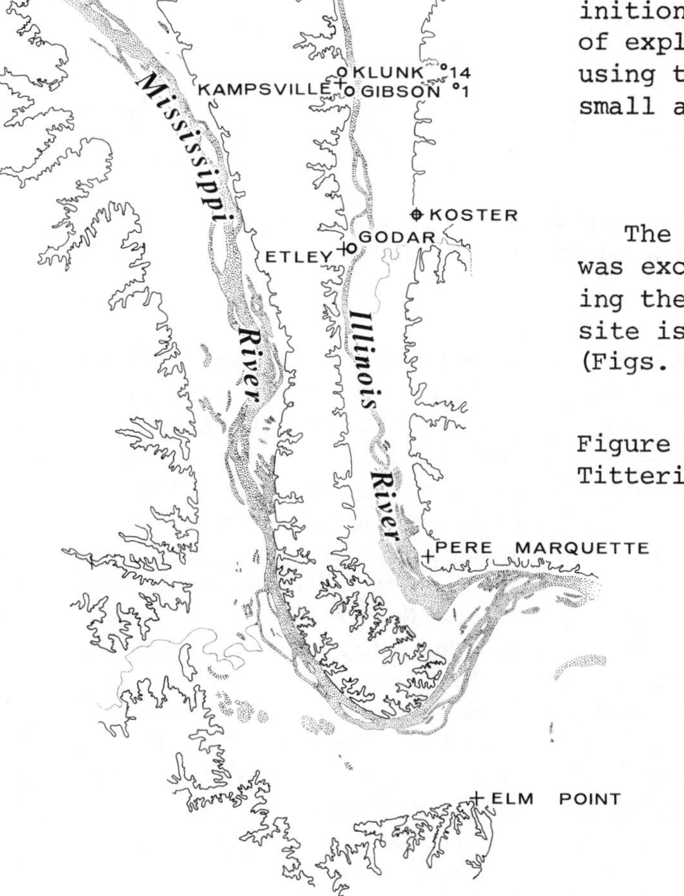

Figure 2. Map of excavated Helton and Titterington phase sites (detail).

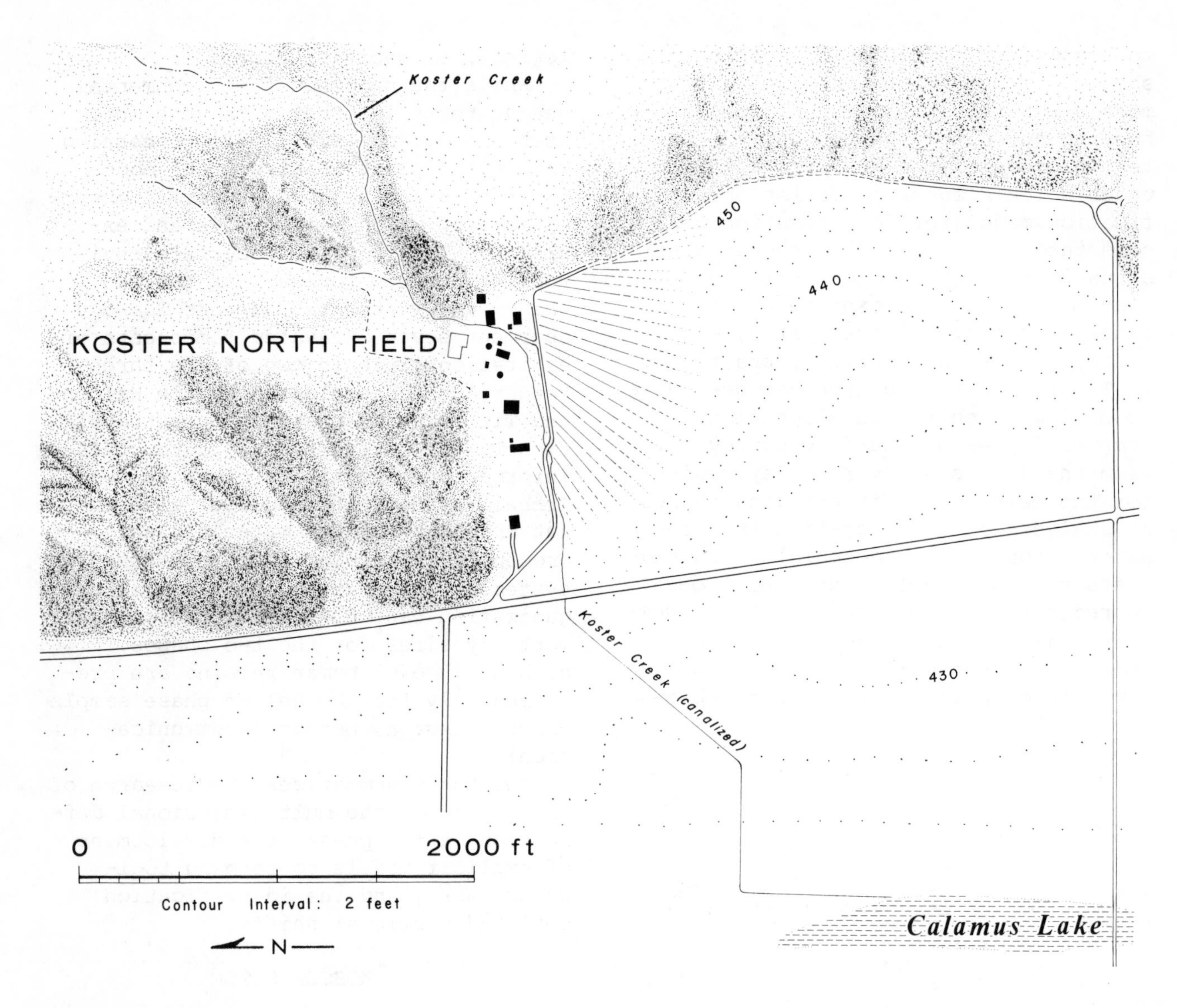

Figure 3. Map of the Koster site. Approximate location of the main excavation area is indicated by the L-shaped area in the North Field.

Woodville Township T9N R13W. Situated along the bluffs at the eastern margin of the Illinois River valley (Fig. 3), North Field lies on the lower slopes of a small steep-sided valley at its entrance to the Illinois Valley. The Koster mound group (Perino 1973a:Fig. 73) was a series of mounds and knolls along the bluff crest forming a large "L" around North and East Fields. Rubey's (1952) geological study of the area includes a photograph from Spankey Hill (Pl. 16a) showing the floodplain of the Illinois River and the uplands of sec. 21, T9N R13W. The old stone house at the Koster can be clearly seen near the center of the photograph.

Houart's preliminary report (1971: 1-3) on the 1969 field season describes East Field and South Field at Koster site, while Perino (1973a) has published a report on the Koster mound group which he excavated in 1961 and 1962. North Field has been excavated by the Northwestern University Archeological Program, under the direction of Stuart Struever, in the 1969 to 1976 field seasons. The North Field excavation plan for 1969 and 1970 is shown in Fig. 4. For the strategy of excavation, see Brown and Struever (1973).

Excavations in seven North Field

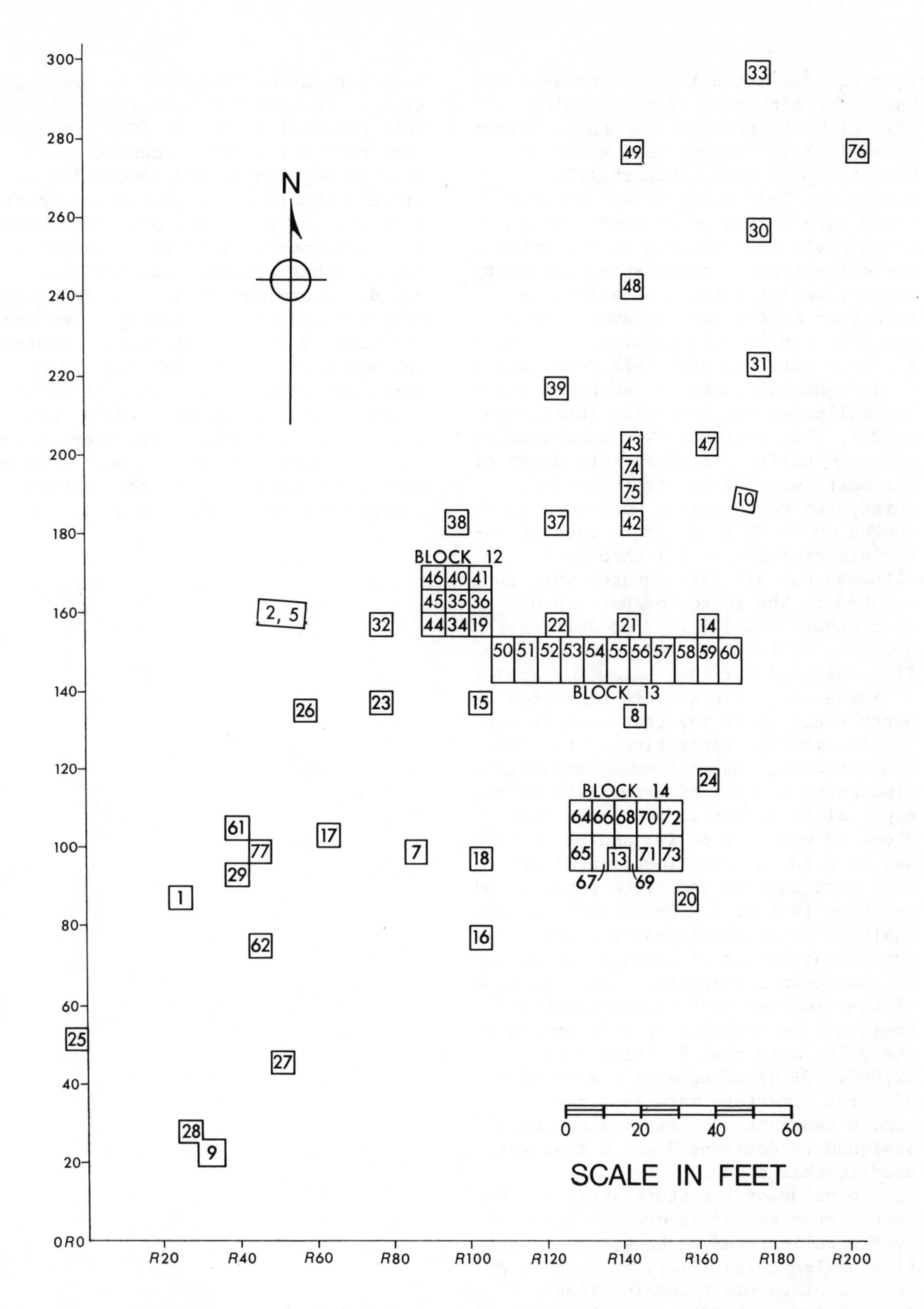

Figure 4. North Field excavation plan of Koster, 1969-1970. The "macroblock" excavation area of subsequent field seasons largely encompasses Blocks 12, 13, and 14.

test squares began in 1969 and were the basis for tentative identification of six cultural "horizons" spanning Helton phase Archaic through Late Woodland-Mississippian times (Houart 1971). During the 1970 field season excavations were initiated or continued in 36 North Field test squares to determine where the Archaic components were best stratified. The cultural strata in each test square were excavated in 3- and 6-in levels, all excavated materials were screened with ½-in mesh, and a ¼- or ½-bushel basket of screened earth was collected for flotation (Struever 1968a). All features were excavated as separate units. Profiles were drawn of the north wall of all test squares. Thirty-two test squares were sunk to depths up to 10 to 12 ft to recover materials from Horizons 1 through 6, although not all test squares were excavated to the bottom of Horizon 6. Four others (8, 10, 14, and 30) were dug down 25 to 30 ft revealing another five cultural horizons below Horizon 6.

Three large blocks were excavated in North Field where the test squares indicated maximum separation of the various horizons, thus following Struever's discussion (1968b) of excavation strategy. Block 12 was 18 x 18 ft across; Block 13 was 12 x 66 ft; and Block 14 was 18 x 30 ft. The location of the 1970 test squares and block excavations is shown in Fig. 3. The stratigraphic analysis of this material was done under the direction of James A. Brown at Northwestern University. Although some of the isolated test square materials could not be included in this artifact analysis, more than 2 metric tons (2,000,000+ g) of materials exclusive of burnt limestone were examined. App. B tabulates the excavation units assigned to Horizons 4 and 6 that were used in this study.

The value of the stone artifacts and debris from Koster is greatly enhanced by the well-preserved bone, shell, and fish scales (Hill 1972), an abundance of carbonized plant remains (Asch, Ford, and Asch 1972), natural populations of snails (Jaehnig n.d.), pollen (Schoenwetter 1972), and a large feature population (Wolynec, in preparation). Because the Koster site is so well stratified (Butzer 1973), the various cultural horizons can be dealt with as physically and temporally distinct assemblages of artifacts, debris, food refuse, features, and environmental indicators. This study examines two of these assemblages, Horizons 4 and 6, as unmixed components from the Koster North Field locality. The combination of good stratigraphic control, well-preserved environmental indicators, and large collections of artifacts provide a wealth of data for studies of prehistoric behavior, human biology (skeletal remains were recovered in Horizon 6), and the natural environment and man's use of it.

2

Artifact Analysis: Problem Orientation and Methods

PURPOSES AND REQUIREMENTS OF THE ANALYSIS

IT HAS long been assumed that culture serves two functions: (1) as a mechanism of adaptation to the environment, and (2) as a mechanism of adaptation to the environment of society. The mechanism of adaptation to the natural environment is manifest in tools and facilities and the various ways of using them to extract raw materials and energy from the environment used by a group of human beings. The mechanism of adaptation to the social environment deals with the realm of ideas, as symbols and status markers; the creation and maintenance of social institutions; the establishment and maintenance of channels of expression of psychological variables; and the various methods of utilizing these ideas, symbols, institutions, and pathways of expression. The task of the archeologist is to observe and document these multitudinous aspects of culture in the prehistoric record and to develop predictive models for the selection of various strategies of adaptation to the natural and social environments. To accomplish this task, as set out by Taylor (1948), White (1949), and recently restated by Binford (1968), two premises are considered.

The first premise is that the basic unit of study in archeology is neither artifacts, facilities, sites, regions, nor chronologies. The basic unit is the maintenance, extractive, or social task performed in the past, under cultural guidance, to permit adaptation to both the natural and social environments (Binford and Binford 1966). To standardize terminology, an *extractive task* pertains to removal of energy or raw materials from the environment, a *maintenance task* involves the manufacture and repair of tool kits, and a *social task* is an action performed to develop and maintain the sociocultural order of a society (Binford and Binford 1966).

The second premise is that only analogous parts of different systems can be compared. This is Eggan's method (1954) of controlled comparisons. This second premise is expanded upon in Chapter 3 where dimensional analysis is used to determine comparability of prehistoric data.

The first premise allows the archeologist to set up his data at a fundamental level to test models of past human behavior. For example, instead of the category "base camp" which tends to be a catchall term, one can set up a typology of site types by the various combinations of activities which occur at each. This permits a finer analysis of "base camp" since base camps are not necessarily identical for different systems of adaptation. As a second example, instead of considering *site* location in a settlement pattern, one could determine where specific tasks were performed on the resource landscape, indicating which resources were being exploited and how a society partitioned itself to perform various combinations of tasks at specific sites.

Having chosen these problem orientations and premises, the analysis of artifacts will require the following considerations:

1. There must be an explicit model of maintenance, social, and extractive tasks.
2. The model of these tasks must predict the products, by-products, and materials involved in these tasks.
3. There must be an impartial technique to differentiate one task from another when there is an overlap in tool use.
4. There must be independent evidence documenting the performance of these tasks in the past so that the model can be tested and improved.
5. The artifacts, products, by-products, and raw materials must be identified in the archeological record, taking into account the vagaries of preservation and recycling of materials.

Because artifacts best reflect only certain aspects of past human behavior, such as tool use and tool repair in task performance, information will more likely be gained from the archeological record concerning adaptation to the natural rather than the social environment. If one were using mortuary site remains or house floor patterns instead of portable artifacts, then one would be in a better position to study adaptation to the social environment by comparing burial programs (Saxe 1970) or changes in house shape (Tuck 1971).

MODELS FOR TOOL-USING BEHAVIOR

Binford and Binford (1966)

A basic characteristic of stone tool assemblages is the great variability in the frequency of occurrence of each tool type. This variability, expressed either in percentages or presence and absence, must be quantified and explained. The current popular method is to construct cumulative frequency diagrams for each assemblage and discuss the shape differences between curves. Bordes and de Sonneville-Bordes (1970) have perfected this technique for paleolithic assemblages in Europe. They explain major differences in Mousterian assemblages as cultural differences among four ancient "tribes." This cumulative frequency technique has been introduced into the Midwest by Montet-White (1968:Figs. 63 and 64) who compared Woodland assemblages and was used by Klippel (1971:Fig. 25) to compare Archaic assemblages from Graham Cave and the Booth site. Both Montet-White and Klippel explain the observed differences in terms of intensity of activity performance rather than "tribal" differences. The most extensive attempt to compare cumulative frequency diagrams in terms of activities rather than style is Binford and Binford's "Preliminary Analysis of Functional Variability in the Mousterian of Levallois Facies" (1966). In that article, they reexamine Bordes' suggestion (best stated in Bordes and de Sonneville-Bordes 1972:62) that differences in Mousterian assemblages reflect four ancient "tribes." They develop an argument that differential task performance is an alternative explanation to Bordes' interpretation. Their argument is based upon two assumptions (Binford and Binford 1966:291):

1. The form and composition of assemblages from geologically undisturbed contexts are directly related to the form and composition of human activities at a given location.
2. The minimal social processes and organizational principles exhibited by human groups today were operative in the past.

Because Binford and Binford wished to demonstrate that the variability between Mousterian assemblages was a direct consequence of human activities rather than stylistic differences, they developed a list of functions for Bordes' tool types. Then a multivariate technique - factor analysis - was employed to discover regularities in the data explainable as maintenance and extractive tasks. The resultant factors (Binford and Binford 1966:245-259) were interpreted as a number of suggested activities: maintenance tasks, which included the manufacture of tools from nonflint materials and cutting and incising for food processing, and extractive tasks, which included killing and butchering of animals and shredding of plant materials. Taking these five factors, Binford and Binford reordered the cumulative frequency diagrams made famous by Bordes and de Sonneville-Bordes so that behaviorally related artifacts were grouped together. Then they explained the shape differences in the reordered cumulative frequency diagrams in terms of their five factors rather than stylistic differences.

Binford and Binford's innovative study failed to have much influence for several reasons. First, the published article contained neither enough procedural information (Cowgill 1968:372) nor raw data to reproduce their results. Second, there have been few attempts (Freeman 1968; Binford 1972) to correct the procedural problems of doing factor analysis. Third, Binford and Binford have presented an *alternative explanation* to Bordes'theory rather than a tested model requiring independent confirmatory evidence. As a consequence, neither Bordes (1969) nor others have accepted this alternative explanation.

The Mark II Model

I would like to denotate Binford and Binford's 1966 approach as the *Mark I model* for tool-using behavior. I intend to refine this model and call it *Mark II*. The first task of revamping is to produce an a priori list linking together tools, tasks, and resultant products and by-products. For maintenance and extractive activities, respectively, Tables 1 and 2 set out the proposed relationships of tasks, the tools used in each task, the items made during the task, and the debris or by-products of that task. Table 3 is concerned with social tasks.

Of course, there is no source available on how or which specific maintenance, extractive, or social tasks were performed by Archaic peoples at Koster and elsewhere. As it stands, the Mark II model is a melange of various ethnohistorical sources concerning the manufacture of tools and processing of environmental materials for food and items of material culture. However, the Mark II model as presented in Tables 1 through 3 meets the first two requirements for this artifact analysis (p. 12, *left*): explicitness and a proposed (and testable) relationship between specific tasks, tools, and by-products or trash.

The major sources for the present Mark II model are Osgood's tabulation (1940) of the material culture of the Ingalik, a Northern Athapascan group in Alaska; Roger's study (1967) of the material culture of the Mistassini in southcentral Quebec province; Swanton's descriptions (1946) of Indian cultures of the southeastern United States; and Blackwood's fine photographs and descriptions (1950) of the Stone Age technology of a New Guinea group. A number of additional sources that do not deal with a single group or geographical area include LeRoi-Gourhan (1943, 1945) with 1,199 line drawings of objects and methods of use, Hodges (1964) for the working properties of various raw materials, and Forde (1963) for the relationship between economy and many aspects of material culture. There is much literature on the manufacture and use of chipped-stone tools, including Reese (1957), Ellis (1940), Crabtree (1967a, b, 1968, 1970), and their reconstructed use especially as discussed by Semenov (1964). Special activities such as quarrying are covered by Bryan (1950) and Holmes (1919) for cherts and obsidian while Moorehead (1912) discusses the quarrying and aboriginal uses of hematite.

The Problem of Multipurpose Tools

The third consideration for this artifact analysis - that there should be an impartial technique to differentiate one task from another when there is an overlap in tool use - becomes very im-

TABLE 1

Mark II Extractive Tasks

Task	Tools Used	Debris
Trapping	Traps	Traps Certain faunal remains
Hunting	Projectile points Bannerstones, boatstones, and birdstones Knives Bola stones	Broken tools Faunal remains
Fowling	Plummets Net weights	Avifaunal remains Broken tools
Fishing	Leisters Hooks Netting needles Net weights Boats	Aquatic faunal remains Broken tools
Quarrying	Hammerstones Pry bars Excavation tools	Smashed debris Broken preforms, points, tools Cores Fire-broken rock (optional)
Lumbering	Axes Celts Adzes Wedges	Broken tools Lumber
Hide and leather preparation	Large scrapers Beamers Scrapers Flakes Knives	Discarded and broken tools Wear patterns
Nut and seed preparation	Manos Metates Nutting stones Hammerstones	Discarded and broken tools Nut and seed remains
Preserved meat preparation	Manos Metates Knives Choppers	Discarded and broken tools
Vegetable fiber and food preparation	Choppers Pulverizers Digging sticks Hoes Manos Metates Knives	Discarded and broken tools Plant remains Opaline gloss

TABLE 2

Mark II Maintenance Tasks

Task	Tools Used	Items Made	Confirmatory Evidence
Manufacture of chert tools	Antler flakers Hammerstones Cores Sandstone abraders	Points Knives Scrapers Perforators Preforms	Exhausted cores Waste flakes Tools broken in manufacture Worn-out tools used in manufacture Unfinished forms
Manufacture of ground stone tools	Chert hammers Sandstone abraders Hammerstones	Axes Metates Net weights Nutting stones Plummets	Chert hammer and other tool fragments Stone flakes Pulverized stone Worn-out tools used in manufacture Unfinished forms
Manufacture of shell items	Burins Drills Flakes Sandstone abraders Perforators	Pendants Spoons Wampum Tools Hoes Fish lures Fishhooks	Cut shell fragments Broken tools Worn-out tools Unfinished forms
Manufacture of wood items	Saws Knives Axes Adzes Wedges Scrapers Drills Flakes Perforators Burins Sandstone abraders	Tool hafts Structures Containers Shafts Digging sticks Animal traps	Broken and worn-out tools Incomplete forms
Manufacture of woven items	Shuttles Needles Awls	Clothing Baskets Nets Snares	Broken and worn-out tools
Manufacture of hide and leather items	Flakes Drills Microdrills Bone awls Needles	Clothing Shelter Containers Laces Foot gear	Discarded and broken tools Incomplete forms
Manufacture of bone and antler items	Incising tools Polishing tools Perforators Burins Sandstone abraders Sharpening stones	Points Awls Needles Fishhooks Weaving tools Ornaments Antler flakers Shaft wrenches Beamers	Broken and worn-out tools Incomplete bone and antler forms Bone and antler blanks and scraps

TABLE 3

Mark II Social Tasks

Social Task	Tools Employed	Items Made	Confirmatory Data
Red paint manufacture	Hematite Scrapers Flakes Abraders	Rubstones Paint cups	Scraps of hematite Stained tools
Facilities Burials Use of ornaments	The various tasks performed in the social realm generally outside the realm of specific tool use which can be tested with the simple linkage arguments of tools, tasks, and confirmatory information.		

portant when we examine the Mark II model. Many tools are hypothesized for use in more than one task. Figs. 5 and 6 indicate that many tools, especially those used in maintenance tasks, occur within more than one set (i.e., within more than a single circle or ellipse). For example, sandstone abraders are involved in the following maintenance tasks: making chert tools and items of ground stone, shell, wood, bone, and antler. The same problem occurs with extractive tasks. Manos and metates are used in meat preservation (pemmican), in processing nuts and seeds, and in pulverizing other vegetable foods.

There are several ways to deal with the multipurpose tool problem. Winters (1969) divided his tools into task-specific and multipurpose tools so that he had nine classes of task-specific tools and one class of multipurpose tools. Wilmsen (1970) sets up general classes of functional tool types based upon the edge angle of unifacial tools. He then characterizes an occupation by the frequency of occurrence of various edge angles. Binford and Binford (1966) could identify multifunctional tools from their correlation matrix if their samples were large enough. All three of these solutions have problems. Winters makes no provision for testing his a priori assignments of tools to multiple and restricted task classes. Wilmsen has very low specificity in the types of tasks being performed, making his analysis less useful in comparisons of sites for settlement-system analysis. Binford and Binford, unfortunately, do not discuss multipurpose tools, possibly because their functional typology is oriented toward an action (cut, crush, pierce, etc.) rather than a number of specific actions.

The following solution is proposed for the problem or multipurpose tools: the use of the *theory of sets*. The theory of sets was developed by George Cantor during the nineteenth century. A *set* is any well-defined collection of objects. "Well defined" means here that it is possible to determine readily whether an object is a member of a set or not. A variety of notations are available to perform operations on sets. Figs. 5 and 6 are graphic depictions of sets showing how objects (artifacts and debris) are shared by various sets (specific tasks). Selby and Sweet (1963:Chap. 1) cover various aspects of sets and their conventions are used here.

Let us make the following definitions for a synthetic situation:

1. Let (a, b,...,i) be functionally defined tool types.

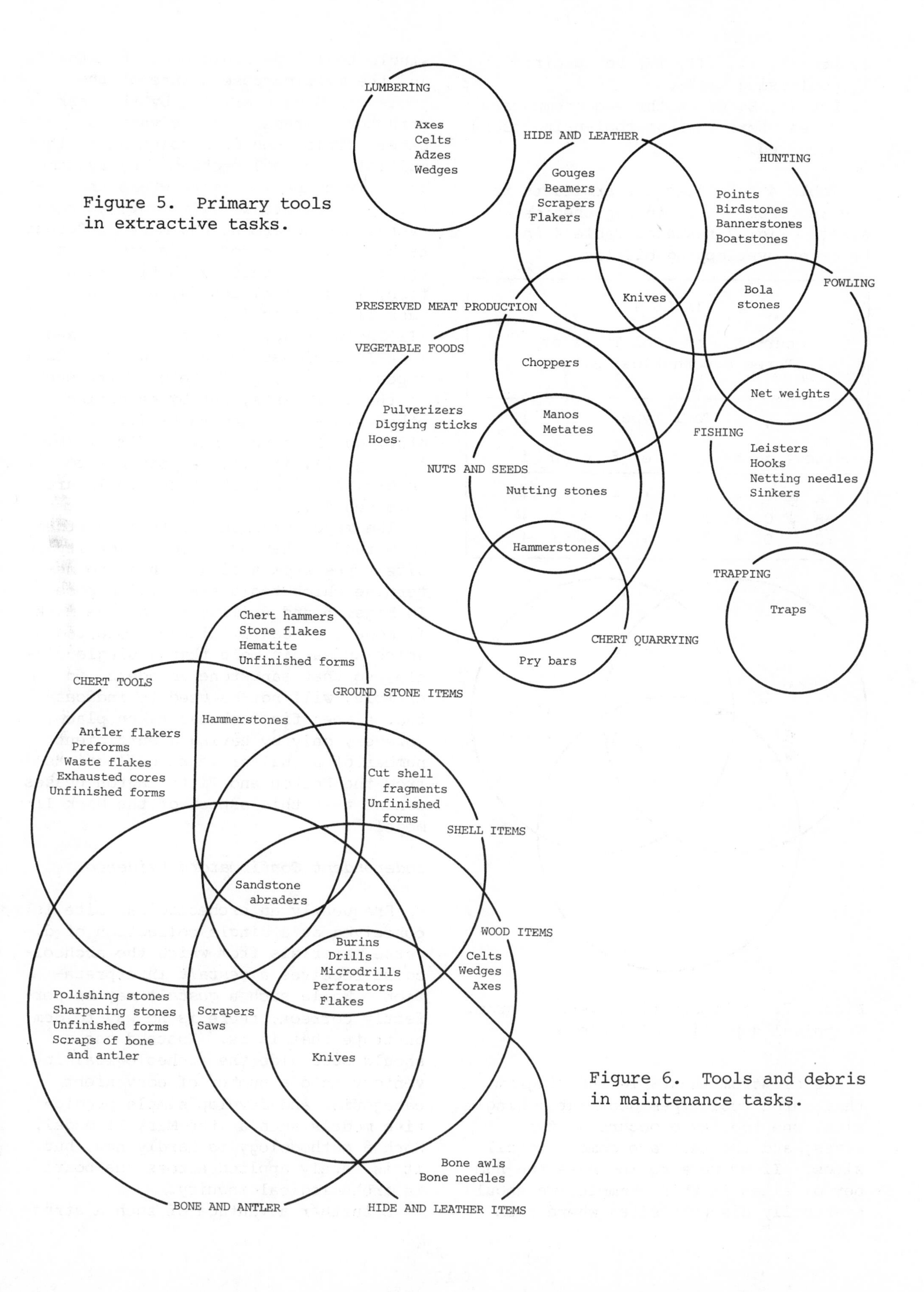

Figure 5. Primary tools in extractive tasks.

Figure 6. Tools and debris in maintenance tasks.

2. Let (I, II, III, IV) be specific tool-using tasks.
3. Let (A, B, C) be three contemporary sites where various tool-using tasks occurred.

Table 4 tabulates the artifacts recovered from the three hypothetical sites. Fig. 7 restates Table 4 in terms of overlapping circles.

TABLE 4

Occurrence of Tool Types at Three Hypothetical Sites

Site	a	b	c	d	e	f	g	h	i
	Tool Type								
A	+	+	+	0	+	+	+	0	+
B	0	+	+	0	+	+	+	0	+
C	0	+	0	+	+	+	+	+	+

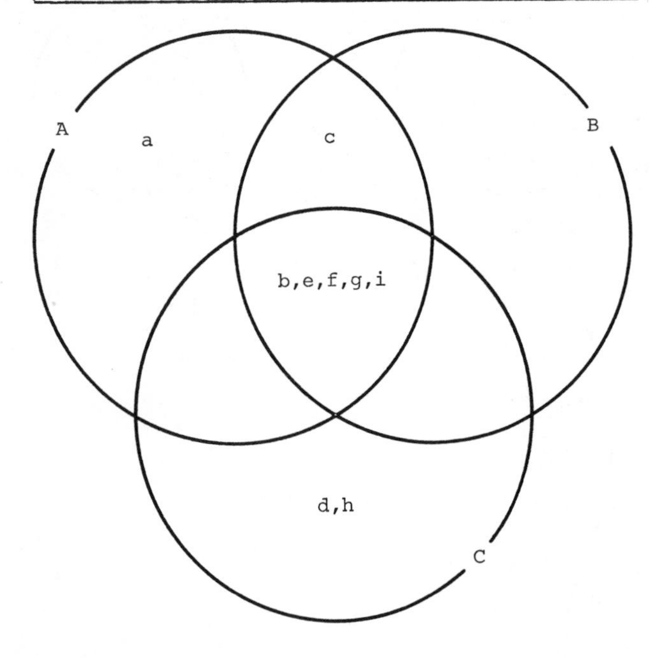

Figure 7. A hypothetical Venn diagram. Graphical depiction of Table 4.

We see from the table and diagram that three tool types occur at a single site, one tool type occurs at two sites, and the rest are common to all sites. If we were to increase the number of sites in this example, we should eventually discover sites where each single tool type could occur by itself, and the multipurpose nature of the tools would be clarified by the task structures present at the various sites. This then is a solution to the multiple-use tool problem. By systematically comparing sites where the activity structure is different, we can eventually determine how many different tasks a specific tool type may be involved in. In this synthetic situation, Task I includes (a, e, f, g, i), Task II includes (c, e, f, g, i), Task III includes (d, h, e, f, g, i,), and Task IV includes (b, e, f, g, i). Tool types (b, e, f, g, i) belong with each of the four tasks, but by selecting other sites with new tasks (V, VI, etc.) which do not include all of (b, e, f, g, i), it will be possible to determine which tasks these tools are involved in.

The major drawback of this set theory method is having enough diversity in site types from a single phase to determine which tools are multipurpose. In Figs. 5 and 6 illustrating the Mark II model, we can eliminate those tools which appear in more than a single circle, so that sandstone abraders, for example, will not be used to indicate that a specific task has taken place. However, only by having a sufficient number of actual artifact collections from the Helton and Titterington phases can we *test* this aspect of the Mark II model.

Independent Confirmatory Evidence

Frequently an archeological site is conceived as a single collection of diverse materials from which the archeologist receives a *gestalt* interpretation. While such a *gestalt* may be perfectly correct, there is no way to demonstrate that it is. Instead one should subdivide the archeological inventory into a number of convenient categories and develop simple predictive models such as the Mark II model. Such a methodology is hardly new, but it is rarely applied across the board in archeological inquiry.

A further advantage of such a structuralist approach is that the "absolute frequency of occurrence" problem is broken down into two parts: the tasks performed and the number of repetitions of each performance. Techniques such as cumulative-frequency analysis (Bordes and de Sonneville-Bordes 1970) combine the variety of tools present at a site with the frequency of occurrence of each one so that (1) comparisons between assemblages are in terms of mixed variables (tasks combined with frequency of repetitions) rather than specific acts of human behavior (tasks alone), (2) multitask tools are not corrected for, and (3) differences in assemblages are difficult to explain because one does not know if different tasks are being performed or if the same tasks are merely done with different relative intensities.

ARTIFACT TYPOLOGIES

Because the questions being asked in this analysis have to do with the documentation of behavior at archeological sites, it is necessary to maximize the observability of the behavior under study by careful selection of categories for the archeological materials. While one would like to develop an attribute list which would automatically sort tools and debris into strictly functional and/or technological categories, Sackett (1966:360) has suggested that

> ...no attribute system attempts to provide an exhaustive inventory of the variables relevant to its artifact group, and no doubt a mixture of technological, functional, and stylistic elements are reflected in each of them.

Because of this problem of separating technology, style, and function in the attribute lists, it is necessary to develop a methodology to exert as much control as possible over the materials at hand. The first order of the analysis is to be able to identify the products of the phases under study. Hence, forms meeting the following requirements are discovered in the collections, and they are then usable as *phase-diagnostic* artifacts. Such artifacts are --

1. Uniquely produced by a single phase.
2. Recognizable despite morphological variability of the entity.
3. Consistently preserved at sites and occurring with high enough frequency to be widely available.

Ceramics are widely used as phase-diagnostic materials because they meet these requirements so well - so well in fact that typologies of other tools and debris types have been largely ignored (Binford 1963a). Because the Archaic of the Central States region is nonceramic, little systematic work has been done on potential chronological indicators of the successive Archaic phases in this region. The exceptions are projectile points from deep stratified deposits (Fowler 1959; Klippel 1971; Ahler 1971) and from other sources such as surface finds (Scully 1951; Perino 1962). While projectile points have been useful indicators of phase association in the Central States area, there exist archeological sites lacking such stylistically obvious materials because of the specialized nature of the site, sampling error, and predation by collectors. Therefore, it is necessary to have as extensive a list as possible of phase-specific artifacts to avoid systematic exclusion of certain site types. The following three classes of formal variability are suggested as potential sources of additional phase-diagnostic materials:

1. Technological variation in making chert tools..
2. Variation in the type of blank selected for a specific tool type.
3. Morphological variation within a single functional tool type.

It has been argued (Binford and Papworth 1963; Binford and Quimby 1963; Fitting 1967; Judge 1971; Montet-White 1968) that there are a number of possible techniques to turn unmodified chert into cores, flakes, tools, and the like. Systematic differences can be observed in raw material selection, core preparation, flake selection, heat treatment, and platform modification (Jelinek 1966; Wilmsen 1970). By comparing the *sequential* steps of manufacture used within different knapping traditions, one can distinguish the presence of these different techniques in the archeological record. For example, Middle Woodland blade technology leaves behind heat-treated polyhedral cores while the materials of the Archaic deposits at Koster indicate a lack of refined, heat-treated polyhedral cores. Heat treatment of preforms seems to occur regularly in the materials of the Helton phase while heat treatment is very rare or absent in materials from the Titterington phase.

Because these different knapping traditions produce different products for many of the knapping stages, the selection of suitable forms or blanks for modification into specific functional tool types may vary among cultures. The same holds true for reworking artifacts. During the Helton phase projectile points are frequently modified into hafted endscrapers (Fig. 45), but during the Titterington phase such modification is rare or absent (Fig. 33).

The third approach is the traditional examination of the retouched pieces: projectile points, knives, scrapers, drills, specialized grinding stones, hoes, axes, etc. By controlling for differences in manufacturing and function, one can search for morphological differences within a single functional/manufacturing type which will reflect chronological differences.

While these three classes of variability attempt to uncover and identify the vagaries of stylistic behavior, it remains to create typologies which identify the functional tool categories so necessary in defining tasks at sites. The following eight steps are suggested --

1. Assignment of the entity to a knapping tradition and a location within a manufacturing trajectory.
2. Tentative identification of the retouched edges and surfaces and working edges and surfaces.
3. Consideration of functional properties: size, material, weight, etc.
4. Assignment of the entity to a tentative functional category or a nonfunctional one, e.g., a debris category.
5. Comparisons with published functional tool typologies.
6. Observation of confirmatory wear, resharpening, and breakage patterns following Frison (1968), Semenov (1964), Shafer (1970), Schiffer (1972), and others.
7. Assignment of the entity to one or more probable functional classes.
8. Prediction of activities the tool was involved in and testing with the Mark II model.

In the nineteenth century it was scientifically acceptable to assign tool names such as hand ax, burin, scraper, and the like to stone tools (cf. Abbott 1881). In fact, some early experiments were performed to determine the relative efficiency of these named tools, e.g., Smith's experiments (1893) in chopping wood with axes. However, wear pattern analysis and tool function experiments indicate some problems in the direct assignment of a functional name to a given object (cf. Ahler 1971 on the form and function of projectile points). Rather than play Proteus vs. Procrustes, it seems wiser to assign each artifact from Koster into the "best" category by employing the above eight steps. The next section of this chapter attempts to follow the suggestions set out here by discussing in turn manufacturing stages, tool and debris categories, and the use of tools.

CHIPPED STONE MATERIALS

Koster Lithic Analysis Procedures

Following the methodology suggested above, the first step in lithic analysis is to define the processes and sequential steps used in the manufacture

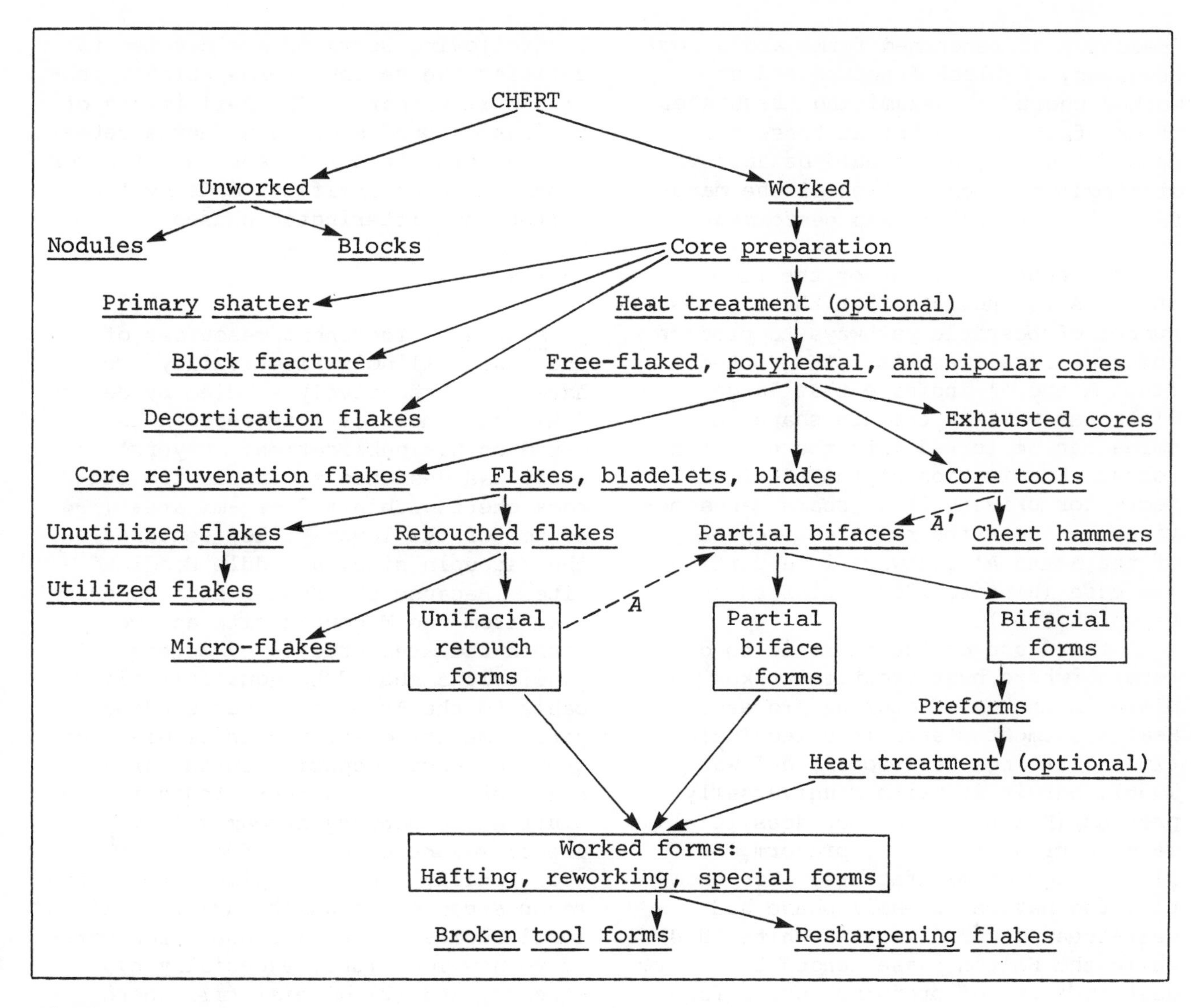

Figure 8. Model for manufacturing chert objects.

of the entities under study. Then, once manufacturing and other technological variables are better understood, the analyst can concentrate on the variables which reflect first functional and then stylistic considerations. While one cannot prove that manufacturing, function, and style are independent variables, one can at least hope that manufacturoid, functionoid, and styloid variables will be close enough to the theoretical concepts so that useful results will be obtained.

Fig. 8 is a manufacturing and use flow chart for the lithic analysis of the Koster site materials. It is a logical extension of Schiffer's model (1972) of use and reuse of archeological materials; it is also an extension of Judge's trajectory model (1971) for the manufacture of fluted points; and it is, in a sense, a manufacturer's diagram of how to produce certain products from the raw materials and techniques at hand.

Fig. 8 serves a multiple function. First, it aids in identifying which stages of the manufacturing process are being performed at any one site. For example, a quarry site or a preliminary processing station would not have the complete range of knapping stages, probably lacking many retouched categories (Bryan 1950). At the other extreme, a site located at great distance from chert outcrops would have a high frequency of retouched forms and a low frequency of block fracture and unworked chert. By examining the stages of manufacture present at these two types of sites, one should be able to distinguish which portion of the manufacturing trajectory was performed where.

The second function of the flow chart is to indicate that there are a number of possible pathways to produce the same final results. The dotted lines A and A' indicate that large flakes as well as certain shapes of cores can be turned into the same final forms. Examination of the final objects for primary flake scars can sometimes indicate the relative frequency of the A and A' pathways in a particular case (Binford 1963b; Binford and Papworth 1963).

A third use of the chart is to determine where heat treatment takes place in the manufacturing process. Heat treatment starts in Paleo-Indian times (Fitting, DeVisscher, and Wahla 1966), but it is neither universally present (Klippel 1970) nor does it always occur at the core, preform, or flake stage of manufacture. For example, the Havana-Hopewell phase had heat-treated cores (Montet-White 1968) while the Helton phase tended toward heat-treating of preforms just before the removal of final shaping flakes. Titterington phase peoples tended not to heat-treat their cherts.

The fourth function of the flow chart is to indicate that a number of waste products and unfinished forms will be left behind for the archeologist to deal with. Indeed it seems almost axiomatic that not every biface discovered at an archeological site is a discarded tool. Many may be nothing more than a "substandard" preform which was not recycled into a form different from the one originally intended by the manufacturer.

The flow chart is again only a preliminary summarization of observations made at two components of the Helton phase and one component of the Titterington phase at the Koster site. Further research will probably modify it.

The following sections are devoted to defining the various terms which appear in the flow chart. The definitions of various chipped stone and debris categories comprise a reference section for description of artifacts made by the Helton and Titterington phases.

Cherts

Sources. The chert resources of the lower Illinois River valley area have been extensively studied by Meyers (1970) and most of this section is based on his publication. Meyers' study was designed to sample the bedrock chert within a 75-sq-mi area (194 sq km) of the lower Valley centered on the Macoupin site, a Middle Woodland site. Because the Koster site is only 5 km from the Macoupin site and well within the area studied by Meyers, his conclusions should be equally applicable to the Archaic phases studied here. Meyers describes three distinct types of chert deposits in the area: *bed rock* or *in situ chert* found in the bluff and secondary stream valley areas; *weathered* or *residual chert* occasionally found in upland areas; and *redeposited chert* which includes (1) *local cherts* which have been transported to new locations, especially by streams, and (2) *glacial till* where about 2% of the cherts are exotic.

The Koster site is located adjacent to bedrock exposures of chert; it is also adjacent to a minor secondary valley where chert has been redeposited from the Illinoian glacier (Karl Butzer, personal communication). Therefore, the Koster site is located near the present-day known sources of the valuable resource, and not surprisingly the occupations under study indicate heavy use of the local chert resources.

The local chert outcrops cover a huge time range. Meyers (1970: Table 1) lists 33 formations from the Ordovician through the Quaternary in the region of the Hardin and Brussels 15-minute quadrangles of which 15 have some chert in them. However, the most important source is the Burlington limestone with a stratigraphic thickness up to 150 ft (about 45 m) in the area. Meyers (personal communication) notes that only Burlington cherts outcrop within 4 km of the Koster site and remarks (1970:12):

> The Burlington is unusual for the large amounts of white and light-colored cherts it contains....This nodular chert occurs in lenses and irregular beds, one to eight inches thick and from a few inches to several feet long. The chert is highly variable in color and fossil content. On the basis of appearance alone, it closely resembles the common chert debris found on all archeological sites in the lower Illinois Valley region.

Second to the Burlington formation is the Chouteau limestone, only 5- to 10-ft (2- to 3-m) thick in the study area. Meyers (1970:10) defines the physical appearance of the Chouteau chert as follows:

> The black to dark gray chert from the Chouteau Formation is very distinctive in its appearance. It contains numerous micro-fossils and is closely similar to some of the distinctive chert debris found on lower Illinois Valley archeological sites....

The other important source of chert is materials traded into the area during Archaic (Didier 1967) and Woodland times (Struever and Houart 1972), principally Hornstone for the phases considered here. Didier's study (1967: 10-11) of Turkey Tail points covers the importance of this chert, called Dongola, Hornstone, or Harrison County, Indiana flint, as an item of trade. This chert is naturally widely distributed in the St. Louis limestone formation in southern Indiana, southern Illinois, western Kentucky, and western Tennessee, with a number of quarries studied by Fowke (1894, 1928). Fowke refers to this chert as gray, but Dongola is usually dark gray in color and difficult to distinguish from "good quality" Chouteau chert, except that the former tends to be nodular, with concentric bands of a lighter color while the latter lacks these characteristics (Meyers, personal communication). Until ongoing chemical analyses by Meyers at the University of Michigan are completed, the gray chert recovered at Koster site is only tentatively identified as Dongola and probably imported from southern Illinois.

Heat Treatment. A further source of variability in the cherts found at Koster site is the use of heat treatment, or thermal alteration of silica materials. Purdy and Brooks (1971) have performed a number of controlled experiments in heat-treating Florida cherts. Because their results are similar to experiments performed on midwestern cherts (as discussed in Collins and Fenwick 1974), I shall follow their findings. Purdy and Brooks (1971) found that a color change takes place between 240° and 260° C if iron is present as a trace material greater than 1100 ppm. At 2500 ppm of iron, a light- to medium-gray chert (N 6.5 in Munsell color notation) turned pink to pale red (5R 7/2) and a pale yellow chert (10 YR 6.5/2) with 4000 ppm of iron turned to reddish brown (10 R 4/4). The second change observed by Purdy and Brooks (1971:323) occurred between 350° and 400° C after sustained periods at these temperatures:

> Munute amounts of impurities (or compounds of the elements making up the impurities) in the intercrystalline spaces of the chert are probably acting as fluxes (substances promoting fusion) to fuse a thin surface film to the cryptocrystals. This fusion occurs when the melting point (eutectic development) of the impurities is reached, which explains why alteration occurs at temperatures of 350° to 400° C....

This thermal alteration of chert changes the flaking characteristics. Before heat treatment much Burlington chert knaps with dull and faintly grainy flake scars. After heat treatment the same pieces knap with rather vitreous and faintly rippled flake scars. Heat treatment of Burlington cherts has two effects: (1) color changes occur if traces of iron are present, and (2) the chert knaps much more like glass or obsidian.

The third change which Purdy and Brooks observed was the appearance of dull areas on the surface of the heat-treated materials. They suggest that archeologists should find "specimens which exhibit a relic dull area surrounded by areas of extreme vitreousness. This situation suggests that the dull area has not been flaked subsequent to heating whereas the vitreous areas have been" (p. 324).

Finally, Purdy and Brooks discuss fracturing and crazing of chert caused by too rapid heating or cooling or by dripping cold water on the hot chert.

Although Purdy and Brooks are experimenting with Florida cherts, it seems reasonable to apply their conclusions to materials from the Burlington formation because (1) their model is physico-chemical; (2) the characteristics they describe to separate non-heat-treated from heat-treated and burned chert are present on artifacts and debris from the Koster site; (3) experimental heat treatment has been done on local Burlington chert from several stream deposits as well as from the Koster site itself to reproduce archeological materials recovered from Koster; and (4) Crabtree and Butler (1964) have performed similar and complementary experiments with heat-treating chert.

Table 5 summarizes various experimental attempts at heat-treating Burlington formation cherts and observations of heat altered chert from the Koster site. In Table 5, heat treatment refers to purposeful alteration of cherts by indirect heating, probably beneath hearths. Because the Helton phase generally heat-treated bifacial forms, those bifacial forms from Horizon 6 which were crazed, cracked, and lustrous are interpreted as failures in this chert annealing process. *Burned chert* refers to accidental alteration by fire. Apparently tools were frequently lost in the fire at the Koster site, thus sometimes making it impossible to determine if an object was heat-treated before the burning episode.

Weathering. Not all coloration of the cherts at the Koster site can be attributed to outcrop or to heat treatment. Color can also be altered by "sand-ridge weathering," where chert turns a distinctive yellow-brown with a brownish exterior after lying in the bottomlands of the lower Illinois River valley. One can identify tools at the Koster site which apparently were brought to the site from sand ridges and were then partially reworked, which

TABLE 5

Heat Treatment Observations on Burlington Formation Chert

	Heat Treatment		Burned		
	Controlled	Uncontrolled	Superficial	Moderate	Extreme
Exterior	Grainy	Crazed	Darkened	Blackened	Shattered
Interior	Pinkish,[a] lustrous[b]	Crazed, fractured, lustrous[b]	Unchanged	Crazed, pink,[a] lustrous[b]	Fractured, pink to dark purple,[a] lustrous[b]

[a]Depending upon iron content.
[b]Depending upon temperature and length of heating.

removed the darker yellow-brown patination. Unfortunately, at the present time the effect of sand-ridge weathering on the characteristic pink color of heat-treated materials is not known. Collins and Fenwick (1974:136) discuss this problem.

Initial Processing

Manufacturing Debris. When chert is removed from its natural setting, it must be processed to produce useful tool forms. This initial processing involves the following categories listed in Fig. 8: *nodules, blocks, block fracture, decortication flakes, unutilized flakes, cores, exhausted cores,* and *core rejuvenation flakes.*

Cherts can be divided into two general forms: *nodular* and *tabular.* The former tend to be spheroidal and if banding is present the bands tend to form concentric spheroids. The latter is in flat sheets and if banding is present, the bands tend to be parallel. Both forms of chert are present in the research area, which creates a problem in distinguishing between a worked rectangular core and a tabular piece of unknapped chert, so a helpful rule was adopted. The outer margins of the Burlington chert layers grade into the surrounding limestone, so that the outermost chert is granular, sometimes chalky and weathered, and occasionally the omnipresent fossils have dissolved out, leaving holes. Therefore, pieces of chert which were more or less surrounded with this cortex or with limestone were defined as unworked, while pieces with this outer covering broken away were considered worked.

Block Fracture. Following the definitions of White (1963) and Holmes (1919), *block fracture* is the byproduct of removing the low-quality matrix materials from the usable chert. The block fracture found at Koster site tends to be very fossiliferous, usually with the fossils being represented by cavities in the rock, and it varies from rather soft and granular to very hard and chert-like. The characteristic conchoidal fracture of chert is not found on block fracture. Binford and Quimby (1963:286-7) describe this category as primary shatter. Rose Duffield (personal communication) discovered through experimentation that the harder block fracture, with so many open fossil holes that it looked like a sponge, made an excellent abrasional surface for grinding thick mussel shell into pendants and the like. Unfortunately, the only evidence of this operation is the shell powder impacted into the open fossil holes. Because this shell powder is readily removed with a scrub brush and water, this prehistoric use of block fracture is still a conjecture.

Decortication Flakes. Decortication flakes have the same exterior face as block fracture, but the interior face of the former lacks cortex materials and has conchoidal fracture surfaces. If more than 50% of the dorsal surface of a flake has cortex, then that flake is defined as a *decortication flake.* Binford and Quimby (1963:287) suggest that a strong negative bulb of percussion is often present on decortication flakes. However, this characteristic seems to relate to the use of an anvil in working nodules, and therefore was not used in classifying materials at Koster where there is no other evidence of anvil techniques. In general, decortication flakes were not retouched into tool forms.

Unutilized Waste Flakes. After the removal of cortex and preliminary shaping of a core, a number of flakes varying in size from microscopic to over 500 g can be removed from the core. The core is then sent along one of a number of trajectories for further modification or discarded in the midden. The flakes can be further modified through retouch or intensive use modification. However, the vast majority show no macroscopic evidence of utilization, and while these flakes may have been involved in activities such as light cutting and trimming (Binford and Binford 1966:Table 1), there is no way to demonstrate this. Microscopic examination of experimental flakes suggests that incidental use of flake edges for light cutting and trimming of leather and wood would not be identifiable on the "unutilized" waste flakes from Koster. Therefore, all flakes not exhibiting use modification or retouch were classified as *unutilized waste flakes*.

Utilized Flakes. A large number of unretouched flakes have macroscopic evidence of heavy use. That is, they have crushed edges or a row of very small flake scars. Great care was taken to include only prehistorically utilized flakes in this category since excavation with shovel and trowel can cause similar breakage. In general, recent alteration has fine chert powder in the "utilized area" and a lighter color to the flake scars as either a faint patination zone or a thin layer of soil stain was removed by the modern crushing. Unfortunately, some of the prehistoric utilization probably reflects abuse under foot in a heavily walked-on village midden. The utilized flakes may have been used as tools for light cutting and trimming and incidental scraping. Rounding polish was rarely observed on these utilized flakes, possibly indicating that these edges were not placed in permanent hafts.

Retouch Flakes. Both Shafer (1970) and Frison (1967) indicate the value of examining the small retouch and resharpening flakes for evidence of platform modification and direct evidence of where certain tool-using tasks took place. However, due to the ½ in mesh used at the site and the fact that the flotation samples were not systematically analyzed to recover microfragments, the retouch and resharpening flakes recovered tend to be of the largest sizes, including *outrepassé* or *plunging flakes* where the distal end of the retouch flake includes the bifacial edge of the object being retouched.

The distinctive feature of retouch flakes, other than intensive use modification or platform modification, is the prominent lip on the interior edge of the platform. Experiments by Fitting (1967) and Newcomer (1971) suggest that this prominent lipping of the platform reflects the method used to detach these flakes. This method involves soft hammers (antler, bone, or wood) used for either percussion or pressure flaking. The Koster site has produced antler flakers (Fig. 65) suitable for the removal of such flakes. Indeed many thin, narrow flakes have this lipping, especially if the material is heat-treated. However, experiments by Crabtree (1967, 1968, 1970), Ellis (1940) and others indicate that additional variables of raw material, motor patterns, experience, and special tools must be considered in determining how specific types of flakes were made. Furthermore, Speth (1972) would suggest that much of the variation between flakes made by percussion relates to intrinsic properties of the materials being knapped. If the same proves to be true of pressure flakes, then one must be very cautious in describing an artifact in terms of specific modes of knapping.

Cores (Fig. 54). Cores are one of the enigmatic forms in lithic analysis. For the Middle Woodland Fulton technique in the central and lower Illinois Valley region (White 1963), one finds polyhedral cores and polyhedral core remnants that are very distinctive and cannot be confused with the cores of other local phases. However, the two Archaic phases under study here practiced free-flaking of cores rather than producing a standard form and then detaching a series of shaped flakes from it. It was decided that an operational definition would be used to sort objects into the core category. In general a *core* is an object from which flakes are struck. In appearance each core has one or more striking platforms where flakes have been detached. Usually there are striking platforms which can be no longer used because of foreshortened flake scars making the striking platform obtuse rather than the desirable acute shape. However, because new striking platforms can be made it is very difficult to determine that a core has been permanently discarded.

Certain types of free-flaked cores are distinctive. *Bipolar cores* are placed upon an anvil and when struck some flakes are detached which have striking platforms at both ends (Binford and Quimby 1963:294). Another distinctive type is the *block core* (Binford and Papworth 1963:83) which "has a relatively flat face from which flakes are removed." However, neither special core type appears at the Koster site, probably because of the vast quantities of chert locally available.

Lacking such special forms of cores, it was decided to define a core as "any irregular chert object that has been flaked on one or more edges, but is not itself an obvious flake." This definition was designed to eliminate broken and unfinished bifaces and outrepassé flakes from the category of core. As a result, the definitional category of core has neither an upper or lower boundary for size. The term *irregular* has meaning only after preliminary sorting has defined the categories of *crude bifaces* and *crude partial bifaces*. Obviously we have a problem of intent. The core is a source of flakes while a bifacial form indicates a tool or blank in-process. While there will always be some disagreement as to the assignment of any particular item to the appropriate class, the criteria discussed here were systematically applied so that internally consistent data have been collected. Resorting of materials indicates that the criteria can be impartially applied.

Exhausted core and *core rejuvination flakes* are two categories that are very difficult to apply because of the lack of formal regularity of the cores recovered from the Koster site. While these categories exist and can be documented at sites with special core forms, it was decided to ignore them for this analysis because of the very subjective nature employed in putting the definitions to use.

Examination of Fig. 8 indicates that cores can be further modified. An outstanding example is the use of a core as a hammer, i.e., as a pecking tool rather than as a source of flakes (Fig. 55). Chert hammers are discussed under the heading "Pulverizers." A second example is the use of cores as choppers (Fig. 56).

Retouched Forms

Degree of Refinement. A *retouched form* is any flake or core-tool that has been further modified through chipping after removal from a core or once the cortex has been removed from a core-tool. In general this retouch can be divided into three gross categories: *crude, medium,* and *refined* (Figs. 50, 51, 52). These categories were chosen in response to the following observations. After watching different individuals (who had been trained by different "experts") at work, it became obvious that once a suitable flake had been struck from either chert, glass, or obsidian, it was worked into a rough form, which Binford and Quimby (1963) refer to as a *phase blank* or Montet-White (1968:31) describes as a *preform* which she defines as "any bifacially retouched artifact which has not been completed." Montet-White points out that this definition takes into account the various degrees of finish which a preform can show. Pi-Sunyer (1967) includes a photograph of a graduated series of preforms while Klippel (1969: Fig. 13) shows drawings of the successive stages in the manufacture of core tools at the Booth site.

Once the preform has been "roughed out," further flakes are removed to thin the form and refine its shape. When the final shape has been achieved, hafting modification is performed and the piece is finished. The latter operations tend to remove much smaller and thinner flakes so that the categories of *crude, medium,* and *refined* tend to reflect this multistaged operation of reducing flakes to refined, symmetrical forms. Because there are a number of different tools and techniques available to perform these operations, it was decided to use directly measurable attributes of flakes and flake scars rather than impose a terminology of percussion versus pressure flaking that Fitting (1967) and others use.

The category of *crude retouch* can be readily observed on roughed-out blanks, such as Klippel's stages A and B (1969: Fig. 13) where the retouch scars are broad (2 cm or more), long (frequently traveling two-thirds of the way across the form) and tend to have very pronounced ridges along the edges of the flake scars; e.g., these scars are deep with rather abrupt terminations. The platforms of these crude retouch flakes tend to be rather thick (about 3 mm or greater) and usually rather wide (greater than 5 mm).

At the opposite end of the scale is *fine retouch*. For the materials under study at the Koster site, the most refined chipping is found on projectile points and hafted scrapers. These fine retouch scars tend to be rather shallow, about 1 mm deep, usually having a small platform less than 2 mm thick and frequently less than 5 mm wide. For the heat-treated forms, these refined flakes frequently have a number of very fine ripples in them, which Purdy and Brooks (1971:324) attribute to the glasslike nature of heat-treated chert. While the fine ripplelike surfaces of retouch flakes may relate to heat treatment, fine retouch is not restricted to heat-treated materials. Retouch flake scars of similar refinement are usually found on non-heat-treated side scrapers and endscrapers as a series of nearly identical flake scars. Fine retouch also tends to remove the scalloped edge of crude retouched forms - compare Fig. 50 with Fig. 52.

Medium retouch lies between these two extremes. For this study arbitrary ranges were set up to delimit a middle zone by flake scars 1 to 2 cm in maximum width, usually 2 to 3 mm deep, approximately 5 to 10 mm wide at the edge of the object, and rather irregularly oriented when compared to fine retouch.

Therefore, the categories of retouch attempt to distinguish the various processes of roughing out blanks, thinning and refining these blanks, and final shaping and hafting of the finished forms in terms of what can be observed on the artifacts themselves.

Having established the criteria for defining retouch as crude, medium, and refined, we can now adopt a rule to score objects which have more than one category of retouch on them, e.g., an unfinished projectile point that has fine retouch only along one edge or a rough form which has been carefully retouched at one end to form a special tool, such as a Titterington phase heavy-duty scraper (Fig. 45). The rule is this: Estimate the percentages of the intact edge with crude, medium, and refined retouch. The most common category of edge retouch then determines which group of retouch the artifact belongs to.

Furthermore, the distribution of retouch was scored as *unifacial, partial bifacial,* and *bifacial* with each artifact individually described as to location of the retouch. Unifacial means that one or more of the edges of one side have been retouched. Bifacial means that both sides of all edges have been retouched. Partial biface means that at least one edge, but not all edges, have been retouched on both faces.

Shapes. Examining Fig. 8, the various retouched forms are placed together only by degree of retouch. Other variables concerned with retouched forms include those of shape and function. *Shape* refers to the outline of these forms. For unifaces, the retouched edge is described as *straight, concave, convex,* or *complex,* and the overall shape of the object upon which the retouch occurs, is ignored. For bifaces and partial bifaces, the forms are described as *square ended* (or *platform ended)* and *round ended;* both categories tending to have parallel sides, and irregular shapes. Because of the highly fragmentary nature of the collection due to breakage, reworking, and apparently accidental inclusion in fires, there are also categories to describe *midsections, pointed ends,* and miscellaneous fragments such as *edges* and *corners.*

Because the best-made items in the Koster materials are *symmetrical hafted bifaces,* and because a common item found in Archaic and Woodland mortuary context in the area is the *cache blade* (Montet-White 1968; Perino 1962), the typology of the bifacial and partial-bifacial forms attempts to set up categories which will reflect the transformation of a large flake or a core tool into a finished item.

All of the objects which fit into the classes of *bifaces* and *partial bifaces* were drawn on index cards so that the category *irregular* would not be a mere catch-all for unexplained shapes but could be further broken down if some other manufacturing trajectory was observed. Because of the many broken forms present, pointed ends were coded by degree of refinement as were midsections. Careful note was taken of the probable cause of fracture which includes breakage, fire damage, reworking, and smashing. *Breakage* is defined as a single fracture across the long axis of the object. *Fire damage* is usually seen by irregular fire popping of the surfaces, crazing of the chert, and occasional fire blackening. *Reworking* can be detected by examining the sequence of flaking to see if a reworking flake went through rather than across the object. *Smashing* describes a form broken in several places as if by fury.

The classification of *round* versus *square ended* was directed toward the problem of separating flake tools from core tools, since platforms would provide a convenient source of square ends while the core tool would tend to lack a simple straight end. *Square* versus *round* might also reflect some differences in the manufacturing trajectories of the Helton and Titterington phases (Fig. 33 versus Fig. 52).

For the unifacial retouch forms, it was decided to encode the general shape of the forms' retouched edges as a preliminary test of whether there is a relationship between edge shape and function. Furthermore, observations on the remaining edges of each retouched flake were made to determine if the purpose of the retouch was to create a working edge or merely dull it so that other edges could be more conveniently used as a knife.

TABLE 6

Functional Categories and Functional Forms Made of Chert

Functional Category	Functional Form
Piercing	Projectile points
Perforating	Blunt drills Drills and bits Microdrills
Cutting	Hafted bifaces Backed blades
Incising	Burins Gravers Spurs
Scraping	Scrapers on hafted bifaces Hafted scrapers Scrapers on flakes Gouges
Pulverizing	Chert hammers Choppers

Worked Forms

Functional Categories and Functional Forms. Turning again to Fig. 8, we see that the *worked forms* are defined as those which are hafted, reworked, or have special morphologies believed to relate directly to tool function. While an object anywhere in the trajectory set up in Fig. 8 is a potential tool, worked forms are farthest along the manufacturing trajectory and have the highest specificity of functional parts. Table 6 summarizes the functional categories and functional forms made of chert. There are a number of other functional categories such as *heat storage* using boiling stones and Poverty Point objects; *counter weights* using nets or looms; *mass* using grinding stones, prop rocks, and mauls; *abrasion* including manos and metates and sandstone abraders; and *weaving* using shuttles, needles, and the like. These functional categories include tools *not* usually made of chipped stone. They will be discussed later in this chapter.

For the tool types made of chipped stone, usually chert, these functional shapes can occur on a number of different forms such as waste flakes, crude bifaces, projectile points, and the like. This variation in selection of forms to be modified will aide in identifying the various knapping traditions under study as well as reflect real functional differences. While Table 6 is by no means complete, it does indicate the major functional categories and functional types recovered from the Koster site during the 1969 and 1970 field seasons.

Wear and Breakage. Because the formal typology is set up in terms of functional shape rather than tool type as was done in Tables 1 to 3, it is necessary to consider how to transform the former into the latter. Wear and breakage analysis has become a standard technique to do so. Because similarly shaped items can have very different functions, e.g., one man's working edge may be another's thumb rest, it is necessary to consider the abrasional and breakage patterns expected from repetitive use of tools in their proper tasks. These wear patterns appear as scratches, ablations, deposition of minerals, crushed areas, small hinge fractures along an otherwise well-made edge, dulling of an edge, ground-out areas, and the like. Breakage patterns include penetration through the bottom of a metate, snapping of a blade due to lateral forces, and snapping of drills. Wear and breakage are used as confirmatory evidence. They permit the tentative identification of surfaces and edges used beyond a threshold level; this level is set fairly high because of the manifold ways in which minor alterations can occur.

Scratches, or striations, on tool edges have been intensively studied by Semenov (1964). Others have employed his techniques to find striations on any number of chipped stone artifacts. Unfortunately, striations can be produced in a number of different ways. Sheets (1973) suggests that striations can be made during manufacture as well as during use. Hester and Heizer (1973) suggest that small samples, such as that used by Nance (1971), can give improper interpretations of the use of a single class of artifacts. Unfortunately, they ignore the possibility that the behavior occurring at the site where Nance acquired his sample produced only one of a number of possible patterns of striations on the class of artifacts under discussion. In other cases, striations may not occur because animal fats lubricate the cutting edges and prevent this type of wear (Brose 1975). E. N. Wilmsen (personal communication) notes that cleaning coagulated blood and animal tissue from the cutting edges of flakes can also produce striations at right angles to those produced in the act of butchering a deer. Oakley (1959:Fig. 3; 14-17) suggests that soil movement can also damage artifacts, especially if frost heaving is present. Other sources of striations include excavating, cleaning, and rolling around in laboratory drawers. Even if one could eliminate all but functionally induced striations, the interpretation may be less specific than Semenov would have us believe; e.g., Bordes' critique (1969:18) of Semenov mentions that striations from two different processes, meat cutting and whittling, appear identical.

Microscopic examination of the Koster materials using a 25X stereoscopic microscope with a well-illuminated stage led to inconclusive results because the striations, when observed, tended to be oriented in all directions. It was then decided to change from microscopic to macroscopic observations which operationally moves the threshold of *worn* versus *unworn* toward heavy rather than incidental usage. While the identification of certain acts which only leave striations is made impossible, it eliminates the problem of multicausality of striations.

Ablation was the easiest wear pattern to observe due to the Archaic habit of using a single tool until a wear facet was produced, sometimes as much as 2 mm wide and 2- to 3-cm long, and frequently highly polished. Ablation occurred most frequently on hafted scrapers and some large scrapers. Mineral deposition mostly involved the use of hematite. A number of tools have hematite worked into their working edges, although the reason for this remains obscure.

Crushed areas were frequently found on bifaces. Winters (1969:32) uses this characteristic, along with *small hinge fractures*, to distinguish heavily used knives from projectile points, although he judiciously cautions that chipping techniques can also produce both dull edges and hinge fractures. Small hinge fractures are interpreted as wear rather than the by-products of manufacture when they occur on edges which show signs of use modification before the small flakes were removed.

Dulling, grinding, and *rounding* of the edge are three subjective conditions because many of the hafted tools have been dulled, ground, and/or abraded on those parts which the haft rubs against. Other examples of such edge modification appear in some classes of microtools when portions of tool edges are crushed away rather than flaked away to make the microtools.

The best evidence for determining that edge alteration occurs as a result of use rather than manufacture, is to examine partially resharpened edges and the very small flakes removed during resharpening. Frison (1967) has demonstrated the utility of examining the small flakes removed during reworking and resharpening. Frison found that a single object might evolve into several tool types, leaving behind direct evidence of these other uses in the form of wear on removed edges.

Not all wear relates to the use of objects in maintenance and extractive tasks. Binford (1963b:180) notes a "wear" pattern on Turkey Tail points which, although notched or stemmed to be hafted, are too delicate to be used as knives:

> All specimens exhibited a slight polish along the high ridges of the flake scars on the blade. There was no polish at the tip or on the base. This suggests that the specimens may have been carried around so that the polish resulted from their having rubbed together [or rubbed against wrappings, since the wear is from a soft rather than hard substrate -*TGC*].

This then is a wear pattern but not in the functional sense usually implied since the alteration is probably due to long distance transport.

Just as various manufacturing methods can be discovered through experimental methods, so too is the development of wear and breakage patterns. Experiments with stone tools have been performed by a number of people, including Smith (1893) for axes; Ford, Phillips, and Haag (1955) for microperforators; Semenov (1968) for various tool types; Ahler (1971) for a number of experiments involving the potential uses of projectile points; and numerous other studies involving the replication of wear and breakage patterns. The general criticism of these experiments is that they fail to take into account the multicausality arguments that manufacture, use, abuse, cleaning, reworking, alteration in the soil, and damage between excavation and analysis all contribute somewhat to the final appearance of the artifacts. Therefore, my discussion of the use of various artifacts will tend toward questions of whether an object was used beyond a certain threshold of wear, suggestions of which activities may have led to the observed wear, and recommendations for further research on both the archeological and experimental materials.

Bordes (1969) believes that functional typologies cannot totally replace formal, or any other type, of typologies. Bordes is correct only because his problem orientation is "to reconstruct the collective history of prehistoric humanity" (p. 18) with the implication that there is a single, best typology to do this. Because the problem orientation of the present study is to segregate formal and functional variability, at least two different typologies will be developed. One encodes maintenance and extractive tasks. The other typology attempts to establish stylistic horizons for the region during the Late Archaic period using manufacturing trajectories and shapes of projectile points.

Bifacial and Unifacial Forms

Projectile Points. *Projectile points* are usually defined as symmetrical, pointed bifaces with evidence for hafting. Perusal of Bell (1958, 1960) and Perino (1968a, 1971a) indicates the variety of shapes and forms that are called projectile points and gives an intuitive, if not an explicit, definition of this large and vague class of objects. Fenenga (1953) has attempted to break down this class into *arrows* and *spear points* plus *knives* by demonstrating a bimodal weight distribution. In a far more elaborate study, Ahler (1971) has attempted to determine how many different functions can be performed with hafted projectile points *and* can be observed on prehistoric examples through wear and breakage analysis. Ahler presents a table of nine different categories of activities discovered on a sample of 114 Archaic projectile points from Rodgers Shelter (23BE125) in Missouri (p. 108, Table 55). These activities include --

1. Projectile points.
2. Heavy-duty cleaving and cutting of penetrable material.
3. Light-duty cutting, slicing, and sawing.
4. Piercing, separating, and splitting.
5. Heavy-duty sawing and slicing.
6. Specialized sawing or slicing of soft materials.
7. Whittling.
8. Scraping.
9. Burin slotting, grooving.

About 10% of the Rodgers Shelter points were of uncertain function.

Ahler's analysis indicates that the Middle Archaic points he studied were probably used very much like pocket knives today. If these forms were hafted to long shafts, they could also have functioned as spear tips. Some Nilotic tribes combine the functions of spears and knives into a single tool. The problem of multifunctionality of projectile points is that their task-specific predictive value is greatly decreased. The advantages of projectile points being used in a number of different contexts is that a greater proportion of sites will have projectile points than if these tool forms were very restricted in their range of functions. Because projectile points remain the basic chronological markers for the Archaic, more sites will be datable because a variety of site types will include projectile points in their inventory.

The shape of projectile points is determined by the raw materials used, the knapping technique of the maker, the amount of use and resharpening, and breakage or remodeling into a new functional tool form. App. A includes formal descriptions of the projectile point types from the Helton and Titterington phases as well as a key to distinguish one type from another. Figs. 33 through 44 illustrate the various point types.

Perforators. *Perforators* include tools of a variety of shapes and sizes. *Blunt drills, drills* and *bits,* and *microdrills* fit into this category. *Drills* (Figs. 46 and 47) are usually parallel to nearly parallel and bifacially worked with refined retouch, and they tend to have a rounded or chisel-like distal end. The end is not a needlelike puncturing tool, but tends to have an obtuse cutting edge. It is frequently suggested that these drills are actually over-sharpened hafted knives rather than perforating tools. Morse (1971) suggests that a cache of Dalton points indicates a progression from a convex to a concave knife blade and then finally down to a narrow drill form. Drill shafts are subject to much breakage due to application of lateral forces and they are frequently recovered as bits and hafting elements.

Blunt drills (Fig. 48) tend to be triangular in form and relatively thicker and wider and more strongly tapered than the bit portion of drills. The workmanship tends to be of medium quality rather than the fine retouch found on drills. Breakage is relatively more rare for blunt drills due to the greater thickness and width at the distal end. Blunt drills are also less likely to be found on hafted bifaces but are more common on larger, cruder forms.

Microdrills (Fig. 49) are very small, unifacially or sometimes bifacially worked projections made on a variety of reworked forms. While there are formal similarities to objects called "Jaketown perforators" (Ford, Phillip, and Haag 1955:140-141), the materials from Koster differ in two ways. First, the Koster microdrills are not made exclusively on blades but on a number of different forms. Second, there is a marked difference in wear patterns. Haag states (Ford, Phillip, and Haag 1955:140-141):

> Actually, there is little evidence that the Jaketown objects were used to produce holes; in fact it must be admitted that they gave little evidence as to specific use. At least one specimen is highly polished at the end, but this is a significant exception, because several thousand of these awls bear no evidence of polish as the result of a rotating motion. The ends of the points on most of them are blunted, almost battered, and it seems certain that this tapered end was the working end and not a haft.

The Koster microdrills are almost universally polished into a conical shape at the tip. Many times there are traces of hematite in this conical area of polish. Possibly the Jaketown perforators and the Koster microdrills are similar forms serving in different tasks.

Cutting Tools. Because the act of knapping produces flakes with hard, sharp edges, almost any freshly flaked object can be used to hack away at organic substances. However, for North American materials, the term *knife* (Fig. 53) is restricted to hafted bifaces, although *backed blades* is a term used in Paleo-Indian studies. Ahler's study (1971) of projectile points indicates the great varieties of uses a knife can be subject to and the variety of wear patterns observable on Archaic artifacts. Winters (1969:32) suggests that knives may tend to have more undulation to their edges due to alternate flaking techniques than do projectile points.

Incising Tools. Other microtools are *burins, gravers,* and *spurs.* Although not common, burins have been found in North American archeology. Kelley and Heizer (1962) report on some collected from Santa Cruz Island, Calif. A *burin* is produced when a transverse flake is removed from another flake or blade. The object removed (*lamelle de coup de burin*) is called a *burin spall.* As Kelley and Heizer point out, there are two kinds of burins, *purposeful* ones and *accidental* ones; and either category may wind up showing wear patterns indicating their use as a burin, e.g., incising hard materials. Burins do occur at the Koster site, but at such a low frequency that it is suspected that all of these are accidental creations *(burin de fortune)* although several indicate that they were used as burins.

Gravers and spurs (Fig. 49), in contrast, are relatively common artifacts in the microtool industry at Koster. *Gravers* are defined as broad and flat projections from the edge of a tool blank. Usually worked unifacially, the working portion of the tool is made by crushing and flaking away part of the original edge on either side of a central area between 2 and 5 mm wide. The result is a "miniscraper" or what could function as a burin depending upon whether the relatively short straight edge or the corners of the edge are used. Nero (1957) has published a report on gravers which seems to include the forms described here with an admixture of spurs.

Spurs (Fig. 49) can be manufactured in the same way as gravers, except that there is no corresponding 2- to 5-mm edge. Instead the two sides of the projection come together as a point which can be very acute and sharp. The spur itself tends to be no wider than 4 mm and rarely longer than 8 mm. Some spurs do not come to a point but to a short straight edge oriented at 90 deg to the edge of the rest of the artifact. This short, very sharp chisel edge can be used as a burin to incise hard materials. Comparing the size of the working edges indicates that spurs and gravers are functionally very similar, and there is probably some degree of overlap in function. Nero's definition (1957:300) of graver, "a small, sharp point fashioned on the edge of a flake or a flake implement" would place microdrills, spurs, and gravers under one heading. I prefer three.

Scraping Tools. The act of scraping is defined as pushing a cutting edge across, rather than into, a surface at right angles to the cutting edge. *Scrapers* are special steep-edged tools used in scraping. Wilmsen (1970:71) suggests that edge angles between 66 and 75 deg are found in hafted end-scrapers. This steepness prevents the breaking away of the working edge. Generally the scraper is characterized by steep, nearly uniform unifacial retouch on a segment of a flake or retouched form. However, this steep, even retouch does not automatically assign an object to the category of *scraper*. Other forms with abrupt retouch include *backed blades* (Wilmsen 1970:70) where an edge is blunted by retouch to make the blade easier to hold, while another part of the blade (usually an acute edge) is the working portion. A second exception is one in which even abrupt retouch merely shapes a form, e.g., producing a graver or a spur on a flake, or fabricating a haft element on a tool.

Because the Koster site is located in, on, and adjacent to loessic deposits, and the loessic soils seem to act as abrasive and polishing agents, there is a very distinctive wear pattern on scrapers which have been intensively used. This wear pattern is first seen as a rounding and softening of the scraper edge. Then a polish begins to develop on and adjacent to the working edge. The polish is similar to the "glaze polish" described by Witthoft (1967) except that the polish on the scrapers does not seem to have the optical depth of opaline deposits on agricultural implements such as Mississippian hoes. As the polish develops, the working edge of the tool undergoes ablation, eventually forming a facet up to 2 mm wide and as long as the working edge (2-3 cm). Furthermore, a number of resharpening flakes have been found in which the platform indicates that it was removed from a well-worn scraper.

The Titterington phase has a special *heavy-duty scraper* or *gouge* form (Fig. 45). These tools seem to have a great deal of functional similarity with "Clear Fork gouges" (Hester, Gilbow, and Albee 1973) from the Rio Grande Plain of southern Texas. The Clear Fork gouges, however, tend to be triangular as well as trapezoidal in outline and made on large flakes. Hester, Gilbow, and Albee present a thorough analysis of their gouges involving both macroscopic and microscopic wear patterns. They observe a wear pattern tending toward light dulling and nibbling along the edge. They suggest possible uses for these tools, including hide working, woodworking, and bone working. They feel that woodworking is the best explanation for the high frequency of edge nibbling.

Heavy duty scrapers, or gouges, from

the Titterington phase often have a very distinctive polish on the working edge and on the face above the working edge. Resharpening occurs frequently on these tools and they are reused until dull. Edge nibbling also occurs; hence if the Titterington heavy duty scrapers were woodworking tools, rather than hide working tools, the polish may be caused by the loessic environment of the Koster site. The loessic soils add another variable to the problem of relating wear patterns to past activities.

Pulverizers. Pulverizers can be divided into three classes: *choppers* (Fig. 56) which are used for cutting meat, bone, and vegetable materials; *hammerstones* (Fig. 64) which are used to break bone, to work chert, or to drive stakes; and *chert hammers* (Fig. 55) which are special tools to peck ground stone into special shapes. Winters' (1969:36) offers the following definition of *choppers* as large, crude chert forms with -

> ...one edge prepared by the removal of large flakes from alternate faces to produce a wavy convex or straight edge. The surface perpendicular to the chopping edge is left unthinned, and often shows deliberate crushing of the sharper edge, providing a very effective area for gripping.

Winters' definition was applied to the Koster materials and those objects which met his morphological description *and* had crushing or hinging on the chopping edge were assigned to the category *chopper*.

Chert hammers are lumps and cores used as pecking tools on ground stone artifacts. The shape of the chert hammer tends to become more spherical through time as projections are broken off. Pond (1930) gives a vivid description of the uses of the chert hammer. Experiments by Rose Duffield (personal communication) indicate that pecking with a piece of chert can produce spheroidal chert hammers, grooved axes, and channel basin metates. Bordaz (1970:105) gives the same opinion concerning the function of chert hammerstones.

Because chert hammerstones are fragile, it is very difficult to distinguish between a complete chert hammer and a portion of one. In general, the larger fragments and those having at least a semispheroidal shape were counted as *chert hammers* while small fragments or pounded flakes were counted as *chert hammer flakes*. Experiments by R. Duffield indicate that only moderate force is necessary to crumble away igneous rock and that heavy blows tend to shatter the chert hammer instead of producing faster crumbling of the stone being worked.

GROUND STONE MATERIALS

Ground stone artifacts at the Koster site are principally made of glacial cobbles and native stone. The native stone in the region includes limestone, chert, sandstone, and hematite but these are less important in the assemblage. Hematite quarries in nearby Missouri were studied by Moorehead (1912). The glacial cobbles available in glacial beds near the Koster site and in the beds of Apple Creek and Macoupin Creek represent a wide variety of igneous and metamorphic rock. Among these cobbles are a large number that weigh between 0.5 and 2 kg, with plane-parallel sides and rounded corners. Forms such as these are the basis of the ground stone assemblages at the Koster and Apple Creek sites (Thomas Volman, personal communication). Once these conveniently sized and shaped pieces were selected, there began a continuous gradation between unmodified forms and highly polished manos (Fig. 63) and heavily pecked hammerstones (Fig. 64).

The basic mano form is altered in three ways:

1. By being used as a mano until the faces are well polished.
2. By being used as a percussive tool to knap chert, to shatter bone, or to drive stakes into the ground.

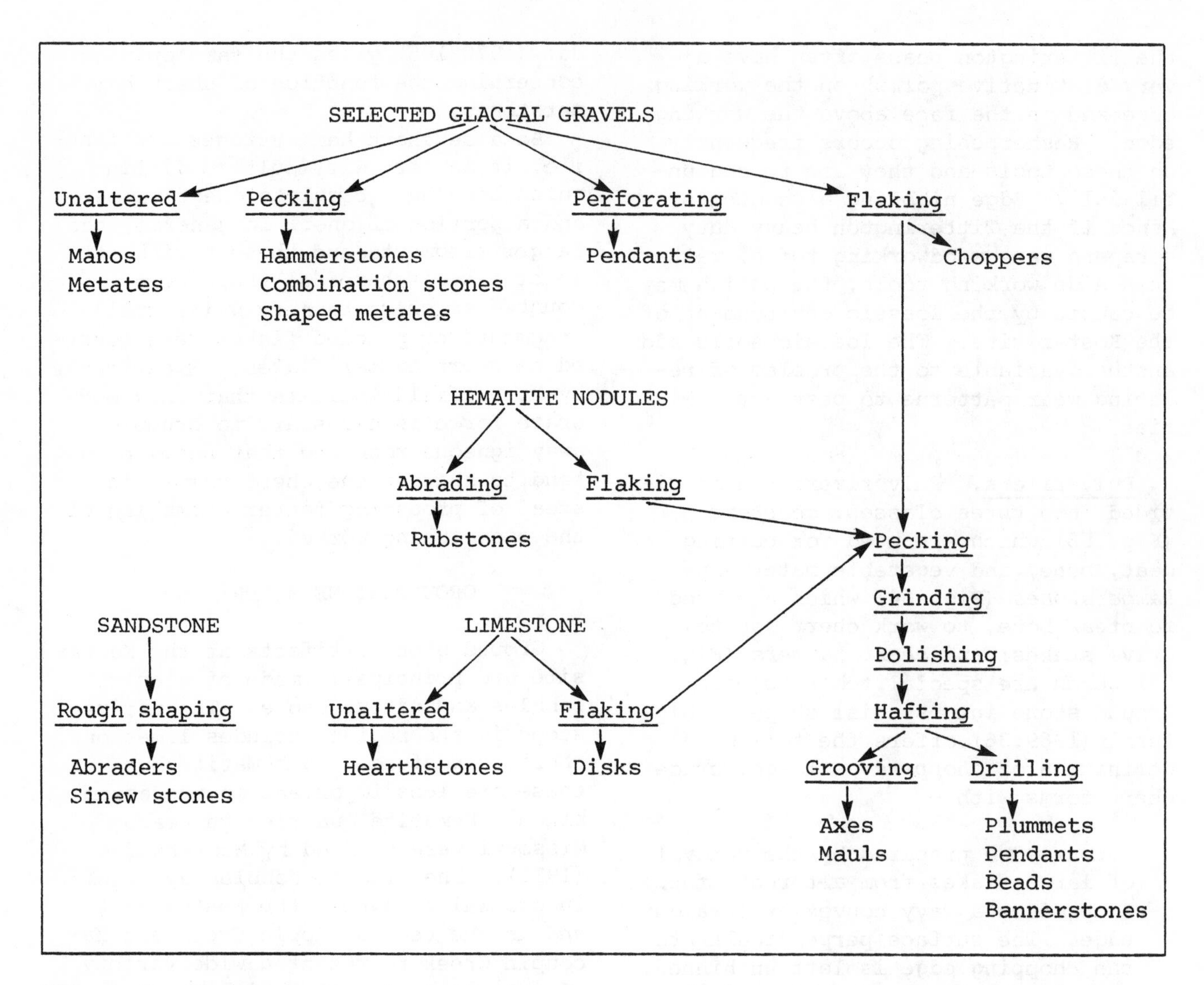

Figure 9. Manufacturing trajectories for ground stone tools made from various raw materials.

3. By being used as both a mano and a hammerstone and so producing a shallow pecked depression in the center of the grinding surfaces - hence the name *combination stone* or *pitted manos* (Fig. 63).

Very large glacial cobbles, weighing at least 30 kg in one case, were made into Channel Basin metates (Fig. 65) while small, flat, water-smoothed pebbles were drilled and made into pendants (Fig. 61).

Glacial cobbles were also put through a complex process of flaking, pecking, grinding, and polishing. These shaped forms include axes (Figs. 57 through 59), mauls, plummets (Fig. 60), pendants (Fig. 61), bannerstones, and beads (Fig. 62). Pieces of hematite were used in this way to produce axes (Fig. 57) and plummets (Fig. 60) while the waste produced from hematite manipulation could be used as rubstones, paintcups, and beads (Fig. 62), and the products of pulverization as a red paint pigment.

Sandstone was used as flat and conical-shaped abrading stones (Fig. 64). Some of these pieces also have slots and grooves probably reflecting their use as sinew stones and awl sharpening stones.

Limestone was used in two principal ways, as hearth stones and as a substitute for hematite. There are sev-

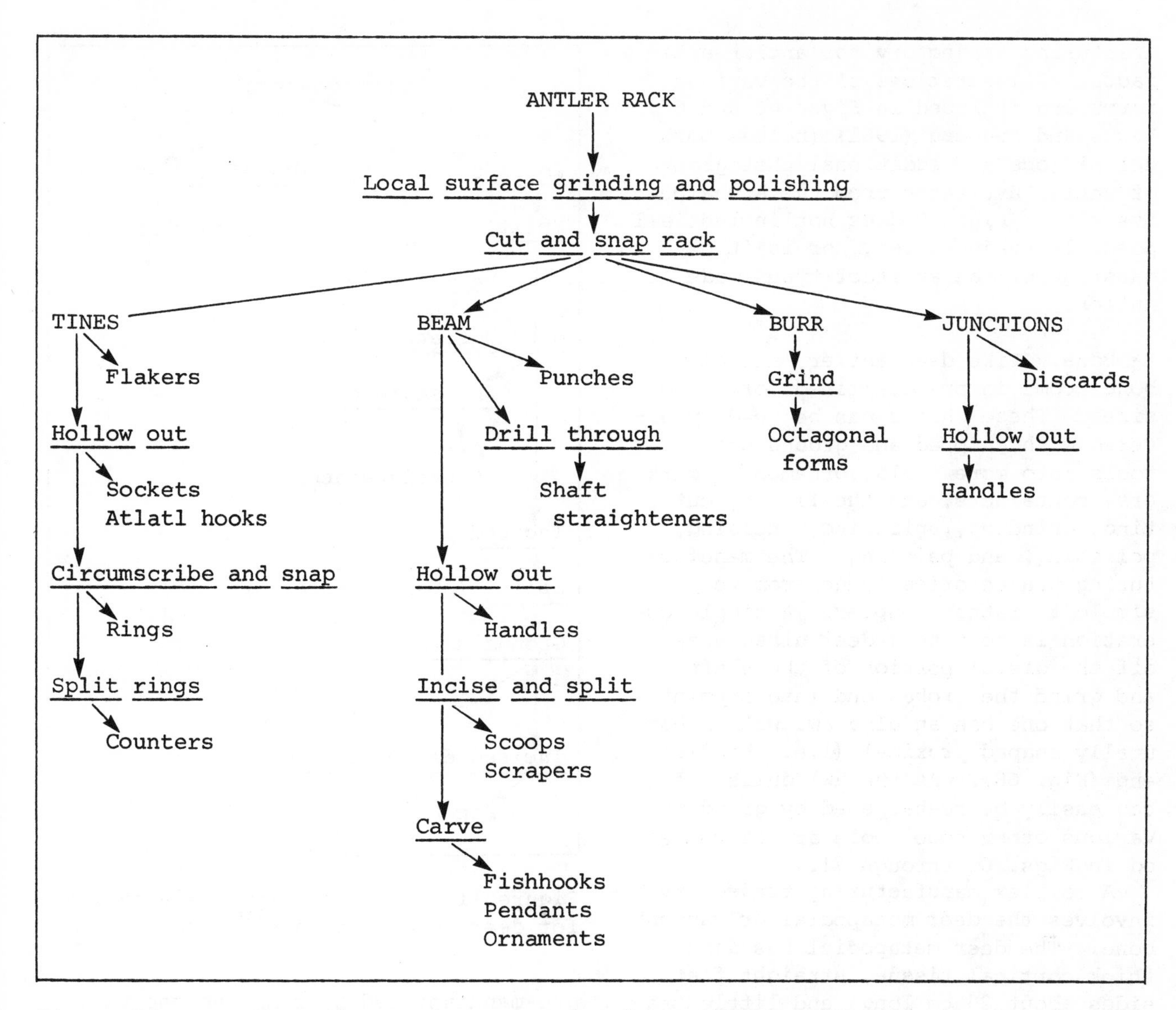

Figure 10. Manufacturing trajectories for deer antler artifacts.

eral limestone plummets from Horizon 6 at Koster as well as a number of perforated but unshaped pieces which may have been used as weights (Figs. 60 and 61).

Fig. 9 is a generalized manufacturing trajectory for ground stone tools. Only the major pathways of manufacture are shown. In general the ultimate fate of any piece of ground stone is to be used as a hearthstone. For example, the majority of axes from Koster are either fire broken or fire fractured to the point of crumbling into hundreds of fragments. The analysis of wear and breakage patterns of these ground stones is to be reported elsewhere.

WORKED FAUNAL ELEMENTS

Antler. Deer antler is composed of several parts: (1) the *base*, including the area of attachment to the skull and the expanded ring or burr above the base; (2) the *beam*, or shaft of the antler; (3) the *junctions* where the beam bifurcates into tines; and (4) the *tines* themselves with a tip at the outward end and a junction or the beam at the other.

Because a single antler can be very unwieldy, it is frequently cut apart by incising a 3- to 4-mm deep groove around the antler and then snapping it in half. Fig. 10 is a generalized manufacturing trajectory for antler artifacts. Illustrations of the various forms are included in Figs. 66 and 67. Lewis and Kneberg (1961) include both definitions and additional photographs of antler artifacts from the Archaic Eva site. Fig. 10 does not include all possible trajectories, nor is it exhaustive of the artifact types made of antler.

Bone. Like deer antler, animal bones come in predetermined forms and sizes. These shapes can be readily altered with chipped and ground stone tools into more tools, ornaments, markers, containers, and the like by cutting, grinding, splitting, incising, polishing, and painting. The manufacturing trajectories range from very simple to rather complex. A simple operation is to take a deer ulna, snap off the distal portion of the shaft, and grind the broken end into a point so that one has an ulna awl with a naturally shaped proximal (i.e., handle) end (Fig. 68). As the awl dulls, it can easily be resharpened by grinding. Various other bone tools are illustrated in Figs. 69 through 71.

A complex manufacturing trajectory involves the deer metapodial or cannon bone. The deer metapodial has dense thick cortical tissue, straight flat sides about 25 cm long, and little trabecular tissue. The metapodial is incised along the long axis until it is cut into two long pieces. Then it can be ground flat, incised again along the long axis, split into two more long, thin pieces, and worked down into a final form such as a bone pin. See Figs. 73 and 74. At several stages in this operation other bone artifacts can be produced. Fig. 11 illustrates the manufacturing trajectory for a variety of bone artifacts made from deer metapodia. Other bones are also used to make artifacts. Fig. 71, for example, illustrates some split deer phalanges and a fishhook made from a split deer phalange. Definitions of bone artifacts closely follow Winters (1969).

Turtle carapaces are a common source of cups or vessels (Fig. 72). These

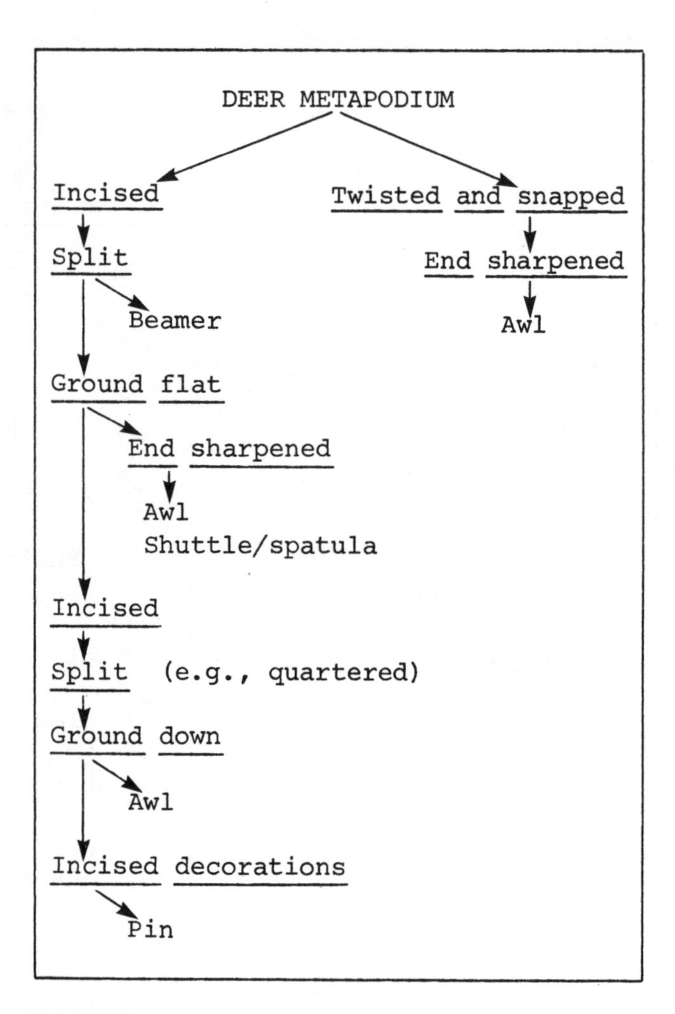

Figure 11. Manufacturing trajectories for deer metapodial artifacts.

are manufactured by removing the plastron, cutting and grinding down the auxiliary buttress behind the front legs and the inguinal buttress ahead of the rear legs, grinding down the various articular surfaces and projections for the legs, and cutting and scraping away the spinal processes along the interior surface of the neural bones. Sometimes small holes are drilled through the edge of the carapace for either suspension or hafting.

Unfortunately, unless the carapace has fused or ankylosed, the separate bones eventually come apart so that many cups are found in fragments. Because of this, turtle carapace cups are defined by associations of worked carapace pieces belonging to no more than one species. The total number of cups recovered is therefore unknown.

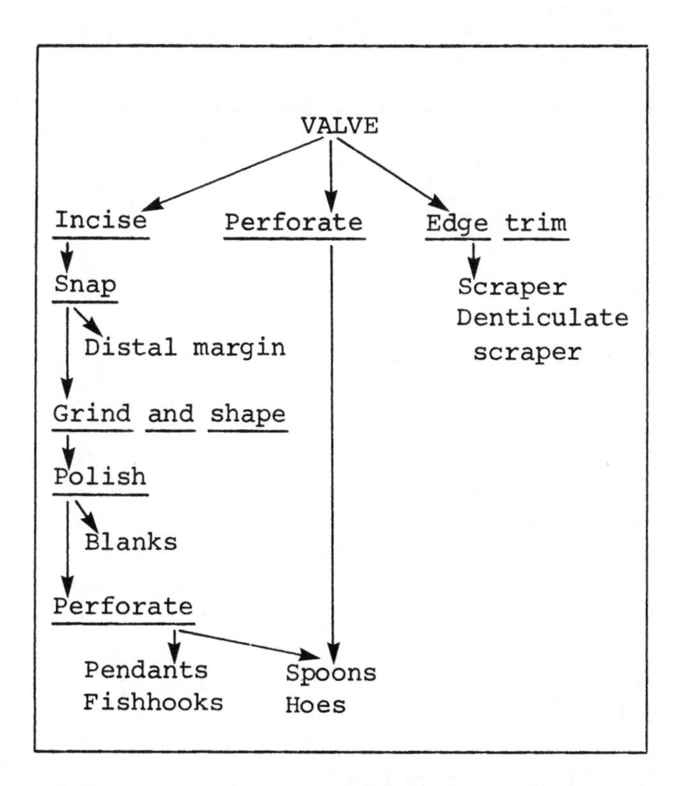

Figure 12. Manufacturing trajectories for worked shell artifacts.

Shell. Freshwater mussel shells have been divided into four anatomical areas: the *hinge* or *umbone*; the *beak*, which protrudes above the umbone; the *body*, or most of the flatter portions of the shell; and the *distal margins*. In general the shell is cut into rough geometric shapes by deeply incising it and then breaking along the incisions. Once broken into proper form, these portions can be further processed by grinding and polishing. The number of categories of cut and worked shell is small and consists mainly of spoons and pendants. One item which might have been used as a denticulate scraper has a series of small teeth or projections along the straight portion of the distal edge. This particular piece is otherwise unmodified. Shell artifacts and scraps of manufacture are illustrated in Fig. 77. Fig. 12 illustrates the manufacturing trajectory.

Teeth. Worked teeth are rare at Koster, the only examples being several large rodent incisors (*Castor*) apparently used as small chisels (Fig. 71). Cut and split mandibles and maxillae are conspicuously absent, in marked contrast to some of the Shell Mound Archaic sites where cut mandibles are common grave goods (Winters 1968). Possibly this lack of cut mandibles reflects the lack of status burials in the refuse middens at Koster during Horizon 4 and 6 times.

SUMMARY

The fundamental unit analysis in processual archeology is neither the artifact nor the site. Instead it is a discrete episode of human behavior called the *task* relating to extractive, maintenance, or social behavior. A single component of an archeological site can be viewed as a collection of trash or refuse *created* by the performance of specific extractive, maintenance, or social tasks. This act of creation comprises three things: the task performed, the tools involved in the performance of that task, and the resultant debris of manufacturing, butchering, cooking, house building, etc. These three things - tasks, tools, and the resultant by-products or trash - are logically linked. The Mark II model, developed in this chapter, defines these links for 17 specific tasks. Before the links can be tested, three problems must be considered:

1. Archeological specimens must be separated into functional types, manufacturing stages, and debris classes, and stylistic variability must be examined. Such typologies are developed in this chapter.
2. Many tools are multipurpose. Set theory is used here to discover the relationship between tasks and multiple- and single-function tools.
3. The study is restricted to tasks which were involved with tool use and performed with sufficient intensity to leave archeological evidence behind. Obviously all of human behavior cannot be compressed into the 17 tasks identified in this study. Other data sets, such as features, will be needed to fill out the model for human behavior in the past.

3

The Titterington Phase

THE TITTERINGTON FOCUS

THE TITTERINGTON *focus* (Griffin 1952: Fig. 200) is a Late Archaic Red Paint burial focus first described by Dr. Paul F. Titterington (1950). Titterington based his interpretations of an Archaic mortuary complex on materials excavated or salvaged from seven sites in the greater St. Louis area and an eighth in Brown County, Illinois. It is characterized by limestone slabs, and side-notched, ogival, and stemmed projectile point forms. Wray (1952) considered the focus slightly later in time, on the border between Archaic and Early Woodland because of the presence of copper artifacts. Montet-White (1968) reviewed the excavated materials for five of the original sites and suggested that three of them - Hartford Church, Etley, and Hemphill - are of a Late Archaic tradition while two others - Godar and Elm Point - are very similar to the Red Ochre complex (p. 103). Perino (1968b:117) excavated a large charnel pit under Mound 14 of the Pete Klunk mound group which contained Godar points and suggested that there should be a Godar focus represented by the Godar site and the charnel pit at Klunk, separate from the Titterington focus.

The 1969 excavations at the Koster site (Houart 1971) suggest that the type of materials from the Etley site occur in Koster Horizon 4, and the preliminary point typologies on the 1970 Koster materials suggest that Godar focus materials occur in Horizon 6. Further analysis confirmed this suspicion. It was decided to break apart the Titterington focus in the following manner. Examining the original trait list of Titterington (1950:Table 1), we see that three sites have only Wadlow and Etley points (Fig. 33): Kampsville, Marquette Park, and Etley. One site, Elm Point, has Etley points and Turkey Tail points. The remaining four sites have a variety of side-notched and other point types (sometimes including Etley and Wadlow points) - Hartford Church, Godar, Gronefeld, and Hemphill. The first four mortuary sites - Elm Point, Etley, Kampsville, and Marquette Park - are assigned to the Titterington *phase*. Fig. 13 shows the location of excavated Titterington Phase sites.

BOOTH SITE: DETERMINATION OF PHASE-DIAGNOSTIC MATERIALS

While the purist might require that one of Titterington's eight sites be used as the "type" site to define the Titterington phase, from a practical viewpoint it is necessary to begin with the Booth site (Klippel 1969), to develop a multidimensional definition of the Titterington phase as proposed in Chapter 1.

The Booth site (23MN242), covering less than 1 acre (0.4 hectares), is located on a ridge above a meander of the South Ford of the Salt River, (NE¼SE¼ NW¼ sec. 29, T 53N R 8W), Monroe County, Missouri, approximately 85 km upstream from the Salt River's confluence with the Mississippi. The site is approximately 100 km due west of the Koster site. It was excavated as part of the Cannon Reservoir salvage operation. Booth is an important site in defining the Titterington phase because it appears to be a single component, because

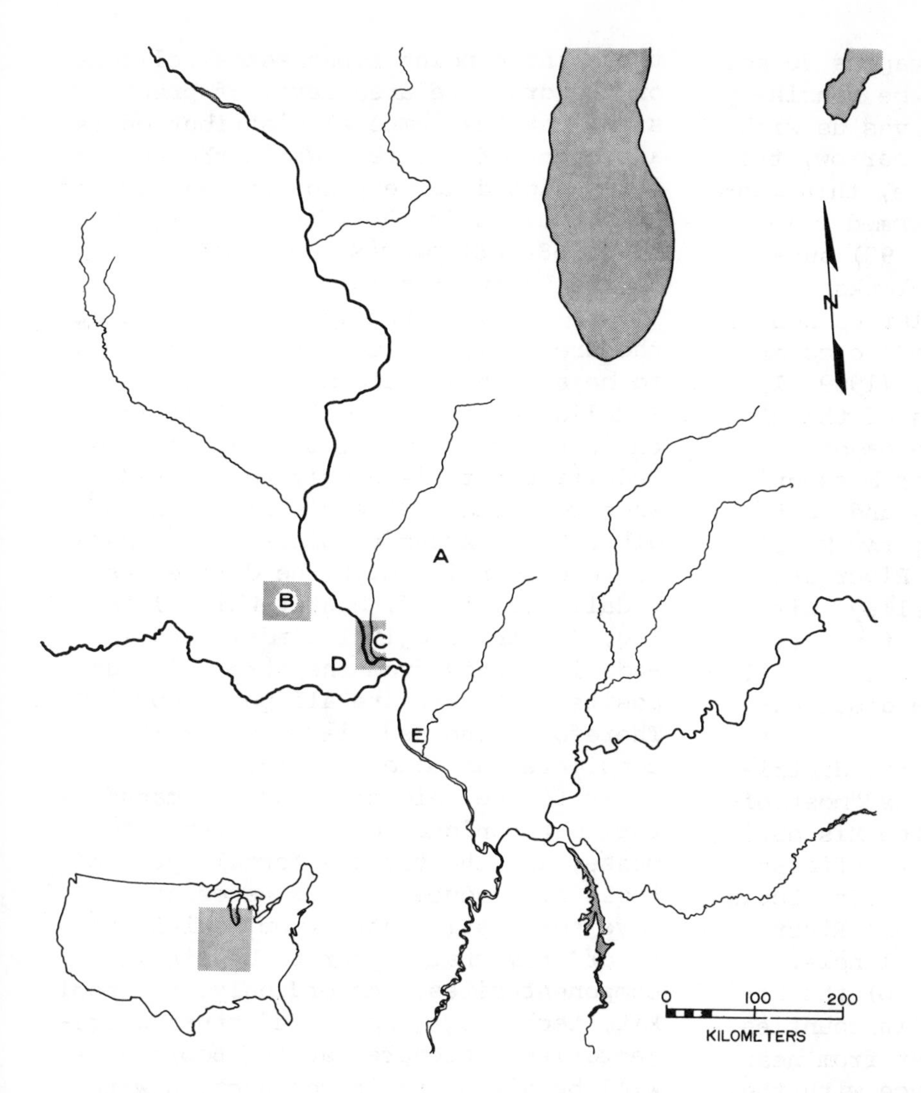

Figure 13. Map of Titterington phase and related sites. (a) Airport; (b) Booth, Collins, Hatton; (c) Elm Point, Etley, Kampsville, Koster, Pere Marquette; (d) Wieman; (e) Modoc Rock Shelter.

a relatively large, continuous area was excavated (2400 sq ft = 0.025 hectares), and because Klippel provides an extensive analysis of the materials.

Excavations at the Booth site recovered a number of well-formed points and blades which Klippel tentatively assigns to the following named categories: Etley (Cats. 1 to 5), Sedalia (Cat. 7), and a thin, rectanguloid biface (Cat. 15) which Klippel (1969:18) compares with similar forms from the Etley site in Illinois. Perino (1968a: 98, Plate 49) refers to these same artifacts as Wadlow points. Other artifacts from the Booth site which may prove to be useful in defining phase membership include a class of thick ovoid bifaces (Cat. 16) which include artifacts with "extensive bifacial polish" (Klippel 1969:18) and resharpened edges. In addition, there is a three-quarter grooved axe (Cat. 33) which in Smith's axe typology (1971) would be a *double-flanged axe*.

Along with these five types of potential style markers of the Titterington phase, Klippel suggests that the manufacturing methods may also be of value: that heat treatment is not used in processing chert (Klippel 1970), that there is a high frequency of large bifacial forms without primary flake scars, and that the manufacturing tradition relates to core tools, rather than flake tools.

While these five artifact types and a specific manufacturing trajectory all occur at what is assumed to be a single component site, we must test the assumption by examining other data sets. Because of their rarity, grooved axes, bannerstones, and copper artifacts cannot be used while special hoes or gouges or heavy-duty scrapers do not elicit enough attention to be consistently mentioned. This leaves us with three large point types: a narrow, thin lanceolate (Sedalia), a wide, thin lanceolate (Wadlow), and a stemmed point (Etley) which Perino (1968a:98) suggests is made from Wadlow blanks.

As a preliminary test, let us see if these three point types tend to covary in time and space. Klippel (1969:51) summarizes the distribution of the Etley point as reflecting the major drainage system of the lower Missouri River west to Grundy County and east into the St. Louis area, up the Mississippi Valley into the Salt River drainage, and up the Illinois Valley, with the greatest concentration of points occurring in the St. Louis area. Bell (1960) gives about the same distribution for the Etley point.

Perino (1968a:98) gives the distribution of the Wadlow point as "most often found in caches along the Missouri River from its mouth to near Jefferson City; up the Mississippi from St. Louis to Quincy; and up the Illinois River from its mouth to Peoria, Illinois." According to Perino (1968a:86) the Sedalia point is also found "in counties bordering the Missouri River from near Kansas City to its confluence with the Mississippi, northward along the Mississippi to above Quincy, Illinois, and in counties northeastward to near Peoria, Illinois."

The geographical distributions of these three point types appear to be similar, considering the vagaries of surface collecting and the appalling lack of precision in naming projectile point types in different geographical areas. To buttress the distributional argument, four other large point types were selected which also occur in the St. Louis area. The Adena point (Bell 1958:4), the Agate Basin point (Perino 1968a:2), the Hardin Barbed point (Bell 1958:4; Luchterhand 1970:27-28), and the Nebo Hill point (Perino 1968a:60) all occur in places well outside the distributional ranges of the Etley, Sedalia, and Wadlow point types.

The geographical distribution of these three point types seems reliable on the drainage area level of precision, yet the temporal distribution is a subject of debate. While the authorities quoted above place the Wadlow and Etley points in the Late Archaic, Perino (1968a:86) places the Sedalia point in the Early Archaic. In Turner's (1965) study of the Sedalia complex at the Green Ridge site, it is considered to be a Late Archaic manifestation. Sedalia points are probably Late Archaic because (1) the distribution of Sedalia points is highly restricted when compared to the distributions of other Early Archaic points, (2) a narrow Wadlow point might be defined as a Sedalia point (cf. Montet-White 1968: Fig. 44, third ogival blade), and (3) Sedalia points from the stratified deposits at Koster are all post-5000 B.C. Therefore, the Sedalia points will be considered as *Late* Archaic.

As to the uniqueness of the manufacturing techniques of the Titterington phase, and the various formal types of tools it produced, it is necessary to have comparative data from sealed strata or from what appear to be single component sites. Accordingly, the tool kit, technology, and manufacturing trajectories discovered at the Booth site will be discussed in conjunction with similar materials and trajectories from the Koster site. A listing of materials from the Booth site is given later in Table 10, along with materials from the Koster site and Modoc Rock Shelter.

KOSTER SITE

Titterington Component Excavations

In Houart's analysis (1971) of the 1969 Koster materials, six cultural horizons were defined on the basis of differential debris density of limestone, chert, and animal bones and certain key artifacts (pottery sherds and point types) in order to tie together discontinuous excavation units. These horizons were assigned numbers 1 (uppermost horizon, Late Woodland-Mississippian materials) through 6 (bottommost horizon, Helton phase materials), with Horizon 4 containing Wadlow points, Wadlow point fragments, a drilled plummet, a gouge, occupational trash, but no features. The 1970 field season at Koster aimed at increasing our knowledge of Archaic Horizons 4 (Titterington phase) and 6 (Helton phase) and to discover if other comparable horizons exist beneath Horizon 6.

During the 1970 field season culture bearing strata at Koster were excavated in arbitrary 3- and 4-in levels and stratigraphic information was collected in two forms: profiles of each square and differential debris density plots of limestone, chert, hematite, sandstone, and sherds. An initial definition of Horizon 4 was developed for the 1970 materials using Houart's methods (1971). It was determined that profile information alone could not identify Horizon 4 since the occupation left behind little or no organic staining. Moreover, the differential debris density plots, which did identify a Horizon 4 occupation with a very high chert-to-limestone ratio, also included some provenience units with sherds and Woodland projectile points. Therefore, the following rule was adopted to eliminate non-Titterington phase materials from the list of Horizon 4 excavation units: A provenience unit was eliminated if it contained European trash, ceramic artifacts, heat-treated chert artifacts, Dongola chert artifacts or flakes (other than Turkey Tail points), or projectile point forms not already assigned to the Titterington phase at the Booth site. Portions of the site which were obviously eroded were also eliminated from the list. Rigid application of the rule left the provenience units listed in App. B for the present analysis of the Titterington phase occupation at the Koster site. In other words, we have produced a conservative assignment of arbitrary excavation units of Horizon 4 to the Titterington phase.

The sample of the Titterington phase at Koster then is represented by six features and a .01 hectare area sampled in 1969 and 1970. Unfortunately, the total extent of the Titterington occupation at Koster is not yet known.

The Tool Kit

The Titterington phase tool kit includes several tools distinct in both morphology and manufacturing techniques. These forms include three point types, and a special heavy-duty scraper or gouge. The total Koster sample of these point types from the 1969 through 1971 field seasons is summarized in Table 7 and the stylistic aspects are discussed in App. A. The 1969 and 1970 excavations recovered 14 heavy-duty scrapers (Fig. 45).

All 14 of the heavy-duty scrapers are made upon quadrangular, straight- to convex-sided bifaces of medium- and crude-quality chipping. Their dimensions are summarized in Table 8. The distinctive trait of these artifacts beyond their general shape is the presence of polished areas both along the scraping edge (11 examples) and occasionally along portions of the central flaking line of one face (6 examples). Scrapers lacking edge polish (three examples) have very fine edge wear flakes removed from the working edge. The working edge of all 14 pieces tends to be a shallow curve, usually bifacially worked, hence the suggestion of Houart (1970) that these tools might have been gouges. The edge polish is usually unifacial (9 examples) and occasionally bifacial (2 examples). Furthermore, resharpening of these tools was practiced because 4 show resharpening which left behind small islands of old polished surfaces.

The wear and resharpening patterns, as well as the size and shape, of the Koster sample of heavy-duty scrapers compare favorably with those from the Booth site. Klippel's (1969:16, 18) Cat. 14:b, d (thick rectanguloid and trianguloid bifaces) and Cat. 16:a-c (thick oval bifaces) include four tools and one fragment which have the same appearance as those from the Koster site, and certain aspects of the wear pattern are similar. The major difference is that one of the Booth examples

TABLE 7

Inventory of Titterington Component Materials at Koster

Item	Refined	Medium	Crude	Total
Bifaces (BF)				36(10)
Square-ended	4(3)	5(1)	1(1)	
Round-ended	-	1(0)	7(4)	
Irregular	2(0)	2(1)	-	
Sections	1	2	2	
Tips	2	3	1	
Edges	1	1	1	
Partial bifaces (PBF)				7(4)
Square-ended		1(1)	-	
Round-ended		-	1(1)	
Irregular		1(1)	1(1)	
Edges		1	2	
Unifaces (UF)				36(23)
Straight	3(3)	3(3)	1(1)	
Concave	1(1)	-	1(1)	
Convex	5(5)	1(1)	1(1)	
Complex	2(2)	5(5)	-	
Resharpening 13				
Chert hammers (all complete)				6
Cores				60
Complete				53
Fire-damaged				7
Choppers				3
Heavy-duty scrapers				14(13)
BF: Square-ended	1(1)	6(5)	1(1)	
BF: Round-ended	-	1(1)	-	
Drills				6(3)
On Etley points				3(1)
On Sedalia points				2(2)
On stemmed bifaces				1(0)
Gravers				2(2)
On irregular PBF	-	1		
On complex UF	1	-		
Stemmed bifaces (broken both ends)				1(0)
Microdrills (on straight UF edge, refined)				1(1)

Note: Numbers in parentheses are complete forms.

TABLE 7 (Continued)

Item	Refined	Total
Scrapers		3(3)
PBF	1	
UF: Convex	1	
UF: Complex	1	

Projectile points	*CP*	*BS*	*BL*	*SC*	*RW**	*TOT*
						42
Wadlow Blades	2	7	2	2	-	13
Recurved (ogival) Wadlows	1	-	-	-	-	1
Etley Points	8	13	-	-	3	24
Sedalia Pts.	2**	-	-	-	2	4

CP = complete, *BS* = base, *BL* = blade, *SC* = section, *RW* = reworked, *TOT* = total
*As drills **Nearly complete

Utilized flakes	9.521 kg
Unutilized flakes	11.085 kg
Block fracture	4.261 kg
Decortication flakes	3.731 kg
Hammerstones	6
Manos (mullers)	8
Combination stones (manos with pecked pits)	5
Axes (three-quarter grooved)	1
Hematite lumps	29
Hematite rubstones	4
Hematite beads	1
Sandstone abraders	7
Worked antler	2
Base portion of cut and snapped antler; discard piece	1
Cut-off tine (chopped off?)	1
Worked bone (midsections of awls?)	2

TABLE 8

Dimensions and Weight of Heavy-Duty Scrapers, Koster Site, Titterington Phase

	n	$\bar{x}$	*s*
Length (mm)	13	74.9	9.3
Width (mm)	14	45.5	5.0
Thickness (mm)	14	20.4	4.2
Weight (g)	13	72.4	19.0

has been reworked into a blunt drill at one end. Perino (1973b) illustrates four rectilinear bifaces which he refers to as celts, but which have many of the characteristics (size, shape, quality of manufacture) of these heavy-duty scrapers. Unfortunately, lack of discussion of confirmatory wear patterns prevents any final conclusions about the functional and cultural affiliations between Titterington phase heavy-duty scrapers and Perino's chipped-flint celts.

Henning's survey (1961) of the Joanna Reservoir (now the Cannon Reservoir) on the Salt River in eastern Missouri includes a tool category, Adze B, which is rectilinear with a thick cross-section. These artifacts may also fit in the category of heavy-duty scrapers because of the characteristic wear pattern (Henning 1961:152):

> On several specimens included in this category [Adze B], both ends have been utilized and resharpened through pressure retouching, producing a chisel or gouge like end. The ends are often worn smooth and polished as though through utilization. It is possible that some specimens were hafted, as polish is evident on the central portions of the tool as well as along the ends.

My interpretation of the function of all of these heavy-duty scrapers, celts, and adzes is that they were used in working on hides and leather, and occasionally on wood. Furthermore, I suspect that these tools are chronologically restricted to the Late Archaic, if not just the Titterington phase, since they do not occur below Horizon 4 at Koster.

Before discussing wear and breakage of the other Titterington phase tools at Koster, it is necessary to discuss manufacturing techniques and the manufacturing trajectory used to make these tools.

Cores are a basic form that reflect manufacturing techniques. The Titterington materials from the unmixed proveniences at Koster include 60 cores. Of these, 52 were of non-heat-treated Burlington chert, 1 was a multicolored chert (non-Burlington), and 7 were fire-broken. None of the 60 appear to have been heat-treated. These cores do not fall into distinct morphological classes since the manufacturing technique used was a free-flaking rather than a prepared-core technique. Hence, it was decided that the best attribute to describe these objects was weight since this reflects size without specifying shape. Fig. 14 is a frequency of occurrence graph in increments of 40 g. Fifty-three core weights are plotted as well as 6 chert hammers, since the chert hammers appear to be made on discarded cores.

Fig. 14 shows a very skewed distribution of core weights with a single mode occurring between 50 and 60 g and a mean weight of 102 g. The following technological interpretation is suggested: There is a lower size limit (as measured indirectly by the modal weight) on cores, below which it is difficult to remove flakes of sufficient size. A second possibility is that shaped cores (core tools) have been removed from the class of cores and what are left are those objects which could not be properly shaped before they became too small. Klippel (1969:Fig. 13) used the term *blocked biface* to describe an intermediate stage in making core tools. Many of the crude and medium bifaces and their fragments may reflect such progressive stages of manufacture, especially since primary flake scars are rare on these larger forms.

Use Modification of Chipped Stone Artifacts

The evidence for use modification has already been discussed for the heavy-duty scrapers. Among the hafted bifaces, the Etley points (Fig. 33) include 8 complete blades. Light abrasion occurs along both edges of 2 of the blades and along a single edge of another. The Wadlow points (Fig. 33) include 14 examples of blades of which 3 show no signs of abrasion, 7 show

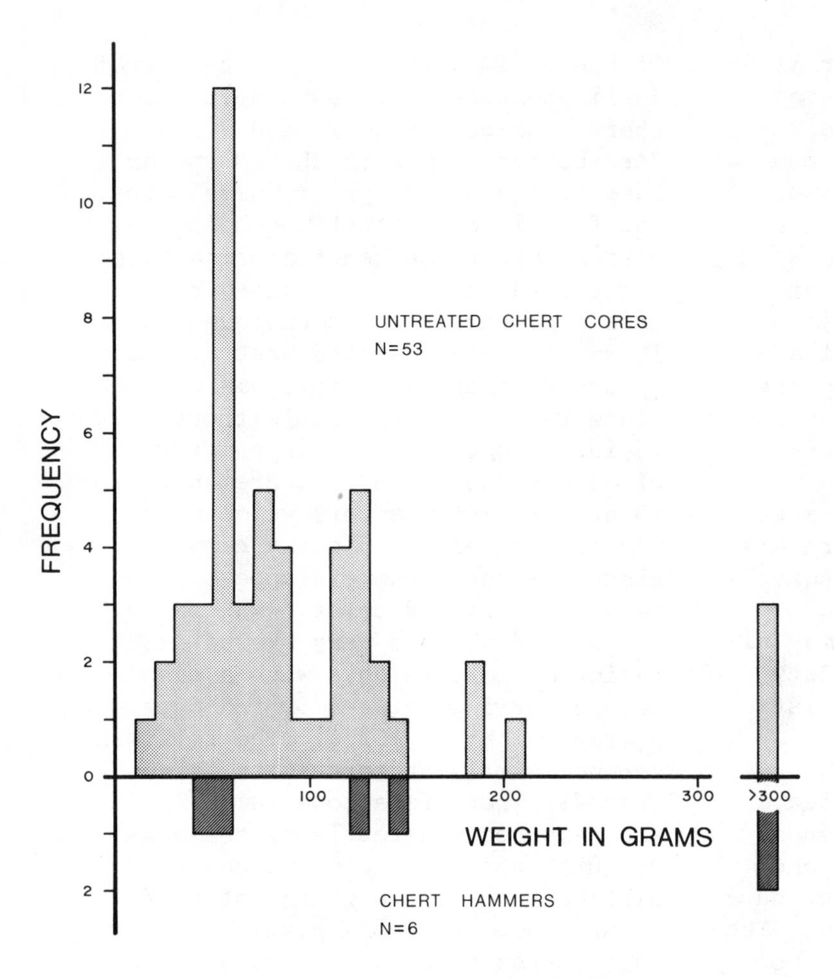

Figure 14. Weight distribution of Titterington phase cores and chert hammers at Koster. By 10-g intervals.

very heavy abrasion on only one edge (which is frequently well rounded from wear), 2 show very heavy abrasion on both edges of the blade, and 2 indicate the formation of wear facets where the scalloped edge of the retouch flake scars have been worn away. The recurved (ogival) Wadlow point (Fig. 33) shows heavy abrasion on both edges of the blade. Despite the heavy wear found on some of the Wadlow blades, none have areas of grinding or polishing on the blades or hafting areas. While Klippel (1969:12) notes that some of the Booth site Sedalia points have ground tips, none of the Koster Sedalia points (illustrated in Fig. 33) have ground tips.

Regarding the complete, square-ended, refined bifaces, these have wear patterns similar to the lanceolate forms: 2 show light abrasion and 1 shows heavy abrasion. The abrasion on these blades tends to occur on the most distal one-third of the blade edge, i.e., surrounding the tip.

There seems to be a general dichotomy between the stemmed and lanceolate forms; the Etley points tend to show little if any obvious wear, while the Wadlow forms and the refined, square-ended bifaces (which show a very definite amount of hafting modification) tend to show extensive if not intensive usage, probably as knives and saws.

For the remaining bifaces, 14 are unaltered, 3 show a medium degree of abrasion and light rounding on the edges, and 1 appears to be taken from a stream deposit because all of the edges are crushed smooth and the flake scars are abraded and smoothed together like a water-washed pebble. Two of the unaltered forms are broken. It is concluded that most of the bifacial forms are unfinished tools, implying that the manufacture of hafted bifaces was going on at the Koster site. In contrast to this, bifacial tips tend to show definite wear patterns; the refined and medium ones all show light to moderate abrasion.

Perhaps these tips are from broken tools, rather than fragments of broken preforms. Midsections and edges of bifaces show an intermediate condition, with abrasion light to absent on refined and medium bifaces, and absent on the crude midsections. The medium and crude edge fragments may be produced by resharpening because their edges show medium crushing and abrasion and one has ochre impacted into its bifacial edge. Upon examining these bifacial forms for hafting modification, one finds that the refined square-ended bifaces and the Wadlow points have heavy abrasion along the sides of the tang portion. Except for one Wadlow point, there seems to be a relationship between hafting modification and intensity of wear pattern.

With respect to the partial bifaces, the square-ended specimen has medium abraded edges and might be a reworked heavy-duty scraper. The round-ended specimen is heavily abraded and rounded on its edges. The irregular forms and bifacial edge fragments appear to have been used as rough chopping and pounding tools.

For the 12 specialized tool forms, there is much evidence for use. Specifically, the 6 drills (Fig. 46) have light to medium abrasion along the sides of the shafts, although the 3 with complete tips are sharp at the distal end, implying that these forms are heavily resharpened knives, or that only the tip portion is resharpened for the task of drilling holes. Both gravers have worn tips; the microdrill shows incipient conical wear on its tip; two of the scraper forms show intensive polishing and rounding of their working edges (hide scraping?). Macro- and microscopically this is very similar to the wear on the heavy-duty scrapers. The third scraper has two scraping surfaces. One shows many hinge fractures from use on unyielding surfaces, such as bone or wood, while the other edge shows only light smoothing of the scraper edge.

The resharpening flakes and thinning flakes include 7 with light abrasion, 4 with medium abrasion and rounding, 1 with crushing probably from manufacture, and 1 with a sharp edge. The size range for these special flakes does not include pieces small enough to have been removed from heavy-duty scrapers; hence no polished edges and surfaces were discovered.

Ground Stone and Worked Fauna

For ground stone, Duffield's analysis (personal communication) indicates that the sole axe is three-quarters grooved (Fig. 57), made of crystalline rock, and heavily battered about the bit end. While the axe from the Booth site is also three-quarters grooved, the similarity ends there, as the Koster example is rather plain, in marked contrast to the Booth example. Table 7 summarizes the various categories of pecked and ground stone recovered in association with the Titterington phase chipped-stone materials. One item of note in the ground stone assemblage is the "nutting stone" or combination stone. These are manos with a shallow pecked pit in the middle of the grinding surface.

Alice Berksen's worked bone, antler, and shell analysis (personal communication) is also summarized in Table 7. The four items indicate that antler was being worked at Koster, although the worked bone (identified by Frederick C. Hill as mammal bone) does not include manufacturing debris. The lack of worked shell cannot be due to scarce resources since one of the cultural features is a large mussel shell lens.

Before discussing the third Titterington phase excavated component, I would like to note that the confirmatory wear pattern analysis has been very useful in several ways. First, it suggests possible uses of the large, heavy-duty scrapers, which otherwise might be placed in the morphological category of chipped-stone celts. Second, it aids in deciphering the manufacturing trajectory for large bifaces by indicating when these forms start to accumulate wear patterns and when alteration through manufacture has ceased. Third, many of the special tool forms are worn, if not worn out, permitting us to compare the results of wear pattern analysis with the results of the Mark II model.

MODOC ROCK SHELTER

Modoc Rock Shelter (Illinois State Museum Number Ra^{S}501) is located "about two miles south and east of the village of Prairie du Rocher, Illinois, in the SW¼ of the SE¼ of Section 26, Township 5 South, Range 9 West, ... Illinois-Missouri Renault Quadrangle" (Fowler 1959b:9). The rockshelter is beneath a 30-m-high sandstone overhang, on the eastern edge of the 6.2-km-wide (4-mi-wide) floodplain of the Mississippi River. The site itself is a deposit of loessic soils and human refuse about 10 m thick, which has been accumulating over the last 10,000 years, with intermittent periods of erosion (Fowler 1959b:16). In a number of ways Modoc Rock Shelter is very similar to the open air site in the Koster North Field. Both are bluff-based sites, protected somewhat from the elements by being in either a box canyon or a rockshelter and very close to running water. Both sites are well stratified because of the accumulation of soil at the sites; and both have been attractive to human occupation for the last 8500 years. Modoc Rock Shelter is about 125 km south of the Koster site. By contrast, the Booth site location is very different, being far from a major river valley, in the uplands, and probably not too far from the interface of upland forests and prairie lands.

Although Modoc Rock Shelter is extensively reported (Fowler and Winters 1956; Fowler 1959a,b) and has been used as a standard reference for the Archaic period in Illinois (Winters 1959; Willey and Phillips 1958:113; Griffin 1968), there are problems in using these reports. For example, Griffin (1968:131) feels very uncomfortable with the Modoc excavations:

> The Modoc shelter was dug in 1-foot levels [Modoc was actually dug in 6-in and 12-in levels (M. Fowler, personal communication). Griffin was misled because the analysis was reported as 1-foot aggregates - *TGC*] and in 5-foot squares, and although the natural soil zones were observed and studied, I have a feeling that the artifact associations, as represented by depth groupings, are not necessarily representative of the specific time they were deposited in the shelter. No intrusive storage, refuse, or burial pits are mentioned, and no reference is made to other means of possible displacement of artifacts. Dr. Fowler has informed me that in the analysis of the material, the specimens from observed pits and other disturbances were not used....

In addition, the small sample size of any single projectile point type led Fowler to base his point typology upon major classes of hafting modification (corner-notched, expanding stem, straight stem, contracting stem, side-notched, stemless, lanceolate, and pentagonal) and a couple of standard types (Hidden Valley Stemmed, Modoc Side-Notched, etc.) rather than upon manufacturing and stylistic differences within a single class of hafting modification. However, because the report is so well illustrated and due to some fortunate coincidences in how certain portions of the site were aggregated into arbitrary depths below the ground surface, it is possible to discuss one of "the short periods of human occupancy" that Griffin (1968:131) speaks of.

Examining Broyles' drawings (Fowler 1959b:Figs. 9 and 10), we can indicate which of Fowler's hafting categories include Wadlow and Etley-like points. Then, Fowler's depth distribution of artifact types (1959b:App. 1) can be used to see whether one or more depth strata contain principally those point categories which exclude side-notched and other forms which seem to relate to the Helton phase or other defined phases. For Etley points, Broyles' illustrations include the following items: Fig. 9, Cat. B (expanding stem), first and second points; Fig. 9, Cat. C

TABLE 9

Projectile Point Stratigraphy at Modoc Rockshelter

Named Type	Fowler's Type	Depth (ft) 12-11	11-10	10-9	9-8	8-7	7-6	6-5	Above 5
Etley	Straight Stem	1	6	7	7	5	3	3	4
Etley	Expanding Stem	1	5	12	14	18	3	3	4
Wadlow?	Stemless	-	5	5	-	5	-	2	-
Wadlow?	Blanks	3	3	2	8	3	-	2	1
	Pentagonal	-	-	1	1	-	-	-	-
	Contracting Stem	-	1	3	3	-	1	-	1
	Hidden Valley	-	-	1	-	-	-	-	-
	Side-Notched	11	24	20	22	20	-	1	-
	Other forms	-	-	2	2	2	1	-	-
	Sherds	-	1	4	15	10	1	1	5

(straight stem), first, fifth, sixth, and seventh points; and Fig. 10, Cat. A (large bladed, straight stemmed), second point. For Wadlow points, there are no direct analogs. Although the following items have the rectilinear bases, they lack the usual length of Wadlow points: Fig. 9, Cat. G (stemless), third and fourth points. Because Wadlow points tend to be broken and broken forms are not, in general, illustrated by Fowler (1959b), I suspect that more likely candidates reside in the Modoc collections.

Table 9 summarizes the point type occurrence by 1-ft stratigraphic units at Modoc Rock Shelter (Fowler 1959: App. I). Table 9 indicates that the Titterington phase and the other categories, especially the side-notched forms, are most common below the 8-ft level. But there is a sudden decrease of all but the Titterington phase categories above 7 ft. I would suggest that the remaining units, 7-6 ft and 6-5 ft, belong to the Titterington phase occupation with later, ceramic bearing horizons above 5 ft. It is unfortunate that the 1956 report (Fowler and Winters) aggregates the materials into large stratigraphic units, one of which, Zone 4, represents a deposit of yellow soils from a depth of 10-5 ft. Zone 4 thus combines what I am calling a Titterington phase component with an earlier one.

As it stands, the 7-5 ft stratum includes enough materials to make preliminary statements about the Titterington phase at Modoc Rock Shelter: the 65 excavation units include 2,372 chert flakes, 6 post molds, 80 typed artifacts, 3,841 vertebrate remains, and 608 mollusk remains (Fowler 1959b: Table 3). Even with this reorganization of Fowler's stratigraphic analysis, the Modoc Rock Shelter sample still has problems: (1) it represents a grab sample rather than a representative sample of the component; (2) it does not include materials from features; and (3) it is somewhat mixed with materials from other components, including two cord-marked sherds and one side-notched point. However, until Modoc Rock Shelter is reanalyzed in terms of natural stratigraphy, it is the sample we must deal with.

Table 10 summarizes the Titterington phase artifacts for the Koster, Modoc, and Booth components according to functional categories.

TABLE 10

Titterington Phase Artifacts by Functional Categories at Koster, Modoc Rock Shelter, and Booth Sites

Functional Category	Tool Type	Koster	Modoc	Booth	(Klippel's Category)
Piercing/cutting	Projectiles, knives	42	14	61	(1-7, 9, 15)
	Utilized fragments	11	17	63	(10:f,r,x; 11:a-aa; 14:d; 16:d,e; 17:a,c,d; 18:a-e)
Perforating	Drills, bits	6	2	15	(13:a-o)
	Bone awls	2 frag.	3+2 frag.	[a]	
	Microdrills	1	-	0	
Cutting	Hafted bifaces	1	0	3	(8)
	Crude knives	-	4	-	
	Unmodified or waste flakes	20.61 kg	2,372	25,897	
	Unifacial retouch flakes	25	-	23	(20-24)
Incising	Gravers	2	1	0	
	Bone gravers	0	1	[a]	
Scraping	Scrapers	3	6	scarce	(p. 29)
	Heavy-duty scrapers	14	-	5	(14:b,d; 16:a-c)
Handles	Antler handles	0	1	[a]	
Pulverizers	Chert hammers	6	-	22	(27:a-v)
	Choppers	3	0	1	(16:f)
	Hammerstones	6	7	3	(32:b-d)
	Manos (mullers)	8	0	8	(29:e-l)
	Combination stones	5	0	5	(29:a-d; 32:a)
	Metates	0	0	6	(31:a-g)
Manufacturing	Cores	60	-	38	(p. 28)
	Rejuvenation flakes	-	-	6	(25:a-f)
	Waste flakes	11.08 kg	2,372	25,897	
	Unaltered bifaces, partial bifaces, and fragments	20	2	47	(10:a-e,g-q,s-w,y-ae; 14:a,e; 17:b,e-i; 19:a-h)
	Resharpening flakes	13	-	3	(p. 29)
	Sandstone abraders	7	3	32?	(30:d-aj)
	Antler flakers	0	4	[a]	
	Antler scraps	2	0	[a]	
Weights	Bannerstones	0	1	0	
Tree felling	Axes	1	1 bit	1	(33)
Debris	Misc. rock, stone	several	-	2,674[b]	(p. 28)
	Features	6	?	0	(p. 33)
	Post molds	0	6	0	(p. 34)
	Burials	0	0	0?	(p. 34)
Ornaments	Hematite beads	1	0	0	
	Snail beads	0	1	[a]	
	Bone pendants	0	2	[a]	
	Tooth pendants	0	1	[a]	
Red paint	Hematite lumps	29	0	1,280[b]	(p. 3)
	Hematite rubstones	4	0	27	(28)

Note: An attempt has been made to make these type categories strictly comparable among the three samples. In cases where a category was not recorded for a site, a dash (-) is used.

[a] Because the Booth site has no preserved bone, bone tool categories are not comparable for all three sites.

[b] Klippel mentions that the local soil contains miscellaneous waterworn chert, stones, and hematite, so that lumps of unmodified hematite may or may not have been transported to the site for modification.

Klippel (1969:48-51) has compiled an extensive list of published Tittering-ton phase components in both Missouri and Illinois, based upon the distribution of the Etley point. In addition, his recent report on the Collins site (23MN223) includes some Titterington phase materials (Klippel 1972). For excavated habitation sites (without badly mixed materials) there are the three components discussed above. For burial stations, there are five components to be discussed: Etley, Kampsville, and Marquette Park in Illinois and Elm Point and Wieman in Missouri. A sixth burial station, Airport, discovered near Springfield, Ill., is currently being analyzed (Donna Roper, personal communication).* There are probably hundreds of other Titterington phase sites in the region, some of which are reported in the literature, and a few excavated. However, these have been excluded from the analysis because of problems of stratigraphic or chronological mixing.

---

*Another possible mortuary site to add to this list has come to my attention since the completion of this manuscript. It is the Hatton Mound in eastern Missouri. Chapman (1975:211, 217) refers to it as another Cuivre ceremonial component, i.e., similar to the Wieman site, where:

> ...burial offerings were a large specialized Etley stemmed, Sedalia-like lanceolate..., drills, a gorget, hematite, galena, corner-notched projectile points, a snubbed-end flake scraper, choppers, chert-core hammerstones, manos, anvilstones, a calcite pendant, a beaver-incisor knife, antler tapping tools, antler flaking tools, a bone flesher, bone punches, bone awls, modified raccoon jaws, a tubular-bone bead, and fragments of copper. The burial of infants and adolescents in a rock and earth mound structure were part of the component assemblage. The structure in which the burials were found was made of chert cobbles and boulders, some weighing as much as 75 pounds. The burials had been placed in a shallow oval depression; they were flexed or bundled or consisted of piles of bones or scattered bones. Artifacts placed with the dead were in caches.

MORTUARY SITES IN ILLINOIS AND MISSOURI

Before discussing the adaptational and trade dimensions of the Titterington phase, its mortuary dimensions should be discussed because these reflect directly upon a number of other dimensions. The original report on the Titterington focus (Titterington 1950) includes seven sites in the St. Louis area, and three excavations of a site in Brown County, Ill. Of these, four sites have been assigned to the Titterington phase because of the presence of only Etley, Wadlow, and Turkey Tail points. Another site, Hartford Church, has been eliminated as mixed with earlier Helton phase materials. The four sites are Elm Point, Etley, Kampsville, and Marquette Park.

Elm Point Site

The Elm Point site was a "red ochre limestone slab-covered burial...in a mound on top of Elm Point, 2½ mi northwest of St. Charles, Missouri..." (Titterington 1950:24). Montet-White (1968b:101-102) states that Titterington's excavations at the site recovered six multiple burials with limestone slab covers. The artifact inventory is listed in Table 11. While Elm Point produced only one Etley point, Montet-White (p. 102) carefully points out that it is a "typical Etley point, a subrectangular stemmed specimen, made on a ogival blade."

Etley Site

The Etley site is located on the Oettle farm, somewhere on the east-facing Illinois bluffs of Calhoun County, Ill., about 3 km north of Hardin (Titterington 1950). Titterington states that the site was composed of two low mounds, each 15 x 6 x 0.5 m (50 x 20 x 1.5 ft). Perino (1968b:117) quotes the site's excavator, Walter Wadlow, as observing that the interments at the Etley site were "placed in radial formation, heads towards the center, under a large slab which was supported by limestone blocks." Wadlow excavated nine such groups of multiple burials, each with three to six extended individuals, accompanied with red ochre, grave goods, and roofed over with limestone slabs. The artifact inventory from the Etley site (Titterington 1950:Table 1; Montet-White 1968: 100) is listed in Table 11.

Summarizing the burial programs of these two sites, Montet-White states (p. 102):

> However incomplete, this information can be used to interpret certain aspects of the burial practices represented at the above mentioned sites. Either single or multiple, the burials were placed in a shallow pit. The bodies were laid in a fully extended position, covered with red ochre, and large limestone slabs were used for roofing the burial pits. No mention is made of secondary burials, and the presence of charred bones indicating cremations is not reported. In spite of the

TABLE 11

Titterington Phase Mortuary Sites: Artifact Inventories

	Elm Point	Etley	Kampsville	Marquette	Wieman
Very large blades	0	0	0	0	1
Ogival blades[a]	0	75	2	21	19
Etley Stemmed points	1	13[b]	1	1	3
Turkey Tail points	47	0	0	0	0
Intrusive points	0	0	0	0	1[c]
Full-grooved axes	1	19	0	} 2	2
3/4-grooved axes	0	6	0		4
Tubular pipes	1	0	0	0	0
Bannerstones	0	3	2	0	0
Engraved shell	0	0	0	2	0
Copper celts	0	3	0	0	0
Copper awls	0	1	1	0	0
Plummets	6	0	0	0	0
Copper plummets	1	0	0	0	0
Diorite spheres	0	0	0	1	0
Hematite lumps	several	0	0	0	0
Total	57+	120	6	27	30
Number of burials	6 gps.	8-9 gps. of 3-6 bur.	1?	2	ca. 40

Note: The Etley and Wadlow points from these five sites tend to be larger than similar forms recovered from habitation sites. However, the manufacturing techniques and the general shapes of these items from both habitation and mortuary sites are identical.

[a]Perino (1968a:98) uses the term Wadlow blade. [b]Perino (1968a:98) has subsequently examined the materials and would type one of the Etley points as a shallow side-notched blade. [c]This is my own interpretation of Bacon and Miller (1957).

conditions in which the sites were excavated, it can be assumed that the latter at least would have been recognized.

Kampsville Site

Titterington (1950:20) reports a single limestone-slab-covered grave near Kampsville, Calhoun County, Ill. which produced two Wadlow points, an Etley point, two bannerstones, and a copper awl. This site is assigned to the Titterington phase because of the presence of Wadlow and Etley points and the absence of other point types.

Marquette Site

The Marquette site (Titterington 1950:20-22) and the Kampsville site are similar. Walter Wadlow, the excavator, told Titterington that there were two parallel burials, the bodies lying on their backs, extended and covered with limestone slabs with 27 artifacts but no red ochre. Titterington describes the artifacts but does not mention any mounded structure over the burials. The site location is loosely described as the far north end of the land then recently incorporated into Pere Marquette State Park, Jersey County, Ill.

Wadlow and Etley points assign this small burial station to the Titterington phase. There are also two incised shell objects called "head ornaments" because each skull had one on or near it. Fig. 15 is a drawing after Titterington's photograph (1950:Fig. 4). The two artifacts are bilaterally symmetric; the incised designs are highly stylized, perhaps anthropomorphic or more likely zoomorphic. The designs are similar, except that one figure has an extra V-shaped element and the other a row of parallel striations along one edge (male and female?). It is not known how these ornaments were worn; there are no suspension holes.

Wieman Site

Another Titterington phase burial station, located in Lincoln County,

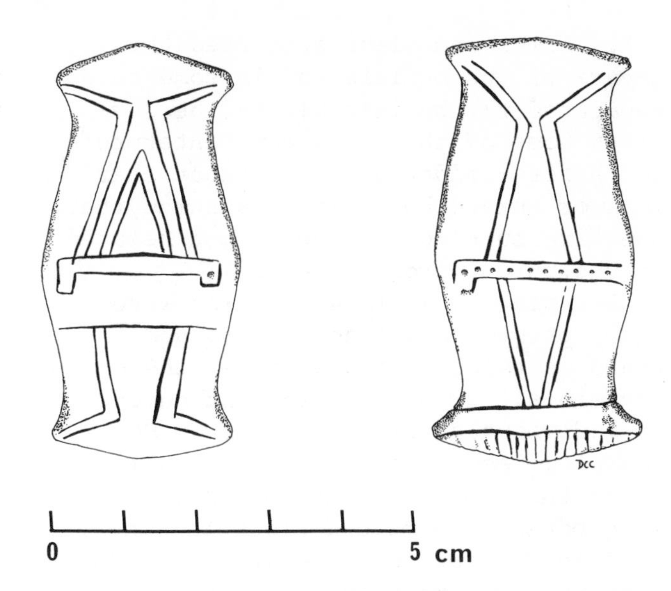

Figure 15. Sketch of shell artifacts from the Marquette site. After Titterington (1950:Fig. 4).

Mo., was excavated by Bacon and Miller (1957). While they refer to the site only by its survey number, 23LN11, I have decided to refer to it by the name of the landowner, Bertha Wieman, following a long standing tradition in American archeology. The Wieman site is located on the crest of a 20- to 25-m-high (60- to 80-ft) hill rising out of the bottoms of the Cuivre River. This hill is located "near highway 47, about one mile east of Troy" (p. 19) which would have placed the site approximately 30 km up the Cuivre River, 85 km from the Booth site (23MN242), and 40 km from the Koster site (the last two distances being straight-line, rather than following the river valley).

Bacon and Miller note that the entire hilltop is covered with a scatter of aboriginal debris and that 30 years of plowing had begun to bring human bone to the surface. The area excavated about this plow-induced exposure included a round 8-ft-diameter burial area with a single layer of burials in the western half and two layers in the eastern half. There was an extension to the northeast where the burials appeared to be stacked three deep (p.

21). Limestone slabs separated the layers of the burials and in some cases separated the burials within the levels. Some of the slabs were interpreted as fire-reddened, but without charcoal or burned bone, it is assumed that the fire burning episode is not related to the burial program (p. 21).

Because the skeletal remains were badly preserved and no one trained in field osteology was present at the excavations, burial position and number of individuals remains obscure. For example, Bacon and Miller (1957:21) noted that in all of the burials the long bones were placed close together, "and in several instances were placed side by side, with another group of long bones placed on top. The effect of this placement was to give the appearance of a careful stacking of the bones." They concluded that this probably reflects bundle burials. Further, "a definite count of the burials could not be made, due to the difficulties in distinguishing separate burials. An approximation would be forty burials" (p. 22).

The Wieman site is assigned to the Titterington phase because the points illustrated by Bacon and Miller are Wadlow and Etley points made of non-heat-treated cherts. In addition, the burial program employing limestone slabs and groups of points and axes placed beneath and adjacent to burials fits the observations made by Titterington, Wadlow, and others for the sites already mentioned. There is no mention of red ochre with the Wieman burials and several pieces of hematite, several hammerstones, and many flint chips recovered from the uppermost part of the fill have been excluded from this analysis. Table 11 summarizes the assemblage.

There were also three chipped-stone artifacts which were anomalous in the following respects: (1) they are described as being made of waxy chert, light gray to pink in color, which I interpret as evidence for heat treatment; (2) these three heat-treated artifacts are distinctly different in shape from Titterington phase artifacts. The exact provenience of two of these artifacts is not known (p. 30) and the authors suggest that these two points relate to the debris scatter on the hilltop. I concur. The last item, a reworked side-notched point was "definitely associated with a burial, may have been the cause of death" (p. 30). In any event, the point will be considered as "intrusive" and excluded from further analysis.

Finally I suspect that the Wieman burials occurred under a mound, like those at the Elm Point and Etley sites because: (1) the superimposition of limestone slabs between burials implies the accumulation of soil rather than the filling of burial pits part way for successive burials; (2) the darker, more compact earth about the burials (p. 33) suggests a buried soil horizon protected from leaching and disturbance by the overburden of the mound itself; and (3) I suspect that 30 years of plowing would have rapidly destroyed the site. Unless new evidence comes to light, I will consider the Wieman site burials to be from a plowed-down mound rather than a cemetery.

ADAPTATIONAL DIMENSIONS OF THE TITTERINGTON PHASE

Tools and Tasks

Figure 16 is a Venn diagram comparing the presence and absence of Titterington phase materials from components at eight sites: Booth (23 MN242), Elm Point, Etley, Kampsville, Koster, Marquette Park, Modoc Rock Shelter, and Wieman (23LN11). The figure is a visual plotting of the information contained in Tables 10 and 11. The three large circles represent habitation type sites, while five smaller circles represent burial stations. Six of the circles show some degree of overlap while two circles, those of Kampsville and Wieman, are concentric to the Etley site. This means that six of the eight sites have some unique artifact types.

Now it is our task to interpret this information. We immediately see that there is a sharp break between mortuary

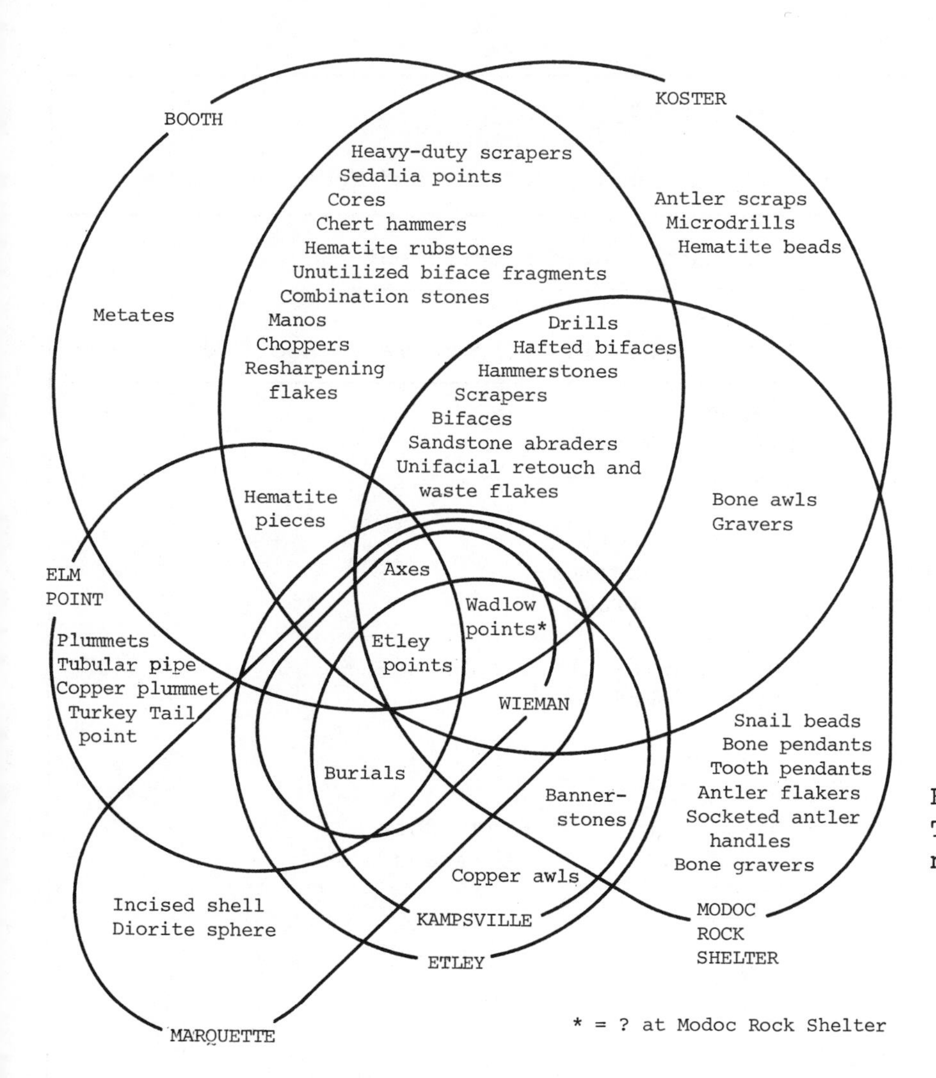

Figure 16. Comparison of Titterington phase components at eight sites.

and habitation sites. Only the latter should be analyzed in terms of the Mark II model for maintenance and extractive tasks, however. Accordingly, the habitation type sites will be discussed.

We see from Fig. 16 that each habitation type site has some exclusive artifacts. Booth alone possesses metates; Koster alone has microdrills and hematite beads; and Modoc Rock Shelter has antler artifacts and a number of ornaments, including a prismoidal bannerstone. For items which appear at all three sites, we have a rather depleted collection of chipped-stone tools. While lack of analytical categories at Modoc Rock Shelter can explain the absence of cores in this common or undifferentiated core of tool types, this ad hoc explanation does not hold for the several categories of ground stone and hematite pieces which Koster and Booth share. Are these differences explainable in terms of the various constellations of maintenance and extractive tasks performed at these sites?

Ignoring for now the ever present problems of sampling bias, sample size, and mixed samples, let us examine Tables 12 and 13. These tables summarize the maintenance and extractive tasks as defined by the Mark II model, for the three Titterington phase components. A zero (0) indicates that there is no evidence that the particular tool-using task is present at the site. A question mark (?) indicates that the Mark II model defines a task as present due to one or more key artifact types, but there is no confirmatory evidence that this task actually took place at the site. A plus sign (+) indicates that the presence of the particular task has independent confirmatory evi-

TABLE 12

Titterington Phase Maintenance Tasks at Booth, Koster, and Modoc Rock Shelter

Task	Tools Present	Confirmatory Evidence Present			Booth	Kos.	Modoc
		Unfinished Items	Debris	Worn Tools			
Chert tool manufacture	Hammerstones Sandstone abrad. Antler flakes	Bifaces Preforms	Cores Waste flakes		+	+	+
Ground stone tool manufacture	Chert hammers Hammerstones Sandstone abrad.		Chert hammer frags.		+	+	?
Shell item manufacture	Drills Flakes Incising tools Sandstone abrad.	Would require shell manufacturing debris			X	0	0
Wood item manufacture	Knives Axes Scrapers Drills Flakes Gravers Bone gravers Heavy-duty scrapers			Heavy-duty scrapers	+	+	?
Woven item manufacture	None preserved				0	0	0
Hide and leather work	Flakes Drills Microdrills Bone awls			Worn drills and microdrills	?	+	?
Bone and antler tool manufacture	Sandstone abrad. Gravers Retouched flakes		Antler scraps Worked bone		X	+	+

Note: A zero indicates no evidence for a task being performed; a question mark indicates that there is no confirmatory evidence; an X indicates problems of preservation; and a plus is a confirmed task.

TABLE 13

Titterington Phase Extractive Tasks at Booth, Koster, and Modoc Rock Shelter

Task	Tools Present	Confirmatory Evidence Present	Booth	Koster	Modoc
Trapping	None	Fauna	X	O	O
Hunting	Projectile pts. Knives	Point fragments Worn Knives	+	+	+
Fowling	None	Fauna	X	O[a]	O
Fishing	None	Fauna	X	O	O
Quarrying	Hammerstones	All early stages of knapping Cores Primary shatter Chert outcrops	+	+	?
Lumbering	Axes	Worn axes Bit fragments	?	+	+
Hide and leather preparation	Scrapers Heavy-duty scrapers Flakes Knives	Use polish on scraper forms	+	+	?
Nut and seed preparation	Manos Booth: metates Combination stones Hammerstones	Flora	?	?	?
Preserved meat preparation	Manos Booth: metates Knives Choppers	Worn tools Butchered animal bones (indirect)	?	?	?
Fibrous vegetable preparation	Choppers Manos Booth: metates	Worn tools	?	?	?

Note: A zero indicates no evidence for a task being performed; a question mark indicates that there is no confirmatory evidence; an X indicates problems of preservation; and a plus is a confirmed task.

[a]Plummet in Houart (1971:Fig. 10d) is from what is now thought to be geologically mixed context and has been omitted from this analysis.

dence. An (X) indicates that the model is not testable due to preservation problems.

Our first task in evaluating the results is to correct for certain gaps in the data in order to eliminate as many question marks as possible and to make some alterations in the Mark II model. One such gap involves metates. The Mark II model as originally conceived states that a number of grinding and chopping tools (manos, metates, combination or nutting stones, and choppers) are used in three extractive tasks, each involving pulverization (Table 13). The presence of any one of these tools would automatically assign a question mark for these three extractive tasks. However, the Venn diagram in Fig. 16 suggests that the metate does *not* covary with the other tools. In addition, choppers, mullers, and combination stones do not covary with hammerstones since Modoc Rock Shelter has the former but not the latter.

Therefore, the most diagnostic artifact of intensive pulverization is the metate, while the hammerstone would be the least diagnostic. Therefore, the three extractive tasks need to be restated. A portion of Table 13 should be restated as Table 14. The restatement suggests that metates relate to the intensive pulverization of plant and animal remains, while manos and combination stones refer to the processing of nuts and seeds and manos and choppers refer to processing of fibrous vegetable matter. Hammerstones and knives are too generalized to be used as a basis for the task model analysis. Unfortunately, while the metates indicate intensive pulverization, they do not identify the raw material being processed. On the other hand, combination stones (or nutting stones or pitted manos) and choppers do separate nut and seed processing from meat and vegetable processing.

There is a second instance of noncovariation between tools which the Mark II model does not account for. A nontrivial example is the presence of microdrills uniquely at Koster. While the microdrills may be used for boring small holes in various substances, equivalent artifact forms such as bone awls may be equal and alternative so-

TABLE 14

Restatement of Pulverization Tasks: Titterington Phase

Task	Tools			Debris	Booth	Koster	Modoc
	Intensive	Normal	Non-specific				
Nut and seed processing	Metate	Manos Combination stones	Hammerstones	Nuts Seeds	? Intensive	+ Normal	0
Preserved meat processing	Metate	Manos Choppers	Knives	Fauna	? Intensive	+ Normal	0
Fibrous vegetable production	Metate	Manos Choppers		Other flora	? Intensive	? Normal	0

Note: This restatement of the three pulverization tasks is an example of an explicit model producing feedback information when tested with archeological materials. It also indicates the value of the Venn diagram in separating multipurpose tools into task-specific ones.

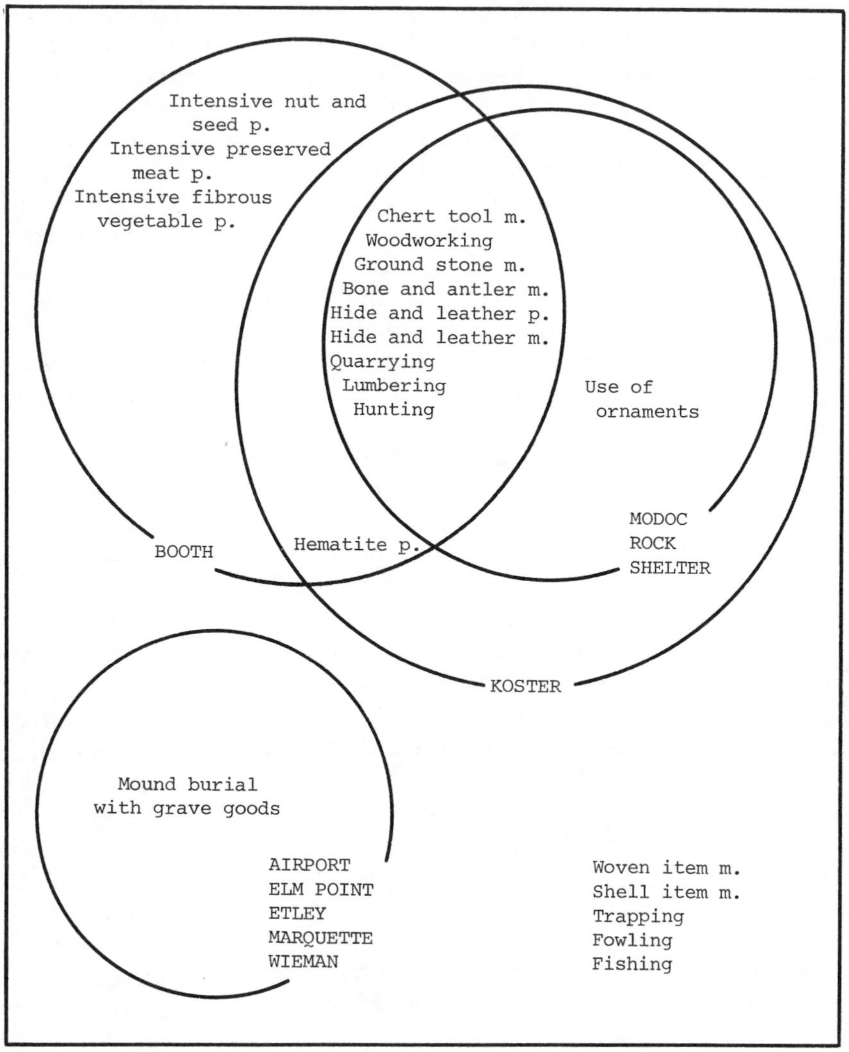

Figure 17. Universe of Titterington phase tasks.

Intensive nut and seed p.
Intensive preserved meat p.
Intensive fibrous vegetable p.
Chert tool m.
Woodworking
Ground stone m.
Bone and antler m.
Hide and leather p.
Hide and leather m.
Quarrying
Lumbering
Hunting
Use of ornaments
BOOTH
Hematite p.
MODOC ROCK SHELTER
KOSTER
Mound burial with grave goods
AIRPORT
ELM POINT
ETLEY
MARQUETTE
WIEMAN
Woven item m.
Shell item m.
Trapping
Fowling
Fishing

m. = manufacturing
p. = preparation

lutions to the problem of poking holes in leather. Then again, the chert microdrills possibly serve a special function in a subcategory of woodworking. Unlike the metates, which I consider a critical tool in any intensive work of pulverization, the microdrills may be reflecting too fine a distinction for the Mark II model. Here again, the Mark II model is being *tested* against the data, rather than providing a blanket explanation for the data.

Obviously, not all of the behavior at these three sites can be completely explained in terms of maintenance and extractive tasks. While the social tasks model is very embryonic, it can be noted that the Booth and Koster sites have worked and ground hematite, while Modoc Rock Shelter has a number of pendants and a prismatic bannerstone.

To compare these three sites along adaptational dimensions, it is merely necessary to take Tables 12-14 plus the above comments and make another Venn diagram, Fig. 17, which illustrates the Titterington phase task universe. The universe includes all the tasks in the Mark II model while each circle includes the tasks present at that site. I have arbitrarily decided to change all question mark scores (?) to pluses (+) since the lack of preservation at Booth site and the lack of specific debris classes at Modoc Rock Shelter biases against pluses and for question marks.

Fig. 17 indicates that our sample of eight Titterington phase components falls into three categories: (1) Mortuary sites; (2) Short-term bivouacs with an orientation towards hunting, quarrying, working hides and leather, and maintenance of the tool kit; and (3) Short-term base camps with an orientation toward hunting, animal processing, vegetable processing, quarrying, and maintenance of the tool kit. One could further subdivide this classification with (la) multiple and (lb) single burial mortuary sites and (3a) intensive and (3b) normal food processing activities at short-term base camps.

The habitation sites have a common core of maintenance and extractive tasks, but this core does not include the full range of anticipated possibilities: nine tasks form a common core, but five tasks are not represented at the sites. The presence of ornaments at Modoc Rock Shelter and Koster or the processing of hematite at Booth and Koster do not seem to be central to our understanding of how these sites functioned along adaptational dimensions. To explain why we have three somewhat different types of habitation sites requires a certain amount of environmental reconstruction, now that we have developed a solution to the problem of which tasks occurred at these sites.

Environmental Reconstruction

Titterington phase materials come from a geological area described in Missouri by McQueen (1929) as a glaciated till plain with a gentle and rolling surface, except near the larger streams and rivers where there is moderate dissection; and in Illinois by Rubey (1952) as mostly a glacial till plain extending eastward from the Illinois Valley and dissected by streams. Across much of this plains area is the Prairie Peninsula, a mosaic of upland prairie openenings among oak-hickory woodlands with mesic deciduous forest along the valley slopes (Wight 1968: 78).

Bearing these brief descriptions in mind, the Booth site is presently located in an oak-hickory forest zone that stretches out into the prairie vegetation and sparsely forested areas of the till plains (Klippel 1969). For the Koster site, Zawacki and Hausfater's (1969) reconstruction of the early nineteenth century vegetal zones indicates that the Illinois floodplain was a mosaic environment of river, forest, bottomland prairie, backwater lakes, and sloughs. The Koster site itself is located in a somewhat drier bluff-base hardwood forest zone. Above the bluffs is an oak-hickory-elm forest which then thins out into a barrens of mixed forests and grasslands, eventually becoming true, upland prairie. Modoc Rock Shelter is located in an environmental situation analogous to that of Koster. But what were these local situations like during the second and third millennia B.C.?

Asch, Ford, and Asch (1972) present two lines of evidence that there has been considerable continuity in the general picture of level prairie lands dissected by forest-covered slopes and valleys. The first line of evidence is that a high correlation exists between the distribution of nineteenth century forests and land slopes greater than 4% throughout Illinois. While the Prairie Peninsula in general may suggest a drier, more variable climate than do the forested areas to the north and south, the local distribution of forest and prairie apparently relates to local topography. Their second line of evidence is based upon macroplant remains from Koster which indicate that by 7000 B.P. most of the modern tree species were present in the lower Illinois Valley area and stayed there. While the wood charcoal sample for the Titterington phase (Horizon 4 in Asch, Ford, and Asch 1972:Table 1) is very small, Yarnell's study (1964) of a number of midwestern sites indicates that no major changes in vegetation have occurred during the last 4000 years. In summary then (Asch, Ford, and Asch 1972:22):

> The occurrence of trees, sometimes even mesic associations, on slopes in the much drier prairies west of Illinois suggests that dry

conditions in Illinois would not easily dislodge trees from the slopes of the lower Illinois Valley though on the gentler slopes prairies might prevail.

While it would be foolish to copy maps of vegetation for this century and relabel them 2000 B.C., it seems reasonable, using the data presently available, to assume that the Booth site was in or near an oak-hickory forest zone which jutted out into the Missouri prairie due to the downcutting tributaries of the Salt River system, and that the Koster and Modoc Rock Shelter sites were fronted by a mosaic of prairie, forest, and wet lands; that there were parallel bands of forest above and below the bluff crests; and that the uplands became progressively more prairielike and less a deciduous forest as distance increased from the main valley.

Exploitation of Plants and Animals

Against this reconstructed environmental background, let us examine the direct evidence of which resources were being exploited. Booth site has neither preserved flora nor fauna. Modoc Rock Shelter has a faunal report by P. Parmalee, broken down into 1-ft intervals. Although present, flora was not systematically collected. The Koster site has a preliminary paleoethnobotanical report (Asch, Ford, and Asch 1972) and a preliminary identification of faunal materials for the Titterington phase (Frederick C. Hill, personal communication). Hill's analysis of the faunal remains is based upon a total of 622 bones and 1,790 shells from the screened units, of which 282 were identified to the family, genus, and/or species level. An additional 18 bones and 1 shell were recovered from the flotation units, of which 14 were identifiable to the family, genus, and/or species level. The excavated faunal materials from this component are scarce and generally in poor condition such that only the thicker-shelled mussels were preserved. The tabulations of Hill's analysis are included as App. C. Hill's conclusions are tentative until further data can be collected from the Koster site. His summary of the presently available data is as follows:

> Utilization of the ponded portion of the river and associated backwater lakes is evidenced by the presence of the particular fish and mussel species assemblage. Although the soft shell turtle is aquatic, the exact habitat from which they were hunted is not certain since it is impossible to determine which of the species is present in the remains. Waterfowl remains would be expected to be more numerous with the emphasis placed on aquatic resource exploitation. However, their scarcity is probably due to a seasonal factor rather than the avoidance of this resource. While the raccoon, deer, and turkey represent woodland animals, the deer is more closely associated with the woodland-prairie ecotone, while the other two species tend to be found in greater numbers within the forest proper. Thus if we look at the species list simply in terms of number of animals from each of the various available resource zones, we find the river itself to be the single major contributor of faunal resources. However, the large amount of food supplied by the deer establishes the forest-prairie ecotone as the major resource zone in terms of pounds of meat supplied.
>
> Season of occupation indicators are few in horizon four [the Titterington phase sample - *TGC*]. Unfortunately, no mussels were complete enough to allow for season of death determination nor were fish scales available for this estimation. The only evidence available for season of occupation estimates is that provided by the large numbers of mussels. It is assumed that they could be collected during the summer or fall due to their greater availability at these times.

Other interesting results of Hill's analysis include his observations on the butchering practices of deer:

> Only two deer bones showed evidence of butchering processes. One of twelve toe bones was cut on its ventral surface probably during removal of the cannon bone. One of three distal femur heads was knife scored where the knee joint was severed during the butchering process. It appears that the deer was butchered elsewhere and brought back to the site in pieces. The head and vertebrae were not included in the sections brought back to the site or if they were these bones were later discarded elsewhere.

Hill also notes that none of the nine antler fragments included a base portion; hence "it was impossible to determine if they represented shed antlers."

Hill's faunal analysis tends to augment the conclusions of the Mark II analysis of the Koster artifacts. The absence of fishing tackle (hooks or net weights) seems reasonable if fish were being taken from ponded areas rather than the Illinois River itself. The absence of plummets, (the plummet reported by Houart [1971] has been assigned to a mixed zone) which I assume to be fowling net weights, and the presence of waterfowl elements suggest three possibilities: (1) Waterfowl may have been hunted without nets using plummets as weights; (2) because the waterfowl seem to be less important, considering the heavy use of aquatic resources, fowling may have been so rarely performed that plummet usage was not intensive enough to leave behind these artifacts at Koster; or (3) plummets do not relate to fowling nets. The heavy use of deer agrees with the Mark II model. Unfortunately, a major source of protein - shellfish and fish - was not predicted because the tools (if any) used in collecting them did not preserve at Koster.

The floral analysis of Asch, Ford, and Asch (1972) is based upon 89 pieces of wood charcoal and 1.7 gm of carbonized nutshells. The major sources of firewood are *Quercus* sp. (oak), *Juglans* sp. (black walnut and butternut), *Fraxinus* (ash), and Ulmaceae (elm and hackberry) (Asch, Ford, and Asch 1972: Table 1). *Carya* sp. (hickory and pecan) and *Acer* sp. (maple) represent minor sources. Comparing this prehistoric distribution of firewood with reconstructions of historic vegetation for the major wooded ecological zones of the lower Illinois Valley (Asch, Ford, and Asch 1972:Table 2), the best fit would be the 1815-1820 observations of the hillside-talus forest whose tree types in descending order of abundance were Ulmaceae, *Quercus* sp., *Juglans* sp., *Acer* sp., *Fraxinus* sp., *Carya* sp., and *Tilia* sp. (basswood). Except for basswood which has an exceptionally low heat value as a firewood (Zawacki and Hausfater 1969:25), we see a reasonable correspondence considering the small sample available. The 1926-1930 observations on this zone give similar results except for the low frequency of ash. I would conclude that firewood was being gathered from the same hillside-talus-slope forest zone in which the Koster site is located, this being the simplest explanation.

For the nut analysis, Asch, Ford, and Asch (1972:8) note that flotation samples yielding no nuts came primarily from excavation units lying between cultural horizons or from the Titterington phase occupation. While this low density of carbonized nut remains reflects nut processing rather than intensive nut processing (since there are no metates at Koster) at a short-term occupation, four types of nuts are recorded: hickory, pecan, acorn, and hazelnut (Asch, Ford, and Asch, Table 3). This variety of nut types reflects exploitation of a number of different resource zones and different nut crop seasons. Following the discussions in Asch, Ford, and Asch (1972:9), hickory nuts and acorns are available from the upland forest and hillside-talus-slope forest, pecans are restricted to the floodplain forest, and hazelnuts are almost exclusively limited to the upland zone (cf. Zawacki and Hausfater 1969:Tables). To add to this diversity of resource location, there is variation in the season of availability. For instance, the peak for pecan is about one month later than for most of the other nuts and acorns (N. Asch, personal communication).

Therefore, because these nuts come from several different resource zones and are harvestable at different times, I suggest that stored nuts were being processed at Koster during the Titterington short-term occupation rather than nut gathering being a major activity there. Again, this interpretation seems to be in line with the Mark II model analysis of the tool assemblage.

Table 15 summarizes the fauna from Modoc Rock Shelter for depths between 5 and 7 ft (Fowler 1959b:Tables 7 and 8). Here again we have a rather small sample of remains, with a situation in which identification of elements was difficult, only a small portion giving us information about resource exploitation. While the minimum number of individuals is not given, one would anticipate that deer and elk represent the most important source of meat while fish and shellfish are least important. Waterfowl and waterbirds are well represented and there is a relatively high frequency of amphibians and reptiles. Turkey, quail, and prairie chicken are also present. Like the faunal assemblage from Koster, we find that the two major resources being exploited are woodland animals (raccoon and turkey in the forest; deer and elk in the woodland-prairie ecotone) and aquatics (waterfowl, fish, and mussels). The presence of large mammals, such as elk and deer, suggests that like Koster, Modoc Rock Shelter represents a primary exploitation of the forest and forest edge situation around Modoc Rock Shelter and up Barbeau Creek into the upland forest, with a secondary exploitation centered around the floodplain and river.

Once more, the Mark II model did well for the land mammal hunting, but gave no indication of the exploitation of fowl, fish, or mussels. Here again, habitat-specific information about the fish and mussels might indicate that tools would not be needed to collect them. However, the migratory waterfowl present a problem in interpretation since no plummets were recovered from Modoc Rock Shelter for the Titterington phase occupation. Unfortunately, until we have an example in which presence of plummets covaries with the absence of waterfowl, the Mark II model is untested in its assumption that plummets are fowling net weights.

Fowler (1959b:44) would suggest a fall or winter occupation at Modoc Rock

TABLE 15

Titterington Component at Modoc Rockshelter: Faunal Inventory

	Number of Elements
Mammals	
Deer and elk	172
Raccoon	12
Opossum	2
Others	27
Unidentified	3,299
Total	3,512
Fish	
Total	37
Amphibians and reptiles	
Total	136
Birds	
Waterfowl	42
Water birds	3
Turkey	4
Quail and prairie chicken	5
Passenger pigeon	2
Others	2
Unidentified	138
Total	196
Mussels	
Total valves	40

Shelter due to the presence of migratory waterfowl and fully formed deer antler. Further evidence for a cold season occupation comes from the features at Modoc described by Buettner-Janusch (1954:86) as thick, wide beds of white ash and interpreted by James Brown (personal communication) as heating beds to make camping at the rock shelter more comfortable during late fall or winter. Panchromatic and infrared photographs of these features are shown by Buettner-Janusch (Fig. 32). (Note: the Modoc Rock Shelter was originally named Barbeau Creek Rock Shelter [Buettner-Janusch 1954].)

It is unfortunate that carbonized plant remains were not systematically collected from Modoc Rock Shelter because the Mark II model predicts the absence of carbonized nuts and seeds. Unfortunately, the model cannot be tested at Modoc.

Finally, turning to Booth site, Klippel's interpretation is that "the site was probably occupied during a season when vegetals [*sic*] were being collected and preserved" (1969:52). If these vegetal resources included nuts and acorns, the occupation would have occurred during nutting time, which would be August through October (Zawacki and Hausfater 1969:Table 10). If there had been preserved and analyzed floral and faunal remains from the Booth site, I suspect that we would have another example of a dual exploitation strategy from a single locality: (1) pursuit of large land mammals such as deer and perhaps elk and smaller game such as raccoon and turkey in the forest-prairie ecotone and (2) the heavy collecting and processing of the nut crop, which required metates for efficient bulk processing, instead of exploiting collectable resources from a riverine-floodplain resource zone.

Malacological Analysis

Binford and Binford (1966:267) suggest that, along with resources, suitable places to live are scattered across the landscape. Hence we might wonder what attracted people to the Koster site to use it as a short-term campsite. In addition to the generally sheltered nature of the location and a perennial spring, archeomalacological analysis by Jaehnig (n.d.:74-77) suggests that the site proper was mostly dry and open, except for localized tree cover near Squares 44 and 45. Since snails reflect very localized conditions and the floral report indicates that the entire region was neither drying up nor blowing away, probably we have a clearing in the bluff-base talus-slope forest, which attracted hunter-gatherers as a suitable campsite.

MORTUARY AND TRADE DIMENSIONS

The five mortuary sites reported here for the Titterington phase fall into two types: multiple burial sites such as Etley, Elm Point and Wieman, and single burial sites such as Kampsville and Marquette Park. The multiple burials occur in mounded structures while the single group burials do not, probably because the mounds are built up over a period of time as more individuals and limestone slabs are placed together, as accretionary episodes. Mortuary goods include oversized chipped-stone tools, axes, and special items of copper, hematite, shell, exotic chert, etc. such as bannerstones, ornaments, plummets, Turkey Tail points, adzes, awls, and diorite spheres. Frequently the various grave goods occur in localized piles near a burial and red ochre is sprinkled over the grave (except for Marquette Park and Wieman).

Because there are no osteological studies of these mortuary sites, it is not possible to determine if natural populations were being buried or if a special age or sex group had access to extensive grave goods and mounded burial. A sixth mortuary site, Airport, located at the Springfield, Ill. Municipal Airport, has some ill-preserved burials which might shed light on this problem (Walter Klippel, personal communication).

The mortuary sites give us our only

information about trade patterns during the Titterington phase. Among raw materials, native copper is present. Titterington (1950) specifically notes that the Turkey Tail points at Elm Point have concentric gray bands, which suggests to me that they are made of Hornstone or Harrison County, Ind. chert. Assuming that the copper artifacts are made of materials from the Upper Great Lakes lode, rather than from local glacial till (Rubey 1952), we have two exotic resources moving into the region, one from the south and the other from the north. On stylistic grounds, the copper artifacts closely resemble contemporary Old Copper artifacts in Wisconsin, while the Turkey Tail points are clearly part of a widely dispersed mortuary and trade complex (Didier 1967).

The presence of both exotic styles and exotic raw materials in mortuary, rather than habitation site, context suggests three things --

1. Binford's suggestion (1962) that copper artifacts functioned as status markers rather than tools is supported, rather than Griffin's contention (1952:356) that these were tools.
2. For at least one Archaic phase, copper tools are occurring in mortuary rather than habitation site context. (See McHugh's comments [1973:74-75] on such occurrences.)
3. The lack of exotic grave goods at the Wieman site may reflect the relatively greater isolation of groups living up secondary streams.

DATING*

As I stated at the beginning of this chapter, phase definition starts with a stylistic definition of certain artifact types. When a number of components have been assigned to the phase and the definition of the phase becomes fleshed out, one can reassess and refine the stylistic definition. This refinement requires larger samples of style markers and, with some luck, several absolute and relative dates. To aid in the refinement of Titterington phase artifact types, Appendix A presents metric data for Wadlow, Etley, and Sedalia points from Booth, Koster, and Wieman sites.

Unfortunately, there are no carbon dates for this phase. However, we may be able to bracket its temporal position. Because the Titterington phase is stratigraphically above the Helton phase at Koster, it must post-date 4800 B.P.. This is in good agreement with the 8-ft-depth carbon date (M-483) at Modoc Rock Shelter of 4720 ± 300 years B.P. (Fowler 1959b:Table 1). If there is a Riverton culture occupation (Winters 1969) at Koster (Houart's Horizon 3), then the Titterington phase ends by ca. 4000 B.P. If there is no Riverton culture occupation there, I would suggest that the Titterington phase occupation is earlier than the Kampsville focus (Perino 1968b:78-84) which has been carbon dated to 920 B.C. (Perino 1968b:115). I would place the Titterington phase earlier than the Kampsville focus (1) because the burial program of the Titterington phase is similar to that of the Helton phase, rather than the Kampsville focus as seen at Mound 7 of the Klunk mound group; (2) because there is very little time between 920 B.C. and the Early Woodland period which is usually assigned to the first millennium B.C.; and (3) because Klippel estimates (1972:59) that Booth site is earlier than the dates of 570 and 660 B.C. assigned to the Early Woodland component at Collins site (23MN223) in northeast Missouri.

Therefore, until carbon dates are available from single-component Titterington phase sites, we can guess date the phase to sometime between 4800 and 4000 or 3000 B.P.

---

*Since the completion of this manuscript a single radiocarbon date (ISGS 329) has been obtained from the Titterington phase Feature 286a at Koster. The date, 3950 ± 75 years B.P., is in excellent agreement with Cook's reasoning in this section - *Ed.*

SUMMARY

Analytical Summary

This study of the Titterington phase has centered around three themes: (1) assigning prehistoric materials to functional, stylistic, and manufacturing categories; (2) testing the Mark II model with these data and using confirmatory plant and animal remains to evaluate the model; and (3) developing a pragmatic definition of the time-space concept of phase within an anthropological view of sociocultural systems.

The chipped-stone materials were very easily placed in Klippel's non-heat-treating tradition on account of both the lack of heat alteration of chert and the generally large, massive forms of the Wadlow, Etley, Sedalia and heavy-duty scraper forms. The functional analysis did well as a means of determining where use modification occurred on a tool and how intensively a task was performed. This agrees with results of tool use experiments (Luedtke n.d.). The stylistic analysis indicates that this phase is somewhat restricted geographically, although how much this reflects localized projectile point terminology and the lack of published materials from adjacent areas is unknown. Comparisons of habitation site point forms and those from mortuary sites indicate similar manufacturing methods, though at mortuary sites the forms tend to be somewhat larger and much less frequently broken. At the same time, there is a special mortuary form, the Turkey Tail point, which apparently does not occur at campsites. It is anticipated that these Turkey Tail points have a much longer continuity in time than the characteristic point forms of the Titterington phase.

Using the typologies discussed above, the Mark II model was used to determine the presence and absence of specific maintenance and extractive tasks at eight sites. Fig. 17 summarizes the analysis. Then animal and plant remains from Koster and animal remains from Modoc Rock Shelter were compared with Fig. 17. For Koster, the firewood analysis suggests that only the local forested zone was being exploited. The carbonized nut analysis reflects either that nuts were collected incidentally while Koster was occupied in the late summer or early fall, or that stored nuts were being used there. Hill's faunal analysis indicates the degree of slippage between tools and hunting activities, although the generalized picture of exploiting only two major resource zones fits with the picture of Koster as a limited extraction locus in a settlement system. At present, there seems little hope in tightening the artifact analysis for netting and trapping because wood, fibers, and nets are not preserved at Koster. Kroeber and Barnett's study (1960) of California fishing techniques suggest the sort of materials one might expect in a situation of better organic preservation.

By comparison with the extractive tasks, the maintenance tasks are much better known since antler, bone, and stone remnants of manufacture were present. It is anticipated that a higher specificity of tasks can be achieved when this analysis is further tested by Renata Wolynec's feature analysis (n.d.).

Modoc Rock Shelter's fauna was rather similar to that of Koster, and the same comments can be applied to that site.

In general, then, the Mark II model tends to err on the side of conservatism rather than introducing unsupported tasks. Modification of the original model was made possible for three pulverization tasks. Levins (1968:4) has suggested that models cannot simultaneously maximize realism, precision, and generality. Hence, to increase realism and precision (since these two aspects are most important in setting up components of settlement systems) we will have to sacrifice generality and make the model more responsive to the way things were apparently done during the Titterington phase. While this does not change the general relationship between tools, tasks, and trash, it does suggest that specific relationships between them are not universal.

As to the dimensional analysis and definition of an Archaic phase, we have some information on all major groups of dimensions except human biology. However, there are some mystifying gaps for certain dimensions. For example, we have isolated three very similar campsites, one in the uplands and two in bluff-base situations. These appear to be all deer hunting camps, with three different levels of nut and seed processing, and some amount of riverine resource exploitation at the bluff-base sites. Long term base camps, typified by organically stained midden and a full range of maintenance and extractive tasks, have not been reported in the literature. The floral and faunal analyses of Modoc Rock Shelter and Koster site indicate that environmental changes during this period would be greatly ameliorated due to the local topography of river valleys and stream cuts; hence, the environment should have readily supported hunting and gathering societies. A second explanation, that this society did not have long-term base camps, seems absurd because the mortuary program indicates a degree of locational stability and trade items from these same mortuary sites indicate involvement with a larger milieu.

Unfortunately, the dimensional analysis does have a general weakness: a lack of carbon dates to test the reliability of depending on a relatively small number of items to assign components to a phase. In addition, there will always be those components which do not have materials that assign them to the Titterington phase, especially very limited activity sites such as a grinding station, a deer butchering locus, or a fishing camp. Winters (1969:137) has remarked on this problem for the Riverton culture. By the same token, it is fortunate that the Wadlow, Etley, and Sedalia points permit assignment of mortuary stations to the phase and that we do not have to worry about another phase defined from mortuary context being the complement of the Titterington phase.

In addition to these three analytical schemes, we have defined the Titterington phase as follows.

Dimensional Summary of the Titterington Phase

1. Stylistic dimension
   a. The defining artifacts are Etley points, Sedalia points, Wadlow blades and certain rectanguloid heavy-duty scrapers.
   b. Manufacturing of chert artifacts seems to follow two trajectories: free-flaked cores and flake tools on the one hand, and bifacially worked cores which develop into large core tools on the other. Heat treatment does not normally occur in either manufacturing trajectory.
   c. Stratigraphic context places the Titterington phase at post-4800 B.P. (end of Helton phase) at Koster and post-4700 B.P. at Modoc Rock Shelter. The geographical extent of the phase seems to be the northern half of Missouri and westcentral Illinois: the dendritic web of eastern deciduous forest (Carolinian province) branching out into the Prairie Peninsula (Illinoian province).
2. Technological dimensions
   a. Manufacture of chert objects includes core tools and absence of heat treatment. The manufacture of ground stone objects closely follows Fig. 9. Until examples of various stages of manufacture of antler, bone, teeth, and shell are available, these aspects of Titterington phase technology are unknown.
   b. A complete inventory of Titterington phase tools is not possible, considering the sample of three campsites and five burial sites.
   c. A complete inventory of tool-using tasks is not possible for the same reason.

3. Adaptational dimensions
   a. The maintenance and extractive tasks analysis has defined two classes of sites: mortuary sites with either single or multiple burial episodes and deer hunting camps with different levels of nut and seed processing, and some degree of riverine resource exploitation at bluff-base situations. The riverine resource exploitation was missed by the Mark II model.
   b. The subsistence-settlement system will be discussed in Chapter 5, since surface survey data can contribute to our knowledge of land usage.
   c. The structure of segmentation of the Titterington phase is unknown.
4. Trade dimensions
   a. Exotic raw materials include Great Lakes native copper and trade cherts probably from Harrison County, Ind. or Southern Illinois. Exotic styles include Turkey Tail points.
   b. It is not presently known what was exported from the region.
5. Mortuary dimensions
   a. The burial program involves the placement of the deceased in limestone slab lined burial pits with frequent grave offerings of special artifacts and red ochre. This procedure is repeated until low accretionary mounds result. It is suspected that not all individuals have access to this mode of burial. Cremation does not seem to have been practiced.
   b. Mortuary sites occur on blufftops or other elevated locations near or in river valleys. The sites tend to have either a single group of burials (1-2) or multiple groups (6-9) of burials (1-6).
6. Human biology dimensions
   a. No data.
7. Sociocultural dimensions
   a. The mortuary sites suggest that the Titterington phase society was not totally homogeneous, but that certain individuals had access to trade items and special mortuary goods (cf. Winters [1968]). However, the three habitation sites do not suggest how the society was organized.
   b. There was active participation in the Turkey Tail distribution network and the associated red paint burial complex.

4

The Helton Phase

STRATIGRAPHIC DEFINITION

WHILE THE Titterington phase component was barely noticeable at the Koster site, the remains of Upper, Middle, and Lower Horizon 6 are striking. For Upper and Middle Horizon 6, field observations indicate a thick midden deposit (over 1 m in some places) of greasy, dark gray to almost black soil filled with cultural debris by the ton, and flecked with charcoal, burnt clay, limestone fragments, and shell (Houart 1971). This midden still has a pungent odor of decay and a high nitrate content (Butzer, personal communication). Along with the formation of this thick midden, prehistoric behavior also left behind a large number (in the hundreds for the 1970 excavations) of features, facilities, possible house floors, etc. Beneath this heavy midden is a brownish-buff zone which contains a high density of features, but with fewer cultural inclusions than the zone above. This brownish-buff zone is Lower Horizon 6.

These three major subdivisions of Horizon 6 are based upon profile analysis by James A. Brown in 1972. Because the site was excavated mostly in arbitrary 3-in levels, a number of excavation units include materials from more than one of these three subhorizons. Table 16 gives the various subdivisions of Horizon 6 and the carbon 14 dates for these zones.

Taking the three unmixed zones of Horizon 6, we must examine two problems:

1. Are there stylistic or technological differences between the zones, e.g., do we have the remains of one, two, or three stylistically different phases?
2. Do these three zones reflect the same range of maintenance and extractive tasks?

Our first test of Problem 1 is to compare the projectile point styles in these various subhorizons. The 1970 sample of points was enlarged with those recovered in 1969 and 1971. These points were visually typed before their stratigraphic relationships were known. App. A defines the various projectile point types. Table 17 tabulates the projectile point stratigraphy within Horizon 6.

Examining Table 17 and noting that the total number of projectile points from each zone reflects the occupational intensity and volume of that zone in the present sample, it appears that (1) not every point type occurs in each zone, although this could easily be due to sampling error; (2) the major point types, Karnak (Fig. 34), Matanzas (Figs. 35-39), and Godar (Fig. 40), are present in each unmixed zone; and (3) the mixed zones do not differ greatly from the adjacent unmixed ones.

Because there are only minor differences between the zones, and Upper Horizon 6 is a very small sample, the rest of the analysis will focus on just two unmixed zones: Middle Horizon 6 and Lower Horizon 6. Even though these two zones do not appear to be stylistically different, the differences in the midden mentioned above suggest that there might be other differences, especially if different tasks were being performed there.

TABLE 16

Stratigraphic Zones and Radiocarbon Dates[a] for Horizon 6

Zone	Soil Zone	Date[b] Lab Number	B.P. ± S.D.	B.C.
Hor. 4/Hor. 6 Upper	Dark gray-buff	Mixed zone, no dates run		
Hor. 6 Upper	Dark gray	ISGS 202	4880 ± 250	2930
Hor. 6 Middle	Dark gray	ISGS 199	5070 ± 90	3120
		ISGS 198	5250 ± 250	3300
		ISGS 235	5140 ± 75	3190
		ISGS 197	5175 ± 85	3225
		ISGS 237	5305 ± 75	3355
		ISGS 233	5440 ± 100	3490
Hor. 6 Main[c]	Dark gray			
Hor. 6 Middle/Lower	Dark gray-brownish-buff	Mixed zone, no dates run		
Hor. 6 Lower	Brownish-buff	ISGS 209	5720 ± 75	3770

[a]The dates are listed in stratigraphic order. Except for ISGS 198, which has a large standard deviation, the dates are internally consistent.

[b]B.P. = A.D. 1950; dates are reported in terms of the Libby half-life.

[c]Horizon 6 Main includes all materials in Upper and Middle Horizon 6.

TABLE 17

Projectile Point Stratigraphy within Horizon 6

Zone	Karnak	Matanzas Modal	Matanzas A	Matanzas B	Matanzas C	Matanzas D	Helton	Godar	E	F	Other	Total
4/6-U	1	6	-	-	-	-	-	-	-	-	-	7
6-U	1	1	-	1	1	-	-	1	-	-	1	6
6-M	32	129	15	16	11	16	7	17	1	7	57	308
6-M/6-L	3	20	2	2	-	-	-	4	1	2	8	42
6-L	1	15	1	3	-	-	-	4	1	-	1	26
6-L/7	-	-	-	-	-	-	-	-	-	-	-	0
Total	38	171	18	22	12	16	7	26	3	9	67	389

A = Faint Side-Notched Matanzas
B = Deep Side-Notched Matanzas
C = Straight Stemmed Matanzas
D = Flared Stem Matanzas
E = Apple Blossom Stemmed
F = Brannon Side-Notched

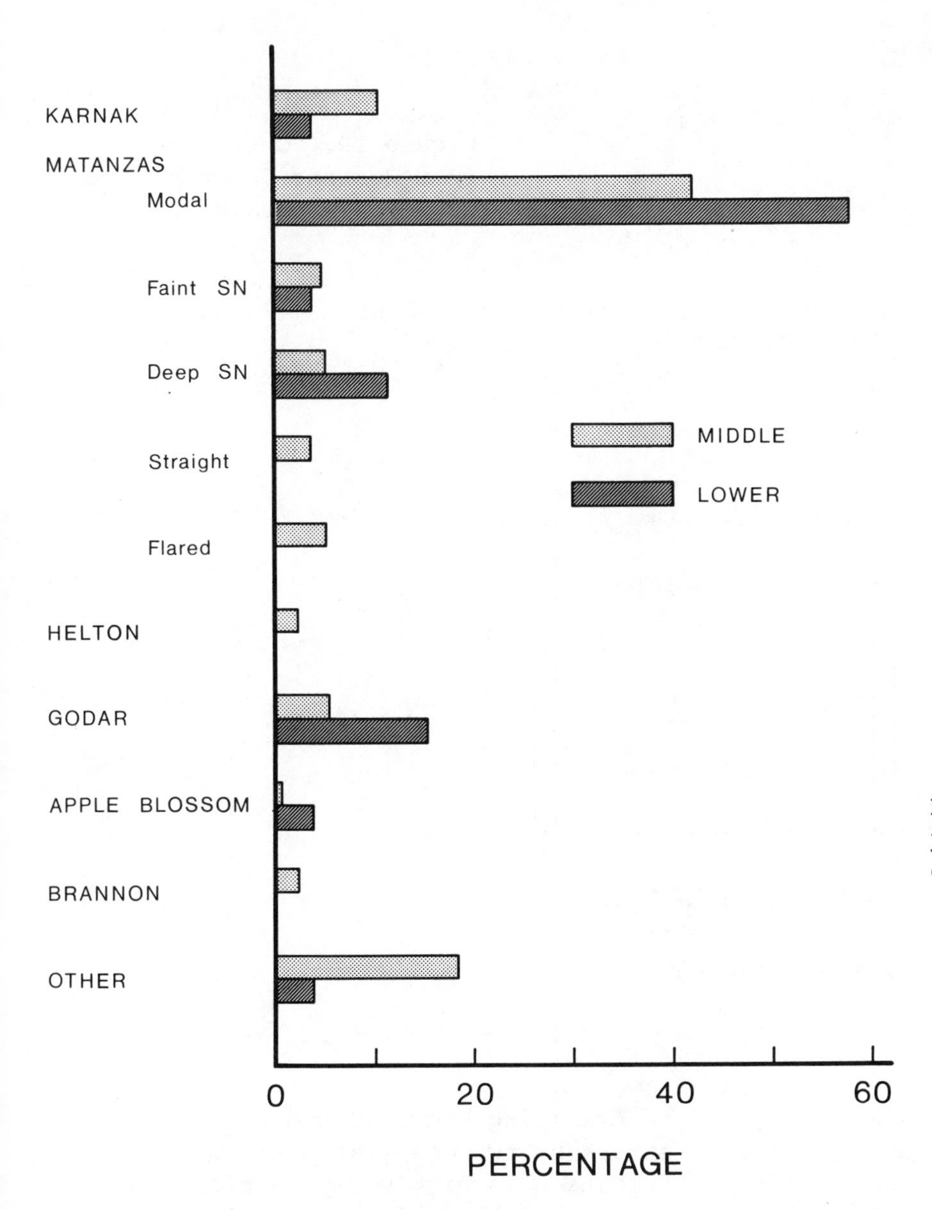

Figure 18. Projectile point frequencies in Middle and Lower Horizon 6.

STYLISTIC DEFINITION

Stylistic definition of the zones will be based upon three artifact categories and a manufacturing trajectory: projectile points, incised bone pins, a special metate form, and the manufacturing trajectory for chipped stone artifacts as measured by discarded core weights. Fig. 18 compares the frequency of occurrence of point types between Middle and Lower Horizon 6. While there are some differences in terms of presence and absence, there are no major changes in the point types.

To check this conclusion, comparisons were made along another stylistic dimension: the manufacturing trajectory of chert artifacts, specifically the distributions of heat-treated and non-heat-treated discarded core weights. All cores from Middle and Lower Horizon 6 were divided into categories of heat-treated, non-heat-treated, fire damaged, and chert hammers. If the two stratigraphic zones represent successive occupations of the same phase, then the distribution of heat-treated and non-heat-treated cores should be similar. As a control on this test we have the Titterington phase materials at Koster which definitely belong to a different manufacturing tradition where heat treatment is absent (Klippel 1972). If Lower and Middle Horizon 6 have somewhat diver-

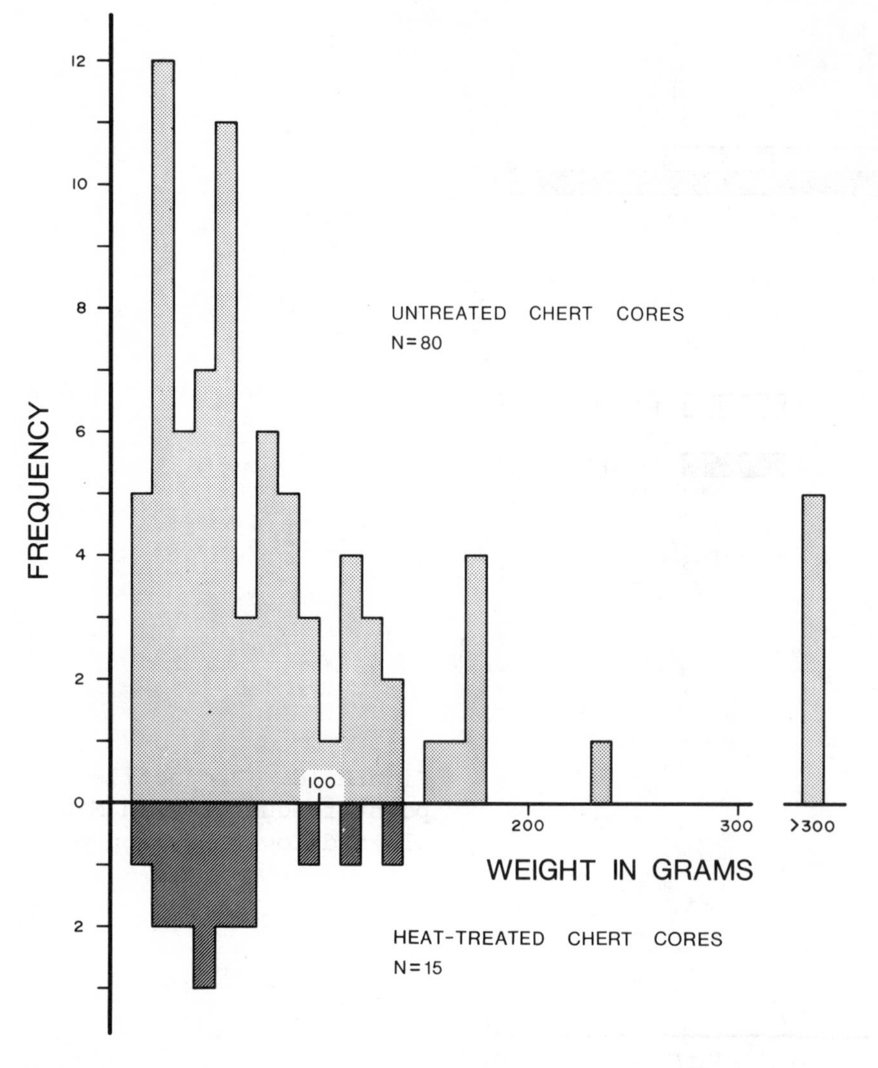

Figure 19. Core weights from Horizon 6 Lower. By 10-g intervals.

gent chertworking technologies, we may have a way of subdividing the stylistic continuum of projectile points to gain finer chronological control during this prehistoric period.

The Horizon 6 cores were sorted into the following categories: *non-heat-treated, heat-treated,* and *fire burned.* (In Struever's terminology [1973] heat-treated cherts are "roasted" and fire burned cherts are "burned.") The fire burned cores were not included in this comparison, even if the core had been heat-treated before being burned. Fig. 19 for Lower Horizon 6 and Fig. 20 for Middle Horizon 6 are graphic representations of frequency of core weights for heat-treated and non-heat-treated chert. The other cores which have been fire crazed, fractured, or broken by fire are tabulated later in Tables 19 and 21.

Examining Figs. 19 and 20, one is struck by two observations: Each distribution is highly asymmetrical toward the left, and the mode is approximately at 35-45 g for all four samples. Because of the large number of categories in the data, a nonparametric statistic, the Kolmogorov-Smirnov Test (Siegel 1956:131-136) will be used to test for any significant differences in weight distributions between heat-treated and non-heat-treated cores in Middle and Lower Horizon 6. The data on core weights are given in App. D. The results of these tests employing a two-sample, two-tailed model are given in Table 18. This table suggests that cores from Horizon 6, either heat-treated or otherwise, are drawn from the same population (or populations with the same distributions), although the non-heat-treated cores from Lower

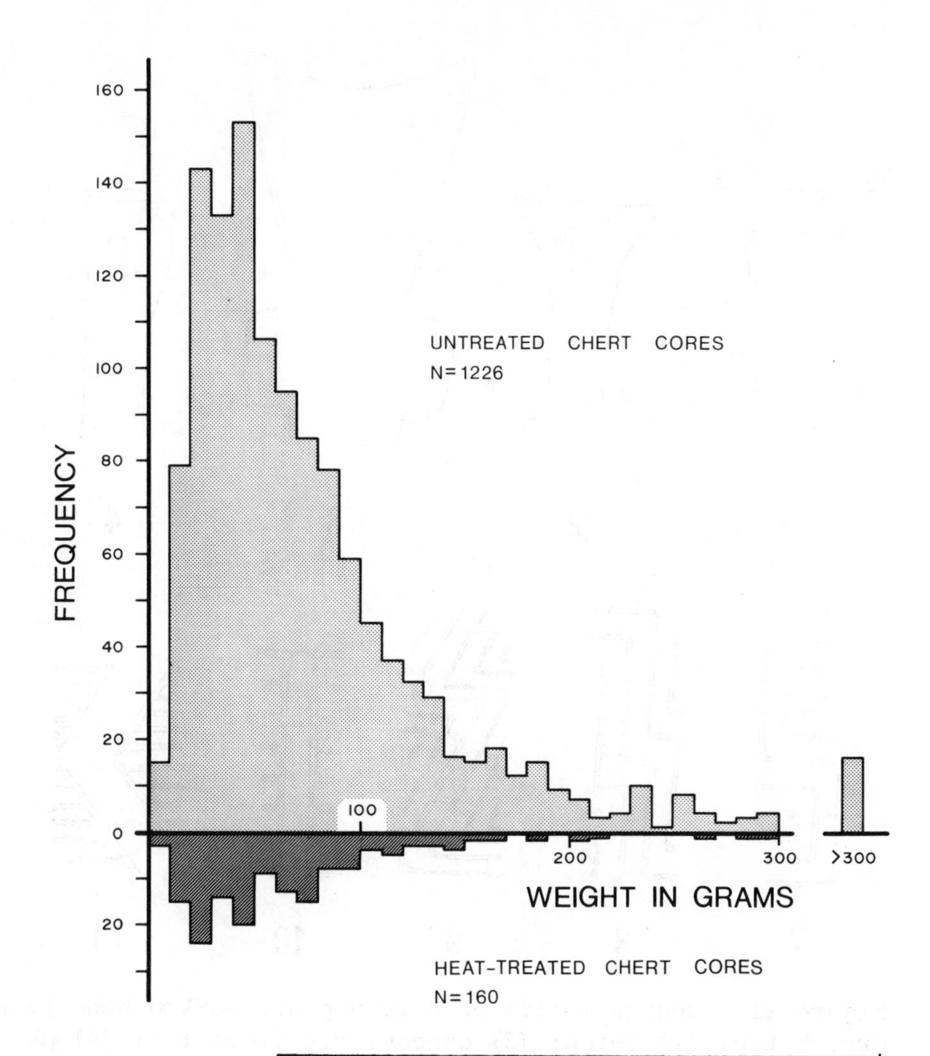

Figure 20. Core weights from Horizon 6 Middle. By 10-g intervals.

Horizon 6 are slightly different from those heat-treated cores in Middle Horizon 6. The Horizon 4 materials (Titterington phase) are *not* drawn from the same population (or populations with the same distributions) as the Horizon 6 (Helton phase) materials (cf. Siegel 1956:127-131). Again, there is some ambiguity between non-heat-treated cores from Lower Horizon 6 and cores from Horizon 4. These comparisons suggest that the same manufacturing trajectory is used in both Middle and Lower Horizon 6, and that this trajectory is not used in Horizon 4.

A third artifact which might aid in separating the two Horizon 6 unmixed strata is the Channel Basin metate. These metates (Fig. 65) are usually made on large igneous cobbles from glacial tills, and weigh from 5 to more than 20 kg. Their characteristic fea-

TABLE 18

Statistical Comparison of Koster Site Core Weights (Kolmogorov-Smirnov Two-Sample, Two-Tailed Test)

	Hor. 6-M HT n=160	Hor. 6-M Non-HT n=1226	Hor. 6-L Non-HT n=80
Hor. 4 Non-HT n=53	D=.2566 p<.001	D=.3045 p<.001	D=.2053 n.s.
Hor. 6-M HT n=160		D=.0685 n.s.	D=.0855 n.s.
Hor. 6-M Non-HT n=1226			D=.0992 n.s.

HT = heat-treated

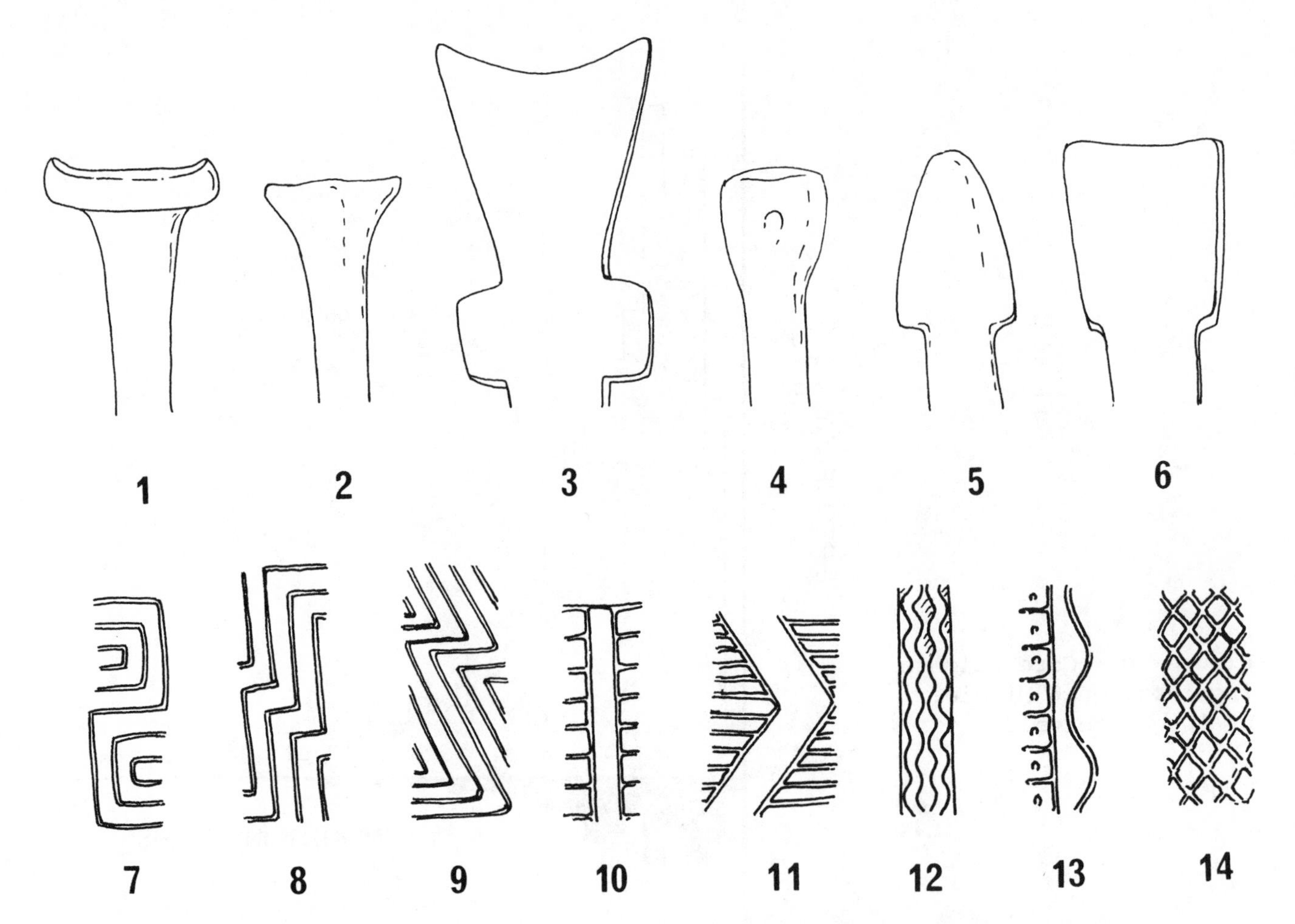

Figure 21. Design motifs of Helton phase worked bone pins, Koster sample. (1) Crutch top; (2) T-top; (3) concave cruciform top; (4) oval top; (5) spade top; (6) square top; (7) concentric squares; (8) concentric steps; (9) concentric S's; (10) zoned bar; (11) zoned zig-zag; (12) running S's in relief; (13) compound design: running S plus dotted squares; (14) cross-hatched design.

ture is a flat semipolished grinding surface around an oblong depression. The depression is between 2 and 3 times longer than it is wide, and it is about ½ to 1/3 as deep as it is wide. It has areas of semipolish along the sides and/or bottom of the groove. In addition, a single artifact usually will have channel grooves on opposite faces. For 8 metates there are a total of 15 grooves. These grooves have the following dimensions (mean and standard deviation): length (n=8) 17.0 $\pm$ 3.2 cm, width (n=7) 6.7 $\pm$ 0.8 cm, and depth (n=15) 2.5 $\pm$ 0.8 cm.

Although there are metates in both Middle and Lower Horizon 6, the Channel Basin type is found exclusively in Middle 6. If the middle and lower horizons represent similar occupations with a high overlap in maintenance and extractive tasks (barring problems of unequal sample size and the fact that even small fragments of Channel Basin metates were absent in Lower 6), this special metate form may represent a minor technological change. Discovery of these artifacts at other sites should elucidate this mystery.

The fourth class of stylistically important objects is geometrically designed bone pins. The 1970 Koster excavations recovered 39 fragments of these objects made of split, ground, and polished bone (Figs. 74-76) and the various stages of manufacture (Fig. 73). Fig. 21 depicts the various design motifs found on these bone pins

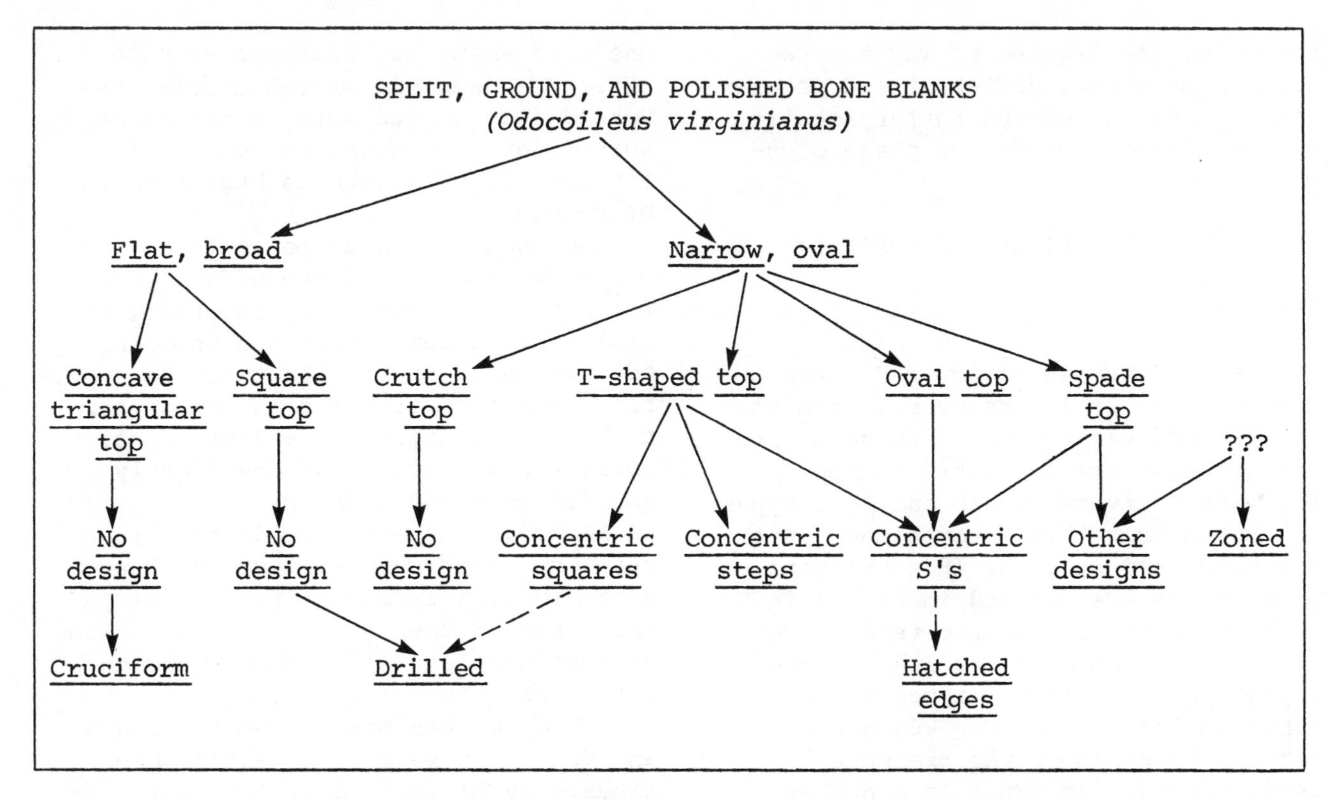

Figure 22. Manufacturing sequence typology of bone pins from Koster.

and Fig. 22 is a tree diagram (Whallon 1972) which reflects the various ways in which these motifs combine. In general these bone pins are marked by (1) simple carved forms which are non-zoomorphic, (2) the presence of repeated shapes and designs, (3) a high degree of symmetry, (4) the very fine quality of manufacture, and (5) the rather simple structure of the typological tree in Fig. 22.

Turning to exact provenience in Horizon 6, the lower zone has only two fragmentary examples, both made of flat bone, one with a crossbar and the other a drilled hole. The middle zone has the other 37 examples which cover the full range of variation present at Koster. Because the worked bone from Lower Horizon 6 is a small sample and fits into both the manufacturing and the formal typology devised for the middle horizon, it seems unlikely that the worked bone will separate these two components.

In summary, four stylistically defined categories were selected to see if there were any phase differences between Middle and Lower Horizon 6. Projectile points indicate that the stylistic differences were minimal. Discarded chert core weight distributions indicate that there is at most a minor change in flintworking technology. Channel Basin metates may separate early from late Helton phase, although this change could reflect either sampling error or the fact that the task requiring the use of Channel Basin metates occurs only in the later occupation. Geometrically-shaped bone pins suggest that there is a very strong continuity in the worked bone assemblage.

Therefore, I can see no justification in assigning these two Koster components to different stylistically defined phases on the grounds discussed above. However, because there is a temporal difference in these components, they should be analyzed as separate samples for the rest of the analysis since the combinations of maintenance and extractive tasks may be different. After the analysis of these two components is complete we can then reexamine the problem of why the two soil zones appear different and determine if the use of the Koster locality changed during the Helton phase occupation.

KOSTER: LOWER HORIZON 6

Inventory

The 1970 sample of Lower Horizon 6 comprises materials recovered from 42 squares and 82 features. These squares and features are tabulated in App. B. The widely diverse trash and tool types collected from these provenience units are tabulated in Table 19. Projectile point types are defined in App. A in both stylistic and metric terms. Core and chert hammer weights are recorded in App. D. Functional types are defined in Chapter 2. Fig 26, a Venn diagram which shows the presence/absence of artifact types at a number of Helton phase components, will be discussed later in the chapter.

Use Modification

The Lower Horizon 6 projectile points indicate heavy breakage. Of the 24 hafted, symmetrical bifaces, 13 are complete and 11 are mutilated. Of the latter, 3 are reworked as endscrapers. The single Karnak Stemmed point (Fig. 34) appears to have been used as a knife because one edge shows light to medium polish and the other edge has been resharpened unifacially. Among the Modal Matanzas points (Fig. 35) with complete or nearly complete blades, 4 have sharp edges, 3 have light abrasion on the edges, and 1 has medium abrasion on both sides of the tip. Of the 2 Modal Matanzas points reworked as end scrapers, 1 shows light abrasion on one working edge; the other shows no abrasion on the rather jagged working edge.

Other Matanzas forms include a sharp-edged shallow side-notched form and the deep side-notched forms, one with medium wear on one side of the blade and one a broken form with a large (1x2 cm) burin flake removed from one face when the blade was snapped off. The deep side-notched point reworked into an end scraper has ochre worked into its scraping edge, which although lightly used is beginning to be rounded.

The complete Godar point (Fig. 40) has sharp edges, and one of the broken forms has been partially reworked, possibly into a burin with the opposing edge ground down and blunted. However, the burin beak itself does not appear to be use-modified. The last point, a small stemmed type, has one lightly abraded edge and a sharp one.

Although the evidence is not clear cut, one might suggest that the lanceolate form, the Karnak Stemmed, was a knife rather than a missile tip, while the Matanzas and Godar forms seem to better fit the latter category.

Table 20 presents the wear pattern analysis of bifaces and partial bifaces. By breaking down the table in-

TABLE 19

Inventory of Helton Component Materials, Horizon 6 Lower

	Refined	Medium	Crude	Total
Bifaces (BF)				50(12)
Square-ended	4(1)	5(3)	3(3)	
Round-ended	1(0)	2(1)	3(0)	
Irregular	-	-	5(4)	
Sections	6	3	2	
Tips	5	3	2	
Edges	3	-	3	
Partial bifaces (PBF)				13(8)
Square-ended	1(1)	2(1)	-	
Round-ended	2(2)	-	-	
Irregular	1(1)	1(1)	3(2)	
Sections	-	-	2	
Edges	-	1	-	
Unifaces (UF)				34(31)
Straight	4(4)	1(1)	1(1)	
Concave	2(2)	1(1)	-	
Convex	1(1)	3(3)	1(1)	
Complex	10(10)	6(6)	1(1)	
Thinning	3	-	-	

TABLE 19 (Continued)

Item	Count
Chert hammers	14(12)
Complete	12
Heat-treated	1
Fire-broken	1
Cores	103(80)
Complete	80
Heat-treated pink	11
Heat-treated purple	4
Fire-broken	7
Polychrome chert	1
Choppers	1(1)
Blunt drills	4(4)

Blunt drills	Refined	Medium
On PBF: Irregular	1	0
On UF: Complex	2*	1

*1 is a double drill

Item	Count
Burins	1(1)
Drills	1(1)
Gravers (on complex, refined UF)	4(4)
Scrapers	7(7)
On reworked projectile	2
On BF: regular midsection	1
On UF: straight	1
convex	3
Spurs (on complex, refined UF)	1(1)
Projectile points	24

Projectile points	*CP*	*BS*	*RW*	*TOT*
Karnak Stemmed	1	-	-	1
Matanzas:				
Modal	8	4	2*	14
Faint Side-Notched	1	-	-	1
Deep Side-Notched	1	1	1*	3
Godar	1	3**	-	4
Apple Blossom Stemmed	1	-	-	1

CP = complete, *BS* = base, *RW* = reworked, *TOT* = total
*As end scrapers
**1 reworked into a burin?

Item	Count
Utilized flakes	19.40 kg
Unutilized flakes	16.31 kg
Block fracture	7.26 kg
Decortication flakes	5.31 kg
Hammerstones	17
Manos (mullers)	7(6)
Combination stones (manos with pecked pits)	19(15)
Metates	2
Axes	3(1)
Three-quarter grooved	1
Fragments	2

TABLE 19 (Continued)

Item	Count
Ground stone fragments	7
Chipped igneous rock	1
Hematite lumps	43
Hematite rubstones	13
Hematite beads	6
Ochre lumps	1
Plummets (hematite)	1
Pendants, stone	5
Pebbles (1 incomplete)	2
Limestone	3
Limestone abraders	1
Sandstone abraders	1
*Worked antler:***	
Manufacturing refuse	7
Surface-altered	2
Worked, function unknown	1
Discarded pieces	4
Tools (flakers)	3
Objects (pendants)	1
*Worked bone:***	
Manufacturing refuse	10
Split phalanges	1
Worked, function unknown	5
Discarded pieces	4
Tools	31
Awls	10
Scrapers	1
Spatulae/weaving tools	1
Fish gorge?	1
Groups of turtle carapace fragments -- cups	18
Objects	4
Tubular beads	1
Bone pins (fragments)	3
Flat, concave-triangular top with crossbar	1
Flat, square top with hole	1
Fragments, not incised	1
*Worked shell:***	
Manufacturing refuse	2
Worked, function unknown	1
Discarded pieces	1
Objects (crude pendants)	1

***All of the worked fauna are broken except the crude shell pendant.

Note: Numbers in parentheses are complete forms.

TABLE 20

Wear Patterns on Bifaces (BF) and Partial Bifaces (PBF)--Hor. 6 Lower

Category	1	2	3	4	5	6	7	8
	Degree of Wear							
Complete forms								
Square-ended BF								
Refined	2	-	-	-	-	-	-	-
Medium	3	-	-	-	-	-	-	-
Crude	2	-	-	-	-	-	-	-
Square-ended PBF								
Refined	1	-	-	-	-	-	-	-
Medium	1	-	-	-	-	-	-	-
Round-ended BF								
Medium	1	-	-	-	-	-	-	-
Round-ended PBF								
Refined	1	-	-	-	-	-	1	-
Irregular BF								
Crude	3	-	1	-	-	-	1	-
Irregular PBF								
Medium	1	-	-	-	-	-	-	-
Crude	2	-	-	-	-	-	-	-
Total	*17*	-	*1*	-	-	-	*2*	-
Broken forms								
Square-ended BF								
Refined	1	-	1	-	-	-	-	-
Medium	-	-	2	-	-	-	-	-
Crude	-	1	-	-	-	-	-	-
Square-ended PBF								
Medium	1	-	-	-	-	-	-	-
Round-ended BF								
Refined	-	-	-	-	-	-	1	-
Medium	1	-	-	-	-	-	-	-
Crude	1	-	-	-	-	2	-	-
Irregular PBF								
Crude	1	-	-	-	-	-	-	-
Total	*5*	*1*	*3*	-	-	*2*	*1*	-

Note: Scoring represents an average of all retouched edges. 1 - none, 2 = n-l, 3 = light, 4 = l-m, 5 = medium, 6 = m-h, 7 = heavy, 8 = polish.

TABLE 20 (Continued)

Category	1	2	3	4	5	6	7	8
	Degree of Wear							
Fragments								
Tips								
Refined	3	-	1	-	1	-	-	-
Medium	1	2	-	-	-	-	-	-
Crude	1	-	1	-	-	-	-	-
Midsections BF								
Refined	3	-	-	-	1	-	-	1
Medium	3	-	-	-	-	-	-	-
Crude	1	1	-	-	-	-	-	-
Midsections PBF								
Crude	1	-	-	-	-	-	-	-
Edges BF								
Refined	2	-	1	-	-	-	-	-
Crude	3	-	-	-	-	-	-	-
Edges PBF								
Medium	2	-	-	-	-	-	-	-
Thinning/resharpening flakes . . .	2	-	1	-	-	-	-	-
Total	*22*	*3*	*4*	-	*2*	-	-	*1*

to complete, broken, and fragmentary forms, we suggest that the complete forms either represented stages of manufacture or were involved in light usage. On the other hand, the broken forms suggest that breakage is related to wear, as more broken forms indicate wear (7) than those that do not (5). The fragments are rather ambiguous because there is less surviving edge for examining wear patterns.

In addition to the artifacts tabulated in the preceding tables, there are a number which have been worked into "special forms" usually described in terms of nineteenth century hand tools. These forms, such as *drill, graver, scraper,* etc. will now be examined for confirmatory wear patterning to see if the nineteenth century lexicon applies:

Blunt drills. Four blunt drills on 3 separate artifacts indicate that 2 were used enough to produce moderate, slightly conical wear on the tip while 2 were used enough to produce a polished drill end (Fig. 48).

Choppers. The single chopper is somewhat crushed along the chopping edge (Fig. 56).

Drills. The single specimen is broken at both ends but it is lightly abraded on one side of the shaft and heavily abraded on the other.

Gravers. Four gravers occur on 2 pieces - 3 on one and 1 on the other. The single graver shows moderate wear, while the triple graver shows wear on only one projection (Fig. 49).

Spurs. A single spur occurs on the same piece as the triple graver. The spur shows no indication of use modification (Fig. 49).

Scrapers. The collection of 7 end scrapers indicates the following distribution of use modification: 3 show heavy crushing of the edge combined with a wear facet in one case and polish above the crushed edges in the two others; 3 show heavy abrasion; and 1 shows a fine polishing facet (Fig. 45).

In general, these are discarded tools and they suggest that a number of tasks are being performed by this component or that working edges of tools have been discarded at the Koster site.

KOSTER: MIDDLE HORIZON 6

Inventory

The 1970 sample of Middle Horizon 6 materials was excavated from arbitrary levels in 62 squares and from 317 features. The list of provenience units is in App. B. The archeological materials from these provenience units are listed in Table 21. As in Lower Horizon 6, there is a wide range and a high density of tool types. Projectile point types are defined in App. A; core

TABLE 21

Inventory of Helton Component Materials, Horizon 6 Middle

	Refined	Medium	Crude	Total
Bifaces (BF)				551(75)
	Refined	*Medium*	*Crude*	
Square-ended	65(11)	69(19)	27(13)	
Round-ended	18(0)	38(14)	12(1)	
Irregular .	10(0)	7(4)	25(13)	
Sections . .	53	54	11	
Tips	71	45	20	
Edges . . .	5	11	10	
Partial bifaces (PBF)				154(51)
	Refined	*Medium*	*Crude*	
Square-ended	6(1)	14(5)	8(5)	
Round-ended	1(1)	9(4)	4(2)	
Irregular .	12(5)	16(9)	29(19)	
Sections . .	2	4	4	
Edges . . .	9	13	23	
Unifaces (UF)				766(766)
	Refined	*Medium*	*Crude*	
Straight .	88(88)	33(33)	10(10)	
Concave .	42(42)	5(5)	1(1)	
Convex . .	136(136)	42(42)	29(29)	
Complex .	224(224)	65(65)	18(18)	
Spokeshaves	12(12)	2(2)	1(1)	
Thinning .	58(58)			
Chert hammers				100
Complete			86	
Heat-treated			10	
Fire-broken			4	
Cores				1520
Complete			1226	
Heat-treated			160	
Fire-broken			136	
Choppers				8
Burins (multiple)				2(2)
On a drill shaft			1	
On a projectile point . . .			1	
Blunt drills				35(35)
T-shaped			1	
On core			1	
On BF:	*Refined*	*Medium*	*Crude*	
Irregular . .	-	1	1	
Tip	1	-	-	

Note: Numbers in parentheses are complete forms.

TABLE 21 (Continued)

On PBF:	*Refined*	*Medium*	*Crude*	
Irregular .	1	-	-	
Fragment .	-	1	-	
Edge . . .	1*	2	1	
On UF:				
Concave . .	1	-	-	
Convex . .	1	-	-	
Complex . .	18*	4	-	

*Double blunt drill
**2 double blunt drills

Drills				34(19)
T-shaped				3(2)
Shafts				9(0)
Hafted biface drills . .				3(3)
On projectile points . .				7(4)
On BF:	*Refined*	*Medium*		
Regular	6(4)	-		
Irregular	2(2)	-		
Tip	1(1)	-		
Edge	-	1(1)		
On UF: Complex . .	2(2)	-		
Gravers				39(39)
On BF:	*Refined*	*Medium*	*Crude*	
Square-ended	-	1	-	
On PBF: frag.	-	-	1	
On UF:				
Straight . .	1	-	-	
Concave . .	1	-	-	
Convex . .	35	-	-	
Spurs				20(18)
On unmodified flake .				1(1)
On PBF:	*Refined*	*Medium*	*Crude*	
Irregular .	-	-	1(1)*	
Edge . . .	-	1(1)	-	
On UF:				
Straight .	1(1)	-	-	
Concave . .	4(3)**	-	-	
Complex . .	12(11)***	-	-	

*2 spurs **1 with graver
***1 blunt drill, 1 graver, 2 spurs.

Hafted bifaces		3(3)
Hafted biface scrapers . . .		12(12)
Hafted scrapers		7(7)
Microdrills		26(26)
On PBF:	*Refined*	
Irregular	1	
Edge	1	
On UF:		
Straight	1	
Concave	1	
Convex	1	
Complex	21	
Scrapers		65(50)
On unmodified flakes . .		1(1)

TABLE 21 (Continued)

On BF:	*Refined*	*Medium*	*Crude*
Square-ended	1(1)	1(0)	-
Round-ended	1(1)	-	1(0)
Tip	-	1(1)	-
Fragment .	7(2)	-	-
On PBF:			
Irregular .	1(1)	-	2(2)
Edge . . .	2(2)	1(1)	1(1)
On UF:			
Straight .	3(3)	-	-
Concave . .	2(2)	-	-
Convex . .	16(13)	1(1)	-
Complex . .	22(17)*	1(1)	-

*1 includes a graver edge

Projectile points 308					
	CP	*BS*	*FR*	*REWRK*	*TOT*
Karnak Stemmed	28	3	-	1 ES	32
Matanzas:					
Modal	84	31	-	1 BD 13 EW	129
Faint SN . .	14	-	-	1 ES	15
Deep SN . . .	5	5	-	6 ES	16
Straight Stem	5	3	-	3 ES	11
Flared Stem .	9	4	-	1 D 2 ES	16
Undifferentiated . . .	1	-	11	1 MB	13
Helton Stemmed	7	-	-	-	7
Godar . . .	7	7	-	3 ES	17
Apple Blossom Stemmed . . .	-	-	-	1 ES	1
Brannon SN . .	2	4	-	1 ES	7
Side-notched .	5	11	-	1 BD 3 D 1 ES	21
Corner-notched	1	-	-	-	1
Stemmed . . .	5	6	-	2 D 1 ES	14
Lanceolate . .	1	3	-	1 D 4 ES	9

CP = complete, *BS* = base, *FR* = fragment, *REWRK* = reworked, *TOT* = total, *ES* = end scraper, *BD* = blunt drill, *D* = drill, *MB* = multiple burin

Utilized flakes	245.58 kg
Unutilized flakes	201.84 kg
Block fracture	77.68 kg
Decortication flakes	75.50 kg
Chert nodules	4
Hammerstones	75(71)
Hematite	4(4)
Other raw material . .	71(67)
Manos (mullers)	152(132)
Combination stones (manos with pecked pits)	88

TABLE 21 (Continued)

Item	Subcount	Count
Metates		70(10)
Axes		40(8)
Three-quarter grooved	3	
Fully grooved	4	
Indeterminate	1	
Fragments (1 hematite)	32	
Ground stone fragments		140
Igneous flakes		1
Hematite lumps		833
Hematite rubstones		116
Hematite beads		58
Ochre lumps		1
Galena		1
Copper beads		1
Quartz lumps		1
Plummets		3(2)
Hematite	1(1)	
Limestone	2(1)	
Pendants (stone)		37
Pebbles: complete	4	
unfinished	10	
Hematite: fragments	2	
unfinished	2	
Limestone (various stages of manufacture)	19	
Grooved stones		2
Worked limestone		21
Sandstone abraders		35
Sandstone cobbles		1
Sand		0.5 liter
Sherds (intrusive)		4
Worked antler:		
Manufacturing refuse		43
Surface-altered	28	
Worked, function unknown	4	
Discarded pieces	11	
Tools		19
Flakers	8	
Shaft straighteners	2	
Perforators	6	
Hollow tines (points?)	2	
Hammer/punch	1	
Objects		5
Tubes/beads	2	
Figure-8 shapes	2	
Incised tips	1	
Worked bone:		
Manufacturing refuse		90
Surface-altered	1	
Split phalanges	1	
Worked, function unknown	31	
Discarded pieces	57	
Tools		267
Awls	117	

TABLE 21 (Continued)

Item	Subcount	Count
Scrapers	8	
Spatulae/weaving tools	7	
Groups of turtle carapace fragments -- cups	128	
Beamers	2	
Objects		73
Tubular beads	2	
Pendants	1	
Pins, shafts, tips (fragments)	70	
Fragments, not incised	33	

Shaft	*Top*	*Incising*	
Flat	Concave-triangular	None	9*
	Square	None	2**
Round	T-shaped	Concentric squares	2***
		Concentric S's	2
		Concentric steps	2
		Indeter. incised	2
	Oval	Concentric S's	3
	Spade	Dot and curves	1
		Concentric S's	1****
	Crutch	Not incised	6
	Missing	Concentric squares	1***
		Concentric S's	3***
		Zoned	2
		Curved lines	1

*5 with cross preserved
**Shafts broken
***1 drilled
****1 with edges hatched

Item	Subcount	Count
Worked teeth (large rodent incisor scrapers)		2
Worked shell:		
Manufacturing refuse		14
Scraps of manufacture	6	
Worked, function unknown	7	
Unfinished pendants	1	
Tools/objects		4
Pendants (1 shaped, 1 crude	2	
Spoons	1	
Denticulates (scraper?)	1	

and chert hammer weights are in App. D; and functional types are defined in Chapter 2. The presence/absence of artifact types are shown later in Fig. 26, a Venn diagram of several Helton phase components.

Use Modification

The very large sample of projectile points, 313 objects recovered during the 1969, 1970, and 1971 field seasons, divide into 15 types and 43 categories. The wear patterns observed on the complete forms are tabulated in Table 22. In addition to these complete forms, there are also broken and reworked forms. Taking all 313 objects, 56% are complete, 29% are unreworked bases and scraps, 12% have been reworked into end scrapers, 2% into drills, 1% into blunt drills, and 0.3% into burins. For the complete forms, the wear pattern analysis presented in Table 22 indicates two trends: (1) the intensity of wear drops off very rapidly, so that most forms indicate light to no visible wear; (2) this trend occurs for all 13 point types analyzed.

Table 22

Observed Wear on Complete Projectile Points--Horizon 6 Middle

Point Type	Degree of Wear						
	1	2	3	4	5	6	7
Matanzas forms							
Modal	46	11	13	5	9	2	-
Faint SN	9	-	3	1	1	-	-
Deep SN	2	1	2	1	-	-	-
Straight Stem	3	1	1	1	-	-	-
Flared Stem	7	3	-	-	-	-	-
Karnak Stemmed	13	5	6	2	2	-	-
Helton Stemmed	3	2	1	1	-	-	-
Godar	4	1	4	1	-	-	-
Brannon SN	1	-	1	-	-	-	-
Untyped forms							
Side-notched	2	2	1	1	-	1	-
Corner-notched	1	-	-	-	-	-	-
Stemmed	7	-	1	1	-	-	-
Lanceolate	1	-	-	-	-	-	-
Total	99	26	33	14	12	3	-

Note: Scoring represents an average for both edges of each complete or nearly complete blade. 1 = none, 2 = n-l, 3 = light, 4 = l-m, 5 = medium, 6 = m-h, 7 = heavy.

Before attempting to interpret these two trends, let us examine Table 23, wear patterns on bifaces and partial bifaces. Complete bifaces and complete partial bifaces indicate the same two trends in wear. Meanwhile, the broken forms and fragments suggest more intensive usage, probably indicating that the likelihood of breakage increases with intensity of use. Because both finished, hafted forms - and unhafted, often unfinished forms - reflect the same patterning of edge wear, I suggest that all of these objects have been used as tools, rather than the former being tools and the latter being rejects from a manufacturing trajectory not to be further used.

Along with the projectile points and various types of bifaces and partial bifaces, there are a large number of forms such as scrapers, drills, and spurs which have been examined to determine type and degree of wear and breakage. They are:

Hafted bifaces. All 3 hafted bifaces have abraded haft areas, but the remaining blades are unaltered, possibly due to resharpening.

Burins. The 2 burins from this stratum are multiple, with a series of four or five burin blows forming a deep V-shaped tool, and showing slight to moderate wear. Other burin flake scars were noticed during the analysis, but because none of these were associated with any wear they were assumed to be accidental.

Choppers. All 8 choppers show various degrees of crushing and abrading

TABLE 23

Wear Patterns on Bifaces (BF) and Partial Bifaces (PBF)--Hor. 6 Middle

Category	Degree of Wear							
	1	2	3	4	5	6	7	8
Complete forms								
Sq.-ended BF								
Refined . .	11	1	-	-	-	-	-	-
Medium . .	11	5	-	1	2	-	-	-
Crude . . .	8	3	1	2	-	-	-	-
Sq.-ended PBF								
Refined . .	1	-	-	-	-	-	-	-
Medium . .	2	3	-	1	-	-	-	-
Crude . . .	2	1	-	-	-	-	-	-
Rd.-ended BF								
Medium . .	6	6	1	1	-	-	-	-
Crude . . .	1	-	-	-	-	-	-	-
Rd.-ended PBF								
Medium . .	1	1	1	-	-	1	-	-
Crude . . .	1	-	-	-	1	-	-	-
Irregular BF								
Medium . .	2	1	-	1	-	-	-	-
Crude . . .	9	1	-	-	-	1	-	-
Irregular PBF								
Refined . .	3	2	-	-	-	-	-	-
Medium . .	5	-	3	-	-	-	-	-
Crude . . .	17	-	1	-	1	-	-	-
Total	*80*	*24*	*7*	*6*	*24*	*2*	-	-
Broken forms								
Sq.-ended BF								
Refined . .	18	2	7	2	8	6	1	2
Medium . .	15	11	4	2	7	7	3	-
Crude . . .	11	-	1	1	-	-	-	-
Sq.-ended PBF								
Refined . .	2	1	-	1	-	1	-	-
Medium . .	4	1	1	-	-	1	-	-
Crude . . .	2	-	-	-	-	-	1	-
Rd.-ended BF								
Refined . .	7	5	2	-	1	2	1	-
Medium . .	13	6	2	1	-	2	-	-
Crude . . .	7	1	-	1	-	2	-	-
Rd.-ended PBF								
Medium . .	3	1	1	-	-	-	-	-
Crude . . .	1	-	-	-	-	-	-	-
Irregular BF								
Refined . .	5	2	-	-	2	1	-	-
Medium . .	2	-	-	-	-	-	-	-
Crude . . .	11	-	-	-	-	-	-	2
Irregular PBF								
Refined . .	1	1	-	-	-	-	-	-
Medium . .	4	3	-	-	-	-	-	-
Crude . . .	-	-	-	-	4	-	-	-
Total	*106*	*34*	*18*	*8*	*22*	*22*	*6*	*4*
Fragments								
Tips								
Refined . .	52	5	6	4	-	-	2	-
Medium . .	21	8	5	2	2	3	3	-
Crude . . .	12	2	1	1	-	2	2	-
Midsect. BF								
Refined . .	28	6	7	4	3	1	-	-
Medium . .	30	3	14	1	-	1	2	3
Crude . . .	7	-	1	-	1	-	1	-
Midsect. PBF								
Refined . .	2	-	-	-	-	-	-	-
Medium . .	1	-	1	-	1	-	-	-
Crude . . .	1	-	2	-	-	-	-	-
Edges BF								
Refined . .	3	-	1	-	-	1	-	-
Medium . .	3	-	1	-	4	-	2	-
Crude . . .	7	-	-	-	1	-	2	-
Edges PBF								
Refined . .	1	-	1	1	-	-	-	-
Medium . .	7	1	1	-	-	-	-	-
Crude[a] . .	12	-	3	-	3	-	2	-
Thinning/re-sharpening flakes . .	14	-	17	1	10	1	11	3
Total	*201*	*25*	*61*	*14*	*25*	*9*	*27*	*6*

Note: Scoring represents an average of all retouched edges. 1 = none, 2 = n-l, 3 = light, 4 = l-m, 5 = medium, 6 = m-h, 7 = heavy, 8 = polished.

[a]Plus one entity which had lost all of its edges through fire breakage.

and some hinge fractures along their working edges. One specimen has edge polish; hence more than a single function may be performed by this class of tool (Fig. 56).

Blunt drills. Two occur on reworked projectile points and the remaining 35 occur on other retouched forms. One has no surviving tip; 1 has a number of hinge fractures of the tip making it more of a push plane than a drill; 6 have sharp tips; 7 have slight wear on the blunt drill tip; 3 show incipient rounding of the tip; 13 show heavy conical wear; and 6 have been used enough to produce polishing on the conical tip (Fig. 48).

Drills. There are 18 drills on retouched forms plus 7 on projectile points. Six have no surviving drill tip; 5 have sharp drill tips; 4 show light abrasion on the drill tip and adjacent areas; 3 have conical wear on the tip; 6 show some degree of medium to heavy abrasion on the drill tip and adjacent areas; and 1 is polished on the tip (Figs. 46 and 47).

Drill shafts. Nine shafts indicate the following: 1 has no tip; 4 have sharp tips; 1 has chisel-like ends but was not used much; 2 are worn on the tip; and 1 has a sharp, reworked distal end. Both the drills and the drill shafts tend to have medium to heavy abrasion along their sides.

When one compares the wear patterns of drills and blunt drills, the drill forms appear to have a number of similarities to hafted knives, bifaces, projectile points, and heavy-duty cutting tools. The blunt drills at least have a tendency toward conical wear on the tip, to the point of polishing, with less-pronounced alterations of the sides of the blunt drill shafts. In other words, many of the drills may be resharpened cutting edges while the blunt drills seem to have been used in a twisting motion to perforate hide or perhaps wood.

Microdrills. Microdrills, gravers, and spurs have a number of similarities because all are small, sharp projections manufactured more or less by accident and then sometimes worked down to rather delicate forms. (See Fig. 49.) Confirmatory wear analysis then permits us to separate accidental forms, spurs, gravers, and microdrills. The sample of 26 microdrills indicates the following wear patterns: 2 come to very sharp points but have no apparent wear; 3 have been damaged at the tip, but adjacent areas indicate characteristic conical wear; 6 show beginning conical wear; 8 show moderate conical wear; 2 show heavy conical wear; and 5 are worn to the point of being heavily polished. Microdrills thus are more directly related to blunt drills than to drills - hardly surprising since microdrills are shaped like miniature blunt drills.

Gravers. Of the sample of 39 gravers, 8 are unworn and hence of uncertain characterization; 5 show hinge fractures under the graver tip, possibly implying use as a push plane on a hard, non-yielding surface; 5 show light abrasion; 10 show medium abrasion; 5 show heavy abrasion; and 6 are polished on the graver tip. (See *scrapers* for comparisons.)

Spurs. Of the 20 spurs in this sample, 11 are unworn; 4 show light abrasion; 1 shows moderate abrasion; 2 are heavily worn; and 2 are polished.

Scrapers are divided into four categories: hafted scrapers, hafted bifacial tools with scraper ends, projectile points reworked into end scrapers (blunts), and scrapers on other chipped-stone forms.

Hafted scrapers. Of 7 specimens, 1 shows moderate edge wear; 1 is heavily hinged as if used on nonyielding surfaces; the remaining 5 show intense polish along the cutting edge and up onto the face of the acute edge. Two of these have developed a thin (1 mm or less) wear facet (Fig. 45).

Scrapers on hafted bifaces. Twelve specimens include 1 unused piece, 1 very heavily crushed on the scraper edge, 1 heavily abraded but not polished, although the edge is very smooth, and 9 polished on the working edge. Only 1 of the polished specimens has a thin wear facet.

Scrapers on reworked projectile points. Thirty-seven specimens include 3 unaltered forms, 2 with crushing on the working edge, 9 abraded on the scraper edge to the point of rounding off that edge, and 23 abraded enough to produce polished areas. Of these 23, 15 have wear facets, some being as wide as 2 mm and as long as 15 mm (Fig. 45).

Scrapers. Sixty-five specimens include 5 unworn samples, one of which must have been resharpened just before being discarded because there are areas of polish beyond the rejuvenated edge. Eighteen show various degrees of edge crushing and hinging, again possibly reflecting their use on nonyielding surfaces; 10 show light abrasion on the edges; 6 show medium to heavy abrasion; and 26 show extensive polishing on and around the cutting edge. Of these 26, 9 have developed a wear facet (Fig. 45).

Multiple tools. In addition to the scrapers made on reworked projectile points, there are 21 artifacts which have two specialized tool forms on the same object. For 10 of these objects, the same specialized tool occurs twice, and for 11 of these objects, different tool types occur. The following results were obtained by examining the wear on the specialized tool forms: Of 5 blunt drills, 4 are smoothed and rounded and 1 is polished. Nine gravers include 1 without wear, 6 showing light abrasions, 1 showing heavy wear, and 1 polished on the graver tip. The single microdrill is moderately worn. Three spurs include only 1 which shows light wear. Finally, of the 3 scrapers, 2 show moderate wear and 1 heavy crushing.

In general, the Middle Horizon 6 sample of tools indicates that these objects were used and discarded at Koster site during the Helton phase occupation.

Worked Fauna

Examining the artifact inventories for the Helton phase occupations at Koster, one is immediately struck by the use of antler and bone mostly for tools complementary to the chipped-stone industry. While there are a few distinct faunal tools, such as antler flakers (Fig. 66) and bone awls (Figs. 68 and 69), there is a lack of specialized forms such as handles, atlatl hooks, telescoped turkey bones (bird calls?), and fishhooks (only one example from Horizon 6). Comparing the worked faunal assemblage of the Helton phase at Koster with the Eva site (Lewis and Kneberg 1961), Koster seems to have a low diversity of worked faunal remains, although some of these types such as bone awls are very common.

One major problem with the worked fauna analysis is the very high degree of breakage during excavation, approaching 100% of the worked bone. When the pieces of antler, bone, shell, and tooth are first exposed, they tend to be both soft and friable and easily damaged by the screens. But once these elements have been dried and hardened, their usually excellent state of preservation becomes apparent and the analysis proceeds without further difficulty.

GEOGRAPHIC EXTENT

If we are to develop a multidimensional definition of the prehistoric cultural system represented by the Helton phase, we must among other things, (1) establish the covariation of tool types in task performance and (2) delineate the subsistence-settlement system. Despite the large sample of artifacts and debris from two sequential base camps at Koster, Koster alone cannot achieve these two important goals. The overlap in tool types between the two Koster components is almost 100%; hence we cannot make much use of Venn diagrams or evaluate certain aspects of the Mark II model. In addition, one geographical locality does not define a settlement system, although a protected bluff-base situation near a secondary valley does permit ready access to all major resource zones.

Projectile Point Distributions

Our first task is to define the stylistic boundaries of the Helton phase by determining the geographical extent of projectile point forms, including Godar, Karnak Stemmed, and Matanzas types, and geometrically-shaped and incised bone pins, similar to those in Figs. 74 through 76. This task is frustrated by the nonstandardized nomenclature used for projectile points and the almost total lack of published descriptions of the geometric bone pins. Each region has its own set of names for local examples of what may be panregional forms. Furthermore, the same term may include divergent forms. For example, Winters (1967:Fig. 4, g and h) illustrates Karnak Stemmed forms from the Wabash Valley which have slight but definite shoulders. Perino (1962:46) has published a photograph of a typical Karnak Stemmed point from Calhoun County, Ill., which lacks any shoulders at all. Karnak Stemmed is *not* a common type in the midwestern literature; hence many examples have probably been assigned to general categories such as lanceolates or knives (Fig. 34).

Matanzas points are on a more solid basis. Munson and Harn (1966:Figs. 2 and 4, Table 1) present both photographic and metric information concerning these points from three surface-surveyed sites in Fulton County, Ill. Similar point types also occur in the American Bottoms (Munson 1971; Harn 1971; Munson, personal communication). Perino (1968a:54) would extend their geographical distribution into "the Mississippi, Missouri, and Illinois waterways in Missouri, Illinois, and Iowa. A somewhat wider form is found in shell-middens along the Ohio River." However, thick, medium-sized, shallow side-notched points with a short hafting element can also be recovered from the next tier of states involving the Mississippi drainage system. While the type may have chronological meaning, even in this large an area, it has ceased to have much cultural meaning from a geographical viewpoint (Figs. 35-39).

The Godar point has suffered just the opposite fate. The continuous distribution of a boldly side-notched form has been chopped up into many local types. Wittry noted (1959:44) that bold side-notched points from Raddatz Rockshelter, Raddatz Side-Notched (Wisconsin), resembled similar forms named Hemphill Notched (Illinois), Osceola (Wisconsin), Graham Cave Notched (Missouri), Black Sand Notched (Illinois) and Madison Side-Notched (Wisconsin). This list of names and locations can be expanded by inclusion of Lewis and Kneberg's Big Sandy (Tennessee) type (1961:34-37) and Perino's Godar (Illinois) points (1963:95). There is a great deal of similarity in these eight point types. For example, one could form a continuum of examples of these point types illustrated in Perino (1968a: Plate 14, Graham Cave; 1971a: Plate 19, Godar; Plate 25, Hemphill; Plate 38, Raddatz) and Bell (1958: Plate 34, Osceola; 1960: Plate 4, Big Sandy). Like the Matanzas point, the boldly side-notched form covers a very large territory.

Turning to the temporal manifestation of these various point forms, the only absolute dates for Karnak Stemmed forms are from Koster. (See Table 16.) The only absolute dates on Matanzas points from a site other than Koster are from the Chrisman site (MacGregor 1954) which gave a rather early shell carbon date of 6490 $\pm$ 300 B.P. and a rather late estimated geological date of ca. 3000 B.P. (Crane and Griffin 1958:1119). Among sites with boldly side-notched forms, Raddatz Rockshelter (Wittry 1959:58-61) dates to between 6000 and 3500 B.P. using both stratigraphic and absolute dating criteria. The Osceola site is dated (Ritzenthaler 1946, 1957) to 3500 B.P. For Graham Cave, Klippel gives a carbon date of ca. 7000 B.P. for a combined sample of Black Sand and Graham Cave Notched points. Black Sand points themselves are frequently assigned to the Early Woodland period, even though Cole and Deuel (1937:139) warn that "there is also a possibility that the artifacts mentioned [the Black Sand points in mound F°77] may be accidental inclusions, as similar objects were found scattered at random through the black sands." Big Sandy types are dated by Lewis and Kneberg (1961:37) at the Eva site to early in the Three Mile component, ca. 5300 B.P. They point out that similar point types at Modoc Rock Shelter are most common at ca. 5200 B.P.

These dates cover a time span of five millennia, although they average about 5000 B.P. Either this boldly side-notched point form was in vogue for 5000-plus years or there are serious contextual and physicochemical problems. Only a major reassessment of the local Archaic chronologies in Wisconsin, Illinois, Missouri, Tennessee, etc., can clarify this temporal problem. In addition, the Graham Cave point may be chronologically distinct because it seems to represent another knapping tradition.

Because the boldly side-notched point (Godar), Karnak Stemmed, and Matanzas points indicate a very large areal extent (central Midwest) and an impossible timespan of five millennia, it is necessary to select a smaller area, and hopefully a shorter timespan, to give an initial definition of the Helton phase.

Helton Phase Components

A principal limitation on delineating a more restricted area is the lack of unmixed components of the Helton phase within 200 km of the Koster site. The nearest Helton-phase-like site to the north is Raddatz Rockshelter (SK 5) Sauk County, Wis., which is nicely stratified (Wittry 1959) with preserved fauna (reanalyzed by Cleland 1966). However, it is about 450 km away in the northern portions of the Carolinian biotic province (Cleland 1966:6) and the faunal revision (Cleland 1966:98-108) indicates the presence of coniferous-forest-preferring species not available in the lower Illinois Valley. Since the primary goal is to understand adaptational strategies in the greater St. Louis area, rather than at the interface between the Carolinian and Canadian biotic provinces, I do not see the utility of including Raddatz Rockshelter in the Mark II analysis of stone tool assemblages.

To the west of Koster is Graham Cave, which has been recently revisited and reanalyzed by Klippel (1971). Klippel has used natural stratigraphic units in his analysis rather than the arbitrary 1-ft levels employed by Logan (1952). Klippel's excavations include materials which resemble Helton phase remains. Specifically, his Fig. 12:e, f and Fig. 14:g look like Matanzas points. Figure 14:a, b, c, d resembles the boldly side-notched Godar point and Fig. 23:j illustrates an incised bone object similar to those from Koster and McCain sites.

Graham Cave is located on the top edge of a talus-slope deposit above the course of the Loutre River, a tributary of the Missouri. The setting of upland prairie dissected by forested deep stream channels (Klippel 1971:Fig. 1) is similar to the region east of the Koster site. Accordingly, the Helton phase does extend as far west as Graham Cave and the appropriate strata will be compared later with the Koster site (Fig. 26).

To the south of Koster we again have Modoc Rock Shelter (Fowler 1959b) as the source of a Helton phase component. Fig. 26 illustrates the relationship of the Modoc samples to those mentioned above. Moving further to the south, we arrive at the Eva site, Benton County, Tenn., with its Big Sandy points in the

Three Mile component (Lewis and Kneberg 1961). However, since Eva is 400 km south of Koster and not involved in prairie-woodland interfaces, it will be excluded from further analysis.

The nearest excavated site east of Koster is McCain (Miller 1941; Dragoo 1958), located on an old terrace of the East Fork of the White River, Dubois County, Ind. There are a number of similarities between the Matanzas points from Koster and the 85 small side-notched points from McCain; other similar forms include drills and hafted endscrapers. (Compare Dragoo [1958: Fig. 29-34] and the illustrations of Helton phase materials in this study.) In addition, there is a strong resemblance between incised bone pins at Koster (Figs. 74-76) and similar artifacts at McCain. However, because McCain is 350 km away and there is some mixing of Woodland materials at the site, the site will be eliminated from further study of the adaptational dimensions of the Helton phase.

Turning now to the mortuary aspects of the Helton phase, there have been a number of mound excavations well within 200 km of the Koster site yielding Helton phase components. The Gibson and Klunk mound groups are on the western bluffs of the Illinois Valley overlooking the present day town of Kampsville, about 15 km north of the Koster site. Gibson Mound 1 includes a low mounded structure beneath a Hopewell period tumulus that contained burials with Godar and other points (Perino 1971b:50). Klunk Mound 14 was built over a large charnel pit containing human skeletal remains and Godar points (Perino 1968b:114-5; 117-8). Further to the north is the Hemphill site, Brown County, Ill., which was included by Griffin (1941) in a study of Hopewell mounds. However, an examination of the tabulations of three excavations at that site in Titterington (1950:Table 1), suggests that the site has a Helton phase component, since the one diagnostic point from the site, a Hemphill point, has some similarities to Godar points. Perino (1971a:Plate 25) has published a drawing of this point and Titterington (1950:Fig. 5:4) has published a photograph.

Finally, 5 km due west of Koster is the Godar site in Calhoun County, Ill. (Titterington 1950), another burial station.

Figs. 1, 2, and 23 locate the various Helton phase sites mentioned in this study.

Other Phase Indicators

Excavations at Koster permitted an initial characterization of the stylistic dimensions of the Helton phase in terms of four classes of artifacts: points, worked bone pins, Channel Basin metates, and core weights. A review of the literature indicates the projectile points are the most efficient phase indicators for published sites because these items are relatively common at sites and are both well reported and well illustrated. Core weight distributions were of no use because this measurement, if performed, usually does not get reported. Channel Basin metates, and metates in general, are also slighted in the literature. This is unfortunate because these large, bulky objects are involved in several important extractive tasks and because there may have been technological changes through time that affected their shape in a regular fashion.

Incised and shaped bone pins, while relatively rare, are frequently reported when present and provide a crosscheck on the Helton phase style zone as defined by projectile points. Pins and related worked bone items have been reported from Arnold Research Cave, Crib Mound, Dillard Stamper Shelter No. 1, Graham Cave, McCain, and Modoc Rock Shelter, as well as the Koster site.

Shippee's (1966:38, Fig. 11h) excavations at Arnold Research Cave, Calloway County, Mo., produced a single incised bone pin fragment with a concave triangular top and a zoned zigzag design on the pin shaft. Unfortunately, this artifact was found above a disturbed burial so that its stratigraphic placement is uncertain.

The Crib Mound (Sp-1) is an Archaic

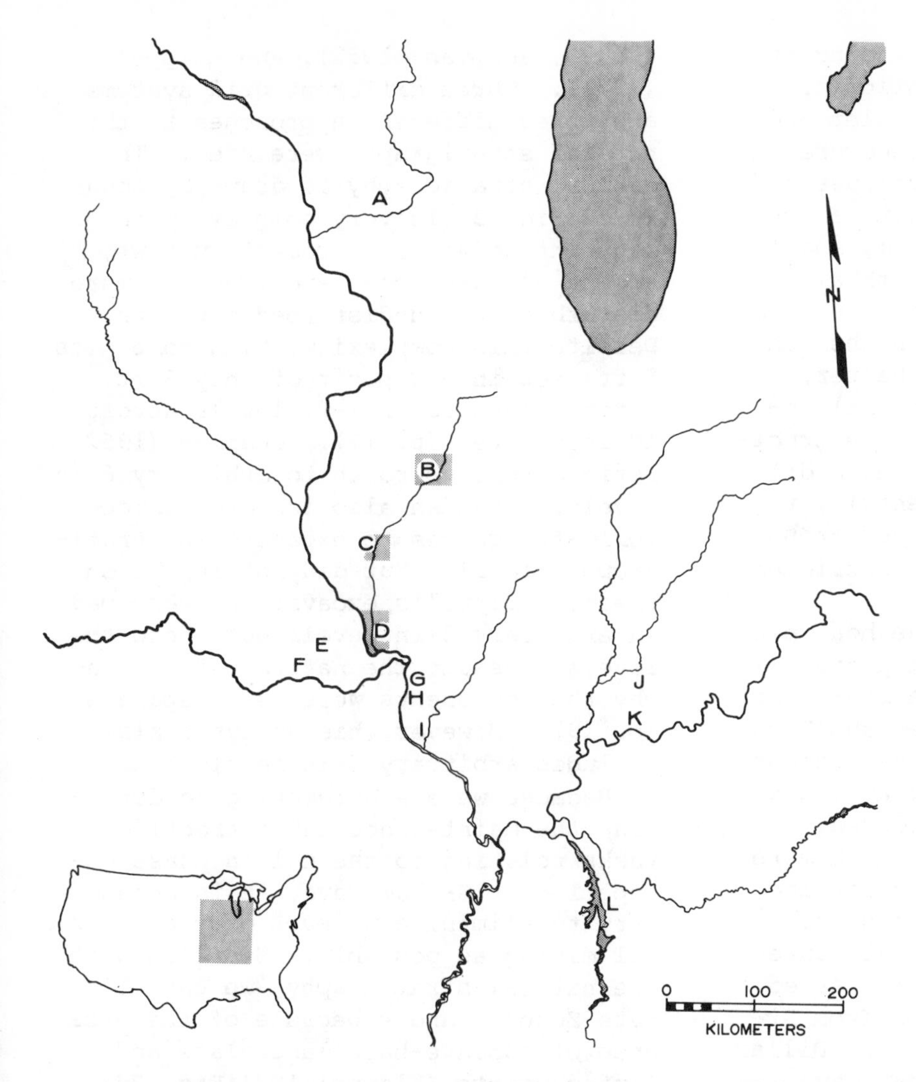

Figure 23. Map of Helton phase and related sites. (a) Raddatz; (b) Black Sand, Lone Barn, Richardson, West Matanzas; (c) Hemphill, Chrisman; (d) Gibson, Godar, Klunk, Koster; (e) Graham Cave; (f) Arnold Research Cave; (g) South Roxana; (h) Poag Road; (i) Modoc Rock Shelter; (j) McCain; (k) Crib Mound; (l) Eva. Not shown: Dillard Stamper No. 1.

shell mound on Corn Island, Huff Township, Spencer County, Ind. (Kellar 1956:42-49, Plate 1). Kellar's Fig. 1 includes a drawing of seven worked and incised bones with a number of characteristic motifs (cf. Fig. 17 and 18): cruciforms with concave triangular tops, and concentric geometric designs including squares, steps, and zigzags. Kellar (1956:48-49) notes that projectile points from Crib Mound resemble those from the McCain site while the worked bone is in the Green River, Ky., Archaic tradition.

The Dillard Stamper Shelter No. 1, Wolfe County, Ky., is a multicomponent rockshelter site with extensive ash lenses and, consequently, excellent bone preservation. Test excavations there by Funkhauser and Webb (1930:266-275, Figs. 27 and 31) recovered an incised bone gorget. This gorget has a double convex herringbone pattern on the outer bone surface and concentric squares design next to a zigzag motif on the inner bone surface. While this bone gorget is not identical to the other examples mentioned here, it still seems to be in the Helton phase tradition in terms of motifs.

At Graham Cave, Klippel (1971:Fig. 23j) illustrates a broken, oval bone pin with an irregular head and a modified concentric Z's design.

The McCain site has produced 18 ornamental pins (Miller 1941:Fig. 3, Plate 11). There are pins with concave-triangular tops with cross bars on flat bone as well as some with waisted-rectangular tops, similar to the concave-triangular forms. There are concentric Z designs on some pins, zoned designs on others. In addition, some pin shafts have notches carved into the sides, something not found at the other sites already mentioned.

At Modoc Rock Shelter, Fowler and Winters (1956:Figs. 8b-d) recovered a fragment with cross-incised lines and hatched zones, a flat pin with a concave-triangular and cruciform, and a modified cruciform object with a drilled top. These objects came from the 10- to 21.5 ft zone. In the summary report on Modoc Rock Shelter, Fowler (1959b:Figs. 11o and 11x) includes two more examples of the cruciform objects, a T-top pin, and a different form which has concentric, rather rectilinear spirals wrapped around the bone object instead of restricted to a single side.

As a cross-check that the bone pin designs found in the Helton phase components at Koster are *not* a pan-Archaic phenomenon, the worked bone from Lamoka Lake (Ritchie 1932), Frontenac Island (Ritchie 1945) and the Port au Choix site (Tuck 1971) were considered. These Archaic artifacts are much more the product of a cutting and carving tradition with much less incising. Carved bone combs come from all three of these eastern sites, while carved bone combs were not reported from Arnold Research Cave, Crib Mound, Dillard Stamper Shelter No. 1, Graham Cave, Koster, McCain, or Modoc Rock Shelter sites. This observation also seems to hold true for the mortuary sites of the Helton phase. Perhaps the "Algonkian influences" from the East did not extend into the Midwest?

If one were to compare the distribution of sites with incised or carved bone pins with sites having Matanzas and Godar-like artifacts, one would see that the worked bone distribution is somewhat concentric to that of the chipped-stone style indicators. Be that as it may, there seems to be little conflict between using points and pins to define the Helton phase in the central Midwest.

GRAHAM CAVE

There are reports of three different excavations at Graham Cave: Logan (1952), Chapman (1952), and Klippel (1971). Three different grid systems and three different approaches to the natural stratigraphy were used. The natural stratigraphy as drawn by Logan (1952:Fig. 3) is very complex, with many intrusive pits, rodent burrows, recent disturbances, and frankly, more disturbed than undisturbed deposits. Despite this complexity, with some pits 5 ft deep in a deposit of only 8 ft, Logan excavated in 1-ft levels across 10-ft squares (p. 17). Chapman (1952) refined this approach to arbitrary 6-in levels. Chapman also isolated three 10x10-ft squares to excavate in stratigraphic levels, but did not report on these. Klippel's excavations were made in arbitrary 3-in levels but where the levels crosscut the natural stratigraphy the components were kept separate (p. 19). However, his analysis also includes arbitrary 6-in levels.

Because we are attempting to determine the maintenance and extractive tasks relating to the Helton phase occupation at Graham Cave, it is necessary to eliminate as much of the temporal mixing as possible. Starting with the natural stratigraphy, we can eliminate Zones 3 and 4 because of the presence of concave-base lanceolate and fluted points (Klippel 1971:Fig. 24). Zone 1 can be eliminated because it is composed of European trash and manure (pp. 15-16). This leaves Zone 2 which ranges in thickness from 1 to 7 ft (p. 16) with its uppermost portions containing sherds and other Woodland materials. However, Klippel's excavations were placed to avoid disturbed portions of the site and the Woodland materials were analyzed separately (p. 21). I believe that there is a Helton phase occupation at Graham Cave in Zone 2 because (1) "Black Sand Notched" points occur in it, (2) the illustrations in Klippel (1971) show a number of characteristic Helton phase artifact forms, and (3) the only Titterington phase Etley point (Fig. 13e) is at the base of Zone 3, obviously out of context. For the Zone 2 occupation, I will combine Klippel's 175 sq ft of natural level materials with 450 sq ft of deposits in Chapman's levels 2A and 2B. Table 24 (pp. 92-93) presents this assemblage (and the assemblages for Modoc Rock Shelter and Koster) in functional categories. While these materials represent only 625 sq ft of excavation at Graham Cave, there is no way to include Logan's material excavated in 12-in arbitrary levels.

MODOC ROCK SHELTER

Modoc Rock Shelter represents another stratified Archaic site which has a major Helton phase component. Examining Broyles's large scale (1:1) illustrations in Fowler and Winters (1956), Godar forms would include Fig. 7(c, k, m, n, p) and 10 (p, q, r); Matanzas forms would include Fig. 7(r) and 10 (d, i, l); and Karnak Stemmed forms would include Figs. 10(n) and 10(o). In addition, the worked bone in Fig. 8(b, c, d) is also similar to materials from the Koster site. Turning to the frequency of occurrence of point types in Fowler and Winters (1956:Fig. 14), we see a major shift in point types between the 5- to 10-ft levels which are dominated by expanding and straight stemmed forms and the 10- to 15-ft levels which are dominated by side-notched forms. In addition, because the 10- to 15-ft zone was carbon dated to between 5280 and 5611 B.P., we would anticipate that the Helton phase component, which is dominated by side-notched forms, is going to occur in this 5-ft-thick zone or will overlap it.

Stratigraphic evidence can be used to further refine this 5-ft-thick zone. Fowler and Winters (1956:Fig. 3) depict three major strata at the site: a sandy clay, overlain with brown loess which in turn is covered with yellow loess. For the deep trench profile, the break between the brown and yellow loess occurs at 15-16 ft below datum. The west pillar profile, however, records this same break at a higher elevation, 12 ft below datum. In other words, there is a 3-ft difference between profiles in the absolute elevation of the stratigraphic break, i.e., the natural soil stratigraphy is sloping. This stratigraphic break is potentially crucial because it should represent a time marker and a buried surface in this area of Modoc Rock Shelter stratigraphy. Fowler (1959b:15-16) used this color change to distinguish his Strata 3 and 4:

> Stratum 4. This differs from Stratum 3 in that it is largely a yellowish-tan rather than brown....
>
> The loess deposits on the bluffs above the shelter are just the reverse of this color sequence, the brown being on the top and the yellow-tan loess below. This area of yellow deposit in the site itself is deepest under the erosional gulley in the bluff above.

Archeological materials from the yellow loess zone must postdate the brown zone sample A date of 5600 B.P. (Fowler and Winters 1956:Fig. 3, p. 32). In other words, the Helton phase occupation ought to occur only in the yellow loess (Stratum 4), and provenience units 12 through 15.5 ft should be excluded because they are contaminated with earlier materials near the west profile. In other words, 12 ft and above would contain unmixed materials.

The next question concerns the upper boundary of this Helton zone. For the Titterington phase occupation, materials between 7 and 5 ft were assigned to this later occupation. Hence the Helton phase is not more than 5 ft thick as far as I can tell from profile and artifact distribution charts. Because there is the difference of 3 ft or so between the two profile drawings of the break between Strata 3 and 4 in the 1956 report, one would suppose that this difference carries over to the top as well as the bottom of the Helton phase zone. Therefore, I shall use 10 ft as the arbitrary cutoff point for "unmixed" Helton phase materials at Modoc Rock Shelter. This gives us a 2-ft rather than a 5-ft-thick zone as seen in two published profiles (Fowler and Winters 1956). This means that the Modoc sample is neither the latter portion or the earlier portion of the Hel-

TABLE 24

Helton Phase Artifacts and Functional Categories at Koster, Modoc Rock Shelter, and Graham Cave

Functional Category	Tool Type	Koster Middle 6	Koster Lower 6	Modoc	Graham[a]
Piercing/ cutting	Antler points	2	0	0	1 (26)
	Projectiles and knives	256	18	51	75 (1-6)
	Utilized fragments	11	0	91	37 (9)
Perforating	Antler perforators	6	0	0	0
	Blunt drills	37	4	-	-
	Drills, bits	36	1	13	8 (14)
	Bone awls	117	10	15	16 (23)
	Microdrills	26	0	-	-
Cutting	Hafted bifaces	3	0	-	-
	Crude knives	0	0	5	-
	Utilized flakes	245.58 kg	19.40 kg	-	103 (12)
Incising	Burins	1	0	-	-
	Gravers	39	1	3	-
	Bone gravers	0	0	1	-
	Spurs	20	1	-	-
Scraping	Scrapers	65	5	95	see: (12)
	Hafted scrapers and scrapers on points	37	3	17	7 (13)
	Shell denticulates	1	0	-	-
	Bone scrapers	8	1	1	5 (25)
	Bone beamers	2	0	-	-
Pulverizing	Chert hammers	100	14	-	-
	Choppers	8	1	2	46 (11)
	Hammerstones	75	17	11	-
	Manos	152	7	0	
	Combination stones	88	19	1	{ 15 (19)
	Metates	10	2	-	5 (20)
	Nutting stones	0	0	0	3 (21)
Manufacturing	Cores	1520	103	+	14 (16)
	Waste flakes	355.02 kg	28.88 kg	12,424	+
	Unaltered bifaces and fragments	551	50	6	186 (10,15)
	Unaltered partial bifaces and fragments	154	13	-	-
	Resharpening flakes	57	3	-	-
	Unifaces	766	34	-	see: (12)
	Sandstone abraders	35	1	0	-
	Worked incisors	2	0	-	-

TABLE 24 (Continued)

Functional Category	Tool Type	Koster Middle 6	Koster Lower 6	Modoc	Graham
Manufacturing (continued)	Antler flakers	8	3	15	3 (24)
	Antler punch	1	0	-	-
	Antler shaft straightener	2	0	-	-
Weights	Plummets	3	1	1	-
	Pebble pendants	33	6	1	-
	Bannerstones	0	0	1	-
Tree felling	Axes	40	3	1	0 (28)
Debris	Misc. rocks, stones	25	1	2	4 (17)
	Worked antler	43	7	8	1 (28)
	Worked bone	90	10	14	-
	Worked shell	14	2	0	-
Features		317	82	present	present
Burials		12		2+	present?
Woven item manufacture	Spatulas	7	1	1	-
Ornaments	Incised and carved bone pins	70	3	1	0 (27)
	Bone beads	2	1	0	-
	Copper beads	1	0	0	-
	Hematite beads	58	6	0	-
	Shell beads	0	0	1	-
	Bone, antler, and tooth pendants	1	1	2	-
	Shell pendants	2	1	0	-
Pigments	Hematite lumps	833	43	0	-
	Rubstones	116	13	0	23 (18)
	Galena	1	0	0	-
Containers	Carapace cups (groups)	128	18	0	-
	Shell spoons	1	0	0	-
Fishing tackle	Hooks	1		0	-
	Gorges	0	1	0	-

Sources: Koster -- this chapter. Modoc Rock Shelter -- Fowler (1959:Table 13, 12- to 10-ft levels). Graham Cave -- Klippel (1971:Figs. 21A, 21B, natural level 2 and arbitrary levels 2A and 2B).

[a] Numbers in parentheses are Klippel's categories.

ton phase occupation, but a mixture of both. Fig. 24 depicts the reinterpretation of the published Modoc Rock Shelter stratigraphy.

To recapitulate, the Helton phase, as stylistically defined at the Koster site, shares a number of stylistic elements with excavated materials 450 km to the north, 95 km to the west, 400 km to the south and 350 km to the east. No doubt these distances could be increased by further excavation and further review of the literature. But by taking a maximum distance of 200 km, to minimize environmental and temporal differences, we are left with two sequential open air components at Koster and two rockshelters: Graham Cave and Modoc Rock Shelter. The artifacts and functional categories for these Helton phase components of these sites are given in Table 24. There are also four mortuary sites: Gibson, Godar, Hemphill, and Klunk. Thus there are eight components to aid in the preliminary definition of the nonstylistic dimensions of the Helton phase.

There have been excavations of other Helton phase components within 200 km of Koster. These include Chrisman site, tested by McGregor (1954), and the predominantly Early Woodland Collins site (Klippel 1972). Unfortunately, both sites are multicomponent. In addition to these two excavated sites, surface surveys in the American Bottoms by Harn (1971:23-24) and Munson (1971: 5) revealed two major base camps, one on Poag Road ($Ms^{V}97$), at the base of the bluffline where Cahokia Creek enters the bottoms, and the other, South Roxana ($Ms^{V}311$), on a natural levee of an old meander of the Mississippi called Grassy Lake. Surface surveys in the central Illinois River valley by Munson and Harn (1966) include three Matanzas-point-bearing sites: Richardson ($F^{V}1111$), West Matanzas ($F^{V}1114$), and Lone Barn ($F^{V}1223$) which are interpreted as "a number of small, temporarily utilized areas which were established at different times at slightly different locations along the terrace margins" (p. 166). However, since there is no guarantee that any of these surface survey sites represents unmixed materials, these five sites have also been excluded.

Figure 24. Schematic illustration of Modoc Rock Shelter stratigraphy for the Helton component. Depth in ft.

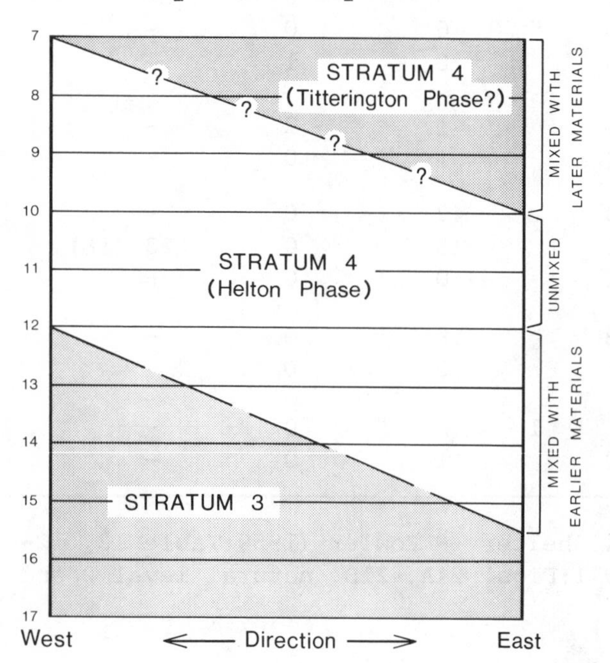

MORTUARY COMPONENTS

Gibson

The Gibson mound group was excavated by Perino and Buikstra in 1969 to recover a complete Middle and Late Woodland mortuary population. While totally excavating these mounds, they discovered a Helton phase component in the form of a low mound beneath the Middle Woodland component of Mound 1. The original size of the Archaic mound cannot be determined due to 3000 years of erosion before the Middle Woodland mortuary activities sealed the earlier mound. Perino (personal communication) states that about 35 points, including two Thebes and one Williams, were found with the Archaic burials. The rest were Godar Side Notched, Hemphill Side Notched, unnotched point forms of the Godar variety, and some drills made on points. Perino (1971a:Plate 25) illustrates four Hemphill points from beneath Gibson Mound 1.

Fig. 25 (p. 98) illustrates the relationship between Gibson Mound 1 and the other Helton mortuary components. Table 25 summarizes the materials covered from these mortuary sites.

Pete Klunk

The Pete Klunk mound group was also excavated by Perino, and beneath Mound 14 a large Archaic charnel pit was discovered (Perino 1968b:114-115):

> The pit was approximately four feet deep, irregular in outline, had a width of twelve feet and a length of fifteen feet...[*it*] had been re-

TABLE 25

Inventory of Helton Phase Mortuary Sites

	Gibson Md. 1	Godar	Hemp-hill	Klunk Md. 14
Burials	+	several	11+	ca. 5
Mound	+	?	+	disturbed
Limestone slabs	0	+	+	0
Large pit	0	0	1	1
Red ochre	0	+	+	0
Agate Basin points	0	+	0	0
Dalton pts.	0	+	0	0
Godar points	+	400[a]	0	2
Hardin pts.	2	+	0	0
Hemphill points	4+	many[b]	1	0
Williams points	1	0	0	0
Bone beads	0	0	1	0
Calcite beads	0	0	71	0
Copper beads	0	0	406+	0
Marine shell beads	0	0	88	0
Pearl beads	0	0	1	0
Rhyolite beads	0	3	0	0
Squirrel incisor beads	0	0	200+	0
Fluorspar tablets	0	0	7	0
Stone tablets	0	0	2	0
Bannerstones	0	24	3	1[c]
Plummets	0	6[d]	3	0
Unfinished plummets	0	0	1	0
Pebble pendants	0	3	0	0
Drilled antler	0	0	2	0
Stone axes	2	25[e]	1	0
Copper axes	0	0	7	0
Copper celts	0	0	3	0
Copper awls	0	0	3	0
Rat-tail spear	0	0	1	0
Copper nugget	0	0	1[f]	0
Galena piece	0	0	1	0
Drills	+	40	0	0
Knives	0	many	0	0
Blunts (scrapers)	0	several	0	0
Arkansas bauxite	0	+[g]	0	0

Note: The Hemphill inventory summarizes the data in Snyder (1898:21-23), Knoblock (1939), Griffin (1941), and Titterington (1950), and ignores the "late" pottery and glass trade bead.

[a] Includes both preforms and finished forms.

[b] Perino (personal communication).

[c] Unfinished [d] Hematite.

[e] Three-quarter grooved. [f] 24 lb.

[g] Perino (1971b:139) used spectroscopic analysis to determine that one of the Godar bannerstones was made of bauxite

filled with clay obtained from a place on the ridge about fifty feet to the north. In the pit were an articulated human rib cage and disarticulated bones of three or four individuals, all found scattered in the fill. Three artifacts were recovered in widely scattered areas of the pit consisting of: an unfinished sugar quartz banner-stone and two side-notched projectile points, identical to those found at the Godar Site...seven miles to the south.

Perino (1973c:Figs. 44, 45) illustrates this situation as well as the three artifacts. Fig. 25 illustrates the relationship of this material to other Helton phase components.

Hemphill

The Hemphill site, about 10 mi east of Versailles, Brown County, Ill., is a badly potted mound group. Dr. John F. Snyder (1898) did some initial probing of one of these mounds, and Knoblock (1939:201-210) reports the activities of the Hemphill brothers in 1933 and 1938. I wish to assign this mound group to the Helton phase because: (1) the Hemphill point, despite its large size seems to fit into the Godar-Hemphill forms (cf. Perino [1971a:Plate 25]); (2) the copper rat-tail spearhead seems to fit into the Osceola assemblage; (3) the absence of other point types or ceramics.

Tabulations of the Hemphill excavations, minus one glass bead dated to the Historic period, are in Table 25 while Fig. 25 illustrates the relationship of this site to other Helton phase sites.

Godar

The Godar site is located on a low terrace at the foot of the western bluffs of the Illinois Valley, about 3 km north of Hardin. Artifacts from the site were used to name the Godar point (Perino 1963:95) and the Godar plummet (Perino 1961:43). Titterington (1950:22) notes that Al Godar had pitted portions of an area 60 ft square, recovering 400 points, 40 T-drills, 25 grooved axes (up to ten lbs apiece), 24 bannerstones, 6 hematite holed plummets, 3 perforated pebbles, and 3 small tubular rhyolite beads. Some of the projectile points had been rehafted, others had been made into endscrapers ("blunts"). Excavations by Titterington in 1943 substantiated that numerous artifacts but no burials were recovered from a depth of 1 to 2.5 ft while all of the burials were found at a depth of 3.5 to 4 ft "on a hard clay deposit and were covered by varying amounts of red ochre and limestone slabs."

Not all of the artifacts from the Godar site can be assigned to the Helton phase. Perino (personal communication) states that the Godar collection, now at the Gilcrease Institute in Tulsa, Okla. did contain Dalton, Agate Basin, and Hardin points which like the early points found under Gibson Mound 1, indicate "that earlier 'found' points were added to the mortuary goods." Perino also notes that neither Matanzas nor Karnak Stemmed points were recovered from any of these mortuary components of the Helton phase. This may reflect upon the social functions of these three artifact forms, i.e., that only the Godar type was considered for grave goods.

Burials in Habitation Sites

In addition to interment and/or processing of the dead at these four sites, Helton phase burials also occur at habitation sites, including Crib Mound, McCain, Koster, Modoc Rock Shelter, and possibly Graham Cave. In general, these habitation site burials did not receive grave goods and certainly not elaborate amounts of copper, bannerstones, axes (although Burial 10 at Modoc Rock Shelter had a three-quarter grooved axe), point caches, and the like. In a preliminary analysis of the Koster sample of burials, Buikstra (personal communication) suggests that these individuals do not represent a normal population but a very skewed age/sex sample of the young, the old, and the crippled, i.e., people of low economic importance or low achieved status. A similar tendency may occur at Modoc Rock Shelter and the McCain site. Appendix E (prepared by Buikstra) tabulates the Koster 1970 burial sample, combining Middle and Lower Horizon 6.

HELTON PHASE BURIAL PROGRAM

The Helton phase is characterized by a complex burial program. Burials occur at all seven components (with various degrees of reliability for each site). These locations include bluff-base, blufftop, and secondary valley sites. For mortuary sites, burials appear to be under limestone slabs with associated red ochre pigment. Artifacts occur in caches near or about the burials. A relatively small number of burials are reported from these sites and there seem to be far more artifacts than burials. It seems likely that low mounds were usually built over burial areas, although after 5000 years very little mound would be left and it might escape notice. The burials at habitation sites seem to be characterized by shallow interments in the midden, few if any grave goods, and no limestone slabs; i.e., probably lower status burials.

The charnel pit at the Klunk site suggests that burial and reburial may have been practiced at this early date of 5000 B.P., because Perino recovered portions of an articulated burial and scattered parts of other individuals as if incomplete exhumation had occurred.

In comparing the Helton phase burial program with that of the Titterington phase, we note the lack of Turkey Tail points in the former. But in general for the mortuary sites of the two phases, there is great continuity in the presence of limestone slabs, red ochre, groups of artifacts, presence of exotic or trade materials, and the general impression that relatively important people were being buried. Lack of excavated Titterington base camps prevents us from comparing the disposal procedures for the rest of the population.

TRADE DIMENSIONS

The mortuary sites provide the best view of the trade dimensions of the Helton phase. Items not locally available are found at Hemphill and Godar sites. The Hemphill inventory includes copper artifacts and a nugget, marine shell, fluorspar, and galena. Slate is present at both of these sites while at Godar, rhyolite and bauxite from near Hot Springs, Ark., are present. The bauxite identification is based on spectroscopic analysis of a bannerstone (Perino 1971b:139). Materials from Koster site include a single copper bead and what appears to be Dongola chert (represented by two projectile points and a few small thinning flakes).

Evidence of trading to the south includes the Arkansas bauxite, the southern Illinois fluorspar, and the Dongola chert. Evidence of trade to the north would be the native copper and the copper rat-tail spearhead from Hemphill site which resembles Wisconsin Old Copper artifacts. The other minerals could have come from a variety of sources beyond the lower valley. Because the habitation sites have very few exotic raw materials or artifacts, I would suggest that these trade items are directly linked to the status system indicated by the burial program, simultaneously acting as status markers as well as goods of restricted access. The analysis of the distribution of carved and incised deer bone pins suggests that there is direct contact between distant groups, although these pins are not related to the mortuary program and we do not know the social context in which they appeared.

Further information about the trade system and the mortuary program include a comparison of the types of tools found at mortuary sites. Fig. 25 is a Venn diagram showing the presence and absence of each artifact type from Gibson Mound 1, Godar, Hemphill and Klunk Mound 14. The tools reflect hunting, fowling, heavy woodworking, and some maintenance tasks (awls, drills, and scrapers), all of the former stressing

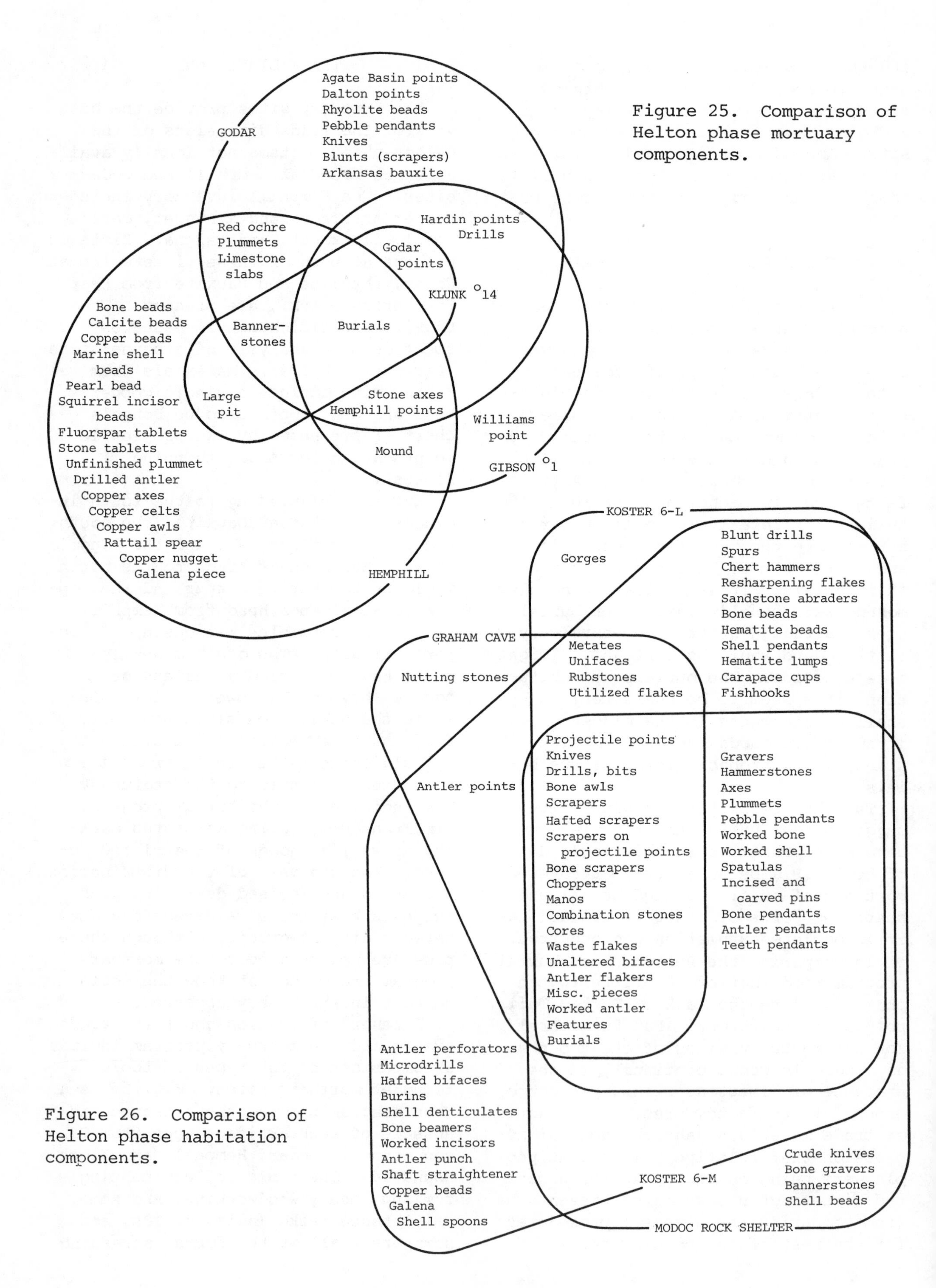

Figure 25. Comparison of Helton phase mortuary components.

Figure 26. Comparison of Helton phase habitation components.

mobility and prowess. The ornaments are almost exclusively pierced for suspension as jewelry or atlatl weights, or are unfinished. Unworked raw materials, which are rare, include the large copper nugget from Hemphill. Again, the tool kits recovered from these mortuary sites seem to stress the tasks of the physically fit.

ADAPTATIONAL DIMENSIONS

Tools, Tasks, and Trash

Fig. 26 is another Venn diagram, illustrating the presence and absence of each artifact type listed in Table 24 from two components at Koster, Graham Cave, and Modoc Rock Shelter. The tool assemblages of these four components are represented by four ellipses, each with a shared focus at the center of the configuration and a nonshared focus around the periphery of the figure. Each site has both unique and ubiquitous artifacts.

The explanation for Fig. 26 stems from a variety of sources: sampling error, confused stratigraphy, stylistic differences, alternative tools to perform the same function, and the performance of various maintenance, extractive, and social tasks. The discussions of these three sites indicate the extent to which one can control for these various sources of assemblage variability other than actual, prehistoric behavior. The behavioral explanation for Fig. 26 is presented in Tables 26 and 27 and in Fig. 27. For Tables 26 and 27, a zero (0) indicates that there is no evidence from tools that the particular task is present at the site. A question mark (?) indicates that there is no confirmatory evidence. A plus sign (+) indicates that the task is confirmed by independent evidence.

For the extractive tasks, I have incorporated the revision of the Mark II model for grinding tasks, making a distinction between casual and intensive processing. The distribution of the pluses, question marks, and zeros reflects the strengths and weaknesses of the revised Mark II model. The model is strongest when the confirmatory information is present in the form of manufacturing debris, unfinished forms, animal and plant remains, and other entities which are separate from the tools themselves. The model is only partially tested with worn tools because (1) no new information is gathered about tool function, since worn tools are assumed by replicative studies to have been used in certain tasks and (2) we cannot distinguish between those tools being used at the site of deposition and tools that were brought back to the site, unhafted, and discarded there.

The model fails, of course, when there is no preserved confirmatory information, e.g., the making of woven objects. However, there are indications that the model can be further improved by making it more specific and more realistic. For example, chert tool manufacture could be broken down into several stages of manufacture: roughing out, refining blanks, finishing touches, etc. depending upon the manufacturing trajectory for a given phase. For Helton phase, a convenient breaking point would be the thermal alteration episode, cf. Sheets (1975) for subdividing a manufacturing trajectory.

Fig. 27 is another Venn diagram which compares the various maintenance, extractive, and social tasks present at the Helton phase sites under study. We immediately see that Modoc Rock Shelter and Graham Cave components are subsets of the range of tasks observed at two components of the Koster site. The four mortuary sites form their own, separate task set. Examining the central area of overlap in Fig. 27, (the intersection of Modoc Rock Shelter, Graham Cave, Koster 6-M, and Koster 6-L), we see a familiar cluster of eight tool-using tasks. This cluster is very similar to the combination of tasks for the Titterington phase in Chapter 3. This situation stems from two factors: First, there is a common core of activities relating to hunting, butchering, maintenance of the chipped stone tool kit, and the processing of

TABLE 26

Helton Phase Maintenance Tasks at Graham Cave, Koster, and Modoc Rock Shelter

Task	Tools Present	Confirmatory Evidence Present: Unfinished Items	Confirmatory Evidence Present: Debris	Confirmatory Evidence Present: Worn Tools	Graham	Koster 6-M	Koster 6-L	Modoc
Chert tool manufacture	Hammerstones Sandstone abrad. Antler flakers	Bifaces Preforms	Cores Waste flakes		+	+	+	+
Ground stone tool manufacture	Chert hammers Hammerstones Sandstone abrad.	Unfinished forms	Chert hammer frags.		0	+	+	0
Shell item manufacture	Drills Flakes Incising tools Sandstone abrad.	Unfinished shell forms	Worked shell		0	+	+	0
Wood item manufacture	Knives Axes Scrapers Drills Flakes Gravers Bone gravers Heavy-duty scrapers Microdrills Antler shaft straighteners			Axes Gravers Microdrills Scrapers	?	+	+	?
Woven item manufacture	Shuttles, etc. Pins and needles				?	?	?	?
Hide and leather work	Flakes Drills Microdrills Bone awls Bones with flattened ends			Drills Microdrills Bone awls Bones with flattened ends	+	+	+	?
Bone and antler tool manufacture	Sandstone abrad. Gravers Retouched flakes Sinew stones		Cut and snapped bone and antler		+	+	+	+

Note: A zero indicates no evidence for a task being performed; a question mark indicates that there is no confirmatory evidence; and a plus is a confirmed task.

TABLE 27

Helton phase Extractive Tasks at Graham Cave, Koster, and Modoc Rock Shelter

Task	Tools Present		Confirmatory Evidence Present		Graham	Koster		Modoc
						Middle 6	Lower 6	
Trapping	None		Fauna		0	0	0	0
Hunting	Projectile points Knives		Point fragments Worn knives Fauna		+	+	+	+
Fowling	Plummets		Fauna		0	+	+	+
Fishing	Weights Fishhooks Fish gorges		Fauna		0	+	+	+
Quarrying	Hammerstones		All early stages of knapping Cores Primary shatter Chert outcrops		?	+	+	?
Ochre grinding	Ochre stained grinding tools		Rubstones		+	+	+	?
Lumbering	Axes		Worn axes Bit fragments		0	+	+	+
Hide and leather preparation	Scrapers Heavy-duty scrapers Flakes Knives Beamers		Use polish on scrapers		?	+	+	?
	Intensive Tools	Normal Tools	Non-specific Tools	Debris				
Nut and seed preparation	Metates Nutting stones	Manos Combination stones	Hammerstones	Nuts & seeds Worn tools	? Intens.	+ Intens.	+ Intens.	? Normal
Preserved meat preparation	Metates	Manos Choppers	Knives	Fauna Worn tools	? Intens.	? Intens.	? Intens.	? Normal
Fibrous vegetable preparation	Metates	Manos Choppers		Worn tools	? Intens.	? Intens.	? Intens.	0

Note: A zero indicates no evidence for a task being performed; a question mark indicates that there is no confirmatory evidence; and a plus is a confirmed task.

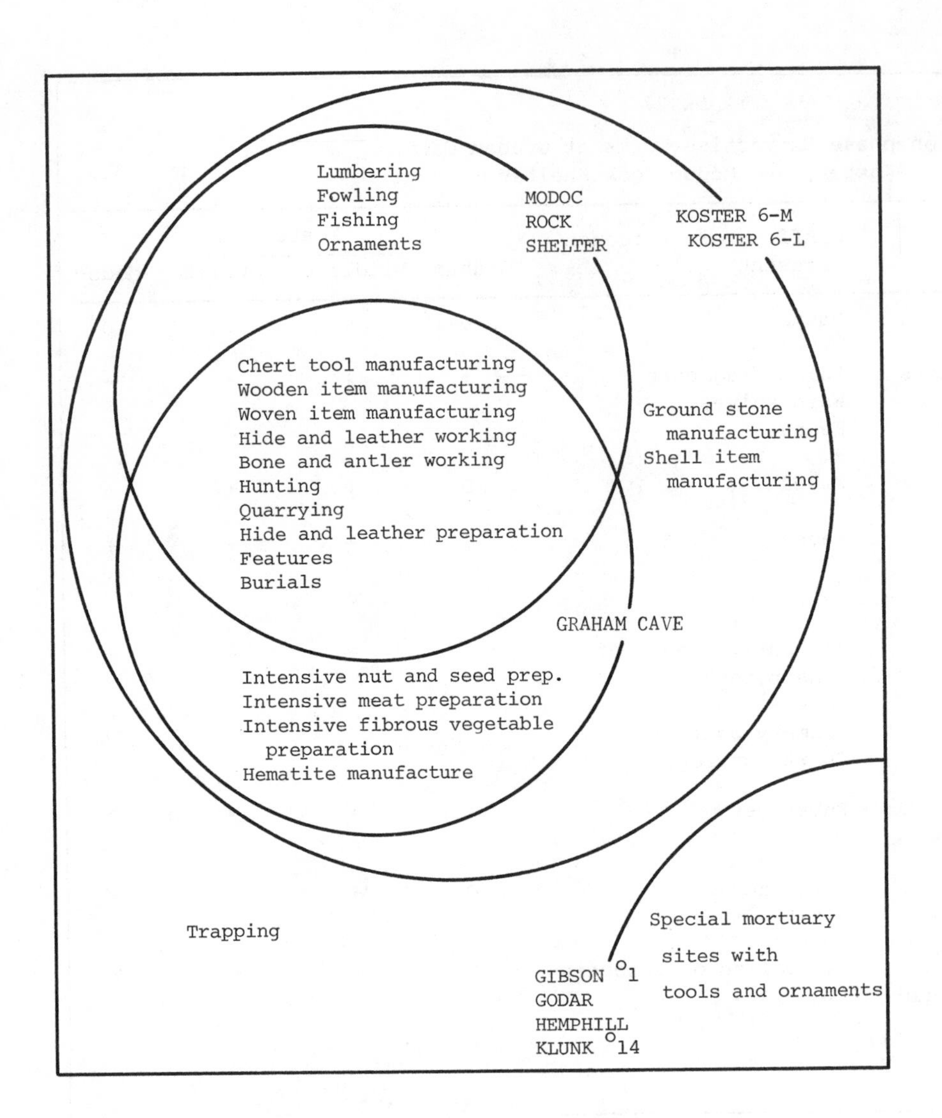

Figure 27. Universe of Helton phase tasks.

animal parts. Second, without hunting it would be virtually impossible to assign such a site to any specific nonceramic phase because there would be no projectile points.

Moving outward from this central cluster of tasks, we have Graham Cave which seems to be a hunting station with intensive grinding of foodstuffs and hematite. The lack of other subsistence activities is not surprising. Farnsworth (1973:26) reconstructs the prehistoric resource base of the Macoupin Valley as being rich in nuts, seeds, and deer during certain seasons of the year, while "backwater lake fish populations and migratory waterfowl were essentially absent." Since the Loutre River is topographically similar to Macoupin Creek (i.e., a small downcutting stream in a peneplain) Farnsworth's interpretations should also apply to the Graham Cave area. Hence the lack of tools for fowling and fishing seems reasonable at Graham Cave. The Booth site is in a similar ecological setting, and it too lacks evidence for fowling and fishing. Unfortunately, lacking reports on flora and fauna (other than worked bone), it is possible only to speculate that Graham Cave was occupied during the fall. Large mammal hunting and nut and seed gathering and processing seem to have been the most important extractive activities and these are related to the fall season. Graham Cave would then serve as a base station with natural shelter. The very large number of unaltered bifaces - 186 or 33% of the total assemblage tabulated in Table 24 - suggests that a large number of spare spear tips could have been efficiently made to replace those broken during hunting and

TABLE 28

Helton Component Fauna at Modoc Rock Shelter

	Number of Elements
Mammals	
Deer and elk	482
Raccoon	24
Opossum	12
Others	122
Unidentified	10,588
Total	11,228
Fish	
Total	207
Amphibians and reptiles	
Total	345
Birds	
Waterfowl	58
Water birds	8
Turkey	4
Quail and prairie chicken	8
Passenger pigeon	0
Others	24
Unidentified	249
Total	351
Mussels	
Total valves	508

butchering.

Turning to Modoc Rock Shelter, we see a different orientation of extractive tasks. Here fowling, fishing, and lumbering replace the intensive manipulation of nuts, seeds, fibrous vegetables, and meat to make pemmican. Parmalee's faunal report (Fowler 1959b: Tables 7 and 8) tabulates a number of major species by 1-ft increments. Table 28 presents these data for the 12- to 10-ft strata. Examining this listing of screen-recovered fauna (½-in mesh), we note a great deal of similarity to the fauna from the Titterington phase at Modoc Rock Shelter, except that mussels seem to be relatively more important. Again, two major resource zones are being exploited: There is a primary exploitation of the forest and forest edges, probably around Modoc Rock Shelter and up Barbeau Creek, to hunt deer and elk, and a secondary exploitation of the floodplain for waterfowl, fish, and mussels.

For the Helton component, there is a plummet and a perforated pendant which should indicate fowling, and the ratio of bird to mammal bone is 3.1:100. The Titterington phase occupation has no such artifacts, but the ratio of bird to mammal bone is 5.6:100. In other words, the assumption that such perforated objects necessarily indicate fowling is not well supported. In general, however, the Helton component at Modoc Rock Shelter has a greater diversity of tool types and, consequently, suggests more activities than the Titterington occupation there.

As with the Titterington occupation, there is a lack of metates for the intensive processing of nuts, seeds, and vegetable fibers. Possibly this reflects the season of occupation. The features from this zone continue upward as ashy lenses of hearths (Brown, personal communication), perhaps indicating harsher weather, although the large number of mussel valves suggests a season other than the dead of winter. Unfortunately, there is no study available of carbonized plant remains from Modoc Rock Shelter. Hence, we cannot directly assess the significance of the lack of metates. As for the plummet and the pebble pendant, we may have a sample too small to permit conclusive statements.

The two Helton phase occupations at Koster site seem to combine the activities of Modoc Rock Shelter and Graham Cave as well as the manufacturing of items of ground stone and shell. This suggests that it is more of a permanent campsite than these two other ephemeral occupations.

Frederick C. Hill's analysis (in preparation) of the faunal remains from the two Helton phase components at Koster is far too complex to be covered here in any detail. His results confirm the predictions of the Mark II model, specifically that fowling, fishing, and hunting, as well as mussel collecting, were performed by those people living at the Koster site during the Helton phase occupations.

Combining the Helton phase components at Koster, the paleoethnobotanical report of Asch, Ford, and Asch (1972) presents an analysis of 2834 pieces of wood charcoal and 292.7 g of carbonized nut fragments. Starting with the wood charcoal, the percentage frequency of wood types is (combining both feature and midden proveniences), in declining order of importance: *Quercus* (oak), Ulmaceae (elm and hackberry), *Juglans* (black walnut and butternut, *Carya* (hickory and pecan), *Fraxinus* (ash), *Acer* (maple), and minor types. Asch, Ford, and Asch (1972:8) suggest that this selection of firewood reflects exploitation of the upland forests where *Quercus* and *Carya* are abundant and of the bluff-base and floodplain forests where Ulmaceae is common.

But, as they point out, such interpretations are based upon small sample size and assumptions about environmental stability during the last 7000 years. The use of firewood must have been extensive at Koster during this time period because the major cultural constituent of the Helton phase middens is fire cracked rock, mostly limestone, which was excavated by the ton in 1970.

Turning to carbonized nutshell fragments, the Helton occupations at Koster are marked by a 96.7% frequency of *Carya* (Hickory) (Asch, Ford, and Asch 1972:Table 3). This is the highest relative frequency of hickory for all horizons at Koster. Because it is unlikely that the local nut crop was 96.7% hickory, there seems to be very high selection for this particular nut type, perhaps for its high protein composition when compared to acorns (cf. Asch, Ford, and Asch, Table 5). This large sample of carbonized nutshells seems to fit nicely with the large number of metates (12 complete plus 60 fragments of others) for Middle and Lower Horizon 6.

What is surprising about the carbonized plant remains is the very low frequency of seeds, such that Asch, Ford, and Asch (Table 6) tabulate more recent seeds than carbonized ones in the flotation units. If seeds were an important part of the Helton phase diet, they were not being processed in such a way as to leave behind accidental burnt-seed masses like those discovered at the White Hall phase occupation of the Newbridge site in the lower Illinois Valley (Struever 1968c:305). Finally, there is no evidence that the domesticated forms of *Iva annua* var. *macrocarpa* (Yarnell [1972] presents a recent review concerning the giant marshelder) were present at the Koster site ca. 5000 B.P. (Asch, Ford, and Asch 1972:16); nor were any other domesticants recovered among the carbonized remains.

Thus the faunal and floral analyses of the Koster components of the Helton phase tend to confirm the predictions of extractive tasks for the Mark II model, although again food gathering tasks which require no tools (or for which tools did not preserve), such as mussel collecting, went unpredicted. It is fortunate that mussel shells are so obvious. Remains of the man-of-the earth root (*Ipomoea pandurata*) are not.

Malacological Analysis

A site's location reflects access to resources as well as suitability to the performance of certain tasks. One index of why a site was chosen would include the local vegetation cover. Jaehnig's snail analysis (n.d.:74) permits a look at the local environmental setting during the time of the Helton phase occupation of the Koster site:

> In Horizon 6, then, we have again an invasion of a dry talus slope

forest on the site. The orderly increase in the dry forest snail frequency looks very natural and precludes the assumption that the snails were present at the site because they were transported there by man while clinging to various materials brought in from a forested environment. This interpretation is corroborated also by a look at the absolute frequency which shows different pictures in different deposits in Horizon 6. The variation will be even greater once all of the data are presented.

Hence the Koster site probably was a mosaic of a dry talus-slope forest and some grassland, with very local variation, and a general drift toward more forest cover. Certainly a situation providing both clear areas and some shade would be conducive to the establishment of a base camp.

SUMMARY

Analytical Summary

This chapter has continued the study of stylistic, functional, manufacturing, and locational aspects of chipped-stone and other artifacts. The Mark II model was given its second independent test against real prehistoric data. The definition of the Helton phase was based upon a number of dimensions: style, technology, adaptation, trade, mortuary practices, human biology, and sociocultural dimensions.

The chipped-stone materials represent a composite manufacturing system. Many of the symmetrical hafted bifaces and 10% of the cores are heat-treated, but most of the other worked forms are *not* heat-treated, unless they are reworked points or flakes from heat-treated cores. The manufacturing trajectories are thus different from the non-heat-treating system of the Titterington phase, and, among other things, this results in a different frequency distribution of core weights. The functional analysis indicates a wide variety of wear patterns, especially in degrees of wear, such that there seems to be neither an upper limit nor a lower limit to when a worked edge is discarded.

In addition, the "projectile points" show much of the wear variability described by Ahler (1971) for earlier materials at Rodgers Shelter in Missouri. The stylistic analysis included chipped-stone tools called Godar, Karnak Stemmed, and Matanzas points; incised bone and carved bone pins showing geometric patterns; a special metate form; and the frequency distribution of core weights. The points and the pins indicate that the Helton phase, unlike the Titterington phase, is not so obviously restricted to a small portion of the Mississippi riverine system. Side-notched, medium-thick, heat-treated points are found throughout the Midwest and into the East. The geometrically incised and shaped bone pins from Arnold Research Cave, Crib Mound, Dillard Stamped Shelter No. 1, Graham Cave, Koster, McCain, and Modoc Rock Shelter sites share a high degree of similarity, as do other aspects of the worked bone, antler, and shell assemblages.

There is additional evidence for long distance communication and trade in raw materials. Raw materials come from a wide geographical area: bauxite from near Hot Springs, Ark.; Dongola or gray chert from southern Illinois, Indiana, or Kentucky; native copper from the Great Lakes, marine shell probably from the Gulf Coast; and galena from somewhere. Some of these imported raw materials include finished artifacts, such as the copper "rat-tail" spearhead from Hemphill site which resembles Wisconsin forms. Other artifacts which suggest long distance contacts include bannerstones (see Knoblock [1939:159-170] for tentative distribution maps of bannerstone types which occur at Modoc Rock Shelter, Godar, Klunk Mound 14, and Hemphill sites) which seem to have rather large style areas, although the specific data base is questionable. One important trade item which is conspicuously absent is the Turkey Tail point and the associated mortuary complex. While Dongola chert was being used very sparingly at Koster, it was being made into secular point forms rather than specialized mortuary blades.

Using the tool typologies developed in Chapter 2, a revised Mark II model was subjected to a second, independent test to determine the maintenance, extractive, and social tasks at eight components of the Helton phase. This array of tasks is illustrated in Fig. 27. These sites were selected so that we would be analyzing the adaptational strategy for a single region. Inclusion of sites from Indiana, Wisconsin, and Tennessee would only have confused the picture. Animal and plant remains from Koster site and animal remains from Modoc Rock Shelter were compared with Fig. 27. For Koster, the firewood analysis suggests that a wide variety of trees were exploited from both the forest zone above the site and from the adjacent floodplain.

The presence of massive quantities of fire cracked rock suggests that much wood was consumed at Koster during the Helton phase. The carbonized nut and seed analysis indicates that *Carya* (hickory) was being heavily utilized and that seeds, if used, were not being dry-parched since more recent than carbonized seeds were recovered in flotation. Hill's faunal analysis indicates that a rather wide spectrum of animals from the Koster site was exploited and the presence of large quantities of mussel shell would not have been predicted from the tool kit. The floral and faunal analyses support the interpretation of the two Helton phase occupations at Koster site as long term, multiseasonal occupations.

Modoc Rock Shelter's faunal analysis indicates that two major resource zones, the adjacent uplands and the nearby floodplain, were being exploited. This fits into the picture of this occupation being a somewhat more restricted extraction and tool-kit-repair locus than Koster site. Again, there is reasonable agreement between the faunal remains and the prediction of the revised Mark II model, although further studies must be done on fowling net weights. The Helton phase and Titterington phase occupations of Modoc Rock Shelter are quite similar in the spectrum of tasks performed and in their faunal remains. This situation is very different from that found for these phases at the Koster site.

For Graham Cave, the lack of recovered floral remains and the lack of a report on the faunal remains hampers our understanding of the site. However, it seems to be a meat and nut extraction station, not unlike Booth site.

The revised Mark II model worked very well, especially when worked antler, bone, and shell items are included in the artifact inventory. The new distinction between intensive and normal processing of various substances by pulverization clarifies the role of metates and other grinding implements. It now seems quite reasonable to deal with more explicitly defined tasks, e.g., to divide hunting into large mammal and small mammal, assign tools to these two categories, and then assign specific game as confirmatory evidence.

The mortuary program for the Helton phase includes two classes of sites: (1) specially prepared facilities, either charnel structures or mounded areas, which are reserved for those individuals who have access to exotic materials and extensive grave goods, and (2) habitation sites where burial tends to be in unmarked, unaccoutered graves. Extrapolating from Buikstra's comments in App. E, we seem to be dealing with a society based upon achieved, rather than ascribed, status. This fits the general notion that the Helton phase was a semisedentary hunting and gathering society without hereditary rankings.

The Helton phase then will be defined as follows:

Dimensional Summary

1. Stylistic dimension
   a. The defining artifacts are Godar points, Karnak Stemmed points, Matanzas points, geometrically

shaped or incised bone pins, and Channel Basin metates.

b. Manufacturing chert artifacts follows three trajectories: (1) the use of non-heat-treated cherts, (2) heat treatment of about 10% of the cores, and (3) heat-treating projectile point preforms. The two types of cores are free-flaked.

c. Absolute dates place the Helton phase in the range of 5500 to 5000 B.P. at both Koster and Modoc Rock Shelter sites. The geographical extent of the phase, as determined by the distribution of the characteristic point forms and bone pins, includes western Missouri, Illinois, Indiana, Kentucky, and probably portions of southern Wisconsin and northern Tennessee. However, because this area is too large to provide a coherent view of adaptational strategies, the in-depth analysis of the phase was restricted to the Prairie Peninsula region.

2. Technological dimensions

a. Manufacture of chert objects involves the heat treatment of preforms and about 10% of cores. The industry is less obviously a core-tool industry than that in the Titterington phase. Manufacture of ground stone objects closely follows Fig. 9. The manufacture of antler, bone, and shell artifacts follows Figs. 10 and 11 and the manufacturing descriptions in Chapter 2.

b. A complete inventory of Helton phase tools is probably approximated by the Koster plus Modoc Rock Shelter samples where the greatest deficiencies would be unpreserved organic remains such as baskets, handles of wood, etc. Unfortunately, until a standard list of tool types is developed, one is never certain that an artifact is absent from a published inventory or included in another, broader category.

c. Archeological evidence has been presented indicating that the Helton phase reveals all of the maintenance, extractive, and social tasks listed in Chapter 2 except trapping.

3. Adaptational dimensions

a. The task analysis has defined three habitation site types: (1) hunting and gathering stations for deer, nuts, and seeds; (2) hunting and gathering stations for deer and floodplain resources; and (3) base camps from which a very extensive number of maintenance, extractive, and social tasks are performed.

b. These three habitation site types may reflect localized use of seasonal resources. The subsistence-settlement system will be discussed in Chapter 5.

c. The structure of segmentation is unknown.

4. Trade dimensions

a. Exotic raw materials include Great Lakes copper, Arkansas bauxite, trade cherts from southern Illinois or Indiana, possibly marine shell from the Gulf Coast, galena and fluorspar from Illinois, and various rare stones used in making bannerstones. Exotic styles include Old-Copper-form artifacts.

b. Exported items have not been identified, although the bone pins are a possibility.

5. Mortuary dimensions

a. Mortuary sites seem to be related to mound building over limestone-slab-covered graves. These graves occur in both bluff-base and blufftop situations. These sites appear to be reserved for those individuals who have access to exotic materials and items. Burial also occurs at habitation sites, but for a different segment of the population and is not associated with grave goods. There may be postmortum manipulation of the dead, e.g., the charnel pit at Klunk Mound 14.

b. All mortuary sites are located on the western edge of the Illinois Valley. This distribution is assumed to be a sampling error.

6. Human biology dimensions
   See App. E and Buikstra (in preparation).
7. Sociocultural dimensions
   a. The distribution of bone pins suggests long distance contacts between local groups. This contact does not appear to be part of a mortuary practice, in direct contrast to the Turkey Tail system present in the Titterington phase. I suspect that the pins are part of a trade system.
   b. The two classes of interments suggest that certain individuals had access to certain goods and services.

5

Subsistence-Settlement Systems in the Late Archaic

ADAPTATIONAL SHIFTS: HELTON TO TITTERINGTON TIMES

THE FIRST goal of this study was to develop a more up-to-date definition of *phase* and Chapters 3 and 4 presented two Archaic examples of this multidimensional definition of the phase. The second goal of this study, the developing and testing of a model to translate assemblages into tasks, has been achieved for two Archaic phases, and at the present time a revised model is being developed for the other Archaic occupations at the Koster site. The third goal now must be discussed: to consider the evidence for a shift in adaptation between Helton and Titterington phase times, say the third millennium B.C. The documentation of this shift proceeds from the better data (excavated materials) to more impressionistic data (surface survey studies) by testing our interpretations with each successive data set. Once the shift is documented, we can then only speculate on why the shift occurred because the crucial evidence has not yet been collected.

ACTIVITIES AT KOSTER

The Koster site represents a single locality where a number of sequential occupations occurred. Because of the depositional history of that locus, these occupations tend to be well separated by zones of sterile or nearly sterile soil. Within each zone of occupation there is a minimum of mixing with other zones. The remains from 5000 B.P. are physically separated from those of 4000 B.P. This fine stratigraphy and continuity of location permit an excellent first approach to Archaic subsistence-settlement systems.

Let us start with a compound null hypothesis, that (1) there was neither change in the subsistence-settlement system nor (2) change in how the Koster locality was utilized. Table 29 lists activities at Koster within the lower and middle occupation zones of the Helton phase and the occupation zone of the Titterington phase.

Examining Table 29, we see a high degree of similarity between the two stratified components of the Helton phase. Both have very complex combinations of activities, probably reflecting use of the location as a base camp strategically located with respect to a number of resources. The site is near outcrops of chert; it is at the edge of the floodplain of the Illinois River just below the blufftops and uplands; it is situated in a somewhat sheltered area near a perennial spring and lies 1 km from the mouth of a large secondary valley (Macoupin). Because of the great continuity of these two Helton phase occupations, one is tempted to conclude that very little change has taken place. Both play the same role in the subsistence-settlement system under the same distribution of local resources. However, when we turn to the Titterington phase activities, listed in Table 29, we note very low similarity with the Helton phase list.

The Helton phase habitation site is complex, potentially even a permanent base camp. In contrast, the Titterington phase component is a hunting camp with some collecting and tool kit maintenance. Its occupation is ephemeral.

Therefore, at least part of the initial null hypothesis is incorrect. There is a marked change in how the Koster locality was used during the Helton and Titterington phases. The other portion of the null hypothesis, that there is no change in the subsistence-settlement system, cannot be tested from a single site. After all, the Titterington base camp may not be at Koster because it was at *another* bluff-base situation, e.g., Titus/Upper Macoupin (Jaehnig 1974:Fig. 26). Therefore, let us make a second test of the null hypothesis. If we find that the structure of segmentation is similar, then we will have confirmed the second portion of the null hypothesis.

TABLE 29

Activities at Koster from Artifact Analysis

Task	Titterington	Helton 6-M	Helton 6-L
M. chert tools	+	+	+
M. ground stone tools	+	+	+
M. shell items	0	+	+
M. wooden items	+	+	+
M. woven items	0	+	+
M. hide and leather items	+	+	+
M. bone and antler items	+	+	+
Trapping	0	0	0
Hunting	+	+	+
Fowling	0	+	+
Fishing	0	+	+
Quarrying	+	+	+
Lumbering	+	+	+
Prep. hide and leather	+	+	+
Intensive p. nuts and seeds	0	+	+
Intensive p. preserved meat	0	+	+
Intensive p. vegetable fibers	0	+	+
P. red ochre or hematite	+	+	+
High status burials	0	0	0
Low status burials	0	Both	

M. = manufacturing, P. = production.

STRUCTURE OF SEGMENTATION

Because there are a number of similarities between these two phases, as both are preagricultural, one would not predict a major change in the subsistence system, especially if a seasonal round is being followed in adjustment to seasonal variation in resources (cf. Zawacki and Hausfater 1969). What may be different is the settlement system. That is, there may be a number of different ways to segment a society on the landscape while pursuing the same or similar subsistence tasks.

Various ways to determine the structure of segmentation of prehistoric society (Struever 1968c:285) are provided by (1) information on where specific maintenance, extractive, and social tasks occur in the region; (2) a typology of sites; i.e., where combinations of one or more activities occur at a single locus; (3) seasonal information about when a given locality was occupied; and (4) data on the horizontal extent of social groups, such as Struever's maximum subsistence-settlement group (1968c:297).

The first kind of information is given in tabular form in Table 30. The table summarizes the geographical distribution of 19 separate tasks for the excavated Helton and Titterington phase sites. The table contains two types of information: first, whether a task occurs in a specific resource zone, and second, whether one or both phases indicate performance of that task in a given zone. Although only two of the three resource zones and only seven components are available for study (not counting mortuary sites), 18 of a possible 19 tasks occur in the valley margin zone while 14 of a possible 19 tasks occur in the secondary valley zone. Tasks which occur only in the valley margin zone are manufacturing shell items, fowling, and fishing, that is, those activities which are dependent upon riverine resources. In other words, the distribution of tasks upon the landscape seems to be related to the distribution of resources. Unfortunately, there are not enough excavated sites to provide a finer control over this problem.

The second way to determine the

TABLE 30

Tasks and Resource Zones: Helton and Titterington Phases

Task	Resource Zones					
	FP		VM		SV	
M. chert tools			H	T	H	T
M. ground stone tools			H	T	-	T
M. shell items			H	-	-	-
M. wooden items			H	T	H	T
M. woven items			H	-	H	-
M. hide and leather items			H	T	H	T
M. bone and antler items			H	T	H	T
Trapping			-	-	-	-
Hunting			H	T	H	T
Fowling			H	-	-	-
Fishing			H	-	-	-
Quarrying			H	T	H	T
Lumbering			H	T	-	T
P. hide and leather			H	T	H	T
Intensive p. nuts and seeds			H	-	H	T
Intensive p. preserved meat			H	-	H	T
Intensive p. vegetable fibers			H	-	H	T
P. red ochre or hematite			H	T	H	T
Status burials			H	T	-	T
Totals	0	0	18	11	12	14

FP = floodplain, MV = valley margin, SV = secondary valley, H = Helton phase, T = Titterington phase, M. = manufacturing, P. = production.

structure of segmentation involves the development of a site typology. Table 30 suggests that the two phases have a somewhat different way to organize the distribution of tasks on the landscape. If we were to make the comparison of these tasks as similar (present in both phases) or different (present in only one phase), we have 11 similarities and 4 differences, with the Helton phase being slightly more complicated in its organization. Looking at specific combinations of tasks, Table 31 indicates the common core of tasks for each phase and the other combination of tasks which occur at a single occupation. Table 31 is developed directly from the Venn diagrams in Figs. 17 and 27. This table suggests that the common core of tasks for the two phases is about the same in complexity, although the specific tasks are not identical. For the other combinations of tasks, the Helton phase seems to deal in larger blocks of tasks (4, 4, 2, 1) than the Titterington phase (3, 1, 1). These differences suggest that there are some differences in the structure of segmentation between the two phases.

Turning now to the third method to separate different structures of segmentation, Table 32 presents guestimates of the seasonal uses of the various excavated sites in the sample. Both phases make fall use of secondary valleys, and fall and/or winter use of the valley margin zones. However, there is no information about where the Titterington phase spring and summer sites are located.

Thus considering only the data from excavated sites, the second half of the original null hypothesis is supported. There seems to be no major systemic change in the subsistence-settlement systems of the two phases. There may be some differences in the structure of segmentation of these societies, but this might reflect unequal sampling rather than real differences.

While there may be great systemic similarity between the Helton and Titterington phase subsistence-settlement systems, it remains to be demonstrated that the distribution of activity loci

TABLE 31

Combination of Tasks: Helton and Titterington Phase Sites

	Helton Phase	Titterington Phase
Common core of tasks	Hunting Chert tool mfg. Bone and antler mfg. Hide and leather prep. Hide and leather goods mfg. Woodworking Woven item mfg. Quarrying Features Low status burials	Hunting Chert tool mfg. Bone and antler mfg. Hide and leather prep. Hide and leather goods mfg. Woodworking Quarrying Lumbering Red ochre production Ground stone mfg. Features
Other combinations	I Intensive nut and seed prep. Intensive meat pulverization Intensive vegetable fiber mfg. Red ochre production	I Intensive nut and seed prep. Intensive meat pulverization Intensive vegetable fiber mfg.
	II Fowling Fishing Lumbering Use of ornaments	II Use of ornaments
	III Shell item mfg. Ground stone mfg.	III Status burials
	IV High status burials	
Missing tasks	Trapping	Trapping Low status burials Woven item mfg. Shell item mfg. Fowling Fishing

TABLE 32

Seasonality of Site Use

Component	Spr.	Sum.	Fall	Win.	Zone
Helton					
Koster 6-L	X	X	X	X	VM
Koster 6-M	X	X	X	X	VM
Graham Cave			X		SV
Modoc RS			X		VM
Titterington					
Koster 4			X		VM
Modoc RS			X	X	VM
Booth			X		SV

VM = valley margin
SV = secondary valley

(sites) across the landscape are similar, especially if one considers the fact that there may have been changes in the food resource zones between 5000 and 4000 B.P. Let us now turn to a new data set, surface survey, to see if there are distributional changes in landscape use.

LOWER ILLINOIS VALLEY SURFACE SURVEY

Limitations

The Northwestern University surface-survey files for the lower Illinois Valley region through 1973 includes typed materials for 702 sites. This material has been collected since 1959 (Struever 1968b). The completeness, and more importantly, the representativeness, of the survey leaves much to be desired for three reasons: (1) the survey is oriented toward ceramic-bearing sites (Struever 1968c; Farnsworth 1973); (2) collector survey is used (Goldstein, n.d.; Farnsworth 1973) as well as systematic survey; and (3) sites may be buried or washed away in the floodplains of the Illinois River and tributary streams. Let us examine the problems of the survey data.

The orientation toward ceramic-bearing sites has tended to exclude Archaic sites and aceramic Woodland sites (see Farnsworth 1973:34). Despite this bias, almost 20% of the sites recorded have Helton and/or Titterington phase materials (projectile points). Unfortunately, if Archaic sites occur in zones lacking ceramic-bearing sites, such zones will be underrepresented for Archaic sites. However, the bias is against *Archaic* sites per se rather than the Titterington or Helton phases specifically so that there is not an obvious bias for either.

Collector survey is a technique designed to discover new sites at a rapid rate so that much material can be collected to answer certain types of problems, e.g., initial impressions about settlement patterns (Struever 1968c). Research by Goldstein (n.d.) indicates that collectors have certain home territories so that areas can be quickly covered. Unfortunately, it is not clear how well these "grab samples" compare with systematic survey results. The other limitation on collector survey is that sites without much collector interest, such as Winters' grinding stations (1969), tend to be ignored.

The third problem with the survey data is the concept of *surface*. The present-day exposed surface of the lower Illinois Valley region is not necessarily the same as the surface in the past. For example, at the Koster site some of the buried horizons are under more than 10 m of deposit. Other bluff-based examples of buried Archaic horizons include Worthy-Merrigan and Titus. For the lower Illinois Valley floodplain, the Peisker site has a buried Archaic horizon. For a more general viewpoint of the alluvial accumulation in the river valleys of the surface survey area, in describing the "Pearl District" (which extends as far south as Eldred, Ill. but not quite to the Koster site), Willman (1973:Fig. 7) remarks that the Cahokia alluvium, accumulated since 14,000 to 15,000 B.P., is "generally less than 40 feet thick in the Illinois Valley, less than 20 feet thick in tributary valleys" within a few miles of the Illinois. North of the Pearl District, Miller (1973:17) estimates that for the Sangamon drainage there has been an average of 3 m of accumulation in the last 14,500 years near Springfield. South of the Pearl District, in the bottoms due west of Koster, is a soil called McFain silty clay formed in a lakebed deposit (Downey, Grantham, and Fehrenbacher 1974:29-30). A radiocarbon date of 2890 B.P. was obtained on mussel shells from 1.3 m below the present surface of this deposit (Brown, personal communication; Coleman 1974:111). In addition to these sedimentation problems, Macoupin Creek may have eroded away many sites in the last 10 km of its floodplain (Ira Fogel, personal communication).

The problems of sedimentation in the river valley bottoms are further complicated because some glacial washout sandridges and other elevated areas have not been covered by the alluvium; hence Luchterhand's study (1970: Table 7) of Early Archaic point types includes examples from the Illinois floodplain.

Because a surface survey per se cannot correct for buried sites or sites eroded away, no matter how systematic the data collection, a rule, based on the following reasoning, is suggested to correct for this bias: There is a general tendency for soil to be washed down from the uplands to the bottomlands. Therefore, one would expect that older sites are more apt to be buried in the floodplain than more recent ones, while in the uplands most materials would be at or near the present-day eroding surfaces. Certainly Luchterhand's study (1970) of Early Archaic points indicates that materials will remain in the upland areas for 8,000 to 10,000 years. Accordingly, if the survey data indicate an increased relative use of the bottomlands by the Titterington phase, one would not know if this is a reflection of aboriginal behavior or the relatively greater burial of Helton phase sites by the alluvium.

Having considered these three limitations on the surface-survey data, I feel that the analysis of these data are at least suggestive, and provide an adequate first test of distributional changes in landscape usage. At the same time, I would not wish to directly compare the Archaic results with Struever's reconstruction (1968c) of Early and Middle Woodland subsistence-settlement systems bacause (1) the survey area has greatly increased since 1968 and (2) aceramic Woodland sites have been excluded from most of the survey; hence, portions of the Woodland systems are not necessarily represented in the survey files.

Methods

The surface survey materials have been entered into an archeological site survey retrieval system file at Northwestern University. This computerized file has been organized to serve three goals (Brown and Houart 1975:114): (1) cataloging, (2) monitoring, and (3) analysis; and the RIQS retrieval system is used to fulfill these three major goals. This present study is an attempt to exploit the survey files to gain new information about the Archaic and to improve the definitions of certain survey items, especially topographic description.

The survey file was queried for the location of all sites having any of the following six classes of projectile point types: (1) Etley; (2) Sedalia, Nebo Hill, and Wadlow; (3) Karnak Stemmed; (4) Matanzas and Helton; (5) Godar, Raddatz, and Faulkner; and (6) Osceola. The definitions of these point types are not exactly identical to those listed in the appendix, but they are considered close enough for our purposes. When a site file had any of these point types, a printout was generated with the site name, site number, drainage, topographic setting, legal description of site location, and the catalog number of each point type under examination. An abbreviated form of this printout appears in Appendix F. The site locations are mapped in Fig. 28.

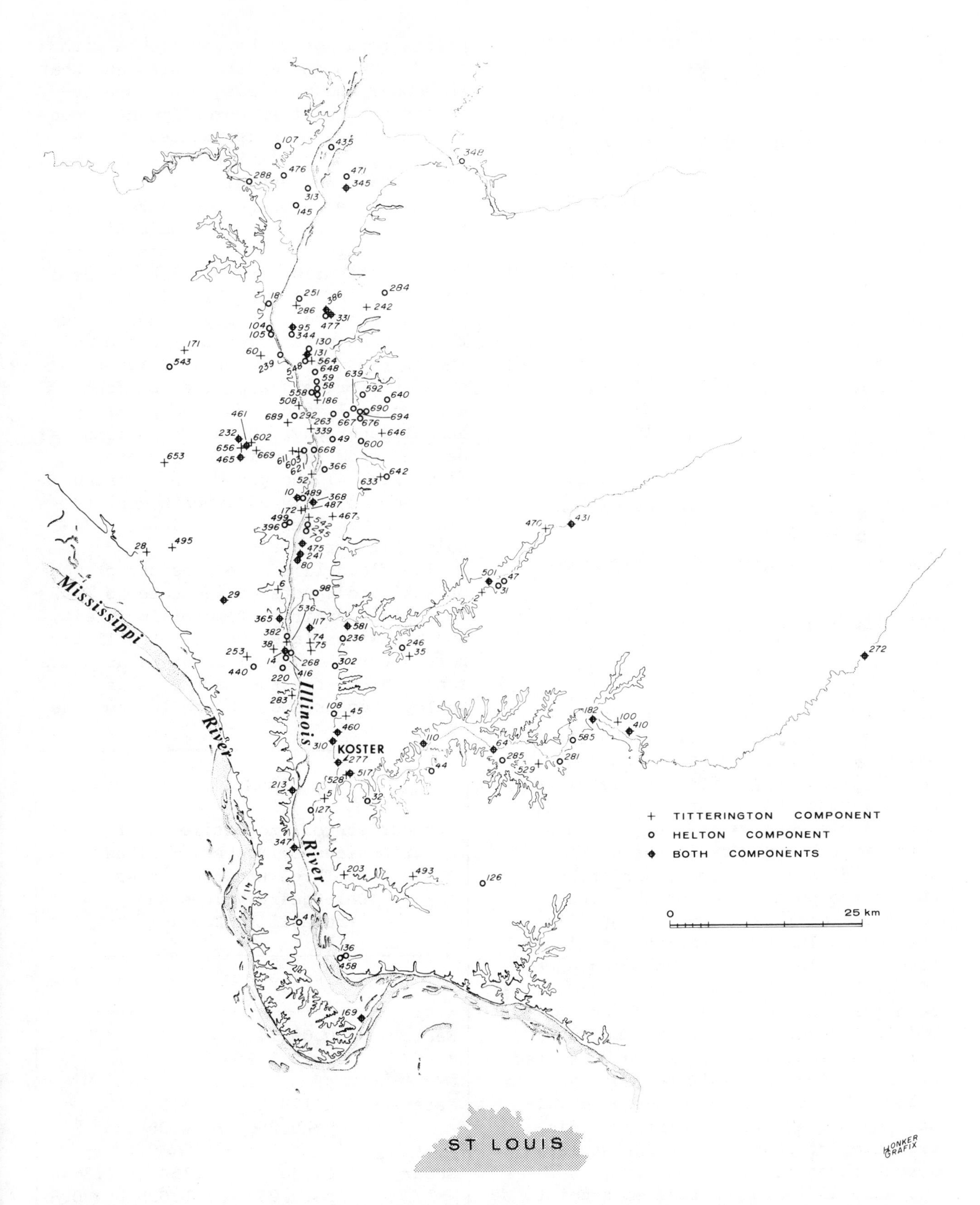

Figure 28. Map of Helton and Titterington phase sites located by surface survey through 1973. Sites are identified by RIQS catalog number.

TABLE 33

Distribution of Point Types by Number of Sites in Each Resource Zone

No.[a]	Point Type	No. of Sites FP	VM	SV
107	Etley	5	7	12
108	Sedalia-Nebo Hill-Wadlow	11	19	31
109	Karnak Stemmed	1	4	5
110	Matanzas	15	22	13
111	Godar-Raddatz-Faulkner	19	25	12
112	Osceola	3	4	2

FP = floodplain; VM = valley margin; SV = secondary valley

[a]Refers to category no. in RIQS file.

Distribution of Components

The initial test of the surface-survey data was to determine if all six point types occurred in all resource zones (to be defined below) and if point types assigned to the same phase had significantly different distributions across the resource zones. If, for example, Wadlow and Etley points were distributed very differently, this might indicate functional differences in the two point forms or that the point definitions in the survey files are too inclusive of earlier and later forms. Table 33 shows the occurrence of point types by number of sites in each resource zone. Absolute number of points per zone was not used because different sampling techniques were used on the various sites in the survey files. Table 34 shows chi-square values and probability of different distribution of projectile-point styles across three resource zones.

Table 33 indicates that each point type is represented in each resource zone. Table 34 demonstrates that Wadlow and Etley points are very closely associated, that the Wadlow and Etley points tend *not* to be associated with the Matanzas and Godar points, and that the Godar and Matanzas points are associated. In other words, point types within a phase are associated, while point types from different phases are, in general, not associated.

The three resource zones are: (1) the floodplain of the Illinois River; (2) the valley margin including a strip of land one mile wide on either side of the bluffline of the Illinois Valley; and (3) secondary valley areas. These three zones were selected for the following reasons: ease of definition; size of a primary exploitation zone; and regional topography and plant and animal geography. Zonal definition is derived from Zawacki and Hausfater (1969:Fig. 4) who present a distribution map of early nineteenth century plant communities for the lower Illinois Valley region.

The floodplain zone consists of what Zawacki and Hausfater indicate as floodplain prairie, floodplain forest, and backwater lakes between the Illinois River and the hillside-talus slope zone, which, for the east side of the valley, begins about one mile from the

TABLE 34

Comparison of Projectile Point Distributions by Number of Sites Across Three Resource Zones (Chi-Square Values and Probability Levels)

	Etley	Wadlow	Matanzas
Wadlow	0.09614 $p < 0.995$		
Matanzas	4.179 $p < 0.250$	7.179 $p < 0.05$	
Godar	6.538 $p < 0.05$	11.154 $p < 0.005$	0.364 $p < 0.8$

Note: Chi-square values have 2 degrees of freedom.

Figure 29. LAND SAT imagery of the lower Illinois Valley region.

bluff crest. For the west side, the hillside-talus slope zone reaches almost to the present day channel of the Illinois River, so that the floodplain zone occurs west of the river only in the northern and southern third of the research region. The valley margin zone includes Zawacki and Hausfater's (1969:Fig. 4) hillside-talus slope zone below the bluffs and the first mile of the upland forest zone back from the bluff crest. The secondary valley regions include all other areas: the rest of the upland forest zone and the barrens and the upland prairies as well as the secondary valleys themselves. A fourth category - "uplands" zone - was discarded because most of the uplands are heavily dissected by secondary and tertiary valleys (see Fig. 29) and most of the survey work has been restricted to secondary valleys per se.

Having defined these zones, the author decided to employ a catch basin idea in scoring a site as belonging to one of the three zones. Examining the faunal remains from Modoc Rock Shelter and Koster sites suggests that both the adjacent floodplain and adjacent upland areas were being exploited from a bluff base location. Hence, a valley margin zone would best represent the known behavior of the Helton and Titterington phases. Likewise, the tabuulation of tasks at Booth and Graham Cave sites indicates that secondary valley sites are not involved in floodplain resources but in a variety of "upland" tasks. Unfortunately, the lack of excavated floodplain sites does not allow us to determine the relationship between living in the floodplain and exploiting the valley margin zone. The concept of catch basin or catchment comes from work done by Munson, Parmalee, and Yarnell (1971) and Roper (1974) on the relationship between the available resources within a certain distance of an archeological site and the variety of resources actually present at the site in the first case, and the distribution of sites in the second.

Unfortunately, it would be very difficult to accurately reconstruct the past distribution of vegetation zones for 4000 and 5000 B.P. in the research area. Hence it was decided not to score each site for the surrounding 1-, 2-, or 3-mile-radius circle centered on the site but to assign it to one zone or another. This zonal assignment was simplified by the topography of the area. The Illinois floodplain has a series of parallel sandridges suitable for habitation sites and separated by lower, swampy areas unsuitable for habitation sites. Parallel to the sandridges, but separated from them by lower areas, is the bluff-base zone. Hence, the areas suitable for habitation sites are long parallel stretches of elevated land, rather than a homogeneous stretch of the floodplain. Fig. 28 clearly shows this phenomenon of floodplain and valley margin sites forming long parallel lines running north and south. App. F records my assignments of each site to a resource zone. I did not use the survey file assignments due to inconsistencies in terminology.

Fig. 28, the distribution map for sites of the Helton and Titterington phases, suggests two things: first, that the floodplain and valley margin zones have received the most attention by the surveyors and second, that there is no clear-cut pattern of differences regarding the distribution of sites for these two phases: Both phases use the same resource zones. But when one tests the relative use of these two zones, there are significant differences. Table 35 indicates that for all three resource zones, the Helton phase has a majority of its sites in the floodplain and valley margin zone while the Titterington phase reflects more even distribution across the landscape. Table 36 contrasts a combined floodplain and valley margin zone with the secondary valley zone. Here, the Helton phase has about two-thirds of its sites in the combined zone, while the Titterington phase has only one-half of its sites there.

Because the earlier phase, Helton, has a relatively greater number of sites in the areas likely to have had some deposition, it is unlikely that these results are a reflection of the depositional history of the region. If there were relatively more Titterington phase sites in the main valley, we would not be able to distinguish changes in relative land use and burial of the earlier phase sites in the floodplain. Taking this sedimentological argument one step further, the Helton phase sites are probably underrepresented in the floodplain survey, which would increase the directionality present in Tables 35 and 36.

TABLE 35

Occurrence of Sites by Three Resource Zones (Chi-Square and Probability Level)

Phase	Illinois Valley	Valley Margin	Secondary Valley
Helton (n = 99)	29	41	29
Titterington (n = 72)	15	22	35

Chi-square = 6.649; probability < .05; degrees of freedom = 2

TABLE 36

Occurrence of Sites by Two Resource Zones (Chi-Square and Probability Level)

Phase	Main Valley	Secondary Valley
Helton (n = 99)	70	29
Titterington (n = 72)	37	35

Chi-square = 6.642; probability $< .01$; degrees of freedom = 1

From this examination of the relative distribution of surface survey sites, it appears that there are significant differences in the settlement *pattern* of the Helton and Titterington phases. However, I do not believe that there are significant differences in the settlement *system* since the excavated site data indicate a high degree of overlap in the presence of maintenance, extractive, and social tasks. What is the significance of this change in settlement pattern?

ENVIRONMENTAL CHANGE: AN HYPOTHESIS

If the Helton and Titterington phases share similar subsistence-settlement systems, but there are differences in the pattern of site distribution, I would hypothesize that we are observing cultural responses to environmental changes between Helton and Titterington phase times; and from an environmentalist's viewpoint, there is good reason to expect increased relative use of the secondary valley resource zone in Titterington phase times. The Helton phase, which is dated at Koster between 5500 and 5000 B.P., would be placed in the latter half of the Hypsithermal Interval while the Titterington phase, which is guess-dated to about 4000 B.P., would occur in post-Hypsithermal times (cf. Wright 1968:84; Geis and Boggess 1968:90). This Hypsithermal Interval, or climatic maximum, is recently described by Wright (1974:11):

> The simplest paleoclimatic interpretation of the postglacial pollen sequence for the Western Great Lakes area calls for relatively rapid warming and drying to a maximum about 7,000 years ago, followed by a leveling out for a few thousand years, and then a gradual reversal back to the climatic level of about 9,000 years ago.

During the warmer and drier Hypsithermal Interval one would anticipate a retreat of upland forest toward more sheltered areas, especially on steeper slopes (Asch, Ford, and Asch 1972:22) and expansion of the prairies into areas vacated by forest. This change may have made the uplands, and possibly the secondary valleys, relatively less productive in mast crops and forest-related animals (deer, turkey, etc.). In other words, this climatic change model suggests that there are relatively more Titterington phase sites beyond the main valley simply because these outlying areas were enriched by a climate cooler and wetter than during the Helton phase.

Rather than speculate further about what changes occurred between Helton and Titterington times, another hypothesis is proposed: If the subsistence-settlement *systems* of the Helton and Titterington phases are equivalent, then the observed changes in relative land use merely reflect alterations in the natural environment caused by the Hypsithermal Interval.

The test of this hypothesis will require the collection of more environmental and archeological information. At present the hypothesis is not testable.

The hypothesis is important because it considers the problem of what causes a hunting and gathering system to deviate into intensive harvesting and horticulture (Struever 1968c). Flannery

(1968) has examined the deviation amplifying response of certain genetically unstable plants (maize) to a change in a subsistence-settlement system. Any time there is a dislocation in a settlement system, there is always the possibility that the response to the dislocation will encourage other deviations to occur. For example, the expansion of the Titterington phase into a relatively richer environment may have led to a population increase, which in turn may have led to greater use of second line foods (Asch, Ford, and Asch 1972), when the primary foods were locally underavailable, and predisposed the system towards intensive collecting and harvesting. Such chains of causality must be taken into consideration when shifts in land use are identified in the archeological record.

6

Trend or Tradition?

DEFINITIONS OF THE ARCHAIC STAGE

THERE ARE but two major syntheses of the Archaic period in eastern United States, one Willey and Phillips' *Method and Theory in American Archaeology* (1956), the other Caldwell's *Trend and Tradition* (1958). Willey and Phillips define the Archaic *stage* as (1956:107-8):

> ...migratory hunting and gathering cultures continuing into environmental conditions approximating those of the present. ...there is now a dependence on smaller and perhaps more varied fauna. There is also an apparent increase in gathering; it is in this stage that sites begin to yield large numbers of stone implements and utensils that are assumed to be connected with the preparation of wild vegetable foods....The specialized techniques of gathering and preparation of wild foods...suggest a medium in which early experimentation in plant domestication could take place.... Furthermore, certain cultures that we classified as Archaic in our first paper because they had no agriculture appear to have achieved stable settlement patterns and other prerequisites of the Formative without that stimulus. Lack of agriculture, therefore, is no longer a negative criterion in our formulation of the Archaic stage.

Willey and Phillips then develop a trait list of various tool types for the Archaic stage, but admit that much evidence is lacking, especially in terms of houses, storage pits, and "other appurtenances" of settled existence. They also indicate that there are exceptions to the general rule of a nomadic lifeway in the development of specialized subsistence economies in the coastal and interior waterside environments or to localized seed gathering in the North American Great Basin and the Southwest (p. 111).

Caldwell gives the following definition for the Archaic stage of Eastern Woodlands history (1958:18):

> ...as the time when primary forest efficiency was achieved. During the five thousand or so years of Archaic duration ending in most regions about 2000 B.C. we find a trend toward greater hunting efficiency. With the progressive development of new food resources the seasonal economic cycles become established. Finally, there is evidence of an increasingly settled and materially richer life.

Caldwell sees primary forest efficiency as one of three subsistence adaptations, the other two being acorn manipulation and specialized shellfish economy. Primary forest efficiency represents hunting in the forest as opposed to the Paleo-Indian adaptation of hunting in plains or savannah. Caldwell measures this development of hunting techniques in the forest by "the development of the shouldered javelin point [which] promoted greater hunting efficiency [in the forest] and that this was achieved during the Archaic" (1958:13). The specialized shellfish economy is seen as an Archaic development which provided a constant source of dietary protein and permitted at least seasonal reuse of choice localities. Acorn dependence is not discussed in detail, probably because there was little ethnobotanical evidence in preflotation days. Caldwell sees a continual increase in the complexity of material culture and, when a specialized shellfish economy is combined with primary forest efficiency, a high degree of seasonal sedentism could have been achieved (Caldwell 1958: 11-14).

These two definitions of the Archaic stage are hampered by the general lack of radiocarbon dates for the Archaic period, by the general lack of published accounts of Archaic habitation site excavations, and by the general neglect of climatic considerations such as the Hypsithermal Interval. They are further hampered by the rather nonquantitative approach to what is the dividing line between sedentary and nomadic, meat-predominating versus vegetable-predominating diet, simple and not-so-simple material culture, etc. In general, both definitions of the Archaic stage make the following assumptions about the archeological "record":

1. Increased dependence upon gatherable resources.
2. Increased sedentism through time.
3. Increased complexity of material culture
   a. New tool introduction for new subsistence activities.
   b. New artifact forms reflecting increased cultural complexity.
4. A very slow rate of change, such that Caldwell allows Paleo-Indian peoples five millennia to adapt to a new environment and become the Woodland Indians.

The explanations offered for why these assumptions are true include:

1. Man had to suddenly readapt to Holocene climates.
2. Exploitation of sedentary resources increased man's sedentism.
3. Sedentism created leisure time for "culture building."
4. This three-stage development would create situations in which demographic increase could occur, agriculture would become an important subsistence necessity, and sedentism would be complete. In other words, the Formative stage is achieved.

Unfortunately, when Willey and Phillips examine the specific archeological record for America north of Mexico (1956:111-139) they are hard pressed to document *any* of their four assumptions other than increased complexity of material culture through time. In fact, they are willing to discount much of the early Archaic archeological evidence bearing carbon dates that "seem excessively early" (p. 114). Obviously, they cannot and do not test their explanations for the "observed" changes in the Archaic temporal period. Caldwell does not do much better. He does attempt to demonstrate that one development of the Archaic was the diffusion sphere or interconnected historical structure which greatly increases the rate of diffusion of cultural innovations. This diffusion sphere subsequently broke down into regional traditions (cf. Caldwell 1958:Fig. 3). However, Caldwell does not document his assumptions or his explanations.

In sum, Willey, Phillips, and Caldwell all superimpose their own ideas and interpretations on a badly documented archeological record and see a long term *tradition* of a hunting and gathering adaptation slowly following a *trend* towards sedentism, agriculture, and the panoply of Formative and Classic.

TESTING THE ARCHAIC STAGE MODEL

On the trivial level, it would be simple to demonstrate that the Archaic stage model is factually wrong in the lower Illinois River valley region. Twenty years of excavations and surface surveys, plus the employment of flotation (see Asch, Ford, and Asch 1972), clearly indicate that developmental trends are not continuous but rather oscillatory for subsistence base, artifact diversity, and the areal extent of style zones. What is needed is not a refutation of the specifics of the Archaic stage model, but a new conceptual framework to assess the variability present in the Archaic period. This new conceptual framework is based upon two concepts: first, that the archeological record must be used to test one's explanations about the past rather than to illustrate one's assumptions; second, that comparisons should be drawn between analogous aspects of cultures rather than by trait lists at one extreme or by stages of complexity at the other.

In this study I have attempted to develop and to test such a conceptual framework using artifacts from the Koster site as the basic data set. The multidimensional phase provides an opportunity to perform controlled comparisons between prehistoric cultures. The Mark II model for explaining behavior through artifacts is an experimental method of making controlled comparisons between archeological sites. These comparisons are made in terms of specific task performance and combinations of tasks. They also rely on having some notion of where specific tasks are performed on the landscape. These comparisons shed light on problems of group organization, subsistence strategies, and site-type typologies.

Other models which permit controlled comparisons include those of the social dimensions of mortuary sites (Brown 1971) which yield information about the specific complexities of a society as manifest in mortuary practices. In fact, much of the New Archeology has consisted of the development of specialized techniques and methods to compare various specific aspects of the archeological record: settlement pattern analysis to compare land use and adaptations, ceramic microstyle analysis to delineate social groups, and human osteological analysis to delineate problems of nutrition, disease, social groups, and population size.

The multidimensional phase attempts to take into account all of these various controlled comparisons so that we can trace the development of specific behavior patterns such as plant domestication, long distance trade, and sumptuary classes as well as the interactions between these various developments.

Willey and Phillips and Caldwell are deductive in their approach. They set up a typological system and then assign a large number of prehistoric cultures to the typological system, with some ad hoc explanations of how a cultural tradition moves from one stage to the next. I suggest that induction is now required to develop a richer typological framework which will take into account (1) the various dimensions of a prehistoric society which are not necessarily lockstep in their individual developmental trajectories, and (2) methodologies to relate the observed changes in one dimension with those in the others. The goal is not to develop a prehistoric record of all of these multitudinous comparisons (which leads to the same pitfall as collecting trait lists) but to develop a theory which explains the *specific instances* known as the archeological record.

This study achieves the first level of typological description. For both the Helton and Titterington phases one can discuss style, technology, adaptation, trade, mortuary practices, human biology, and limited aspects of the sociocultural dimension. Working the descriptions the other way, if one wishes to discuss stylistic developments in the Midwest, one can certainly include examples from these two Archaic phases and make them directly comparable to Hopewell styles or Mississippian styles. The same methodology of controlled comparisons can be done on all of the other dimensions. This study does *not* reach the second level of making comparisons between dimensions, except for changes in the subsistence-settlement system and the trade and mortuary complex systems. Explanations for the changes in the subsistence-settlement system seem to relate to possible environmental changes between 5000 and 4000 B.P. Changes in the trade and mortuary complex systems cannot yet be explained because (1) we do not have enough information about artifacts and goods leaving the lower valley area; (2) we do not know much about the distant groups with whom trading is being done; and (3) only non-quantitative models can be tested at the present time.

Instead of sweeping generalizations about changes in the Archaic period; we end with a framework of dimensions: style, technology, adaptation, trade, mortuary practices, human biology, and sociocultural dimensions. Each dimension in itself must be considered in terms of explaining change through time. Each dimension represents a tradition which has a series of time horizons. This study has focused upon some aspects of these dimensions in order to understand the Koster site and to place the Koster site in a larger, regional framework. A number of analytical techniques have been developed in the process.

It now remains to fill in many of the specific data gaps of these two phases, to revamp the Mark II model for future testing situations, and to extend these analytical systems both backward in time to the Pleistocene/Holocene boundary and forward to the better-known cultures of the Woodland and Mississippian periods.

Appendixes

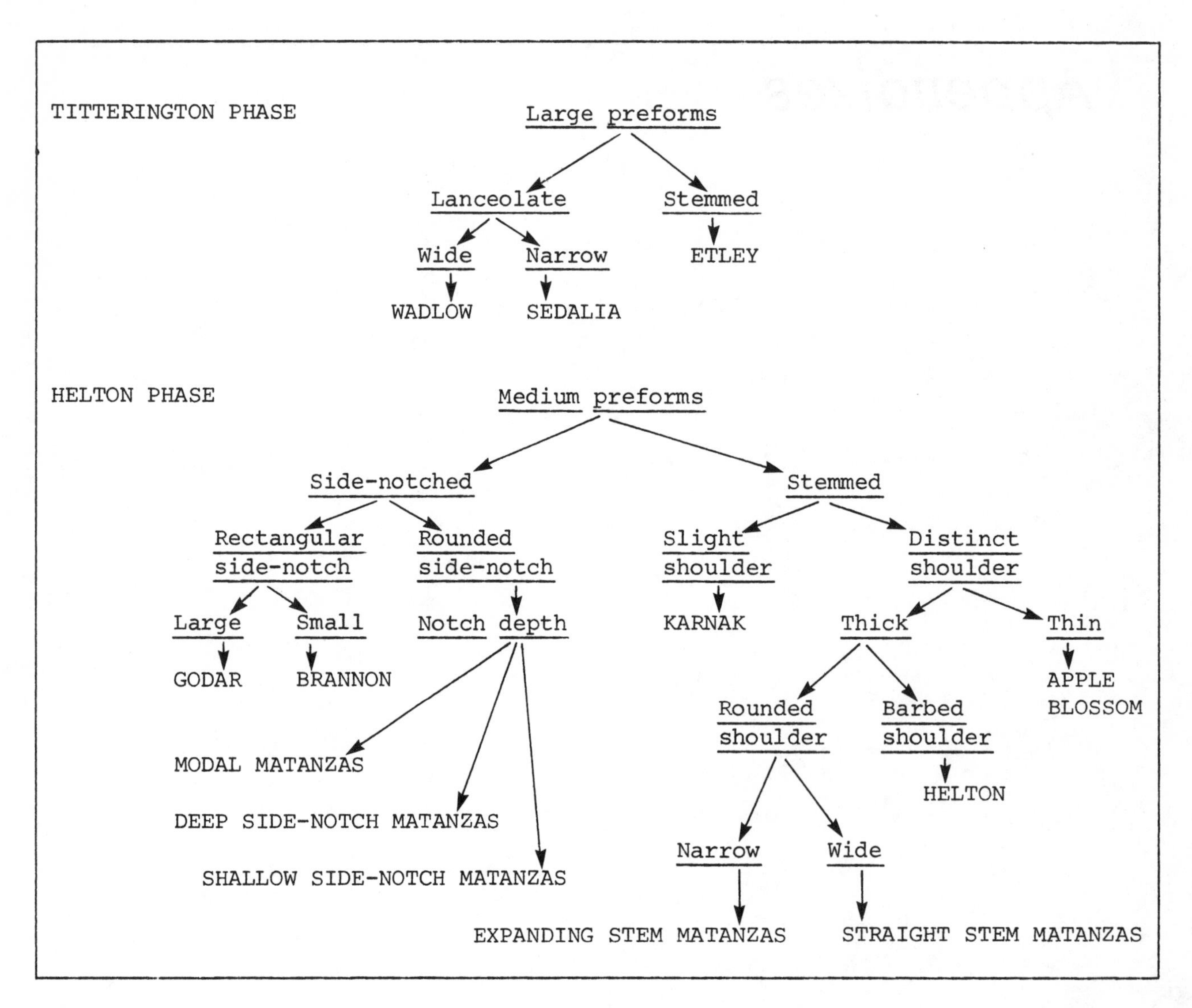

Figure 30. Key to Koster sample of Titterington and Helton phase point types.

Appendix A

Koster Projectile Point Descriptions

KEY TO POINT TYPES

FIGURE 30 is a formal key to the Koster sample of Titterington and Helton phase point types defined in this appendix. The key is set up to separate the point types into the two phases as efficiently as possible. Because the manufacturing trajectories are so distinctly different, it is easy to do this at the first node. Functional considerations, as suggested by the hafting modification, are considered next. At the finest level - i.e., the varieties of Matanzas points - a number of sequential tests are required. These are discussed under the description of the Matanzas points. As more point types are defined, the key will be expanded until a general key to the regional point typology is developed. This key represents an initial step in doing just that.

METHODS

The Koster sample of projectile points from three years (1969-1971) includes 470 typed pieces and larger fragments plus another 100 or so which were either unique in form or too fragmentary to assign to a known type. The points were sorted and resorted into a number of formal categories without knowledge of the stratigraphic relationships between the various objects. As the points were being sorted, all were weighed and measured by Alice Berksen, under my supervision. To avoid bias, the points were never measured as groups of the same visual types. When points were measured twice (as a blind test), accuracy was to the nearest 0.2 cm, 0.1 g, or nearest 6 deg. Each measurement was taken three times and the average value recorded. Individual measurements are given in Table 37.

The measuring formats follow those of Luchterhand (1970) so that a regional data bank will eventually be developed for comparative purposes. However, a few modifications had to be introduced. Luchterhand arbitrarily assigns left and right sides to points. Because there may be some asymmetrical point forms (Sandia points being the extreme case), it is necessary that left and right sides be non-arbitrarily assigned so that statistical comparisons can measure this asymmetry. Accordingly, the following rule was devised: Draw an imaginary central axis of the point from the tip through the center of the hafting element; draw lines parallel to the central axis tangent to the outermost edges of the point. The tangent furthest from the central axis represents the *right* side.

The measurement of maximum breadth was added to Luchterhand's set.

TITTERINGTON PHASE TYPES

Wadlow Points (Fig. 33)

Perino (1968:98; Plate 49) named this point type for Walter Wadlow, an amateur archeologist.

Sample size. Koster (1969 and 1970 excavations) sample includes three complete specimens, seven bases, two broken blades, and two midsections.

Description. (Perino 1968a:98)

> The Wadlow point is a large unnotched blade generally having a straight base and parallel sides. Some variations occur, however, in which the sides are recurved or convex, and some bases are slightly concave or convex. Some points having convex bases may also have rounded basal corners. Those points

TABLE 37

KOSTER PROJECTILE POINT MEASUREMENTS 1969 1970 1971

SEDALIA

PROVENIENCE	TYPE	LAB	AL	BL	TL	SHW	TW	BW	TH	RND	LND	RNW	LNW	RDHI	LDHI	RPHI	LPHI	BR	WT	MW	REW
01 2 7	1 50	1	114	97	16	24		24	106	0	0			165	150	47	60	0	378	29	
02 16 12	2 50	1	129	108	21	24	18	24	104	1	0	18	19	176	169	76	69	2	390	27	
02 29 02	3 50	0	116	89	26	25	16	25	118	0	2		26	170	174	62	62	1	270	25	DRILL
02 37 09	1 50	1							106	0	0					0	0	0	117		DRILL

WADLOW

PROVENIENCE	TYPE	LAB	AL	BL	TL	SHW	TW	BW	TH	RND	LND	RNW	LNW	RDHI	LDHI	RPHI	LPHI	BR	WT	MW	REW
01 2 7	2 40	0						48	145	0	0					0	0	5		63	
01 7 15	1 40	0	134					33	166	0	0			172	162	-8	-18	2	828	39	
01 7 16 A	1 40	1			13	35		35	118	0	0			146	145	0	0	0		37	
01 8 10	1 40	1		29	16	41	32	41	83	2	1	16	16	162	176	-18	-16	1		43	
01 8 13	40	0	103					33	114	0	0					0	0	1	339		
02 14 5	2 40									0	0					0	0	0			
01 16 14	1 40	1							109	0	0					0	0	0		40	MIDSECT
02 18 16	1 40									0	0					0	0	0			
02 29 2	1 40	0						33	138	0	0			174	164	-6	-16	6		40	
02 31 3	1 40	0						26	100	0	0			176	175	-4	-5	1		30	
02 31 13	4 40	0						34	113	0	0			170	172	-10	-8	-8		39	
02 34 4	1 40	1						38	146	0	0			173	161	-7	-19	-8		45	
02 75 12 A	1 40	1	120	98	22	30	29	30	134	1	1	26	14	183	186	79	69	2	546	37	
02 298 A A	1 40	1						26	117	0	0					0	0	-1		37	

ETLEY BARBED

PROVENIENCE	TYPE	LAB	AL	BL	TL	SHW	TW	BW	TH	RND	LND	RNW	LNW	RDHI	LDHI	RPHI	LPHI	BR	WT	MW	REW
01 7 5	120	0	62	51	16	41	17	19	117	-8	-9	17	13	33	21	4	4	1	218	45	
02 15 16	1 120	1			15	32	19	22		-3	-4	15	15	99	67	4	1	2		32	
02 19 15	1 120	1			19	36		23	131	-5	0	12		72	85	-31	0	0		36	
02 20 2	1 120	0	86	72	14	36	23		105	0	-4		15	101	85	0	23	0		37	
02 22 14	2 120	0			17	39	21	22	126	-9	-4	21	18	105	70	13	8	2		40	
02 32 6	1 120	0			18	31	18	19	108	-5	-4	17	21	120	80	1	5	1		33	DRILL
02 33 00	2 120	0			19	41	23	27	129	-5	-5	21	24	81	101	0	-4	2		41	
02 39 10 A	2 120	1	84	65	20	36	27	30	102	-4	-3	18	18	118	131	9	8	0	287	36	
02 39 10	3 120	1							107	-9	0			90		0	0	0			
02 39 10	4 120	1			17		24	26	119	0	0	15	16			12	3	-2			
02 47 4	1 120	0			17	33	17	21	98	-6	-5	19	17	96	73	5	-2	1		33	
02 49 9 A	1 120	0	72	51	19	37	22	25	136	-5	-5	23	21	95	84	4	3	0	294	37	
02 52 6 A	1 120	1			17	37	16	19	89	-9	-6	16	18	66	79	-3	3	2		40	
02 53 9 A A	2 120	1	104	82	22		19	20	106	-4	0	20		112		13	-19	1			
02 53 9 A A	3 120	0	91	78	13	34	17	23	91	-5	-4	11	16	50	92	-3	-6	1		37	
02 53 9 B A	2 120	1	74	47	27	46	28	46	129	-7	-5	27	26	101	106	4	10	2	398	46	
02 53 10 A	2 120	1			19	30	22	24	130	-3	-4	20	20	73	88	-4	6	1		31	DRILL
02 54 7 A	1 120	1	74	58	16		24	25	091	-6	-5	17	16			5	0	4	274	34	
02 56 5 A	1 120	0	72	53	24	35	23	24	139	-3	-4	16	19	111	124	-2	19	-9	207	30	
02 56 8 A	1 120	1	90	74	16	30	20	24	123	-5	-4	16	15	101	111	19	17	0	335	31	
02 74 10	1 120	0			15	38	25	25	132	-3	-4	14		74	64	5	9	2		38	
03 107 2	1 120	1	99	88	12	32	18	19	102	-6	-4	11	11	73	56	12	2	2	361	36	
03 116 2	1 120	0	98	85	16		21		110	0	0			54	88	0	3	0		38	
02 SURFAC	16 120	0			18	37	23	26	112	-5	-6	16	21	70	70	2		1		37	

EXPLANATION OF COLUMN HEADINGS

PROVENIENCE = PROVENIENCE LABEL ON EACH SPECIMEN.
01 = 1969 FIELD SEASON
02 = 1970 FIELD SEASON
03 = 1971 FIELD SEASON
TO RIGHT OF EXCAVATION YEAR CODE, THE FIRST GROUP OF NUMBERS REFERS TO THE SQUARE NUMBER AND THE NEXT GROUP OF NUMBERS REFER TO THE SQUARE LEVEL.
IF THE SECOND GROUP IS A LETTER (A,B,C, ETC. THEN THE FIRST GROUP OF NUMBERS IS A FEATURE NUMBER AND THE LETTERS REFER TO A SUBDIVISION OF THE FEATURE.
AFTER THE LEVEL NUMBER OR THE FEATURE LETTER, THERE ARE TWO COLUMNS OF A≠S.
THE FIRST OF THESE TWO COLUMNS REFER TO SUBDIVISIONS WITHIN A LEVEL. THE SECOND COLUMN REFERS TO ARTIFACT NUMBERS. IF A PROJECTILE POINT WERE DISCOVERED IN SITU, IT WAS ASSIGNED AN ARTIFACT NUMBER. TO THE RIGHT OF THE ARTIFACT COLUMN IS A COLUMN OF NUMBERS WHICH ASSIGN EACH OBJECT FROM A SINGLE PROVENIENCE AN UNIQUE DESIGNATION WITHIN THAT UNIT.
TYPE = NUMERIC CODE TO AID IN SORTING DATA CARDS INTO GROUPS.
LAB = DEFINITION OF RIGHT EDGE OF FORM AS SEEN FROM FACE WITH (≠1≠) OR WITHOUT (≠0≠) LABEL

UNITS OF MEASUREMENT = ALL LENGTHS IN MILLIMETERS. THICKNESS IN TENTHS OF MILLIMETERS, ANGLES IN DEGREES.

AL = AXIAL LENGTH
BL = BLADE LENGTH
TL = TANG LENGTH
SHW = SHOULDER WIDTH
TW = TANG WIDTH
BW = BASAL WIDTH
TH = THICKNESS
RND = RIGHT NOTCH DEPTH
LND = LEFT NOTCH DEPTH
RNW = RIGHT NOTCH WIDTH
LNW = LEFT NOTCH WIDTH
RDHI = RIGHT DISTAL HAFT INCLINATION
LDHI = LEFT DISTAL HAFT INCLINATION
RPHI = RIGHT PROXIMAL HAFT INCLINATION
LPHI = LEFT PROXIMAL HAFT INCLINATION
BR = BASAL RADIUS
WT = WEIGHT
MW = MAXIMUM WIDTH
REW = REWORKED. DRILL = DRILL, END = ENDSCRAPER, MIDSECT = MIDSECTION

TABLE 37 (CONTINUED)

KARNAK STEMMED

PROVENIENCE	TYPE	LAB	AL	BL	TL	SHW	TW	BW	TH	RND	LND	RNW	LNW	RDHI	LDHI	RPHI	LPHI	BR	WT	MW	REW
01 8 34 1	20	1			25	24	14	23	87	2	2	23	23	173	172	-31	-39	1		22	END
02 14 29 A 2	20	1			24	24	11	24	102	2	1	22	20	171	170	-39	-45	2		24	END
02 15 18 1	20	1			23	27	14	27	110	1	0	25	23	164	166	-22	-34	0		27	
02 16 17 2	20	1			29	29	29	16	170	0	1	31	26	161	171	-27	-36	1		28	
02 16 18 2	20	0	80	59	22	24	13	24	104	2	0	22	19	162	168	-49	-32	2	210	24	
02 16 23 A 2	20	0	72	52	20	23	16	24	116	1	0	19	18	173	177	-49	-33	2	165	23	
02 17 11 1	20	0	74	54	20	27	11	27	120	1	1	24	19	164	158	-40	-51	0	264	28	
02 37 25 4	20	0			20	22	14	22	107	-1	1	17	16	163	164	-29	-21	1		25	
02 41 18 A139	20	0	78	65	13	21	10	19	98	0	2	13	15	169	164	-67	-45	0	170	22	
02 43 19 A 2	20	0	73	57	16	21	16	21	96	0	-1	17	14	167	176	-33	-23	-1	176	21	
02 43 21 A 2	20	0	90	59	31	26	15	26	101	1	0	30	30	170	169	-36	-31	1	245	26	
02 50 25 A 2	20	0	88	71	17	22	13	22	130	1	1	18	15	173	168	-48	-32	2	286	24	
02 52 6 2	20	0			20	26	19	26	108	1	1	20	18	172	173	-37	-27	2		25	END
02 53 11 A 2	20	1	62	41	21	24	15	24	93	-1	-1	22	20	164	163	-30	-15	0	158	24	
02 61 11 A 1	20	0	101	78	23	25	12	25	126	1	1	22	25	173	159	-39	-32	1	352	27	
02 64 1 4	20	0			25	28	23	27	129	-1	1	25	24	179	176	-28	-31	1		27	
02 64 4 A 2	20	0	75	50	25	26	18	25	92	-1	-1	25	19	168	162	-21	-23	2	206	25	
02 64 5 A 1	20	0	64	48	16	21	13	21	103	1	0	16	14	162	173	-50	-41	1	156	21	
02 65 6 A 1	20	0	70	48	22	23	16	23	89	1	1	22	20	179	174	-32	-28	2	168	22	
02 71 1 A 1	20	0	72	50	21	24	14	24	82	1	2	20	22	174	172	-27	-28	1	160	26	
02 77 9 A 2	20	0	95	70	25	18	17	19	102	0	1	23	24	180	175	-25	-13	1	201	19	
03 100 11 1	20	1			11	20	14	20	118	0	1	10	11	169	154	-31	-31	2		21	
03 100 11 2	20	0	63	47	16	23	16	21	102	0	-1	12	17	165	163	-25	-11	-1		25	
03 103 16 A 1	20	0	66	48	17	20	15	20	92	1	1	14	15	177	174	-32	-29	2	130	20	
03 108 26 1	20	1	49	29	20	23	11	22	99	2	1	20	19	169	169	-50	-39	0	103	23	
03 111 20 A 3	20	0	55	27	28	21	15	21	79	1	1	27	27	179	176	-10	-25	-1	109	21	
03 111 20 2	20	1	78	63	14	23	18	23	101	-1	-1	14	12	146	135	-31	-20	2	217	25	
03 112 1 1	20	0	83	59	24	26	10	26	98	1	1	23	26	164	166	-36	-34	0	273	31	
03 116 10 1	20	0	82	61	20	23	15	23	91	1	1	22	18	166	173	-50	-31	1	192	25	
03 117 20 A 1	20	0			26	23	13	22	95	2	1	25	27	176	169	-40	-43	1		22	
03 119 26 1	20	0	66	50	16	22	16	22	106	1	0	14	14	182	170	-37	-30	0		22	
03 125 22 A 2	20	1	88	68	19	22	13	22	101	1	0	19	18	173	169	-34	-27	1	217	22	
03 125 25 A 1	20	1	61	44	27	20	10	20	101	1	1	16	15	162	166	-38	-63	2	146	23	
03 130 3 1	20	0	93	61	32	26	13	26	120	1	1	33	31	175	167	-25	-45	1	284	27	
03 130 5 1	20	0	71	48	23	24	14	25	99	1	0	22	20	158	167	-38	-30	2	184	25	
03 132 4 2	20	1			19	25	14	25	109	1	1	17	19	149	163	-49	-53	2		27	END
03 132 7 2	20	0	74	40	34	27	11	26	61	3	2	33	34	174	17	-37	-34	0	107	27	
03 137 4 A 1	20	1	79	57	22	22	11	21	116	1	0	23	19	158	163	-41	-27	1	242	24	
03 137 4 A 2	20	0	66	51	14	20	13	20	104	1	0	15	15	171	171	-37	-49	0	152	22	
02 772 A A 1	20	0	77	59	18	24	17	25	96	1	1	19	13	169	166	-31	-34	2	196	26	
03 233 A A 1	20	1	78	54	23	27	12	27	110	2	2	21	24	172	173	-46	-36	1	220	27	
03 291 A 1	20	1	67	46	20	20	12	20	98	0	1	20	19	171	173	-39	-45	1	138	21	
03 300 I A 1	20	1	87	69	17	23	11	22	112	1	0	19	15	168	160	-45	-38	-1	290	30	

MODAL MATANZAS

PROVENIENCE	TYPE	LAB	AL	BL	TL	SHW	TW	BW	TH	RND	LND	RNW	LNW	RDHI	LDHI	RPHI	LPHI	BR	WT	MW	REW
02 2 5103 1	16	0	46	35	11	20	14		78	0	-1		8	122	134		26	0		19	
01 5 14 3	16	0	54	45	08	18	14		95	0	-2		5	121	122		41	0		19	
01 5 17 1	16	1	47	35	12	21	18		86	-1	0	10		159	166	30		-1		21	
01 8 29 4	16	1	43	32	12	19	15		88	-2	0	8		132	151	29	13	0		19	
01 10 29 1	16	0	43	29	12	18	14	19	91	-2	-3	9	11	125	150	18	44	1	67	18	
02 13 27 1	16	0	56	47	9	20	15	18	65	-2	-2	8	7	134	134	34	43	1	88	21	
02 21 25 1	16	0	34	24	9	20	15	21	80	-2	-2	6	7	146	134	47	46	2	54	20	
02 21 32 A 1	16	0	42	30	12	21	16	21	76	-2	-1	6	6	118	120	64	58	2	70	21	
02 21 35 A 1	16	0			11	20	16	20	90	-2	-2	9	8	126	144	31	49	1		20	
02 21 35 1	16	0			14	23	17	23	91	-3	-3	12	11	130	142	43	58	2		23	
02 22 26 4	16	1			11	17	15	17	78	-1	-2	6	7	137	155	62	17	1			
02 22 27 A 1	16	0	49	37	12	19	25	28	95	-2	-2	6	9	130	151	22	50	0	97	19	
02 22 36 A 1	16	1	54	40	14	21	15	18	106	-3	-3	10	14	130	146	32	20	-1	119	11	
02 22 41 A 1	16	0	67	57	10	20	15	18	103	-2	-2	9	9	134	148	20	19	-1	144	20	
02 24 19 A 1	16	0	72	60	12	18	13	16	101	-2	-2	10	9	113	147	11	55	1	130	19	
02 24 26 1	16	0	56	43	13	21	14	21	89	-4	-3	10	11	129	140	39	45	1	117	22	
02 27 2 1	16	1	58	47	11	21	16	20	81	-2	-2	8	9	135	141	33	24	1	113	26	
02 31 24 1	16	0			12	22	18	22	78	-1	-2	6	9	120	151	29	44	2		21	
02 32 18 1	16	0			14	20	15	18	96	-2	-2	11	10	149	118	35	44	1		20	END
02 33 10 1	16	1	60	50	10	20	14	19	88	-4	0	8		100	129	48	51	2		21	
02 34 14 A115	16	0			12	19	15	19	77	-2	-2	10	7	160	130	26	46	0		19	
02 35 17 A198	16	1	48	39	9	18	14	16	81	-2	-2	6	6	136	145	16	30	1	75	18	
02 36 8 2	16	1			11	20	15	20	93	-2	-2	7	8	118	130	41	49	1		21	
02 36 13 A142	16	1	28	17	11	19	16	20	88	-2	-2	8	7	118	143	30	43	2	52	19	
02 36 15 A187	16	0	40	31	8	16	15	16	89	-1	0	5	4	147	153	13	33	2	51	16	
02 36 16 2	16	1			9	16	14	18	92	-1	-1	6	6	163	161	33	37	0		18	
02 36 18 A219	16	1	56	46	10	17	13		75	0	-2		8	144	148	0	50	0		18	
02 37 15 A 1	16	1			12	19	15	18	50	-1	-2	8	9	145	150	24	35	1		19	
02 37 22 A 1	16	1	51	40	11	18	13	17	74	-2	-2	9	8	126	128	25	59	1	72	19	
02 43 16 1	16	0	50	37	13	21	16	13	90	-3	-3	10	10	132	156	53	63	0		21	
02 43 22 2	16	1	59	48	12	20	17		87	0	-2		9	147	149	0	29	0		21	
02 43 30 1	16	0			13	21	16	22	97	-3	-3	9	10	140	110	44	50	2		22	
02 44 17 17	16	0			12	20	18	19	98	-1	-2	9	10	162	170	8	19	-1		20	END
02 45 7 2	16	1	60	49	12	21	17	21	72	-3	-2	10	9	139	130	41	49	1	100	21	
02 45 15 1	16	0	55	38	17	21	16	17	97	-1	-2	16	11	157	172	14	29	-1	102	20	
02 45 17 A 47	16	0			10	22	17	20	83	-2	-2	9	7	121	131	26	54	1		19	
02 46 16 2	16	0	39	17	12	20	15	20	67	-2	-2	9	9	147	133	37	37	2	53	20	
02 46 17 1	16	1	62	48	14	22	15	21	84	-3	-3	12	13	132	130	44	29	0	122	21	

TABLE 37 (CONTINUED)

MODAL MATANZAS (CONTINUED)

PROVENIENCE		TYPE		LAB	AL	BL	TL	SHW	TW	BW	TH	RND	LND	RNW	LNW	RDHI	LDHI	RPHI	LPHI	BR	WT	MW	REW
02 47 17		1	16	1			10	18	15	18	69	-1	-1	7	7	130	146	28	43	1		18	
02 47 20	A	1	16	1	67	56	11	22	18	20	97	-2	-1	30	39	142	141	10	21	3	140	22	
02 47 22		2	16	0	32	18	14	20	18	21	77	-1	-1	9	11	166	170	13	28	1	56	20	
02 47 22		3	16	0	50	37	13	20	13	20	80	-4	-3	8	8	124	116	58	52	2	91	23	
02 47 23		1	16	0	48	37	11	18	16	21	63	-2	-1	10	7	169	161	27	42	1	63	18	
02 48 21		1	16	1	48	37	11	20	15	20	72	-2	-2	9	7	144	143	24	42	0	72	20	
02 48 23		1	16	1			12	21	15	21	84	-3	-2	7	8	101	140	48	39	2		22	
02 48 24		2	16	1			10	19	12	16	76	-3	-3	8	10	124	123	28	19	1		21	END
02 48 28		1	16	1	47	37	10	20	14	18	83	-2	-2	7	7	120	113	48	51	2	91	20	
02 50 23	A	2	16	1	43	33	10	22	15	17	70	-3	-2	7	7	128	136	59	36	2	69	23	
02 51 20	A	2	16	1	46	36	10	20	14		78	0	-2		9	124	129	0	43	0		21	
02 51 23	A	2	16	1			14	19	14	19	69	-2	-2	10	10	142	129	52	39	2		19	END
02 51 24		2	16	0	45	34	10	18	14	18	83	-3	-2	8	7	130	138	54	47	1	71	19	
02 52 15	A	1	16	1			12	23	18		93	0	-2		7	157	96	0	25	0		24	END
02 52 15	A	2	16	1	53	41	12	20	17	21	87	-2	-2	8	9	159	145	28	47	1	98	20	
02 52 22		6	16	0	50	41	09	19	17	19	83	-1	-2	6	6	168	136	36	40	-1	84	20	
02 53 14		1	16	0	48	37	12	19	16	18	107	-1	-2	8	8	150	145	10	45	2	100	18	
02 53 18		1	16	1			13	18	14	18	84	-2	-2	11	10	140	152	36	46	1		18	
02 53 19	A	2	16	0			12	19	14		90	0	-2		8	149	129	32	0	0		19	
02 53 19		3	16	0	65	57	8	19	15		100	0	-2		6	125	137	24	33	2		19	
02 53 20		3	16	0			9	16	14	14	107	0	-1		7		158	0	20	-1		17	
02 53 23		4	16	1	38	29	9	20	16	18	81	-1	-1	7	7	134	157	33	41	2	62	19	
02 53 24		5	16	1	45	34	12	19	14	17	98	-2	-2	7	9	132	134	18	31	1	77	19	
02 53 26		1	16	1	57	45	12	22	16	21	103	-3	-2	8	8	126	130	42	43	2	139	22	
02 53 26		4	16	1			11	19	16	19	101	-1	-1	9	9	143	153	13	27	1		20	
02 53 27		2	16	0			11	17	13	18	105	-2	-2	9	7	147	143	46	54	1		18	END
02 54 17	A	2	16	0	52	40	12	21	17	19	89	-1	-1	9	7	162	147	43	18	2	101	21	
02 54 23	A	1	16	1			12	19	15		81	0	-2		10	134	137	0	41	0		20	END
02 54 23		4	16	1	57	48	9	18	14	16	66	-1	-1	6	5	129	125	36	24	1	79	20	
02 54 25	A	2	16	0	44	30	14	22	20	22	89	0	-2		9	164	164	28	28	3	108	23	
02 54 26	A	1	16	1			12	22	15		102	-3	0	9		117	135	52	0	0		22	
02 54 26	A	2	16	0	56	42	14	22	15	21	87	-3	-3	10	11	131	120	32	47	-2	119	23	
03 54 33		2	16	1	49	39	10	18	13		76	-2	0	19		158	127	44	0	0		18	
02 55 18		2	16	1			12	21	17	23	86	-2	-2	7	6	130	127	49	51	1		21	END
02 55 24	A	2	16	0	42	35	7	18	16	16	78	-1	0	5		135	144	38	13	2		19	
02 55 26		3	16	1	53	42	12	16	13	18	82	-2	-2	9	9	145	150	35	38	1	77	16	
02 56 17		6	16	1			9	20	16	20	73	-1	-2	5	6	134	120	38	38	0		19	
03 56 29		1	16	0	61	49	12				105	-3	0	11		130		38	0	0		19	
02 57 14	A	1	16	0	57	46	10	20	17	21	86	-2	-2	8	7	136	140	47	38	1	112	20	
02 57 15	A	1	16	1	44	34	11	27	18	17	70	-2	-3	8	6	140	125	59	55	1	55	28	
02 57 15	A	3	16	0	56	43	14	21	16	20	110	-2	-2	9	10	155	142	64	53	3	126	22	
02 57 17		3	16	1			12	20	14	18	73	-2	-2	7	7	118	127	59	42	0		21	
02 58 11		1	16	1	36	26	10	18	14	16	85	-1	-1	8	6	159	126	38	38	0	51	19	
02 58 11		2	16	1	48	36	12	20	15	19	90	-2	-2	7	8	105	111	38	41	3	89	19	
02 58 14		4	16	1	38	26	12		14	18	80	-2	0	9		143		20	35	1			
02 58 16	A	3	16	0	51	40	11	20	18	20	92	-1	-1	6	9	153	167	11	31	2	90	21	
02 58 16		4	16	0			13	18	14	20	85	-3	-3	9	8	141	146	58	39	1		21	
02 58 17		1	16	0	44	34	10	21	15	19	94	-3	-2	7	7	113	128	36	47	1	73	20	
02 58 18		2	16	0			9	21	15	16	90	-2	-2	8	6	116	113	46	15	2		21	END
03 58 19		3	16	1	48	38	10	17	13	19	91	-3	-2	8	6	134	140	48	55	1	89	20	
03 58 19		4	16	0			9	18	14	17	73	-1	-2	8	7	140	138	24	40	1		18	
02 59 8		1	16	0			11	21	10	22	72	-2	-1	7	7	130	130	41	35	1		21	END
02 60 11		2	16	1	56	46	11	19	16		81	0	-2		8	145	137	18	45	0		19	
02 60 11		3	16	1	44	32	12	21	16	19	93	-2	-2	7	8	131	133	35	36	1	97	23	
02 64 8	A	1	16	1	52	42	10	20	15		81	0	-2		8	132	128	0	66	0		21	
02 64 9		2	16	0			13	20	15	21	91	-3	-3	9	8	117	138	28	48	2		21	
02 66 3		1	16	1	48	39	9	16			85	0	-3		8	149	108	0	20	0		16	
02 68 9		5	16	0			14	21	18	21	70	-2	-1	10	12	139	148	38	32	1	1	22	
02 69 7 A		1	16	1	52	39	13	21	15	18	93	-2	-2	21	11	145	132	56	24	0	107	21	
02 74 26		1	16	0	42	31	11	18	13	19	77	-3	-2	9	8	133	129	23	33	2	64	19	
02 76 18		4	16	1	38	26	12	17	15	18	84	-1	-1	8	9	164	166	25	34	1	57	18	
03 100 8		1	16	1			10	17	15	18	67	-1	-2	8	8	161	145	50	23	1		18	
03 104 23		1	16	1			10	19	15	18	82	-1	-2	8	8	144	146	34	37	0		19	DRILL
03 104 24		2	16	0	58	45	13					0	-2	11		138		46	0	0		17	
03 104 30	A	2	16	1	39	30	10	17	12		70	0	-2		7	139	160	0	51	0		16	
03 104 36		1	16	1	51	39	12	20	16	21	100	-3	-2	11	8	150	140	42	36	-1	107	20	
03 106 27		1	16	1	40	31	9	20	14		91	-2	0	7		125	114	40	0	0		20	
03 106 29		2	16	1	53	42	11	16	12	15	103	-2	-2	10	8	154	133	42	40	2	89	16	
03 106 29		3	16	0	46	38	8	18	15	18	72	-1	-2	5	6	137	154	24	50	-1	72	18	
03 106 34		3	16	0	46	38	8	18	15	18	72	-1	-2	5	6	137	154	24	50	-1	72	18	
03 107 21		1	16	1			14	22	16	20	86	-3	-2	12	10	124	121	95	53	2		23	END
3 107 25	A	1	16	0	58	47	11	21	18	20	89	-1	-1	9	7	170	153	38	34	1	113	22	
03 107 25		1	16	0			13	18	13		98	0	-3		13	134	159	0	49	0		20	
03 107 28		2	16	1	46	36	9	20	14	18	69	-2	-2	6	7	130	124	37	59	0	72	21	
03 108 26		2	16	0					12	17	81	0	0					57	54	2		19	
03 109 5	A	1	16	0	39	29	10	17	12		78	0	-2		7	133	128	44		0		18	
03 109 24		1	16	0			09				84	-2	0	6		139		56	0	0		19	END
03 111 20		1	16	0			10	21	16	19	83	-2	-2	18	7	147	135	36	32	0		20	
03 111 32 A	A	1	16	0	47	37	10	19	15	19	73	-2	-1	6	4	108	125	37	48	2	79	19	
03 115 11	A	2	16	1	44	33	11	18	14	17	88	-2	-2	9	7	133	145	52	30	1	72	18	
03 115 13		1	16	0	50	37	13	15	12	15	80	-2	-2	9	13	150	164	28	47	0	49	14	
03 116 7	A	1	16	1			11	20	17	21	85	-2	-2	8	8	125	144	43	40	1		20	
03 117 25		1	16	0	55	44	11	18	14	16	101	-2	-2	9	8	147	149	44	38	1	101	19	
03 118 26		2	16	0	29	20	10	20	16	19	88	-2	-2	8	7	138	155	27	38	0	48	20	
03 119 27	A	1	16	1	66	52	14	23	18	24	95	-2	-2	9	8	151	126	58	61	0	159	23	
03 119 27	A	1	16	1	66	52	14	23	18	24	95	-2	-2	9	8	151	126	58	61	0	159	23	
03 120 20	A	1	16	0			14	19	13	18	86	-3	-2	12	11	146	150	33	24	0		20	END
03 120 22	A	1	16	1	56	44	12	21	18	21	95	-2	-1	9	12	138	169	33	18	-1	145	23	
03 120 23	A	2	16	0	55	44	11	17	14	16	98	-1	0	8		150	152	50	40	0		19	

TABLE 37 (CONTINUED)

MODAL MATANZAS (CONTINUED)

PROVENIENCE			TYPE	LAB	AL	BL	TL	SHW	TW	BW	TH	RND	LND	RNW	LNW	RDHI	LDHI	RPHI	LPHI	BR	WT	MW	REW
03 121 22		2	16	0			9	20	17	20	73	-1	-2	6	7	138	148	32	46	1		20	
03 121 24		1	16	1	62	51	12	18	15	18	88	-1	-2	7	8	149	128	41	49	2	110	20	
03 123 2	A	1	16	1			12	23	17		99	-2	0	10		134	129	47	43	0		23	END
03 125 13	A	1	16	0	74	63	10	20	18	22	98	-1	-2	9	7	155	143	29	40	-1	154	20	
03 125 22	A	1	16	0	48	39	9	19	15	17	74	-1	-2	6	8	121	132	22	44	-1	66	20	
03 126 3	A	1	16	0	51	39	12	18	15	18	83	-2	-1	7	7	139	159	37	43	2	82	18	
03 130 3		2	16	1	40	30	11	19	16	19	95	-1	-2	7	7	144	140	38	40	1	69	20	
03 131 9		1	16	1	46	34	11	18	13	18	82	-2	-3	8	7	150	130	59	73	1	65	18	
03 132 4		1	16	1	60	51	8	19	16	18	89	-1	-1	6	6	136	141	38	25	1	121	23	
03 133 3		3	16	0	24	12	12	22	17	21	112	-2	-2	7	8	137	139	33	69	2	57	22	
03 133 5		1	16	0	56	45	11	19	17	18	88	-1	-1	8	9	124	147	18	19	-1	84	19	
03 134 8		1	16	1	40	38	12	18	14	17	86	-2	-1	9	8	144	160	39	34	1	61	18	
03 135 4		1	16	1	32	21	11	20	13	18	72	-2	-3	8	8	125	113	45	45	2	52	20	
03 135 6		1	16	1			10	17	12		84	0	-2		9	132	146	0	10	0		18	
03 136 3		1	16	1	48	34	14	19	14	16	89	-2	-2	11	10	149	138	46	23	1	73		
03 137 2		1	16	1			13	22	14	20	85	-3	-3	10	10	96	115	60	27	1		22	END
03 137 4			16	0	51	38	13	20	14	16	74	-1	-2	12	9	124	155	28	21	-1	67	20	
03 138 9		3	16	0	45	34	10	19	16	20	75	-2	-1	8	8	146	142	39	28	1	69	19	
03 139 6		2	16	1			10	18	13	18	75	-2	-2	8	7	137	131	47	34	1		18	END
03 139 8		1	16	1			11	18	12	15	87	-2	-2	8	9	119	124	30	28	1		20	
03 140 10		2	16	0			12	21	13	20	91	-4	-4	10	10	117	120	58	33	-1		21	END
03 141 4		1	16	0			15	21	14	20	109	0	-3		13	108	143	40	77	0		22	
03 142 9		1	16	1	42	32	10	20	14	18	61	-2	0	6		110	126	37	43	0		20	
03 142 10		1	16	0	63	49	13	18	14	19	103	-2	-2	13	11	164	150	39	43	1	123	19	
03 143 10	A	1	16	1			12	18	17	21	75	-1	-1	18	9	170	157	31	32	-1		21	
02 183 A	A	1	16	0	37	26	11	16	12	17	64	-2	-2	7	7	134	121	53	43	-2	33	16	
02 198 E	A	1	16	0			12	24	20	24	78	-2	-2	9	6	140	132	29	55	2		24	
02 248 B		1	16	1			9	21	14	17	63	-2	-2	8	6	124	118	44	32	0		22	END
02 259 A	A	1	16	0	51	40	11	21	15	28	87	-2	-2	8	7	107	131	47	48	2	101	23	
02 265 B		1	16	0	26	16	10	19	14	18	85	-2	-2	7	8	110	141	68	39	1	40	20	
02 286 A		1	16	0	36	25	11	18	16	20	77	-1	-2	8	8	130	148	29	39	1	49	18	
02 288 C	A	1	16	1	34	26	9	20	17	20	83	-1	-1	6	7	148	146	38	32	1	57	20	
02 294 A		1	16	1	45	33	13	18	14	17	92	-1	-2	9	12	154	169	24	19	2	82	18	
02 310 B	A	1	16	0	55	44	11	16	13		86	-2	0	10		148	151	44	0	0		16	
02 334 B	A	1	16	1	59	48	11	18	13	17	96	-2	-2	9	9	124	139	49	.24	-1	115	20	
02 360 I	A	1	16	0	43	32	11	17	13	20	77	-2	-2		7	145	142	40	75	1	60	17	
02 420 B		1	16	1	46	35	12	19	14	18	92	-1	-2	7	7	146	126	73	44	-1	104	18	
02 500 A	A	1	16	1	43	34	9	17	15	16	104	-1	0	8	7	160	152	19	44	2	76	18	
02 511 A		1	16	0	34	24	10	19	16		79	-2	0	8		120	135	35	20	0		19	
02 523 D		1	16	1	39	30	9		13	18	85	-2	0	8		123	124	39	31	1			
02 541 D		27	16	0	40	30	10				76	-2	0	6		123		43	0	0			
02 545 B	A	71	16	1	42	31	11	19	15	18	75	-2	-1	8	7	137	136	40	32	2	68	19	
02 557 B	A	170	16	0	52	42	10	20	14	16	72	-2	-2	7	6	116	112	27	46	0	86	20	
02 558 B	A	132	16	1	53	38	15	18	16	19	104	-2	-1	11	10	170	140	26	32	3	117	18	
02 576 A	A	221	16	0			11	18	15	17	78	-1	-2	9	8	138	147	54	43	1		17	
02 642 A	A	3	16	1	46	35	11	22	15	19	86	-2	-3	8	9	138	129	29	60	1	86	21	
02 703 A	A	1	16	1	47	34	13	22	15	22	85	-3	-3	10	10	117	134	65	45	2	82	22	
02 708 C		1	16	1	50	39	11	15	10	14	88	-3	-2	8	9	128	127	42	41	2	74	16	
02 736 A	A	1	16	0	61	52	9	17	13	17	74	-2	-2	7	8	141	132	24	50	1	80	18	
02 761 B	A	1	16	1	54	44	10	23	20	22	91	-1	-1	6	7	127	132	26	28	1	110	23	
02 800 B		1	16	0			13	21	20	22	74	-1	-1	9	9	149	173	16	63	3		21	END
02 827 A	A	1	16	1	50	36	14	20	14	18	108	-3	-2	8	10	135	152	38	52	3	105	20	
03 857 B	A	1	16	0	52	44	09	18	12		85	0	-2		8	127	110		40	0		18	
03 881 B	A	1	16	1	34	24	19	20	17	19	75	-1.	-2	5	6	149	129	31	47	1	50	20	
03 923 A	A	1	16	1			12	20	13	18	80	-3	-3	9	8	127	124	45	44	0		22	END
03 925 A	A	1	16	0			11	11	17	22	78	-2	-2	9	10	128	139	22	29	1		21	
03 927 WX	A	1	16	1	68	53	14	22	16	20	120	-2	-2	11	13	116	164	23	25	3	173	22	

DEEP SIDE NOTCH MATANZAS

PROVENIENCE			TYPE	LAB	AL	BL	TL	SHW	TW	BW	TH	RND	LND	RNW	LNW	RDHI	LDHI	RPHI	LPHI	BR	WT	MW	REW
01 5 17		2	13	0			12	22	17	19	108	-3	-2	9	7	130	127	35	41	4		23	END
02 22 39		1	13	1			15	23	12	23	115	-5	-5	12	12	136	126	60	47	2		23	
02 31 13		1	13	1			14	26	16	23	82	-4	-3	12	38	129	120	37	56	2		27	
02 45 7		1	13	1			14	25	16	22	115	-4	-4	11	12	110	119	58	57	1		27	END
02 48 20		1	13	0	62	46	16	23	17	21	101	-2	-2	13	11	168	150	26	63	1	174	24	
02 52 22		4	13	1			15	23	19	21	94	-2	-1	11	11	125	165	11	35	2		23	END
02 59 8		2	13	0			12	20	14	18	86	-3	-3	10	9	137		48	47	2		21	END
02 64 1		2	13	0			14	24	10	26	112	-3	-3	10	10	125	143	41	45	2		25	EN4
02 64 5		1	13	1			27		12	18	86		-3		14		159		35	1		19	
02 65 7		1	13	1			16	24	17	22	85	-3	-3	11	11	128	138	31	55	3		24	END
02 66 13		1	13	1	56	40	17	20	14	21	105	-3	-3	11	11	149	138	51	39	2	114	21	
03 105 27		1	13	0			16	24	20	24	92	-2	-2	12	12	156	149	38	42	1		24	END
03 105 32		1	13	0			14	24	19	23	106	-5	-2	10	12	126	157	48	26	-1		24	END
03 110 10		1	13	0			15	23	17	23	87	-3	-3	11	11	138	127	43	45	1		23	END
03 121 32		1	13	1			13	25	17	22	76	-3	-3	10	10	123	122	33	43	1		27	END
03 127 11	A	1	13	1	60	44	16	23	16	23	93	-3	-3	13	12	134	132	46	49	-1	124	23	
03 132 3		2	13	0	64	50	13	20	11	15	88	-3	-3	11	10	104	99	25	44	0	126	21	
03 132 3		3	13	0	51	39	12	19	17	20	101	-1	-2	7	9	144	159	33	42	1	116	20	
03 135 11		1	13	0	76	62	14	21	13	20	108	-3	-4	10	10	120	92	64	52	2	200	23	
03 137 9		1	13	0			14	13	15	20	82	-4	-3	10	10	109	111	67	69	1		23	
03 140 5		1	13	1	66	50	16	22	13	19	103	-4	-4	12	12	107	132	40	37	1	164	23	
03 142 8		1	13	0	61	48	12	24	17	22	112	-2	-3	10	10	126	128	42	40	-1	164	26	
02 255 B	A	1	13	1	66	54	12	21	13	20	80	-4	-3	9	9	95	121	40	37	1	136	22	
02 296 F		1	13	0			18	24	19	24	143	-3	-2	16	15	145	143	27	30	1		24	END
02 331 B	A	3	13	0	60	57	12	19	13	18	89	-2	-3	10	08	135	112	43	53	2	115	20	

TABLE 37 (CONTINUED)

FAINT SIDE NOTCH MATANZAS

PROVENIENCE	TYPE	LAB	AL	BL	TL	SHW	TW	BW	TH	RND	LND	RNW	LNW	RDHI	LDHI	RPHI	LPHI	BR	WT	MW	REW
01 5 10 2	14	1	50	40	10	17	17	19	99	-1	-1	6	8	169	174	34	27	2	90	17	
01 8 30 A 1	14	1			18	23	19	22	105	-2	-2	12	18	154	161	19	41	3		22	END
02 20 31 1	14	0			16	26	24	27	141	-2	-1	13	10	162	172	20	31	2		26	
02 23 19 3	14	0	65	57	8	19	15		100	0	-2		6	125	137	24	33	2	136	19	
02 35 13 3	14	0	46	34	13	16	14	16	89	-1	1	9	11	169	152	40	20	2	56	15	
02 36 16 A195	14	1	65	52	13	19	17	21	93	-1	-2	11	9	164	132	21	69	1	128	19	
02 37 23 2	14	1	43	29	14	23	19	20	79	-1	1	10	13	160	138	5	15	1	125	22	
02 45 16 3	14	1	54	43	11	15	14	15	94	0	-1	9	9	180	161	1	30	1	77	16	
02 51 21 2	14	1	43	29	14	23	19	20	79	-1	-1	10	13	160	138	5	15	1	125	22	
02 52 22 3	14	1	41	31	10	20	19	19	95	-1	-1	9	8	163	163	8	26	1	77	20	
02 56 25 A 2	14	0	62	49	13	19	16	18	99	-1	-1	10	12	147	160	24	16	1	122	19	
02 58 16 A 1	14	1	57	47	11	18	17	19	85	-1	-1	7	8	145	153	43	41	1	98	18	
02 64 8 2	14	0	47	36	12	19	19	23	88	-1	-1	6	7	134	161	64	52	3	82	19	
02 66 6 1	14	1	58	44	14	21	20	23	106	-2	-1	10	8	169	178	20	47	3	148	21	
02 68 9 1	14	1	53	41	12	16	15	19	106	-1	-1	8	7	172	141	35	32	2	90	17	
02 73 9 A A 1	14	0	73	59	13	22	19	22	120	-1	-1	9	14	154	175	20	45	-1	199	21	
02 74 24 4	14	0			12	23	19	19	101	1	-1	12	8	148	174	13	10	1		24	END
03 119 25 A 3	14	1	58	48	10	19	16	18	113	-1	-1	11	6	174	169	31	20	1	133	19	
03 135 6 2	14	0	56	44	12	15	14		73	0	-2		10	167	162	25	40	0		16	
02 281 C A 1	14	1	47	37	10	17	14		76	-1	0	6	8	130	170	23	7	0		17	
02 298 A A 3	14	0	66	49	17	20	19	20	104	0	-1	12	14	181	178	26	42	3	129	20	
02 575 A A225	14	0	50	40	10	15	14		83	0	-1		10	161	174	14	28	0		14	
03 860 A 1	14	0	60	48	11	20	18	20	96	-1	-1	7	6	170	156	53	37	3	136	20	
03 865 B 1	14	1	44	32	12	18	16	19	82	-1	-1	8	11	165	178	25	25	0	74	17	

FLARED STEM MATANZAS

PROVENIENCE	TYPE	LAB	AL	BL	TL	SHW	TW	BW	TH	RND	LND	RNW	LNW	RDHI	LDHI	RPHI	LPHI	BR	WT	MW	REW
01 8 35 1	12	1	56	43	13	20	16	18	105	-1	-1	9	12	150	149	10	23	2	129	22	
02 13 38 A 1	12	1	61	46	15	19	14	14	11	-2	-1	12	14	124	118	14	8	-1	55	28	
02 15 25 A 2	12	0	60	44	16	20	16	18	86	-2	-1	13	16	149	167	14	5	2	119	21	
02 19 23 A190	12	0			14	19	14	15	88	-2	-2	10	7	137	128	33	20	1		19	
02 23 13 A 1	12	0			15	23	18	19	96	-2	-2	11	13	151	148	47	20	-1		24	END
02 24 26 2	12	0			13	20	16	18	78	-2	-2	10	10	140	135	56	37	1		20	END
02 50 20 5	12	1	90	71	18	26	19	21	103	-3	-2	16	15	145	148	11	4	3	3n8	26	
02 55 17 2	12	1			12	20	14	16	80	-2	-2	12	10	131	128	7	10	0		21	
02 55 21 A 2	12	0			11	21	17		82	0	-1		8	136	117	0	27	0		21	END
02 56 23 3	12	1			14	23	16	20	75	-3	-2	13	9	133	131	41	25	2		22	
02 59 11 A 2	12	0	53	34	19	21	17	21	71	-2	-2	15	16	150	150	58	30	2	147	23	
02 65 10 2	12	0			14	21	15	18	91	-2	-2	12	11	135	135	26	48	1		22	DRILL
03 106 34 1	12	0	55	41	14	18	13	15	103	-2	-1	13	13	164	148	4	2	-1	113	18	
03 122 19 1	12	1	66	49	18	19	14		101	0	-1		12	161	131	12	9	0		21	
03 135 8 1	12	1	55	44	12	22	12	15	93	0	-3		11	100	120	13	26	0			
02 500 B A 6	12	1	43	32	11	21	11	13	76	-3	-3	9	8	95	93	28	30	1	73	22	
02 611 A A 5	12	1			20	24	17	19	103	-3	-2	16	22	141	159	6	13	-1		26	
02 721 A A 3	12	1			16	21	17	20	98	-3	-3	13	14	135	123	23	35	-1		22	

STRAIGHT STEM MATANZAS

PROVENIENCE	TYPE	LAB	AL	BL	TL	SHW	TW	BW	TH	RND	LND	RNW	LNW	RDHI	LDHI	RPHI	LPHI	BR	WT	MW	REW
02 14 35 A 1	11	1			17	28	19	21	60	-3	-3	14	13	132	128	12	20	2		28	
02 15 20 2	11	0	56	34	21	26	19	21	99	-3	-3	15	20	103	147	15	10	2	123	25	
02 42 21 A 1	11	1			17	27	16	21	90	-4	-4	15	14	92	105	20	40	-1		28	
02 54 25 A 1	11	0	61	43	18	28	22	24	79	-4	0	16		52		15	3	2	145	28	
02 56 18 A 1	11	1			17		14	22	111	-4	0	18			77	5	31	1		32	
02 57 17 4	11	1	57	40	17	28	21	24	92	-3	-3	15	13	133	131	32	53	2	154	28	
02 59 12 A 1	11	0	68	53	15	25	19	25	33	-2	-2	13	13	113	122	4	13	-1			
02 65 6 A 2	11	0	63	49	15	28	21	22	88	-3	-2	12	14	99	138	9	13	-1	163	28	
02 67 3 1	11	0	53	38	16	24	21	24	93	-1	-2	13	13	130	140	18	13	3	126	26	
03 104 23 2	11	1	60	38	22	26	16	18	77	-2	-2	19	18	163	153	48	16	1	125	27	
03 129 4 A 1	11	0			16	30	18	20	106	-5	-4	14	15	54	92	8	54	1		32	END
03 134 9 A 1	11	0			18	26	15	26	83	-2	-1	14	7	114	148	21	2	0		26	END

GODAR SIDE NOTCHED

PROVENIENCE	TYPE	LAB	AL	BL	TL	SHW	TW	BW	TH	RND	LND	RNW	LNW	RDHI	LDHI	RPHI	LPHI	BR	WT	MW	REW
02 17 26 1	30	1	37	23	14	22	16	23	58	-3	-3	6	7	79	147	60	68	-1	55	23	
02 41 20 A182	30	0	42	29	13	21	15	19	80	-2	-4	6	7	88	107	47	50	-1	74	22	
02 42 31 1	30	1			17	30	21	31	89	-5	-4	9	8	93	107	66	70	-1		30	
02 44 10 1	30	0			20	28	23	28	95	-2	-3	10	11	144	132	44	34	-3		29	END
02 48 13 1	30	0			18	25	21	29	96	-4	-2	8	7	112	108	52	57	2		25	END
02 54 26 A 3	30	0			16	25	22	27	88	-2	-2	8	11	148	143	30	30	-2		25	
03 55 29 A 1	30	1			16	25	17	26	82	-4	-3	8	9	103	126	67	77	2		25	
02 59 9 1	30	1			16	32	23	33	97	-5	-5	10	7	82	107	74	56	-8		31	
03 59 19 1	30	1			15	27	20	26	75	-3	-3	8	8	93	107	47	62	1		27	
02 64 4 1	30	0			20	23	19	27	71	-3	-3	10	9	114	133	52	40	2		23	
02 68 2 1	30	1	52	38	14	25	20	29	73	-3	-3	8	9	99	128	58	49	-2	91	25	
02 71 6 A A 1	30	1			14	25	17	25	88	-4	-3	7	7	90	98	103	79	0		25	END
02 73 9 A A 2	30	0	57	40	16	30	19	33	72	-6	-6	9	9	88	87	76	81	-1	142	31	
03 64 25 A 1	30	1	42	30	12	27	20	28	81	-3	-3	10	7	27	90	29	69	-2	96	28	

TABLE 37 (CONTINUED)

GODAR SIDE NOTCHED (CONTINUED)

PROVENIENCE		TYPE	LAB	AL	BL	TL	SHW	TW	BW	TH	RND	LND	RNW	LNW	RDHI	LDHI	RPHI	LPHI	BR	WT	MW	REW
03 103 23		1 30	1			16	27	18	28	76	-4	-3	8	10	82	132	88	86	2		28	
03 106 16		1 30	1	41	27	14	32	13	30	92	-6	-6	11	9	100	70	55	69	1	132	33	
03 111 31		30	2								-5	-4					70	70	0			
03 112 7	A	1 30	1			16	27	21		84	-2	0	10		134	139	49		0		28	
03 122 19		3 30	1	58	44	14	25	15	25	64	-4	-4	7	10	103	108	65		1		27	
03 123 12		1 30	0			17	29	18	30	81	-6	-5	6	8	63	78	91	58	1		34	
03 125 18	A	1 30	1	69	54	15	24	19	26	68	-3	-3	9	10	134	122	53	48	0	127	26	
03 128 8	A	2 30	1			18	25	18	27	76	-4	-5	10	10		100	74	65	1		29	END
03 132 11	A	1 30	1	67	41	16	28	21	27	95	-3	-3	12	11	128	133	70	65	-3	136	28	
03 132 12		1 30	1			12	28	29	24	67	-3	-3	8	10	72	92	56	66	-1		29	END
03 135 12		1 30	1			19	27	22	28	82	-2	-2	8	11	148	142	57	49	0		27	
03 137 10		2 30	1			19	26	19	28	80	-4	-3	8	7	91	113	68	68	1		28	
03 137 12		1 30	0	47	34	13	24	15	20	81	0	-4		9	118	102	0	68	1		24	
03 138 3	A	1 30	0	58	43	14	28	19	28	80	-5	-4	8	6	91	88	74	62	1	153	29	
03 138 07		1 30	0	57	37	20	27	22	29	88	-3	-2	10	11	129	143	54	38	1	156	28	
03 150 14	A	1 30									-4	-3					70	80	-1			
02 278 A		2 30	1	63	45	18	26	22	30	107	-3	-3	12	12	146	151	49	56	0	190	25	
03 927 WA		1 30	1	37	21	17	20	16	22	81	-2	-2	6	7	127	109	1	70	3	67	20	
03 332 A	A	1 30	0			15	32	22		105	0	-3		12	92	129	0	45	0		36	
03 363 B		1 30	1			16	28	17	27	69	-5	-6	8	7	72	85	81	85	3		28	
03 PROFIL		1 30	1	54	39	15	28	19	27	68	-4	-3	10	8	108	124	53	58	2	130	28	

HELTON

PROVENIENCE		TYPE	LAB	AL	BL	TL	SHW	TW	BW	TH	RND	LND	RNW	LNW	RDHI	LDHI	RPHI	LPHI	BR	WT	MW	REW
01 8 29 A		1 130	0	61	48	13		19	22	82	0	-2		8		74	25	51	4		28	
02 18 21	A	1 130	0	68	54	16	29	18	23	80	-6	-4	10	14	52	74	19	25	1	174	30	
02 31 13		2 130	1	60				21	24	81	0	0					50	18	3		34	
02 40 11	A	14 130	0	68	54	16		19	24	72	-4	0	10		48		26	18	2		32	
03 109 22		2 130	1	67	50	17	27	19	24	93	-4	-3	9	10	88	103	30	16	3	209	29	
03 110 11	A	1 130	1	57	42	14		16	20	83	0	-4		10		115	9	25	1		29	
03 113 2		2 130	0	47	32	15	26	21	25	77	-2	-2	9	12	134	141	30	39	2	102	26	
03 116 1		1 130	1	66	55	13	35	15	22	84	-6	-5	14	11	47	52	-10	-34	1	163	36	
03 131 4	A	2 130	1	62	47	14	25	18		94	-2	0	9		134	126	64	0	0		26	
03 133 3	A	3 130	0	60	48	14	36	21	25	70	-6	-4	10	10	32	90	16	12	3	164	38	

APPLE BLOSSOM STEMMED

PROVENIENCE		TYPE	LAB	AL	BL	TL	SHW	TW	BW	TH	RND	LND	RNW	LNW	RDHI	LDHI	RPHI	LPHI	BR	WT	MW	REW
02 30 37	A	1 70	0			10	28	17	25	56	-5	-4	9	8	91	84	41	35	1		29	
03 40 28	A	2 70	1	48	36	13	24	14	18	72	-4	-4	13	11	116	92	21	33	1	80	25	
03 42 38		1 70	1	45	34	11	20	14		76	0	-3		10	112	103	0	16	0		22	
03 44 35		2 70	0			12	20	14	18	55	-3	-2	9	14	86	159	36	30	1		20	
03 44 38		2 70	1			13	25	16	18	77	-4	-3	12	12	28	70	16	19	1		26	
03 44 39		1 70	1	41	27	14	23	16	20	75	-3	-2	13	11	110	150	4	34	-1	73	23	
03 45 32		70	1			10	25	12	16	68	-4	-4	10	12	73	108	27	18	0		26	
03 46 28		1 70	0			14	24	15	19	89	-3	-3	12	13	127	95	42	38	-1		24	
03 54 29		2 70																				
03 59 16		2 70	1			13	24	14	19	81	-4	-3	12	10	103	112	19	45	3		25	
03 64 14		1 70	0			9	22	13	16	57	-3	-3	9	8	88	82	24	24	0		24	
03 110 44		70	0			10	22	17	21	73	-2	-2	8	9	110	99	47	35	-1		24	
03 112 29		1 70	0			12	18	14	18	60	-2	-2	10	11	125	141	20	21	1		20	
03 112 32		1 70	0			12	24	15	16	73	-3	-2	11	12	101	102	6	5	1		25	
03 113 32		3 70	0			12	24	17	19	65	-2	-3	10	11	92	90	12	14	2		27	
03 118 33		1 70	1	52	42	10	20	11		85	-4	0	10		99	117	19	0	0		21	
03 120 54		70	0	28	13	15	26	17	21	74	-3	-3	12	12	116	139	62	14	1		27	
03 123 29		1 70	0			10	24	15	19	61	-4	-4	10	8	75	75	17	40	2		27	
03 143 29	A	2 70	1	44	34	10	22	12	14	69	-3	-3	11	8	133	96	29	28	2	71	23	
03 146 23	A	1 70	1	52	40	12	20	10	14	65	-3	-4	9	12	77	99	38	29	3	68	22	
03 154 7		1 70	0			13	23	15	20	79	-4	-3	12	10	104	103	32	32	-1		24	

BRANNON SIDE NOTCHED

PROVENIENCE		TYPE	LAB	AL	BL	TL	SHW	TW	BW	TH	RND	LND	RNW	LNW	RDHI	LDHI	RPHI	LPHI	BR	WT	MW	REW
03 15 48		140	0	19	10	09	21	16	21	60	-2	-2	4	6	104	108	92	43	0		22	
03 41 35	A	1 140	1	49	35	12		18		76	-2	0	5		83	125	51	0	0		24	
03 104 33		2 140	0	48	35	12		15		82	0	-3		8		133	0	63	0		22	
03 105 31		1 140	0	24	13	11	19	14	18	67	-2	-1	7	6	136	143	45	77	2	48	21	
03 118 28		2 140	1	38	26	12	19			78	-2	0	6		128	149	52	0	0		20	
03 130 4		2 140	1	32	22	10	17	11	16	58	-2	-3	7	6	92	115	38	57	1	44	17	
03 132 11		1 140	1	40	29	11	18	12	20	67	-4	-3	6	6	100	120	59	83	0	52	18	
03 132 12		2 140	1			9	22	15	17	77	-2	-2	7	7	124	117	7	24	2		22	END
03 140 4		1 140	1	31	17	14	29	21	29	68	-4	-3	5	7	97	136	47	63	3	65	29	
03 142 10		2 140	1	24	14	10	14	11	16	72	-2	-2	6	6	97	126	47	56	1	32	14	
03 149 19		140	0	24	8	16	26	22	28	70	-2	-2	4	5	127	104	63	71	-1	59	27	
03 149 22		1 140	0			11		17		72	-4	0	5		65		69	76	1		23	BURIN
02 268 A	A	1 140	1	50	42	8	23	17		77	0	-2		6	99	71	38	50	0		24	
02 290 C	A	1 140	0			13	22	18	23	83	-2	-2	6	6	139	114	58	61	1		22	END
02 320 C	A	1 140	0	44	34	10	22	15		79	0	-2		8	95	105	55	26	0		22	

not having parallel sides are widest two-thirds to three-quarters the distance from the base to the point. Blades that have recurved sides may also have needle-like points....

Wadlow points are manufactured from large blocks of white or tan flint found in creeks and washes in the area of discovery....Some undoubtedly were used as knives for the edges are quite worn....Basal edges are never ground.

Perino's sample is from the Etley site. For the Koster sample, all 14 examples are large, thick bifaces showing deep and irregular shaping flake scars which completely remove any indication of the original large form being modified. These shaping flakes sometimes leave behind a discontinuous meandering ridge line down the long axis of the blade. Despite the crudeness of the shaping flakes, the edges of the blades show medium quality retouch so that the outline of the form tends toward smooth curves with minor irregularities of less than 1 or 2 mm observed face on. When examined edge on, there is a regular undulation of a 1 to 5 mm amplitude with larger undulations where deeper shaping flake scars appear.

In transverse cross section the Wadlow points are lenticular, with four flat surfaces which are slightly concave toward the edges.

The breakage rate for these forms is high. Preservation permitting, the following patterns of wear and abrasion were observed: 1 of 9 has basal abrasion; 9 of 10 are abraded on the sides of the tang portion (arbitrarily defined as the last 2 cm of the proximal end), thus indicating hafting. As for the blades, 3 are unworn, 7 show heavy abrasion on only one edge leaving it well rounded, and 3 are heavily abraded on both edges. The faces of the blades show neither polishing or grinding. Impact breaks are lacking.

The quality of cherts selected for these forms varies from fossiliferous and faintly grainy to highly compacted fossil-free chert. The chert is grayish-white with one brownish specimen and one with mineral staining. The points were probably made from local Burlington formation cherts. None of the forms appear to have been heat-treated, except one which was thermally altered after its manufacture.

In terms of the use trajectory of these forms, none of the 14 examples from Koster show any evidence for resharpening or modification into other functional forms such as drills or scrapers.

Varieties. Table 38 presents statistical summaries of width and thickness of Wadlow points from Booth (Klippel 1969), Koster, and Wieman (Bacon and Miller 1957), as well as Student's *t*-test to determine if there are significant differences between means of

TABLE 38

Comparison of Dimensions of Wadlow Points from Booth, Koster and Wieman Sites

	Width (mm)			Thickness (mm)		
	n	$\bar{x}$	*s*	*n*	$\bar{x}$	*s*
Booth	8	42.5	3.2	9	13.8	1.4
Koster	11	40.9	8.3	12	12.4	2.2
Wieman	19	51.4	6.6	19	13.9	2.8

Student's *t*-test, 2-tailed, pooled variance: *t*-score

	Koster	Wieman
Width		
Booth	0.51	3.60**
Koster		3.82***
Thickness		
Booth	2.20	0.12
Koster		1.57

** Significant at the .01 level
*** Significant at the .001 level

these samples. In width, Wieman site Wadlow points are very different than those from Koster and Booth, while the latter two samples are very similar. For thickness, the three samples show no significant differences from one another, even though the Wieman forms are significantly wider. The sample from the Wieman site seems to represent a much broader, slightly thicker form of the Wadlow point. It is suspected that Wadlow points from mortuary sites are also much *longer* than those from habitation sites. For example, the Wieman samples range from 133 to 232 mm in length, and those from the Etley site range from 125 to 320 mm long (Perino 1968a:98).

Other sources of variability include blade shape, some forms being parallel sided and others having sinuous edges called ogival by some (Montet-White 1968:100). In addition occasionally the base is set at an oblique angle to the central axis of the blade.

Typological Relationships. Morphologically related forms include Morton Lanceolate which is convex-sided with a contracting stem (Montet-White 1968: Figs. 11, 12); Godar Preforms (Perino 1971a:38) which tend to be a good deal smaller than Wadlow points and tend to be heat-treated; Red Ochre points (Scully 1951:9; Perino 1968a:72) which are square based and large with very convex sides; and Sedalia points (Perino 1968:86; Plate 43) which seem to overlap in length, width, and shape with Wadlow points. The Godar form seems related to the manufacturing trajectory of the Helton phase, e.g., use of heat treatment, while the other forms are made like Wadlow points but have minor shape distinctions.

Sedalia Points (Fig. 33)

These points were named by Seelan (1961:307) for the town of Sedalia, Mo.

Sample Size. Koster 1969 and 1970 produced the four examples whose measurements are recorded in Table 37. Two had been reworked into drills, and one has a lateral burin scar at the point tip.

Description. These lanceolate points are generally graceful. The primary flaking is done with broad but shallow shaping flakes, leaving behind a very faint central ridge line. As in the Wadlow points, the ridge line is a sometimes discontinuous meander, but frequently the shaping flakes travel more than two-thirds of the way across the blade. The edges of the blade are even and carefully made. Because the sharpening flakes are rather shallow, only light and discontinuous edge retouch was required to manufacture these well-formed edges. Irregularities in the edge are seldom more than 2 to 3 mm when viewed face on. When viewed edge on, the undulations tend to be either 3 or 4 cm long or less than 1 cm, both with a small to medium (1 to 4 mm amplitude).

In transverse cross section the blade is generally lenticular, but the four sides are gently flowing arcs in contrast to the flatter sides of the Wadlow form. The curve of the arc increases rapidly near the edge but flows freely across the midline, unlike the sharp break in the Wadlow points.

As for hafting modification, two of the three surviving bases have moderate abrasion along the base and both edges of the stem, while the third shows no abrasion at all. The corners of the stems of all three examples are slightly rounded.

As in the Wadlow points, the original form of the unknapped chert piece has been completely altered by flaking and there is no evidence for heat treatment. The quality of the chert, Burlington in all four cases, varies from fossiliferous, with open fossil holes, to fine grained smooth chert.

Because of the small sample size and reworking, little can be said about wear patterns.

Varieties. Table 39 summarizes the dimensions of these four points. Unfortunately, the sample is too small for useful comparison with samples from

TABLE 39

Dimensions (in mm) of Sedalia Points, Koster Site, Titterington Phase

	Length	Width	Thickness
Mean	119.7	27.0	10.85
Std. dev.	8.1	2.0	0.64
Sample size	3	3	4

other sites, such as the nine Sedalia points from the Booth site (Klippel 1969: Cat. F).

Typological Relationships. Sedalia points have been assigned to the Early Archaic by Perino (1968a:86) and the Late Archaic by Turner (1965), both on rather thin evidence. Stratigraphic information from Koster indicates a Late Archaic affiliation. As to formal similarities, "they much resemble Agate Basin points, and rougher Agate Basin points have been mistaken for them" (Perino 1968:86). The Sedalia points are similar in outline to Nebo Hill points (Shippee 1948) but are different in transverse cross section, the latter being very much thicker than Sedalia points. As noted above, the broader Sedalia points overlap the range of Wadlow points.

Etley Barbed Points (Fig. 33)

These stemmed, barbed points were named by Scully (1951:2) for the Etley site on the Oettle farm, Calhoun County, Ill. (Perino 1968a:98).

Sample Size. The Koster sample of 1969 and 1970 includes 24 specimens of which 8 are essentially complete, 3 are reworked as drills, and 13 are in various stages of breakage. Table 37 tabulates the measurements of these points.

Description. Etley Barbed points are frequently depicted as very large. Bell (1960:Plate 18) illustrates one example which is 233 mm long and Montet-White (1968:Fig. 44) has a photograph of one about 280 mm and another 275 mm long. However, such is not always the case. Table 40 presents statistical summaries of Etley points from the Koster, Booth, and Wieman sites.

In the Koster sample of Etley Barbed points, there are a number of blade shapes, which show a resharpening progression from parallel-sided to triangular in shape, and a variety of barb shapes from recurved to absent. Such variability in barb morphology is noted by Scully (1951:2). The stems vary between parallel-sided to slightly expanding, with the base being more or less squared off. The shaping flakes are large and expanding, occasionally extending two-third to three-quarters of the way across the blade. In general these flake scars are not as deep as those found in the Koster sample of Wadlow blades but are more like the Sedalia points found there. The Etley Barbed points tend to have a poorly defined ridge line; most often it is merely the distal edge of a thicker-than-usual shaping flake. The edge retouch flakes come in discontinuous groups, frequently with hinge fractures at the distal end. At least half of the blade edges have rather crude and jagged segments between the refined and well-worked sections. In no instance has any portion of the original, unchipped surface been left behind. Hence the core-versus-flake tool controversy cannot be resolved, although I suspect that most of these forms are made of tabular cherts.

Although all these points are made of local Burlington chert without benefit of heat treatment, the best quality chert is rarely used: 14 examples include grainy, coarse chert; 6 are made of fine grade chert; 4 are made of finely grained, rather lustrous cherts. Of the 24 pieces, 2 have been thermally altered after manufacture, and 1 has been reworked.

For edge alteration, the sample of complete blades includes 2 with light abrasion while 1 shows light abrasion on one edge. Of the stem portions, 13 are abraded on the side and base of the

TABLE 40

Comparison of Dimensions of Etley Barbed Points from Booth, Koster, and Wieman Sites

	Length (mm)			Width (mm)			Thickness (mm)		
	n	$\bar{x}$	*s*	*n*	$\bar{x}$	*s*	*n*	$\bar{x}$	*s*
Booth	7	138.7	18.6	23	35.2	4.9	24	10.8	2.2
Koster	12	83.8	13.1	21	36.9	4.0	23	11.4	1.5
Wieman	3	110.3	17.4	3	32.3	3.0	3	11.0	2.0

Student's *t*-test, 2-tailed, pooled variance: *t*-score

Comparison	Length	Width	Thickness
Booth vs Koster	5.64***	1.28	1.08
Booth vs Wieman	2.22	0.98	0.22
Koster vs Wieman	3.02**	1.92	0.42

** Significant at the .01 level
*** Significant at the .001 level

stem, 7 are abraded on only the side of the stem, 3 show no alterations, and 1 is too badly damaged to be examined.

Varieties. There is a great deal of variation in the barb morphology and in the angles forming the stem element. Klippel (1969) illustrates a variety of such shapes, as does this study of the Koster sample. As to the metric attributes, Table 40 lists Student's *t*-tests comparing length, width, and thickness of Etley points from Booth, Koster, and Wieman sites. Thickness is similar for the three samples. Booth and Wieman are similar in both length and width. The Koster sample is significantly shorter.

Typological Relationships. Large points with stemmed hafting elements from the Midwest include Kampsville Barbed (Perino 1968b:Fig. 37), Dickson (Perino 1968a:Plate 9), and rounded stem points such as Waubesa (Perino 1971a:Plate 49), Hidden Valley (Scully 1951:5), and Stilwell (Perino 1971a: 121).

Kampsville Barbed are smaller, more delicate forms without basal grinding. Dickson and Waubesa points have "beaver tail" shaped stems. The Hidden Valley points have a definite contracting stem with a straight base. Stilwell points tend to have expanding stems with rounded corners as well as heavy serrations on the blade edges. Except for the Stilwell points which Perino assigns to the Early Archaic period (Perino 1971a:94), all are in the transitional times between Late Archaic and Early Woodland, with both Kampsville Barbed and Waubesa-like points occurring at the Koster site stratigraphically above the Titterington phase occupation. Hidden Valley points are possibly stratigraphically out of place at the Hidden Valley site (Adams 1941) since other Etley-like forms occur stratigraphically beneath Matanzas-like forms, the opposite of their occurrence at Koster and Modoc Rock Shelter.

General Comments

The three point types assigned to the Titterington phase share the same manufacturing trajectory and are all rather large, non-heat-treated forms with little variation in thickness (except Koster-versus-Wieman Wadlows) within each type but with a great deal of variability in width and especially length. All three types occur in mortuary context as well as habitation-type sites, although the former tend to be larger examples. A fourth point type is the Turkey Tail, made from a banded gray chert, possibly from Harrison County, Ind., rather than the local Burlington.

Micro-style analysis is not recommended for the Wadlow and Sedalia points because the predominantly lanceolate form lends itself to a variety of shapes that are easily modified through resharpening of the blade. (Ogival shapes being reworked into parallel-sided or convex shapes are an example.) Etley points should lend themselves to such analysis because of the great variability of barb and base shapes. It remains to be demonstrated that these variations in stem and barb shape relate to temporal, geographical, or social differences.

HELTON PHASE POINT TYPES

Karnak Stemmed Points (Fig. 34)

Karnak Stemmed points were named by Winters (1967:Figs. 4g, 4h) in his unpublished manuscript on the Cache River Valley for the town of Karnak, Pulaski County, Ill. Unfortunately, the following description of the type is not completely isomorphic with his (Howard D. Winters, personal communication).

Sample Size. Koster 1969, 1970, and 1971 produced 43 examples of which 31 are complete, 4 are reworked into end-scrapers, and 8 are damaged.

Description. These lanceolate points are distinguished by their very high incidence of heat treatment. Of the 43 points, no fewer than 25 (58%) are definitely heat-treated (pink, red, and occasional blue coloration, high luster to the chert, faint and shallow ripples in flake scars), and an additional 8 (18%) are probably heat-treated (faint and shallow ripples in the flake scars and a metallic ring when tapped). The remaining 10 points (23%) are also made of high quality chert but show no signs of thermal alteration.

Heat treatment occurs after the manufacture of the primary flake and before reduction of this flake into a bifacial form. Twelve of the 25 definitely heat-treated specimens have a portion of the primary flake still present. In each case this scar is very different from that made by the shaping flakes: no waviness, a more granular texture, and frequently a darker stained color similar to that observed on the surfaces of experimentally heat-treated cherts. The remaining points provide an additional six examples of primary flake scars. Usually if the primary flake scar is still present, it occurs on only one face.

The blade is generally laurel-leaf-shaped with greatest breadth at between one- and two-thirds the blade length. When resharpened, the blade becomes parallel-sided with greatest breadth at the haft element. Through continued resharpening, the blade is reduced to a rounded triangle no longer than the haft element. Fig. 34 illustrates this progressive alteration of blade shape. As the blade is resharpened, the cross section becomes more and more hexagonal until a diamond-shaped cross section is produced with steep edge angles.

On unresharpened blades, the shaping flakes tend to be very shallow and very long, occasionally travelling across the blade and around the other end. There is frequently no indication of a central ridge line. The flake surfaces of the points feel like highly polished stone because of the smooth surface, shallow flake scars, and a lack of central ridge lines or primary flake scars in many cases. However, there tend to be flaking accidents which leave behind islands of chert surrounded by hinge fractures. These unsightly lumps occur unifacially on 8 blades.

Concerning edge treatment, 21 of 33 complete blades have serrated edges formed by small projections (1 to 2mm) between retouch flake scars. These serrations, when present, occur on both edges of each blade and extend from the tip to the hafting element. Of the 21 complete serrated blades, 9 show definite abrasion of only one edge on the proximal third of the blade, which may reflect stem abrasion carried on beyond the weak shoulder (or an asymmetrical haft). Of the 12 complete blades without serration, 6 are heavily abraded along the entire length of both edges, and 6 are unaltered.

The stem is usually a straight-edged trapezoid with the broader edge attached to the blade portion. Occasionally there are slight ears at the basal end of the stem. The base can be concave or convex, but rarely deviates more than 2 mm from a straight line. All 43 points have heavy to moderate abrasion on both sides of the stem, and all 40 complete bases have moderate to light abrasion.

These forms seem to resist breakage well, perhaps because of their relatively high thickness-to-width ratio. Reworking into endscrapers is noted, but the low breakage frequency (especially when compared to the Wadlow sample from the Koster site) is reflected in the fact that only four were reworked.

Table 37 lists the measurements taken on these points.

Varieties. None reported. Similar lanceolate to faintly shouldered points occur in Missouri (see below).

Typological Relationships. Well-made, heat-treated similar lanceolate forms also occur at Rodgers Shelter (Ahler 1971: Cats. 16-20). But these are dated at least a millennium earlier in Rodgers Stratum 2 than the Helton phase materials in Horizon 6 at Koster site. Table 41 presents a comparison, using the Student's *t*-test for length, width, and thickness. Despite the great similarity in length, widths are

TABLE 41

Comparison of Dimensions of Karnak Stemmed Points at Koster and Lanceolates at Rodgers Shelter

	Length (mm)			Width (mm)			Thickness (mm)		
	n	$\bar{x}$	s	n	$\bar{x}$	s	n	$\bar{x}$	s
Karnak Stemmed	33	75.1	11.7	43	24.3	2.7	43	10.4	1.7
Lanceolates[a]	9	74.8	9.1	22	26.7	3.4	22	7.7	0.9

Student's *t*-test, 2-tailed, pooled variance: *t*-score

Comparison	Length	Width	Thickness
Karnak vs Lanceolate	0.07	3.01**	6.94***

** Significant at the .01 level
*** Significant at the .001 level

[a]Estimated lengths omitted.

different, although by considerably less than one standard deviation, and thicknesses are very different, with a non-overlap of the standard deviations. I would suggest that the differences in thickness indicate that these two groups, despite similar shapes and use of heat treatment in manufacture, are *different* point types, especially when one considers that the Rodgers Rock Shelter sample is not only thinner but wider, implying a more refined manufacturing tradition.

Matanzas Point Cluster (Figs. 35-39)

The Matanzas point cluster is derived from the point type named by Munson and Harn (1966) for West Matanzas, Fulton County, Ill.

Sample Size. The 1969, 1970, and 1971 excavations at Koster site produced 262 measurable Matanzas points which have been divided into five variants:

Modal	183
Deep Side-Notched	25
Faint Side-Notched	24
Flared Stem	18
Straight Stemmed	12

Description. Because of the large sample size, it was possible to subdivide Munson and Harn's Matanzas Side-Notched point into five classes which share the general manufacturing and blade shape for the type. Table 42 indicates the size of these points. All of the points are neatly made. Examining the 175 with complete blades, only 28 (16%) have evidence of a primary flake scar. Such primary flake scars occur when the primary flake is deeper than the final form of the point. The primary flake scar survives as a small area, usually less than 10 mm across, and occurs only on one face. (Two exceptions occur on very thin flakes.) The shaping flakes tend to be neatly made, being about 5 mm across at the edge and slowly expanding across the blade itself. The flake scars are shallow and the borders between flake scars are very low. These shaping flakes tend to be perpendicular to the long axis of the point (and apparently perpendicular to the original flake as well) and form a vague central ridge which blends into a smooth surface. Occasionally, small islands are left where there has been a failure to thin the blade. The edge retouch flakes occur in discontinuous clusters of very small flakes to define a rather smooth edge profile. Serration is rarely present. In cross section the blades tend to be lozenge-shaped, tending toward diamond-shaped in heavily resharpened pieces.

An examination of the edges of the complete blades reveals the following distribution of wear patterns: Of 175 specimens, 53 (30%) have abrasion on both edges, 22 (13%) have abrasion on only one edge, and the majority of 100 (57%) reveal no detectable abrasion. The blades tend to be parallel-sided for the proximal two-thirds and then curve rapidly into the tip. The blades also tend to be highly symmetrical.

Heat treatment of Matanzas points is common. Seventy-one (41%) are definitely heat-treated, 23 (13%) are probably heat-treated, and 81 (46%) are not. Heat treatment occurs after the primary flake stage and before working off of the shaping flakes. This sequence of events can be determined because 29 specimens show primary flake scars with a rather granular texture that is very different from those of the subsequent shaping flakes.

Turning to the haft element, the defining characteristic of the Modal variety is the placement of the shallow side notches very close to the basal margin so that between the notch and the base there is little room for a continuation of the flowing shape of the preform. The curve for the side notch no sooner ends than the curve for the base begins. Fig. 35 illustrates this continuous curve on the stem element. An examination of patterns of abrasion of the Modal form haft elements (for 175 cases), reveals that 98 (56%) were abraded in both notches and

TABLE 42

Comparison of Dimensions of Matanzas Point Varieties at Koster

	Length (mm)			Width (mm)			Thickness (mm)		
	n	$\bar{x}$	*s*	*n*	$\bar{x}$	*s*	*n*	$\bar{x}$	*s*
Modal	127	48.8	9.5	179	19.8	2.1	183	8.5	1.1
Deep Side-Notch	10	62.2	6.6	25	23.2	2.2	25	9.8	1.5
Faint Side-Notch	22	54.7	9.1	25	19.2	2.8	25	9.6	1.5
Flared Stem	9	59.9	12.9	17	22.2	2.6	18	8.6	2.2
Straight Stem	7	59.7	5.0	11	28.0	2.2	12	8.4	2.1
Total	175	53.3	11.5	257	20.6	2.2	263	8.7	1.3

Student's *t*-test, 2-tailed, pooled variance: *t*-scores

	Deep Side-Notched	Faint Side-Notched	Flared Stem	Straight Stem
Length				
Modal	4.37***	2.70**	3.07**	2.80**
Deep Side-Notch		2.33*	0.49	0.84
Faint Side-Notch			1.27	1.37
Flared Stem				0.04
Width				
Modal	7.54***	1.27	4.43***	12.91***
Deep Side-Notch		5.21***	1.34	6.02***
Faint Side-Notch			3.50**	7.51***
Flared Stem				6.10***
Thickness				
Modal	5.30***	4.47***	0.32	0.28
Deep Side-Notch		0.46	2.12*	2.32
Faint Side-Notch			1.77	1.99
Flared Stem				0.87

* Significant at the .05 level
** Significant at the .01 level
*** Significant at the .001 level

TABLE 43

Hafting Dimensions of Matanzas Point Varieties

	Notch Depth (mm)						Notch Width (mm)					
	Right			Left			Right			Left		
	n	$\bar{x}$	*s*	*n*	$\bar{x}$	*s*	*n*	$\bar{x}$	*s*	*n*	$\bar{x}$	*s*
Modal	162	-1.97	0.74	166	-1.97	0.62	163	8.69	2.94	165	8.41	3.01
Deep Side-Notch	24	-3.08	0.97	25	-2.88	0.83	24	10.87	1.73	25	11.84	5.72
Faint Side-Notch	21	-0.95	0.67	24	-0.96	0.75	21	9.29	2.12	24	9.75	3.03
Flared Stem	15	-2.27	0.59	18	-1.83	0.71	15	12.27	2.25	18	12.28	3.64
Straight Stem	12	-3.00	1.13	10	-2.60	0.97	12	14.83	2.04	10	14.00	3.43

	Proximal Haft Inclination (deg)						Basal Width (mm)		
	Right			Left					
	n	$\bar{x}$	*s*	*n*	$\bar{x}$	*s*	*n*	$\bar{x}$	*s*
Modal	170	37.45	13.97	173	39.57	12.80	155	18.92	2.30
Deep Side-Notch	24	41.12	13.11	25	45.16	10.03	25	21.08	2.43
Faint Side-Notch	25	24.76	14.63	25	31.64	14.40	20	19.95	2.63
Flared Stem	17	23.71	17.54	18	20.67	12.90	16	17.50	2.53
Straight Stem	12	17.25	12.40	12	22.33	18.03	21	22.33	2.31

TABLE 44

Comparisons of Notch Depths of Matanzas Point Varieties
(Student's *t*-Test: 2-Tailed, Pooled Variance -- *t*-Scores)

Variant	Modal	Deep Side-Notched	Faint Side-Notched	Flared Stem	Straight Stem
Modal	-	6.67***	6.10***	1.54	4.52***
Deep Side-Notched	6.62***	-	8.48***	2.89**	0.61
Faint Side-Notched	7.34***	8.61***	-	6.19***	6.66***
Flared Stem	0.90	4.41***	3.82***	-	2.19*
Straight Stem	3.07**	0.87	5.37***	2.44*	-

Right notch comparisons above the diagonal; left notch comparisons below diagonal.
* Significant at the .05 level
** Significant at the .01 level
*** Significant at the .001 level

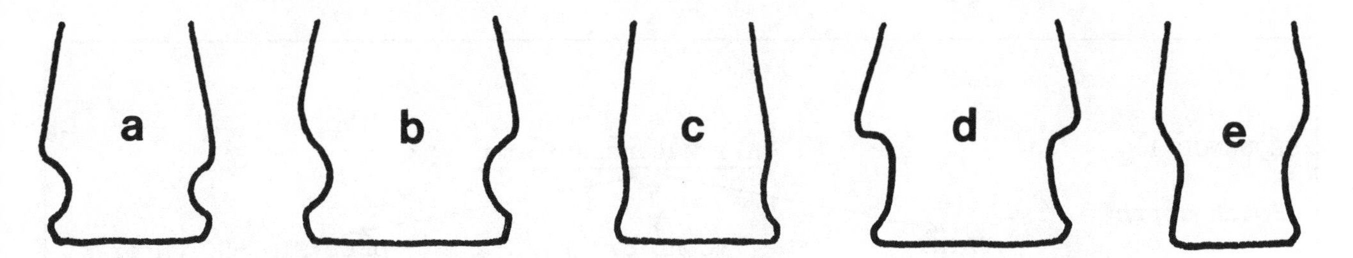

Figure 31. Hafting morphology of Matanzas points. (a) Modal, (b) Deep Side-Notched, (c) Faint Side-Notched, (d) Flared Stem, (e) Straight Stemmed.

the base, 29 (17%) were abraded only in the notches, 20 (11%) were abraded only on the base, and 28 (16%) were not abraded. The base tends to be narrower than the shoulder and varies from slightly concave to slightly convex, although slightly convex (1 mm) predominates as a deviation from a straight base.

The other four varieties of Matanzas points are distinguished by their hafting morphology (see Fig. 31) although, as Table 42 indicates, there are also some differences in width which possibly reflect minor functional differences. If one were to remove the bases from the Matanzas points, it would be very difficult to distinguish among the five varieties. In general, the names of the subtypes are descriptive and Table 43 summarizes some of the measurements in Table 37 for comparative purposes. Upon examining Table 43, it becomes obvious that no single variable will separate the five subtypes. Instead a series of successive sortings will be necessary to key out the various varieties. Upon inspection, there appear to be three ranges of notch depth - Faint Side-Notch at -1.0, Modal and Flared Stem at -2.0, and Deep Side-Notch and Straight Stem at -3.0.

Table 44 presents a series of *t*-tests to ascertain whether notch depth is statistically valid as a sorting variable. Indeed, the results are excellent. The Faint Side-Notch form was different from the four other varieties at the .001 level of probability, while Modal and Flared Stem were not significantly different, nor were Deep Side-Notch and Straight Stem. Other possible comparisons were significantly different at either the .01 or .001 level, except Flared versus Straight Stem, which was different at only the .05 level of probability. Therefore, having assigned a point to the Matanzas point cluster by using the key in Fig. 30, we need to sort first by notch depth. Then, we need some sequential steps to separate Modal and Flared, Deep Side-Notch and Straight Stem, to give us the five varieties, plus an additional test to prevent confusion of Flared and Straight Stemmed forms.

Examining the shapes of the varieties in Figs. 31, 35, 36, 38, and 39, proximal haft inclination should separate Modal from Flared, and Deep Side-Notch from Straight Stem. In addition, proximal haft inclination should separate Flared Stem and Straight Stem. Table 45 presents six *t*-tests to see

TABLE 45

Comparison of Proximal Haft Inclinations for Matanzas Point Varieties (Student's *t*-Test, 2-Tailed, Pooled Variance - *t*-Scores)

Comparison	Right	Left
Modal vs Flared Stem	3.77***	5.96***
Deep Side-Notch vs Straight Stem	5.24***	4.97***
Flared Stem vs Straight Stem	1.09	0.29

*** Significant at the .001 level

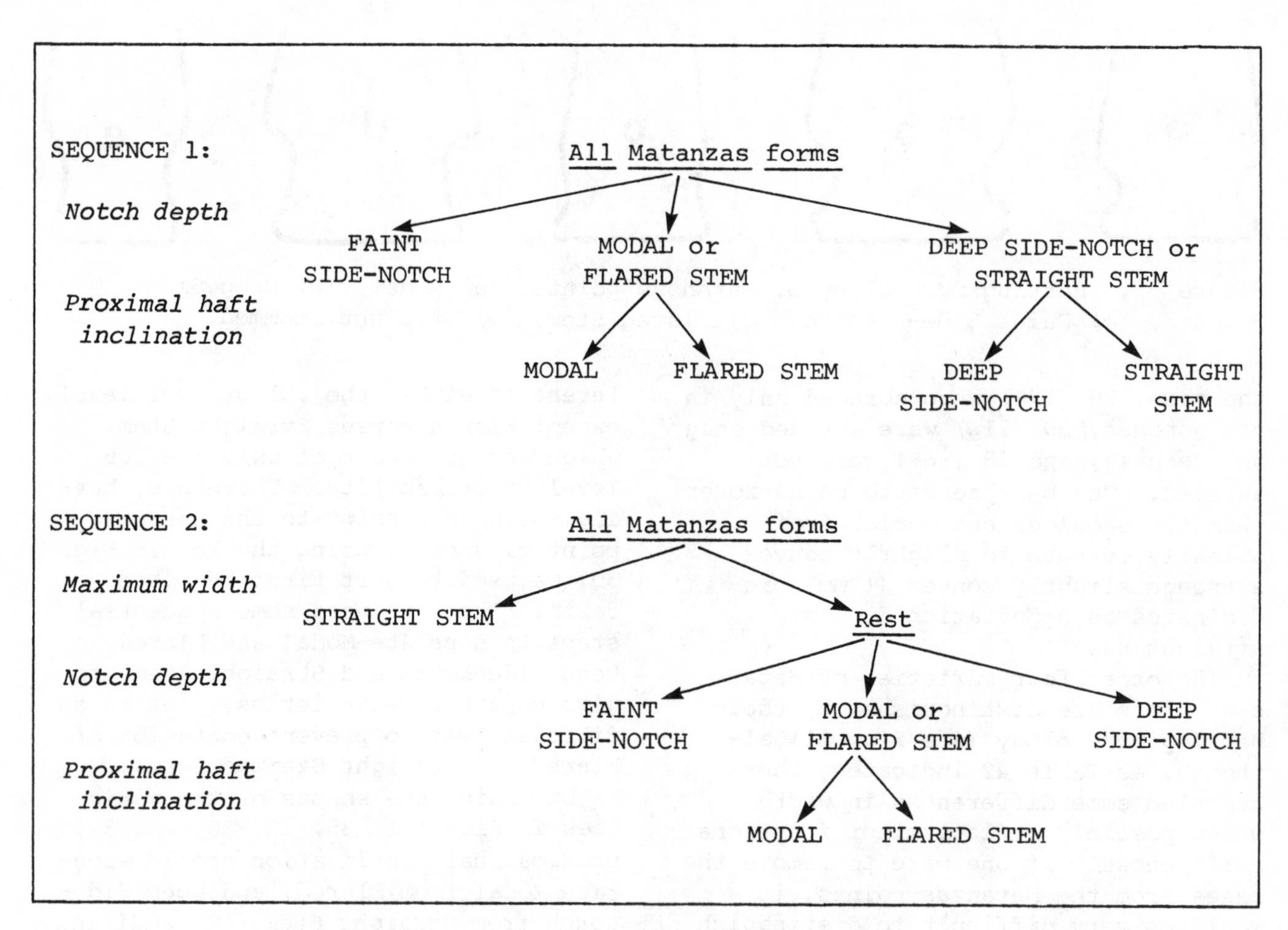

Figure 32. Sorting key for Matanzas point varieties.

if this variable will further subdivide the groups formed by notch depth. Modal and Flared Stem and Deep Side-Notch and Straight Stem were separated at the .001 level of probability, with the mean values separated by approximately one standard deviation or better in the latter case. Unfortunately, Flared Stem and Straight Stem did not separate. In fact, the mean values are separated by less than the 6 deg error of measurement.

This last result reflects upon the problem of quantification of shape differences. While the Flared Stem and Straight Stem forms could be consistently separated by eye, the measurement of the proximal haft inclination could not. In practical terms, I suggest the following: In Table 42, the width of the Straight Stem form is very different from the other Matanzas point varieties. This allows us to separate Flared and Straight Stemmed forms as another step in the keying out process. Also, we have essentially the same stem shape on a narrow blade and a wide blade which makes one group appear to have flared stems and the other straight stems.

The keying procedure for the Matanzas point cluster is presented in Fig. 32 using the following sequence of variables: Sequence 1 - width, notch depth, and proximal haft inclination; Sequence 2 - maximum width, notch depth, and proximal haft inclination. Selection of sequence should be determined by the amount of resharpening in the samples and the number of specimens in which maximum width can be measured.

Varieties. Munson and Harn (1966) present range and mean measurements of Matanzas points from three sites in the Langellier Bottoms, Kerton Township,

Fulton County, Ill. The mean sizes given are similar to those of the Koster sample, but statistical comparisons are not possible. Perino (1968a: Plate 27) illustrates nine Matanzas points which from the drawings would fit into the type as defined here. Houart (1971: Fig. 11) illustrates several points as Helton points but, because the type has already been named, Houart's terminology is no longer being used. Instead, another point type, defined in this appendix, has been given the name Helton point.

Typological Relationships. Matanzas points seem to fit in between unhafted knives and Godar points (or other boldly side-notched points), with the Faint Side-Notched variety sometimes having only the barest trace of hafting modification and the Deep Side-Notched form more or less resembling the Godar point. In the first case, the points may be classified as either knives or preforms and they tend to get buried in functional classifications. In the second case, there is confusion among the various side-notched points called Godar in the lower Illinois Valley region.

Godar Points (Fig. 40)

Godar points were named by Perino (1963:95) for the Godar site, Calhoun County, Ill.

Sample Size. The Koster sample from the 1969, 1970, and 1971 field seasons includes 34 Godar points: 12 complete, 5 reworked into end scrapers, and 17 in fragmentary form. Table 37 lists the measurements and Table 46 summarizes the length, width, thickness, and weight.

Description. Perino (1971a:38) describes the points from the Godar site as medium-sized, broad dart points with parallel sides, and notches as wide as deep and squared to round. "Stems are short and as wide, at the base, as the shoulders." Montet-White refers to these very same objects as Black Sand Side-Notched (1968:99-100), although these now seem to be related to the Helton phase rather than the Black Sand Culture, an Early Woodland manifestation.

For the Koster sample, starting with the manufacturing trajectory, heat treatment occurs about one-fourth the time (9 of 34 examples) when the object is in the flake stage before shaping flakes are removed. Of the 14 complete blades, 6 have primary flake scars on one side. In contrast to the surviving primary flake scars on the Matanzas and Karnak Stemmed points, the surviving portions on Godar points tend to be relatively broad and slightly concave, usually coming very close to one edge of the blade. The shaping flakes tend to be rather broad and shallow, extending from one-third of the way to almost completely across the blade. These shaping flake scars tend to be perpendicular to the axis of the blade and parallel to one another. They are similar to those found on Karnak Stemmed and Matanzas points except that they tend to be broader.

The edges of the blade follow a parallel-sided form which tapers in a full curve toward an obtuse angle at the point. As the blade is reworked, the characteristic broad blade tapers down into a triangular, relatively thick form. The edges of the blades tend to be carefully retouched with nearly continuous, minute flake scars, such that 9 of the 14 complete blades have well-made serrated edges. There is no central ridge line, the shaping flake scars being very shallow and extending to various distances across the blade.

Turning to the hafting element, we find that the parallel sides of the Godar blade continue beyond the side notch, leaving a parallel-sided to slightly contracting stem. As for abrasion on the bases and stems, 21 are ground in the notches and on the base. Of these 21, 18 are also ground along the sides of the stem between the side notches and the base. Only the notches are ground on 5 specimens and 8 indicate no abrasion at all.

TABLE 46

Comparison of Dimensions of Godar-like Points at Modoc Rock Shelter and Koster Site

	Length (mm)			Width (mm)			Thickness (mm)		
	n	$\bar{x}$	*s*	*n*	$\bar{x}$	*s*	*n*	$\bar{x}$	*s*
Modoc: Side-Notched	48	43	9	48	26	6	48	8	1
Koster: Godar	15	52.07	10.55	33	27.39	3.38	33	8.15	1.16

Student's *t*-test, 2-tailed, pooled variance: *t*-scores

Comparison	Length	Width	Thickness
Modoc vs Koster	3.35**	1.20	0.28

** Significant at the .01 level

Varieties. The lack of published measurements of Godar points from other sites in the lower Illinois Valley hampers any discussion of the relationship between the Koster sample and materials from Godar site, Gibson site, etc.

Typological Relationships. There are a large number of named point types which overlap with the Godar morphology. In the Midwest, there are Raddatz, Hemphill, Osceola, Graham Cave, Black Sand, Madison, Big Sandy, and a side-notched category from Modoc Rock Shelter. Comparisons between these various point types is hampered by the lack of description of manufacturing stages, the failure to remark on heat treatment, and the lack of published measurements which can be statiscally manipulated. Fowler's Modoc Rock Shelter report (1959b:App. III) presents the mean length, width, and thickness plus the standard deviation in millimeters for side-notched points which he labels as Raddatz Notched. Unfortunately, his Table 16 which presents these measurements does not include sample size. His Figure 20 indicates a total sample of 60 side-notched or Raddatz points. But his Table 18 indicates that only 48 side-notched points have all three dimensions measured. Assuming that this smaller sample size was used in his Table 16, my Table 46 compares the Modoc Rock Shelter sample of Raddatz points with the Koster sample of Godar points.

Except for a significant difference in length, these two samples could be of the same point type in terms of overall size. Unfortunately, Fowler's illustrations (Fig. 9F) suggest that he has included Matanzas points with the Raddatz-like points. Visual comparisons between the point cluster means in Table 42 and the Godar point means in Table 46 suggest that length and thickness for these two point types are very similar, but that width is different enough to have non-overlapping standard deviations (Student's *t*-test, 2-tailed, pooled variance for width gives a *t*-value of 15.55 which is significant at the .001 probability level). Therefore, in addition to the shape differences in the hafting elements of the Godar and Matanzas points, width is an excellent variable to separate these two types, as indicated in Fig. 30.

Helton Points (Figs. 41, 44)

These points are named for Harlin Helton, a landowner in Greene County, Ill. Use of this name supersedes Houart's (1971) application of the name to points now subsumed within the Matanzas point cluster. Helton points, as currently defined, are not synonomous with Matanzas points.

Sample Size. There are 10 specimens from Koster 1969-1971 of which 5 are complete and the rest virtually so.

Description. They are a wide-bladed form with perpendicular barbs, expanding stem, and a convex base. Metrics are tabulated in Table 37. Six of the points are definitely heat-treated, one may be heat-treated, and three are not. The blade shape is between a rounded triangle and a pointed parabola with the greatest width always occurring at the barbs. The blades have no central ridge line as the shaping flakes are shallow and occasionally extend across the blade; every point has at least one flake scar greater than 1.5 cm long and 1.0 cm wide. Primary flake scars occur on only one point. As with the Karnak Stemmed form, the surfaces of the point are very smooth and even. The blade edges are extensively retouched with short nibbling flakes which produce a smooth and even outline. In cross section the blade is a flattened lozenge with a sharp scallop on both sides of the edge.

Examining the blade edge on, one finds only slight undulation to the blade edge (amplitude of 1 to 3 mm). Regarding resharpening, the points seem to have undergone a series of reworkings of the blade which both shortened the axial length and removed the characteristic pendulant barbs. Reworking also seems to be asymmetrical, so that four points have one large barb and one small, reworked barb. Wear patterns include only two blades with light abrasion along the entire length of both edges.

The barbs are formed by only a few flake scars and then, in six cases, abraded inside the barb and down the tang element. Of these six, three are also basally ground. The stem tends to flare outward to either square or slightly rounded corners. The base is convex and well thinned, although not fluted.

Table 47 summarizes the dimensions of the 10 Helton points.

TABLE 47

Dimensions (in mm) of Helton Points, Koster Site, Helton Phase

	Length	Width	Thickness
Mean	61.6	30.8	8.2
Std. dev.	6.4	4.1	0.8
Sample size	10	10	10

Apple Blossom Stemmed Points (Fig. 42)

These points were named for the Apple Blossom Tavern, Calhoun County, Ill.

Sample Size. Twenty-one specimens were excavated from Koster 1969-1971. Four were complete, three have complete blades, four have been reworked into endscrapers, and the remaining ten are little more than snapped-off stems. Table 48 summarizes the dimensions of these 21 Apple Blossom Stemmed points.

Description. These points are smaller than Matanzas points, somewhat thinner, and have an expanding- to parallel-sided stem. The seven complete blades are parabolic in shape, being nearly parallel-sided at the haft junction but becoming increasingly curved towards the tip. As the point is reworked, the curve is not worked back to the shoulder but merely far enough to produce a new point for the blade. Hence a break develops in the smooth curve where the new and old curves come together. In cross section the points are very thin and, in fact,

TABLE 48

Dimensions (in mm) of Apple Blossom Stemmed Points, Koster Site, Helton Phase

	Length	Width	Thickness
Mean	44.3	24.2	7.0
Std. dev.	8.3	2.4	1.0
Sample size	7	20	20

Student's *t*-test, 1-tailed, pooled variance:

Apple Blossom Thinner Than	*t*-Score
Etley	11.15***
Flared Stem Matanzas	2.94**
Helton	2.91**
Karnak Stemmed	12.56***
Straight Stem Matanzas	2.55*

* Significant at the .01 level
** Significant at the .005 level
*** Significant at the .0005 level

assuming that the Apple Blossom point is usually thinner than the other stemmed forms, a 1-tailed *t*-test indicates that Apple Blossom points are significantly thinner than Helton points, Etley points, Straight Stemmed Matanzas points, Flared Stem Matanzas points, and Karnak Stemmed points. These *t*-scores are listed in Table 48.

The retouch flaking is well done, with a high frequency of parallel flake scars about 3- to 6-mm wide which tend to travel at least to the midpoint of the blade. The central ridge line is not apparent, especially on the six heat-treated examples. Primary flake scars have been removed on all examples. In cross section, the blades tend to be asymmetrical with one side a more rounded curve than the other, although both sides are rather flat. Edge retouch is discontinuous and done with very small flakes. No edges show abrasion.

As for the hafting element, the point approaches a barbed form with the proximal angle of the blade, but the junction of the blade to the hafting element is neither sharp nor abrupt but somewhat rounded. The stem has straight sides which diverge slightly outward toward the base, which tends to be slightly convex (straight to 2-mm convex). Of the 19 examples with virtually complete stems, 3 are lightly abraded on the base and sides, 7 on the sides only, 1 on the base only, and 8 are unabraded.

Brannon Side-Notched Points (Fig. 43)

These points are named for J. Brannon, Greene County, Ill.

Sample Size. Fifteen points of this type were excavated from Koster site, 1969-1971. One is complete, 2 have been reworked into end scrapers, 1 has burin blows along both sides of the edges where the blade has been snapped off, and the remaining 11 are in various fragmentary states.

Description. The Brannon Side-Notched point is a small to medium form similar to the Godar point in general shape yet smaller, especially in terms of the side notches. Heat treatment is common, as 9 of the 15 are definitely heat-treated. None of the heat-treated points give any indication of the surface morphology of the primary flake.

Of the six complete and nearly complete blades, the sides tend to be a continuously increasing curve, i.e., they start as parallel-sided at the notch and become quite curved near the tip. The blade shape is different from the Godar point which is parallel-sided along much of the blade. One of the complete blades has a very large primary flake scar which forms a shallow basin across almost the entire surface of the blade. The thinning flakes tend to be long, thin, and subparallel, usually at right angles to the edges. The

TABLE 49

Dimensions (in mm) of Brannon Side-Notched Points, Koster Site, Helton Phase

	Length	Width	Thickness
Mean	35.25	21.80	7.24
Std. dev.	11.07	3.71	0.75
Sample size	12	15	15

midline is often obscured because of the shallowness of the flakes. The edges show discontinuous retouch and a lack of serrated edges. Two blades have heavily abraded edges and others no abrasion at all.

The side notches are shallow, U-shaped to rather square, and tend to be set at right angles to the long axis of the point. The notch is not cut into a straight lateral edge, like many Godar points, but into the contracting portion of the preform. Examining the stems, we find 12 are abraded on the base, or the sides of the stem, and in the notches, while 3 show no sign of abrasion. Table 49 summarizes the length, width, and thickness of these 15 points, using the information in Table 37.

Typological Relationships. A Student's *t*-test was performed to determine if the width and depth of the side notch were valid measurements to separate these Brannon points from the Godar points recovered at Koster site. Table 50 presents the comparisons, indicating that the differences in notch width are a very significant difference, while differences in notch depth

TABLE 50

Comparison of Dimensions of Brannon and Godar Points at Koster Site

	Notch Depth (mm)						Notch Width (mm)					
	Right			Left			Right			Left		
	n	$\bar{x}$	s	n	$\bar{x}$	s	n	$\bar{x}$	s	n	$\bar{x}$	s
Brannon	12	-2.50	0.90	12	-2.25	0.62	12	5.67	1.07	12	6.42	0.90
Godar	33	-3.67	1.22	34	-3.47	1.13	31	8.64	1.64	32	8.88	1.72

Student's *t*-test, 2-tailed, pooled variance: *t*-scores

Comparison	Width	Depth
Right side:		
Brannon vs Godar	5.82***	3.04**
Left side:		
Brannon vs Godar	4.71***	3.56***

** Significant at the .01 level
*** Significant at the .001 level

are not quite as pronounced.

OTHER TYPES
(Fig. 44)

In addition to the points assigned to the named types listed above, there remains a residuum of untyped points, that is, shapes whose frequency of occurrence at Koster did not permit the defining of a cluster of similarly shaped or made forms. Subsequent excavations at Koster site since 1971 have greatly increased the total sample of projectile points, and it is hoped that this enlarged sample will permit the identification of new types and refinement of old ones.

Appendix B

Provenience Units Used in This Study

TABLE 51

Titterington Component Provenience Units, 1969 and 1970

Arbitrary Excavation Units:

Square	Level	Square	Level
2*	06-09	42	06-07
7*	16-18	43	09-13
8*	10-15	47	04-07
16	13-15	49	07-11
18	15-17	53	09B-10
21	15-20	54	09-11
35	05	55	07-09
36	07	56	06-07
39	09-11	57	03-09
40	03	74	12-18
41	04-06	75	11-13

Features:**

113	Refuse pit
168	Refuse pit
286	Layered shell and limestone in a hearth
298	Refuse pit
313	Naturally filled pit
604	Shell concentration

*Assigned by Houart (1971) to the Titterington component on slightly different criteria.
**Preliminary categories by Renata B. Wolynec.

TABLE 52

Helton Component Provenience Units (Horizon 6 Middle), 1970

Arbitrary Excavation Units:

Square	Level	Square	Level
2-5	101-104	44	11-18
8	38	45	07-17A
10	20-32	46	05-16
13	29-38	47	16-24
14	26-37	48	11-23
15	22-29	49	12-20
16	18-24	50	17-21
17	26-29	51	16-22
18	20-25	52	15-28
19	17-24	53	16-28
20	21-27	54	15-29
21	26-36	55	13-26
22	28-32	56	16-28
23	13A-20	57	11-20
24	15-27	58	09-17
26	07-13	59	05-15
29	06-10	60	09-17
30	10-15	61	10-16
31	10-22	62	08-12
32	11-20	64	03-05
33	09-16	65	03-14
34	10-15	66	02-07
35	09-14	67	03-11
36	09-20	68	03-11
37	18-24	70	02A-03A
38	09-14	71	01A-09A
39	18-24	72	02A-11A
40	08-16	73	01A-08A
41	09-16	74	22-27
42	17-25	76	13-17
43	17-23	77	09-17

TABLE 52 (continued)

Features:			
100	174	506	573a-c
101	175a	507a-e	575a
107	176a	508	579a
108a-d	177a-c	509	583a
109a	178	510a-b	585a
110a-b	182a-b	511	586
111	183a-b	512a	600a-b
112a-b	187a	513a	601a
114a-b	193a-b	514a	602a
115	194a	515	605
116a-b	197	516a	609
117a-d	198a-i	519a	610a-b
118a-b	199a-e	521a	611
119a-b	203a	522a	612
120a	204	523a-d	613
"126"	205a-e	524a-b	614
127a-d	206a-d	525a	615
128a	208a-b	526a-b	616
130	210a-e	528a	617
131	211a	529a-c	618
132	219a	530a-b	619a-b
133	220	531a,c	620
135a-b	227	533a	621
136	228	538a	622
137a-b	229	539a	623
141a-b	231a	540a	624
142	232a	542b-c	625a
143a	233a-e	544a	626
144a	241	545a-b	627
145a-b	245a	547a	628
147	251a	548b	629
149	253	549a	630
150	254	551a	631
153	255a-f	553a	632
154a-b	257	554a	633
157a	267a-b	557a	635a
160	268a-c	558a-b	636a-b
161a-b	270a	561a-b	637
162a-c	278a-c	562b	638a-b
163	279a-c	563a	639
165	281a	(Bur 4)	640
167a-b	500a-h	564a-c	641
169	501a-c	567a	642
170	502	569a	643
171	503	570a	644
172	504	571a-d	645
173	505	572a	646

TABLE 52 (continued)

Features:			
647	682	722	806
648	685	723	807
649	686	724	808
650	687	725a	809
651	688	726a	810
652	689	727a-b	813a
653	690	728	(Bur 8)
654	691	730	814
655	692	732	817
657a-d	693	733	818
658	694	734	819
659	695	735	820
660	696	736	821
661	697	737	822a
662	698	738	823a
663a-b	699	742	824a
664	(Bur 10)	743a,	826a-c
665	700a-b	d,f-k	(Bur 12)
666	702	744	829
667	703	747	830
668	704	748a-b	831
669	705	749	832
670	706	750	833
671	708	760	834
672	711a-b	761	835
673	712	763	836
(Bur 9)	713	771	840a
674	714	788a-c,f	841
675	715a-c	800a	842
676	716a-c	(Bur 7)	843
678	717	801	844
679	718	802	845
680	719	804a,c	846
681	721a	805	847

TABLE 53

Helton Component Provenience Units
(Horizon 6 Lower), 1970

Arbitrary Excavation Units:

Square	Level	Square	Level
8	40-41	38	16-20
10	34-39	39	26-30
13	41	40	17
14	38-41	41	19-22
15	32-33	42	29-32
16	27-32	43	29
18	29-30	44	22
20	29-30	45	18
21	38	46	19
22	38-41B	47	27-28
23	23-24	48	29
24	31-33	50	24-27
26	16	51	23-25
29	17-20	52	29-30
30	26-33	61	18-22
31	24-27	64	10
32	22-23	66	11-13
33	19-22	70	12A-13A
35	19	72	14A-15A
36	20	76	19-22
37	26	77	18-19

Features:

138	236	293	783	904
140	237a-b	299a-b	784	905c
151a-e	238	318	785	906
159a	240	574a-c	795	907
181	248a-b	575	796	908
184	271	576	797	909
185	272a-e	578a	798a	910a-b
186	273a	579	799	911
188a	274a	580a	812	912
191	275a	581a	815	913
207a	276a	750	816	914
214	277a	754	827	915
217	280a	757	828	915b
223a	284a	766	839a	918
224	290	767	(Bur 15)	921
225	291a-b	768	900	925
235	292	778	900a	

Appendix C

Titterington Phase Faunal Materials from Koster, 1970: Preliminary Tabulations, by Frederick C. Hill

TABLE 54

Flotation-Recovered Animal Remains from Horizon 4

	Features				Excavation Units							
	No. of Elem.	Min. No.	Min. % of Class	Min. % of All	No. of Elem.	Min. No.	Min. % of Class	Min. % of All	No. of Elem.	Min. No.	Min. % of Class	Min. % of All
Mammals:												
Scalopus aquaticus, eastern mole	-	-	-	-	1	1	100.00	50.00	1	1	100.00	12.50
Indeterminate	1	-	-	-	-	-	-	-	1	-	-	-
Amphibians:												
Rana sp., frogs	1	1	100.00	14.29	-	-	-	-	1	1	100.00	12.50
Fish:												
Ameiurus sp., bullheads	3	2	40.00	28.57	-	-	-	-	3	2	40.00	25.00
Lepisosteus sp., gars	2	1	20.00	14.29	3	1	100.00	50.00	5	1	20.00	12.50
Centrarchidae, sunfishes	1	1	20.00	14.29	-	-	-	-	1	1	20.00	12.50
Ictalurus sp., catfishes	1	1	20.00	14.29	-	-	-	-	1	1	20.00	12.50
Indeterminate	2	-	-	-	-	-	-	-	2	-	-	-
Indeter. vertebrates:	3	-	-	-	-	-	-	-	3	-	-	-
Mussels:												
Lasmigona complanta, white heel-splitter	1	1	100.00	14.29	-	-	-	-	1	1	100.00	12.50
TOTAL	15	7	-	100.02	4	2	-	100.00	19	8	-	100.00

TABLE 55

Screen-Recovered Animal Remains from Horizon 4

	Features				Excavation Units				All Units			
	No. of Elem.	Min. No.	Min. % of Class	Min. % of All	No. of Elem.	Min. No.	Min. % of Class	Min. % of All	No. of Elem.	Min. No.	Min. % of Class	Min. % of All
Mammals:												
Odocoileus virginianus, white-tailed deer	7	2	66.67	1.89	60	3	37.50	12.50	67	3	33.33	2.46
Procyon lotor, raccoon	1	1	33.33	0.94	3	1	12.50	4.17	4	2	22.22	1.64
Scalopus aquaticus, eastern mole	-	-	-	-	2	2	25.00	8.33	2	2	22.22	1.64
Canis sp., dogs	-	-	-	-	2	1	12.50	4.17	2	1	11.11	0.82
Geomys bursarius, plains pocket gopher	-	-	-	-	1	1	12.50	4.17	1	1	11.11	0.82
Indeterminate	30	-	-	-	333	-	-	-	363	-	-	-
Birds:												
Meleagris gallopavo, turkey	-	-	-	-	1	1	33.33	4.17	1	1	25.00	0.82
Branta canadensis, Canada goose	-	-	-	-	1	1	33.33	4.17	1	1	25.00	0.82
Anas carolinensis, green-winged teal	-	-	-	-	1	1	33.33	4.17	1	1	25.00	0.82
Chen sp., snow or blue goose	1	1	100.00	0.94	-	-	-	-	1	1	25.00	0.82
Indeterminate	32	-	-	-	10	-	-	-	42	-	-	-
Reptiles:												
Terrapene sp., box turtles	-	-	-	-	12	2	50.00	8.33	12	2	50.00	1.64
Trionyx sp., softshell turtles	2	1	100.00	0.94	1	1	25.00	4.17	3	1	25.00	0.82
Pseudemys sp., sliders, or *Graptemys* sp., map turtles	-	-	-	-	1	1	25.00	4.17	1	1	25.00	0.82
Indeterminate turtle	2	-	-	-	21	-	-	-	23	-	-	-
Fish:												
Aplodinotus grunniens, freshwater drum	4	3	37.50	2.83	3	2	50.00	8.33	7	5	45.45	4.10
Ictalurus sp., catfishes	2	2	25.00	1.89	1	1	25.00	4.17	3	2	18.18	1.64
Ictiobus sp., buffalos	1	1	12.50	0.94	2	1	25.00	4.17	3	2	18.18	1.64
Ameiurus sp., bullheads	1	1	12.50	0.94	-	-	-	-	1	1	9.09	0.82
Centrarchidae, sunfishes	1	1	12.50	0.94	-	-	-	-	1	1	9.09	0.82
Indeterminate	51	-	-	-	16	-	-	-	67	-	-	-
Indeter. vertebrates:	17	-	-	-	-	-	-	-	17	-	-	-
Mussels:												
Amblema plicata, blue-point	113	56	60.22	52.83	1	1	20.00	4.17	114	56	59.57	45.90
Lampsilis a. fallaciosa, slough sand-shell	22	14	15.05	13.21	1	1	20.00	4.17	23	14	14.89	11.48
Proptera alata = Potamilus alatus, pink heel-splitter	8	5	5.38	4.72	1	1	20.00	4.17	9	5	5.32	4.10
Quadrula quadrula, maple-leaf	7	4	4.30	3.77	-	-	-	-	7	4	4.26	3.28
Megalonaias gigantea, washboard	5	4	4.30	3.77	-	-	-	-	5	4	4.26	3.28
Uniomeras tetralasmus, pond-horn	3	2	2.16	1.89	-	-	-	-	3	2	2.13	1.64
Fusconaia flava undata, pig-toe	2	2	2.16	1.89	-	-	-	-	2	2	2.13	1.64
Leptodea sp., fragile paper shell	1	1	1.08	0.94	1	1	20.00	4.17	2	1	1.06	0.82
Anodonta corpulenta, stout floater	-	-	-	-	1	1	20.00	4.17	1	1	1.06	0.82
Quadrula pustulosa, pimple-back	1	1	1.08	0.94	-	-	-	-	1	1	1.06	0.82
Actinonaias ligumentina, mucket	1	1	1.08	0.94	-	-	-	-	1	1	1.06	0.82
Ligumia recta, black sand-shell	1	1	1.08	0.94	-	-	-	-	1	1	1.06	0.82
Quadrula nodulata, warty-back	1	1	1.08	0.94	-	-	-	-	1	1	1.06	0.82
Arcidens confragosus, rock pocketbook	1	1	1.08	0.94	-	-	-	-	1	1	1.06	0.82
Indeterminate	1534	-	-	-	85	-	-	-	1619	-	-	-
TOTAL	1852	106	-	99.97	561	24	-	100.04	2412	122	-	100.02

Appendix D

Koster Core Weights

Weight Class, decagrams	Titter-ington	Helton Middle 6		Helton Lower 6	
	NHT	NHT	HT	NHT	HT
0.0- 0.9	-	15	3	-	-
1.0- 1.9	1	79	15	5	1
2.0- 2.9	2	143	24	12	2
3.0- 3.9	3	133	14	6	2
4.0- 4.9	3	153	20	7	3
5.0- 5.9	12	106	9	11	2
6.0- 6.9	3	95	13	3	2
7.0- 7.9	5	85	15	6	-
8.0- 8.9	4	68	8	5	-
9.0- 9.9	1	59	8	3	1
10.0-10.9	1	45	4	1	-
11.0-11.9	4	37	5	4	1
12.0-12.9	5	32	3	3	-
13.0-13.9	2	29	3	2	1
14.0-14.9	1	16	4	-	-
15.0-15.9	-	15	2	1	-
16.0-16.9	-	18	2	1	-
17.0-17.9	-	12	-	4	-
18.0-18.9	2	15	2	-	-
19.0-19.9	-	9	-	-	-
20.0-20.9	1	7	2	-	-
21.0-21.9	-	3	1	-	-
22.0-22.9	-	4	-	-	-
23.0-23.9	-	10	-	1	-
24.0-24.9	-	1	-	-	-
25.0-25.9	-	8	-	-	-
26.0-26.9	-	4	1	-	-
27.0-27.9	-	2	-	-	-
28.0-28.9	-	3	1	-	-
29.0-29.9	-	4	1	-	-
30.0-39.9	1	12	-	3	-
40.0-49.9	2	2	-	1	-
50.0-59.9	-	1	-	1	-
60.0+	-	1	-	-	-
Total	53	1226	160	80	15

HT = heat-treated
NHT = non-heat-treated

Appendix E

Helton Phase Human Skeletal Materials from Koster, 1970: Preliminary Analysis, by Jane E. Buikstra

TABLE 56

Distribution of Koster Helton Phase Skeletal Materials by Age and Sex

Age Group	Male	Female	Unknown
Adults			
50+	2	1	-
40-49	1	0	-
30-39	0	0	-
20-29	1	0	-
Total	4	1	0
Sub-Adults			
10-20	-	-	6
3-9 (children)	-	-	1
0-3 (infants)	-	-	0
Total	0	0	7
Grand Total:	12		

JANE E. BUIKSTRA (personal communication), who analyzed the mortuary sample, compared it with a "typical graveyard population":

> Given the small sample, these comments can, at best, be termed subjective. However, one striking fact is the over-representation of adolescents in this burial series. My impression is that this age grade is one of those least likely to be represented in a graveyard, second only to children 6-12 years of age. Such a configuration, if one were speaking of a single population in a closed unit of time, would suggest either an epidemic or special selection for burial (or non-burial) in the habitation area.
>
> Males are also over-represented in terms of the total series, more so if one adds the fact that at least one of the adolescents is a male. This also speaks of selection in burial practices, but the basis for this selection remains obscure.

Appendix F

Lower Illinois Valley Surface Survey Records for Helton and Titterington Phase Projectile Points

Site	RIQS No.	Tit.		Helton				PH
		E	S	K	M	G	O	
Albert's Hog Ridge	14		2		1			VM
Anthony's Garden	18						1	VM
Audrey	581		1		1			VM
Baytown	28		1					VM
Beach	29	3	2		1			SV
Bear Bridge	31			1				SV
Becker's Ridge	32			2				SV
Benear School	35		1					SV
Benz	38		1					SV
Berry	44					1		SV
Bessie	45		1					SV
Big Bear	47						1	SV
Big Swan School	49				2	1		IF
Bixby East	52		1					VM
Blackburn South	58					2		IF
Blackerby	10	9	6		2	1		VM
Bloomfield	1				2			IF
Bloomsand	59					1		IF
Blue Creek	60		1					SV
Boker	64	2	1		1			SV
Boston-Witwer	592					1		VM
Britten	70				1	2		IF
Brownie Bickers N	74	1						IF
Brownie Bickers S	75		1					IF
Burline	80		1		1			IF
W. G. Chase	95	1			1			IF
Cheney	98					1		IF
Chism	100	2						SV
Ciesler	104					2		VM
Cindy	600				1			VM
Claypool	105				2	1		VM

E = Etley (RIQS Cat. #107)
S = Sedalia-Nebo Hill-Wadlow (#108)
K = Karnak Stemmed (#109)
M = Matanzas (#110)
G = Godar-Raddatz-Faulkner (#111)
O = Osceola (#112)
PH = Physiography
IF = Illinois floodplain
VM = Illinois Valley margin
SV = Secondary valley

Site	RIQS No.	Tit.		Helton				PH
		E	S	K	M	G	O	
Clemmons	602		11					SV
Clouds	603		1					SV
Clytus	107					1		VM
Cole Creek	108					1		VM
Crib	110		1	1				SV
Cypress Land	117		2		1	1		IF
David	611		1					SV
Dependahl	126				1			SV
Devening	127				2			IF
Dolen (N Field)	130				1	1		IF
Dolen (S Field)	131		1		1		2	IF
Duncan Farm	136					1		VM
Elbus	145					1		IF
Ellen	621				1			VM
Flautt	182	1				1		SV
Friendly Lady	186	1						IF
Golden Eagle	169	1	1		1			VM
Gordon	171		1					SV
Gourley	172		2					VM
Guy Sager	203		1					VM
Hamlin	633		1					SV
Hardin School	213		1			1		VM
Hazelwonder	220				1	1		VM
Hillig	232		1			1		SV
Hillview Road	639				1			VM
Hobson	236					2		VM
Holt	640					1		SV
Hoover Brothers	239					6		VM
Howard	241		3		1	10		IF
Hubbard	242	1						SV
Hurricane Creek	245					3		IF
Hurt	246						1	SV
Ila Tash	251					1		IF
Ingersol	253	1	1					SV
Janus	642				1			SV
John Brown	263					2		IF
Kamp	268					1		VM
Kiel	4			1		1		VM
Killebrew	646		1					SV
Killian	272	1			1			SV
Kleinschmidt	648				1	2		IF
Koster	277							VM

Site	RIQS No.	Tit.		Helton				PH
		E	S	K	M	G	O	
Kramer	281				1			SV
Kraut	283		1					VM
Krems	284					1		SV
Krueger	285				1			SV
Krusa	286		4					IF
Laehr	288				1			VM
Landers	292				1			SV
Lesmore	653		1					SV
Levis	302					1		VM
Logan	310		1			1		VM
Loraine	313					1		IF
Loren	656		3					SV
Loy	585					1		SV
Macoupin	5		1					IF
Mauvaise Terre	331		2		1	1		VM
McEver's Creek	339		2					VM
Meisenbach	344						1	IF
Meredosia	345	1			1			IF
Merrigan	347	1			3	1		VM
Merriman	348				1			SV
Morgan	365	3					1	VM
Morgan Slough	366					1		IF
Mound House North	368	1	21	2	2	1		IF
Mud Run	2	1						SV
Oraland	382				1			VM
Oxville	386		1		1			VM
Paul	667				1			VM
Perry	396				1	1		VM
Power Station	410		1			2		SV
Pudy	668			1				VM
Raisin	669		1					SV
Rapp	416					1		VM
Rimbey	431	1	1		2			SV
Rock Island	435				1			IF
Rose	440					1		SV
Russell	676				2			VM
Schallenberg	458					1		VM
Schild-Hilltop	460		1			2		VM
Schnepf	461	2	1	1	2	1		SV
Scott	465		2		1			SV
Shafer	467		1					IF
Shepard	470		1					SV
Shearl	471				1		1	IF
Silver Towers	475		1			1		IF
Sims	476					1	1	VM
Six	477				1			VM
Sowers Mound Group	487		1					VM
Springer	489			1	1			VM
Stamps	493		1					SV
Stark	495		1					SV
Sterling	689		1					SV
Stilwell II	499				1		1	VM
Storm	690			3				SV
Strang	501		2		2	1		SV
Swartz-Florence	508	1						VM
Thaway	694				1	1		VM
Titus	517	1	1			1		SV
Upper Macoupin	528	1	2					SV
Valley Farm	529		1					SV
Vaughn	6	1	5					VM
Vetter	536		1					VM
Vosseler Cribs	542		3					IF
Wabash	543					1		SV
Walnut Creek	548					1		IF
Wendell Freeman	558					1		IF
William	564		1					IF

Appendix G

Koster Artifact Illustrations

Figure 33. *a,b,* Sedalia points. *c,d,* Wadlow Blades. *e-h,* Etley Barbed points. (Titterington phase.) ⟶

a
b
c
d
f
e
CM
g
h

Figure 34. Karnak Stemmed points. (Helton phase.)

Figure 35. Matanzas points. (Helton phase.)

Figure 36. Deep Side-Notched Matanzas points. (Helton phase.)

Figure 37. Faint Side-Notched Matanzas points. (Helton phase.)

Figure 38. Straight Stemmed Matanzas points. (Helton phase.)

Figure 39. Flared Stem Matanzas points. (Helton phase.)

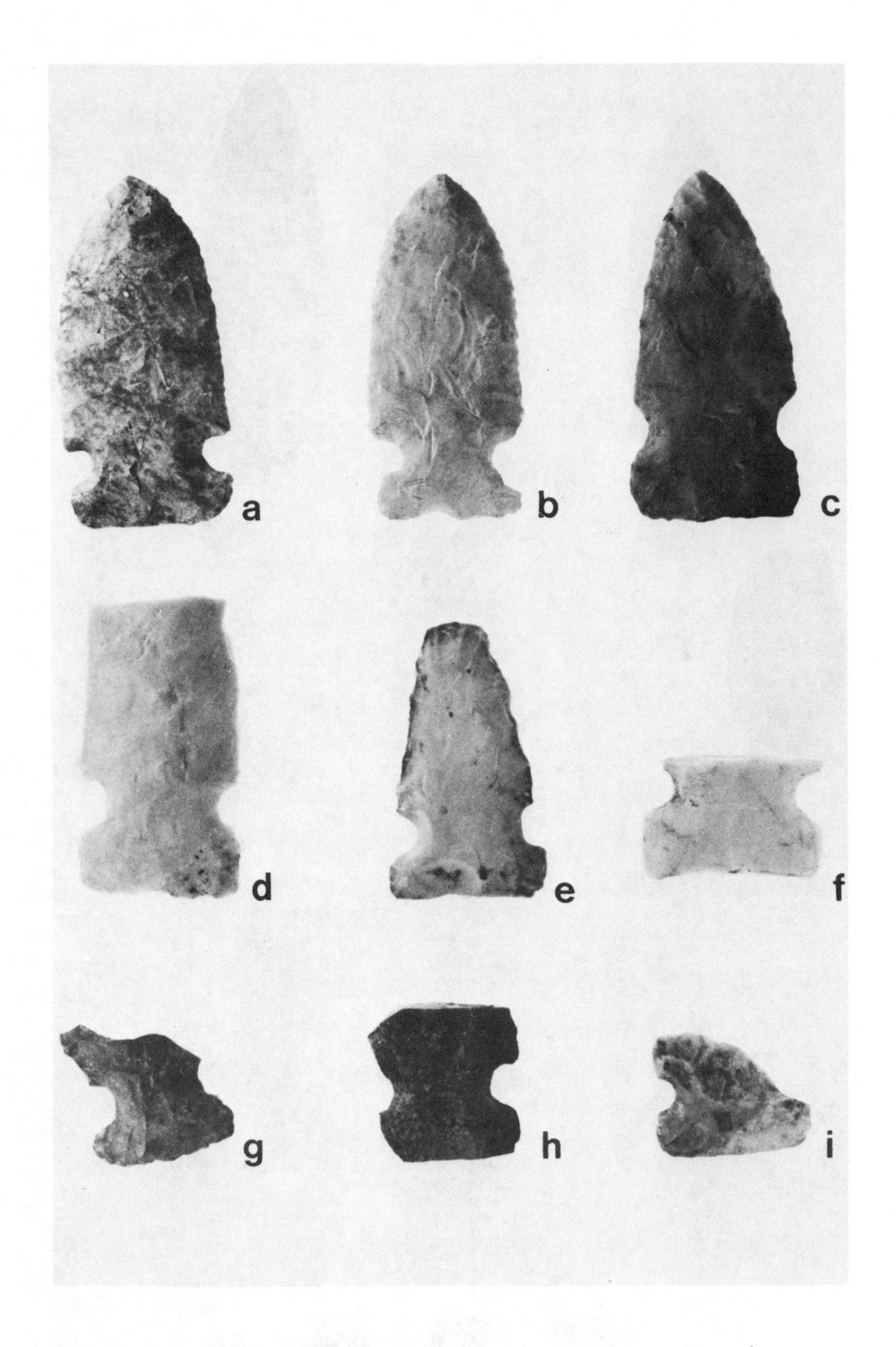

Figure 40. Godar Side-Notched points. (Helton phase.)

Figure 41. Helton points illustrating degrees of resharpening or reworking. (Helton phase.) *Scale in cm.*

Figure 42. Apple Blossom Stemmed points. (Helton phase.)

Figure 43. Brannon Side-Notched points. (Helton phase.)

Figure 44. *a*, Helton point. *b,c,* Side-notched points with basal thinning. *d-f*, knives. (Helton phase.)

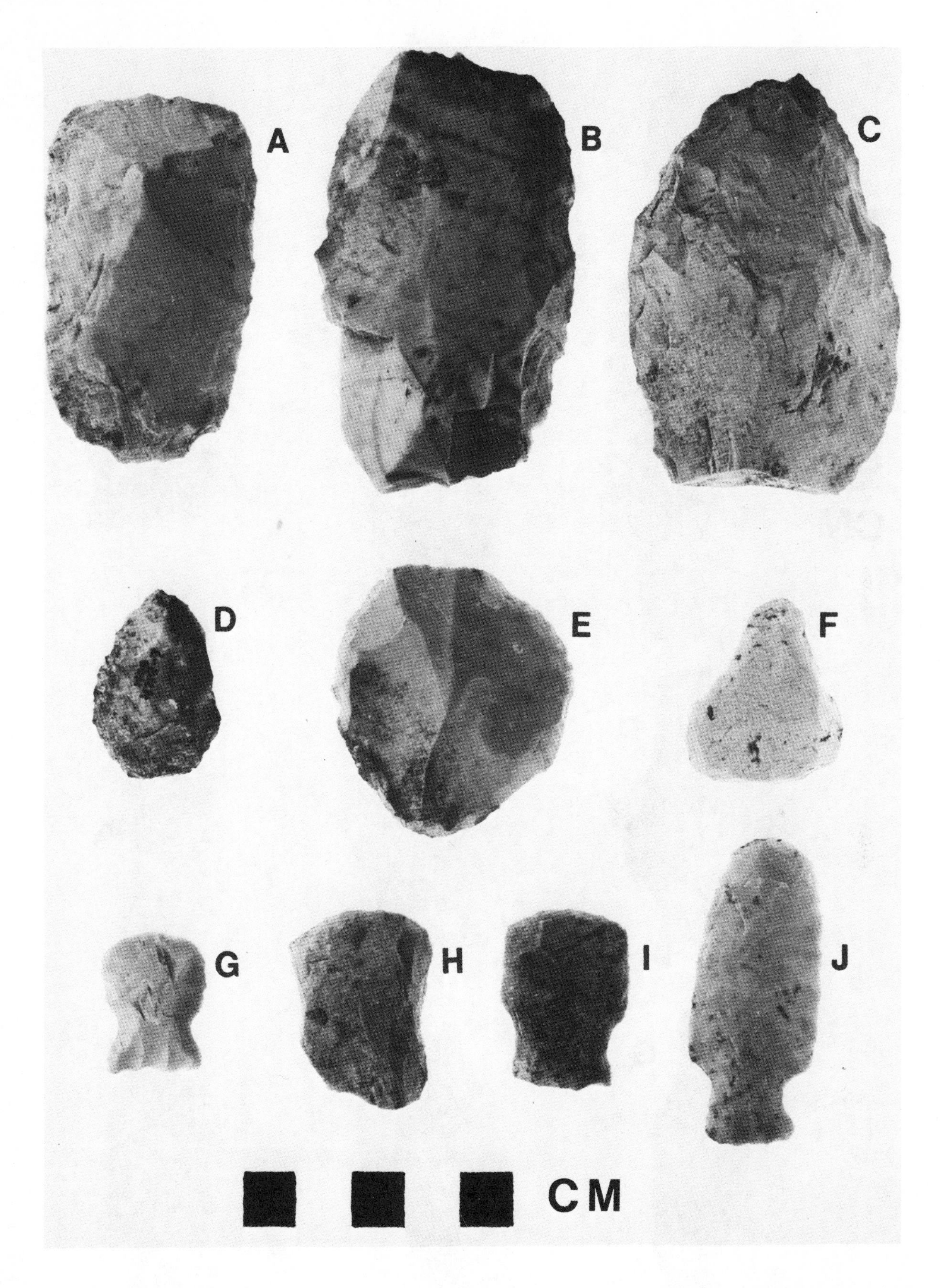

Figure 45. Scrapers. *a*, Heavy-duty scraper. *b*, Side scraper. *c*, Double side scraper. *d*, Side scraper on flake. *e*, Multiple side scraper on flake. *f*, Hafted end scraper. *g,i*, Hafted scrapers. *h*, end and side scraper. *j*, Matanzas point reworked into end scraper. (*a*, Titterington phase. *b-j*, Helton phase.)

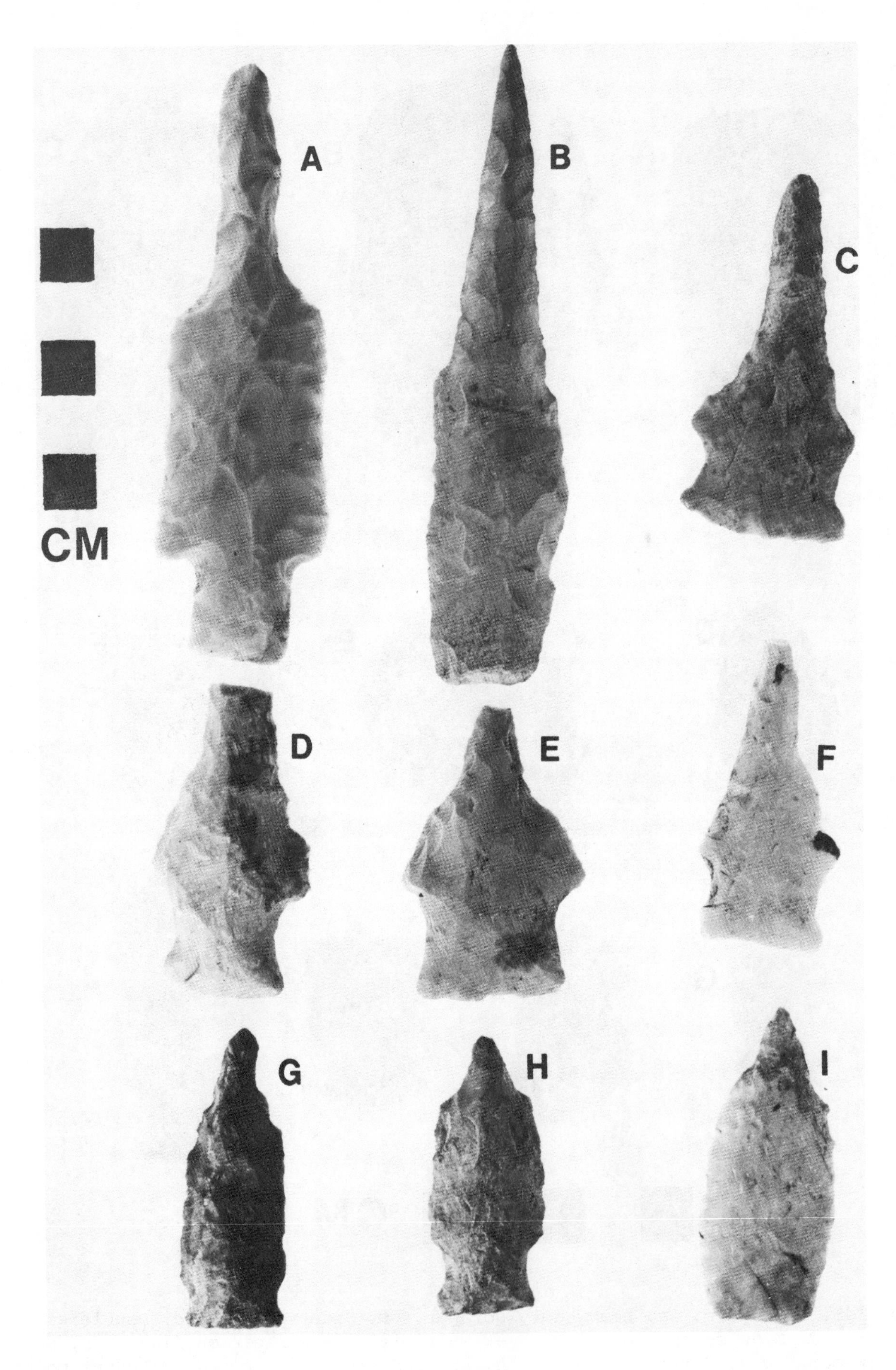

Figure 46. Drills on projectile points. *a*, On Etley point. *b*, On Sedalia point. *c*, On side-notched point. *d-f*, On stemmed points. *g,h*, On Matanzas points. *i*, On Karnak Stemmed point. (*a,b*, Titterington phase. *c-i*, Helton phase.)

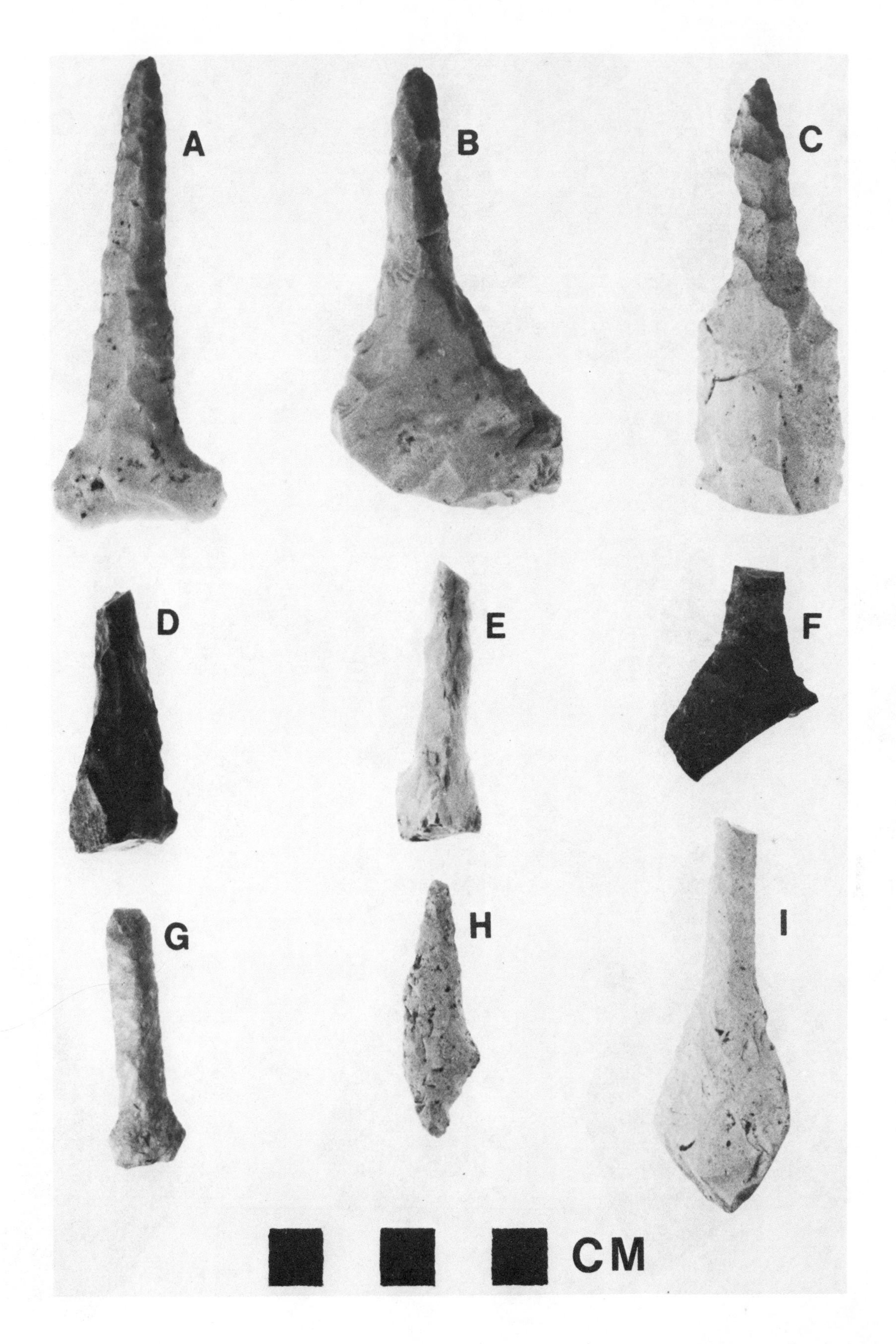

Figure 47. Drills. *a*, T-drill. *b*, On retouched flake. *c*, On parallel sided biface. *d,e*, On triangular retouched flakes. *f*, On broken biface. *g*, Broken T-drill. *h*, On small biface. *i*, On thick biface. (Helton phase.)

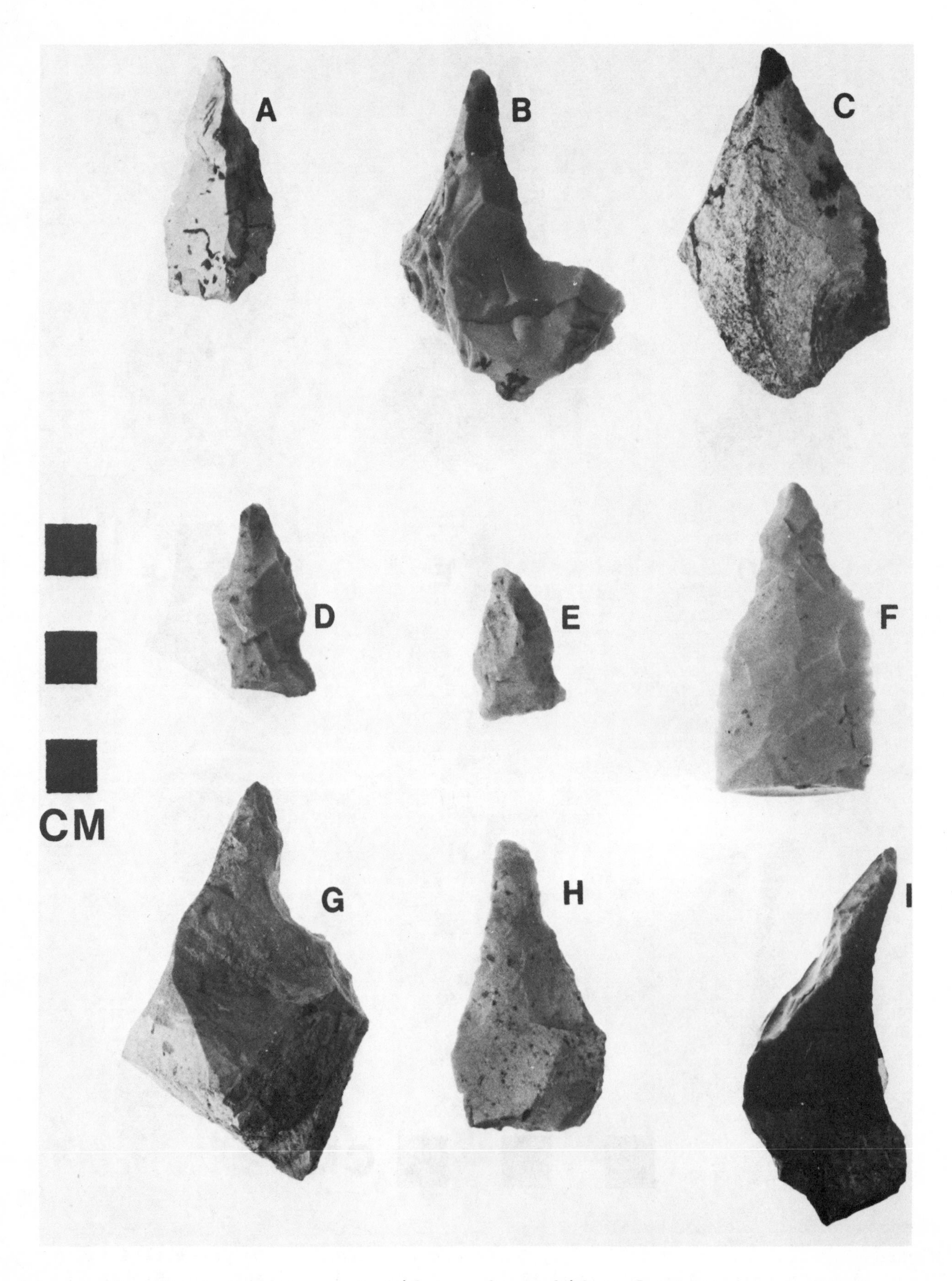

Figure 48. Blunt drills. *a*, On biface. *b*, On biface fragment. *c,g*, On retouched flakes. *d*, On hafted biface. *e*, On Matanzas point. *f*, On broken biface. *h*, On partial biface. *i*, On reworked flake. (Helton phase.)

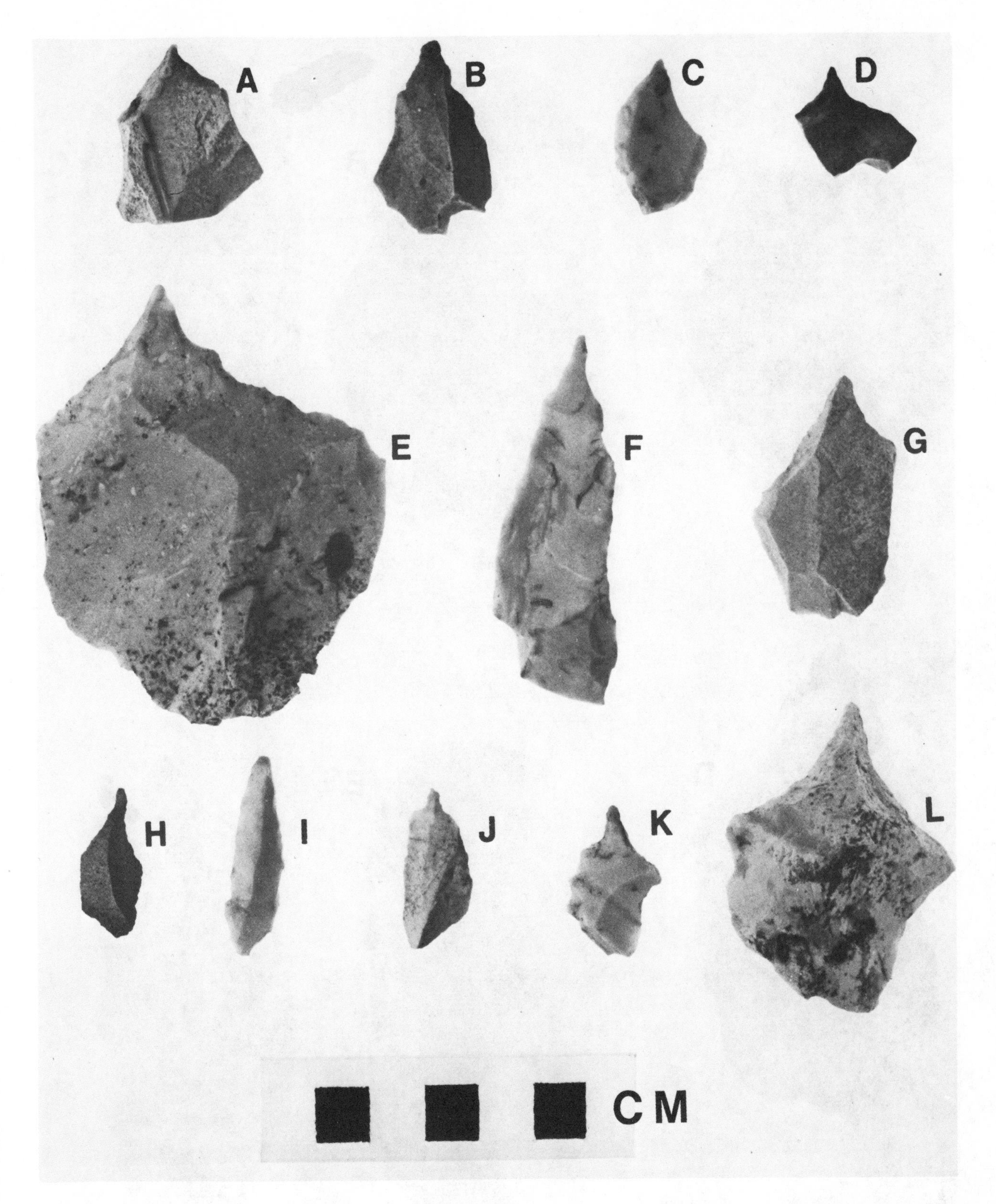

Figure 49. Microdrills, gravers, and spurs. Microdrills: *a*, on flake; *k*, on retouched flake. Gravers: *b,g,h*, on flakes; *e,l*, on retouched flakes; *f*, on biface fragment; *i*, on narrow biface. Spurs: *c,j*, on flakes; *d*, on retouched flake. (Helton phase.)

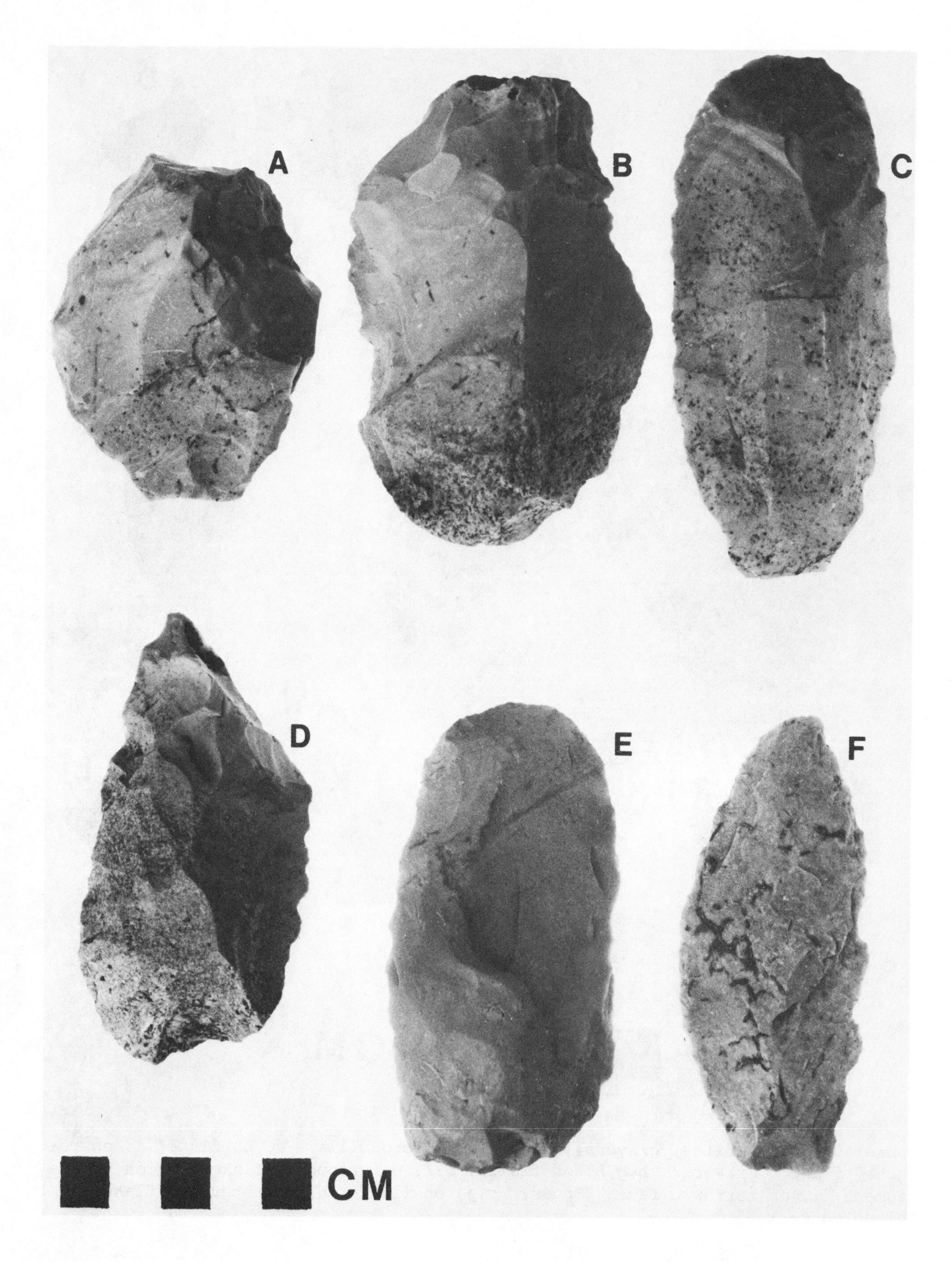

Figure 50. Crude bifaces. (*a-c,e,f*, Helton phase. *d*, Titterington phase.)

Figure 51. Medium bifaces. (Helton phase.)

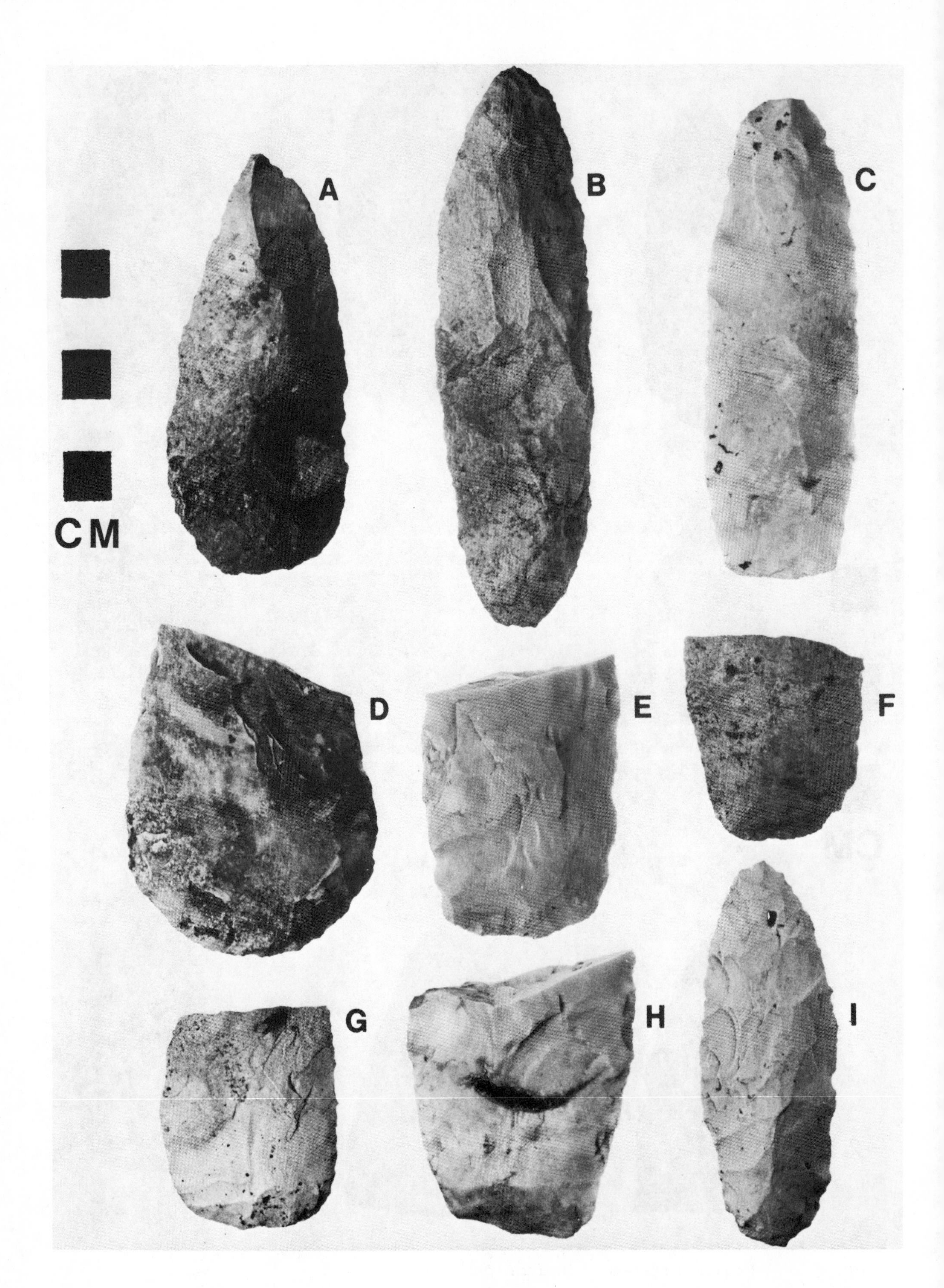
A
B
C
D
E
F
G
H
I
CM

Figure 53. Various knife forms. (Helton phase.)

← Figure 52. Refined bifaces. (*a*,*b*,*d-i*, Helton phase. *c*, Titterington phase.)

Figure 54. Cores. (Helton phase.)

Figure 55. Chert hammers made from discarded cores. (Helton phase.)

Figure 56. Choppers. (Helton phase.)

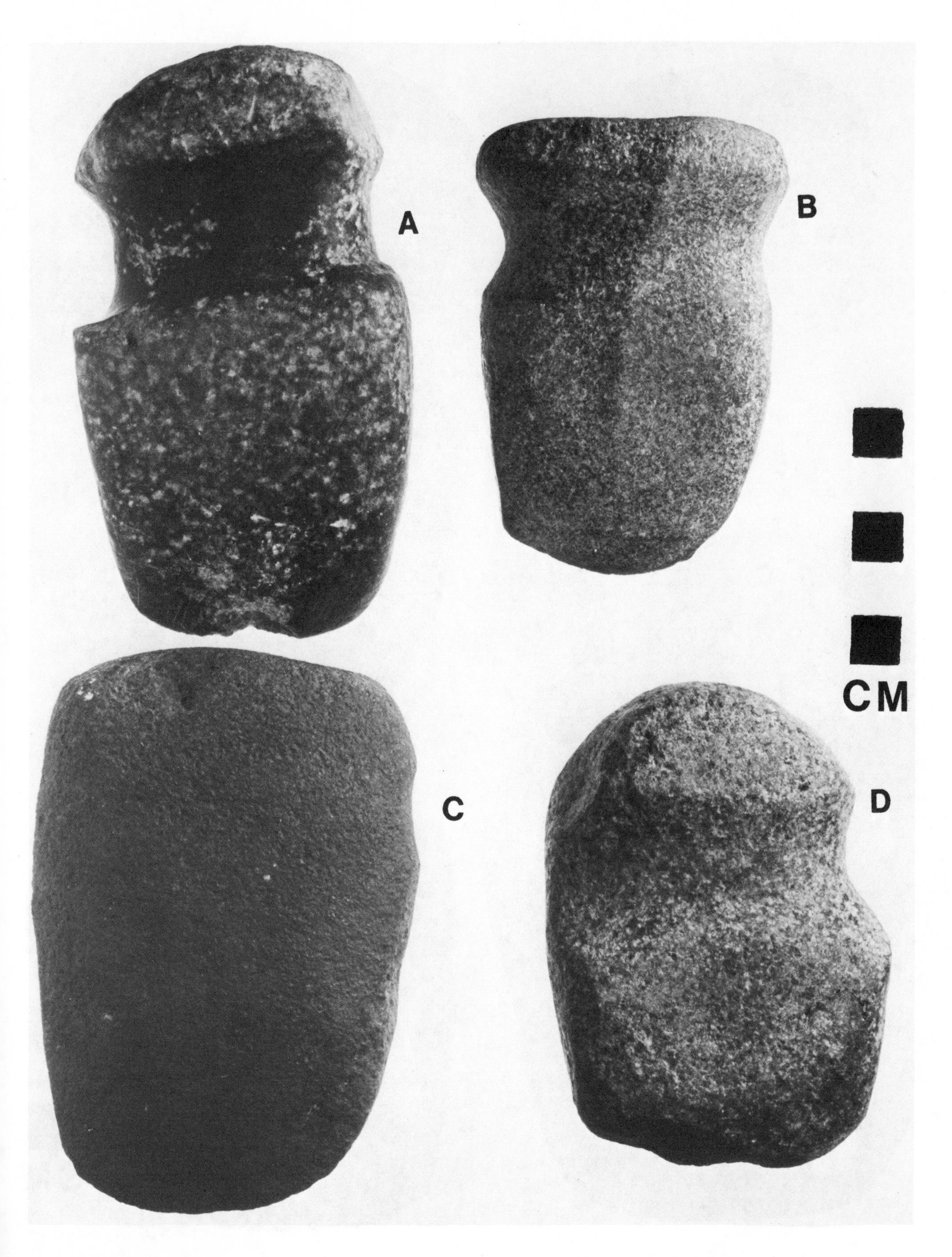

Figure 57. *a,b*, Full grooved axes. *c*, Partial grooved axe (hematite). *d*, Three-quarter grooved axe. (*a-c*, Helton phase. *d*, Titterington phase.)

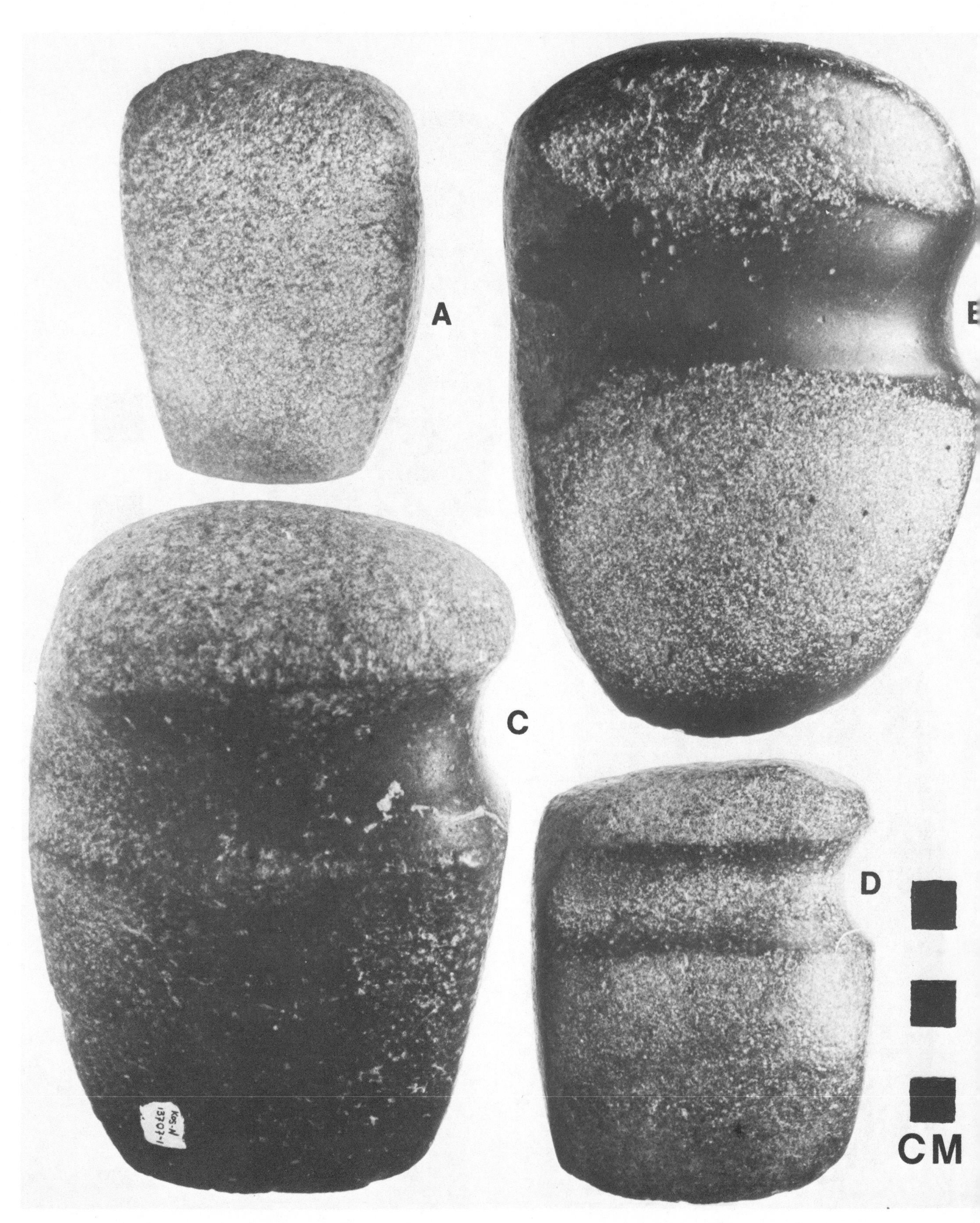

Figure 58. *a*, Unfinished axe. *b-d*, Three-quarter grooved axes. (Helton phase.)

Figure 59. Three-quarter grooved axes. (Helton phase.)

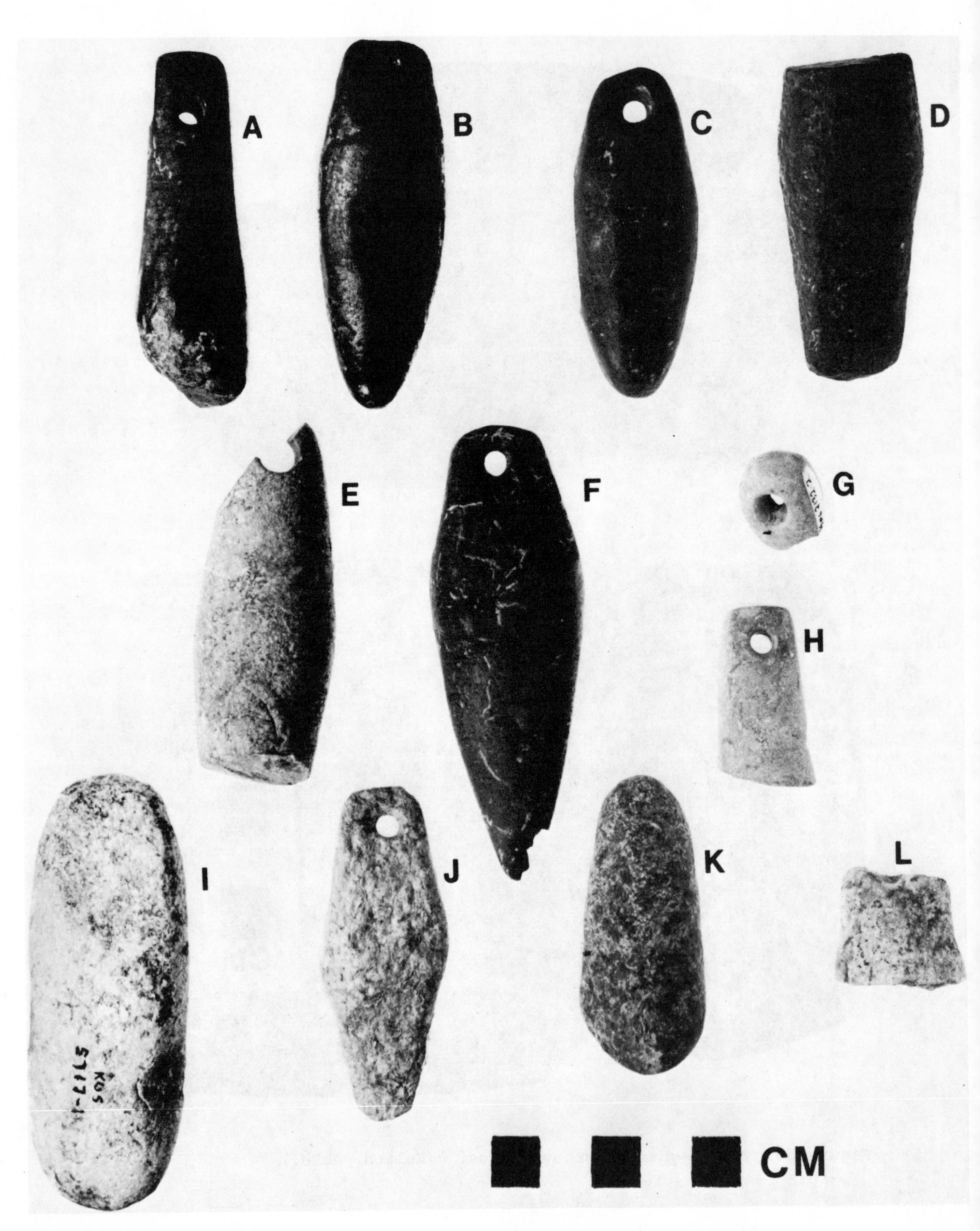

Figure 60. *a-j,l*, Plummets. *k*, Pendant. (*a,c,f*, Godar type, hematite. *b*, Godar type, partially perforated, hematite. *d*, Manufacturing stage, hematite. *e,h,j*, Godar type, limestone. *g,l*, Godar type fragments, limestone. *i*, Limestone preform. *k*, Partially perforated pendant, igneous stone.) (Helton phase.)

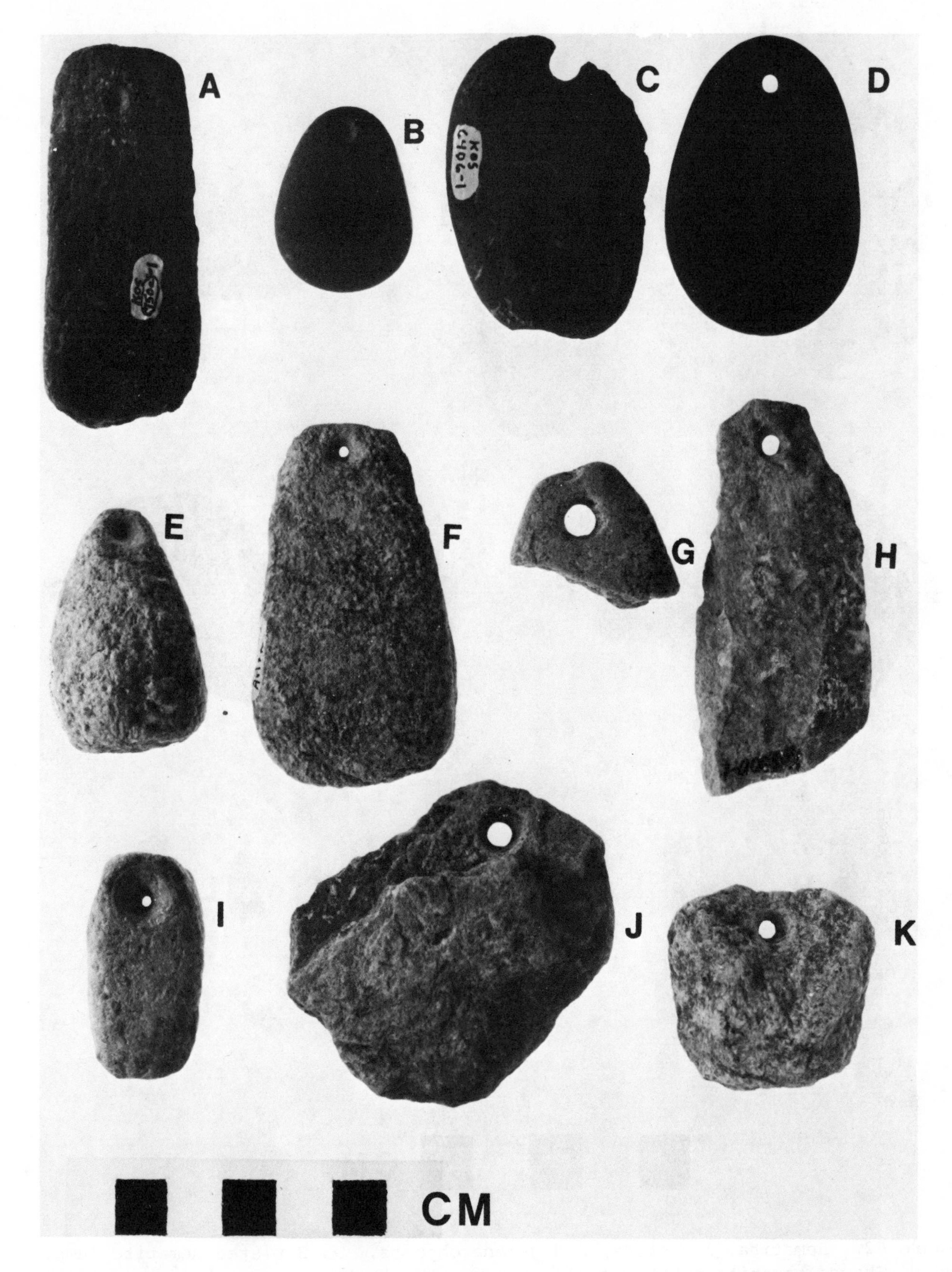

Figure 61. Pendants. *a*, Shaped, pecked, partially drilled. *b*, Unshaped thin pebble, partially drilled. *c*, Unshaped, broken, drilled. *d*, Unshaped thin pebble, partially drilled. *e,f*, Shaped, pecked, bifacially drilled limestone. *g,i*, Shaped, pecked, ground, bifacially drilled, limestone. *h,j,k*, Unshaped, bifacially drilled, limestone. (Helton phase.)

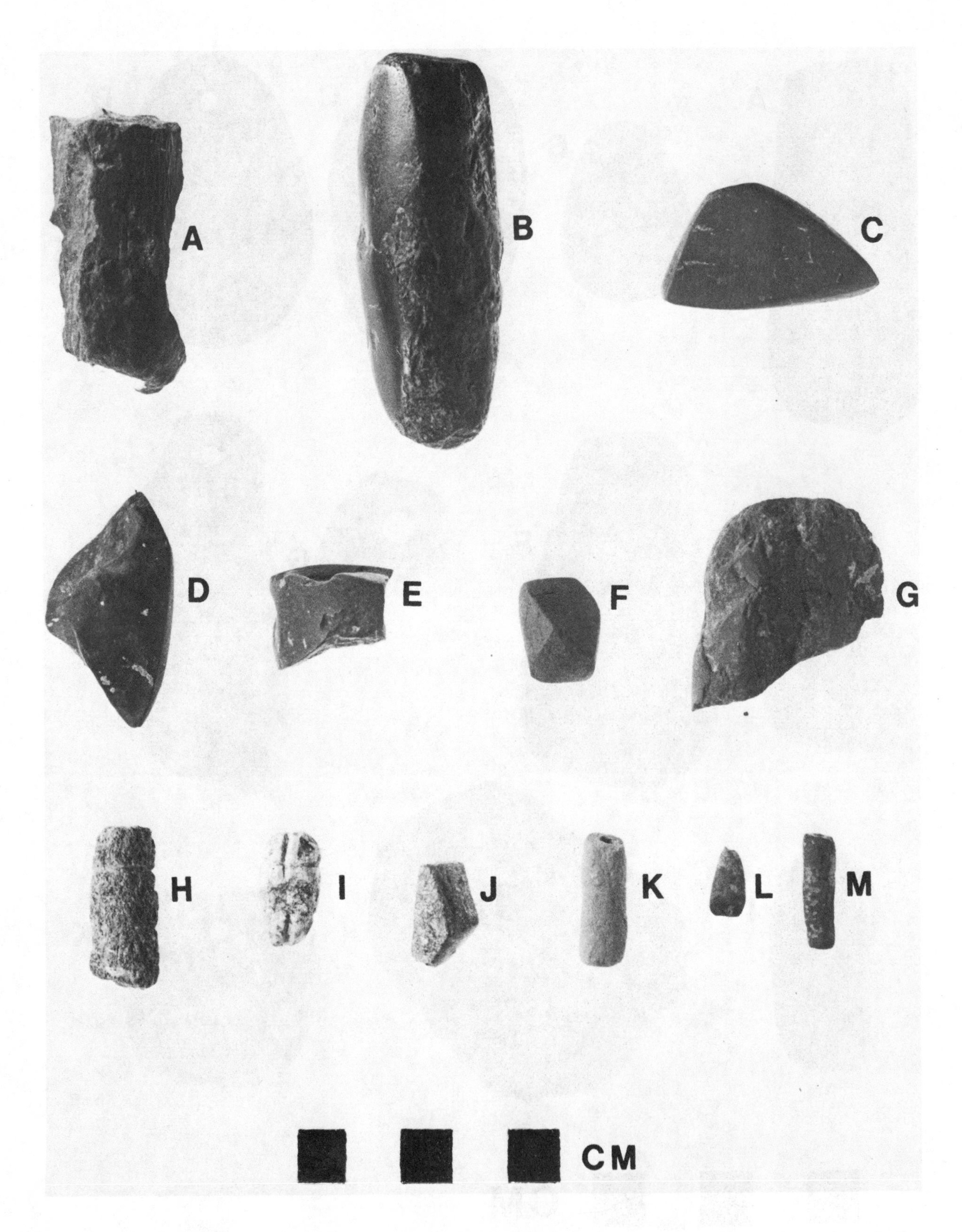

Figure 62. Hematite, limestone, and galena objects. *a*, Striated hematite lump. *b-d,f*, Shaped hematite rubstones. *e,g*, Hematite rubstones. *h*, Incised stone object. *i*, Incised limestone object. *j*, Unworked galena crystal. *k-m*, Hematite concretionary beads. (Helton phase.)

Figure 63. Manos. *a*,*b*, Pitted (combination stones). *c*,*d*, Unpitted. (Helton phase).

Figure 64. *a*, Hammerstone. *b*, Pitted hammerstone. *c*,*d*, Sandstone abraders. (Helton phase.)

Figure 65. Channel Basin metate. (Helton phase.)

Figure 66. Worked bone and antler. *a*, Worked rib, probably scraper. *b*, Scraper on flaked longbone. *c*, Double antler flaker. *d*, Cut and snapped antler tine. *e*, Fire treated antler flaker. *f*, Antler flaker. *g*, Worn and polished rib fragment. (Helton phase.)

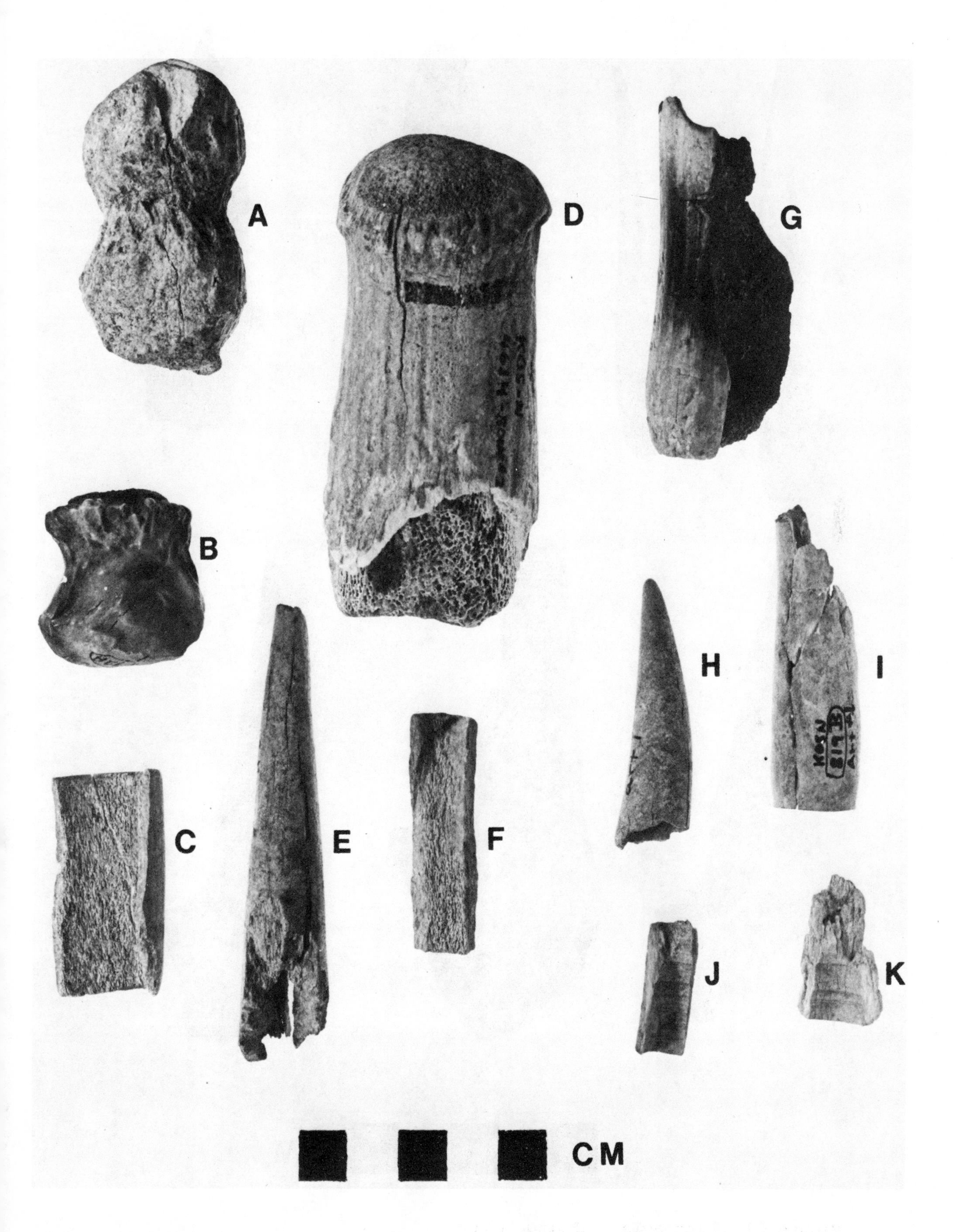

Figure 67. Worked antler. *a*, Figure-8 shaped object. *b*, Burned figure-8 shaped object. *c,f* Broken rings. *d*, Punch. *e*, Hollow point. *g*, Burned shaft straightener with broken hole at top. *h,i*, Projectile points. *j,k*, Interior view of hollowing marks on points. (Helton phase.)

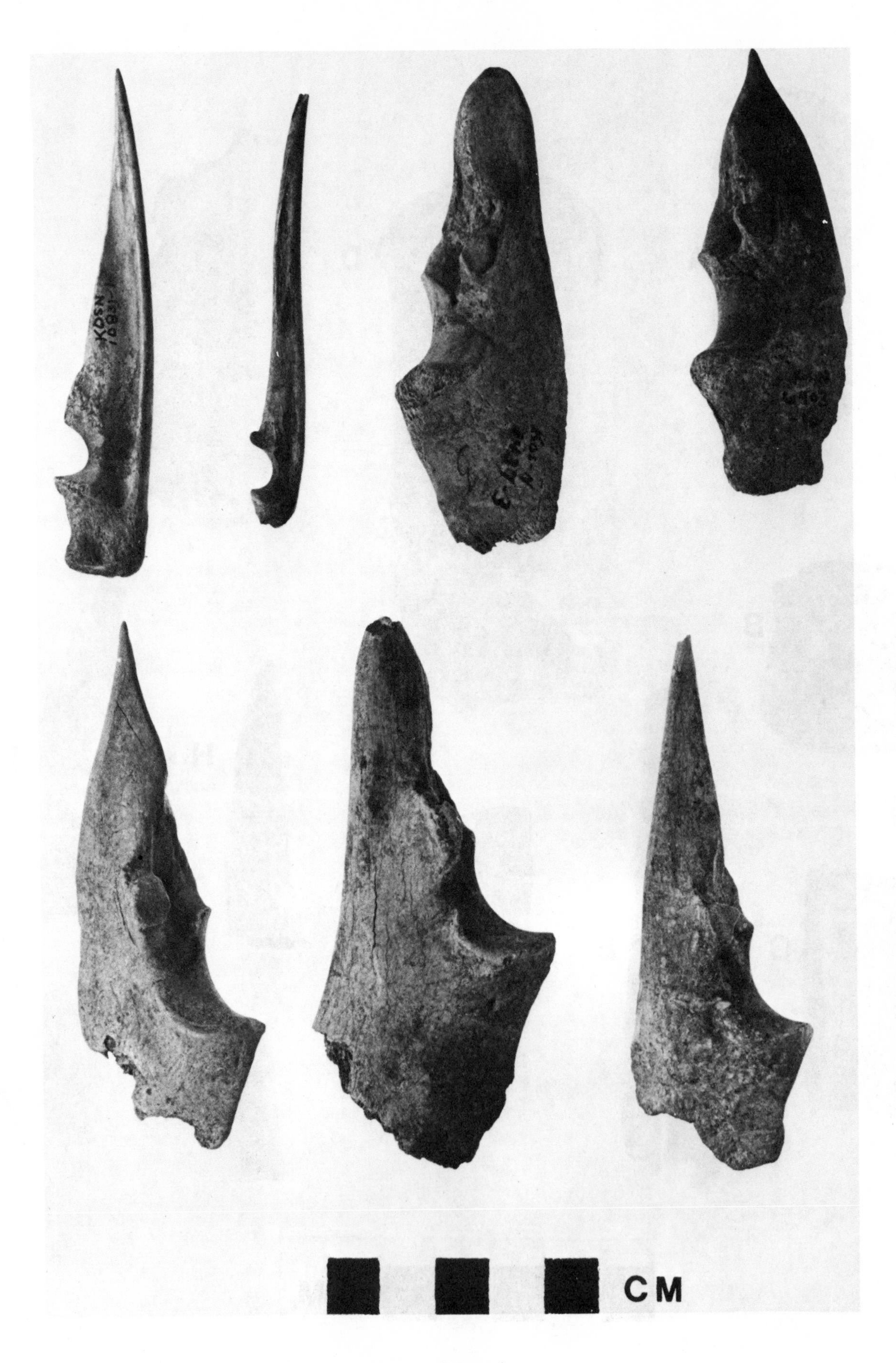

Figure 68. Ulna awls. (Helton phase.)

Figure 69. Awls on various pieces of bone. (Helton phase.)

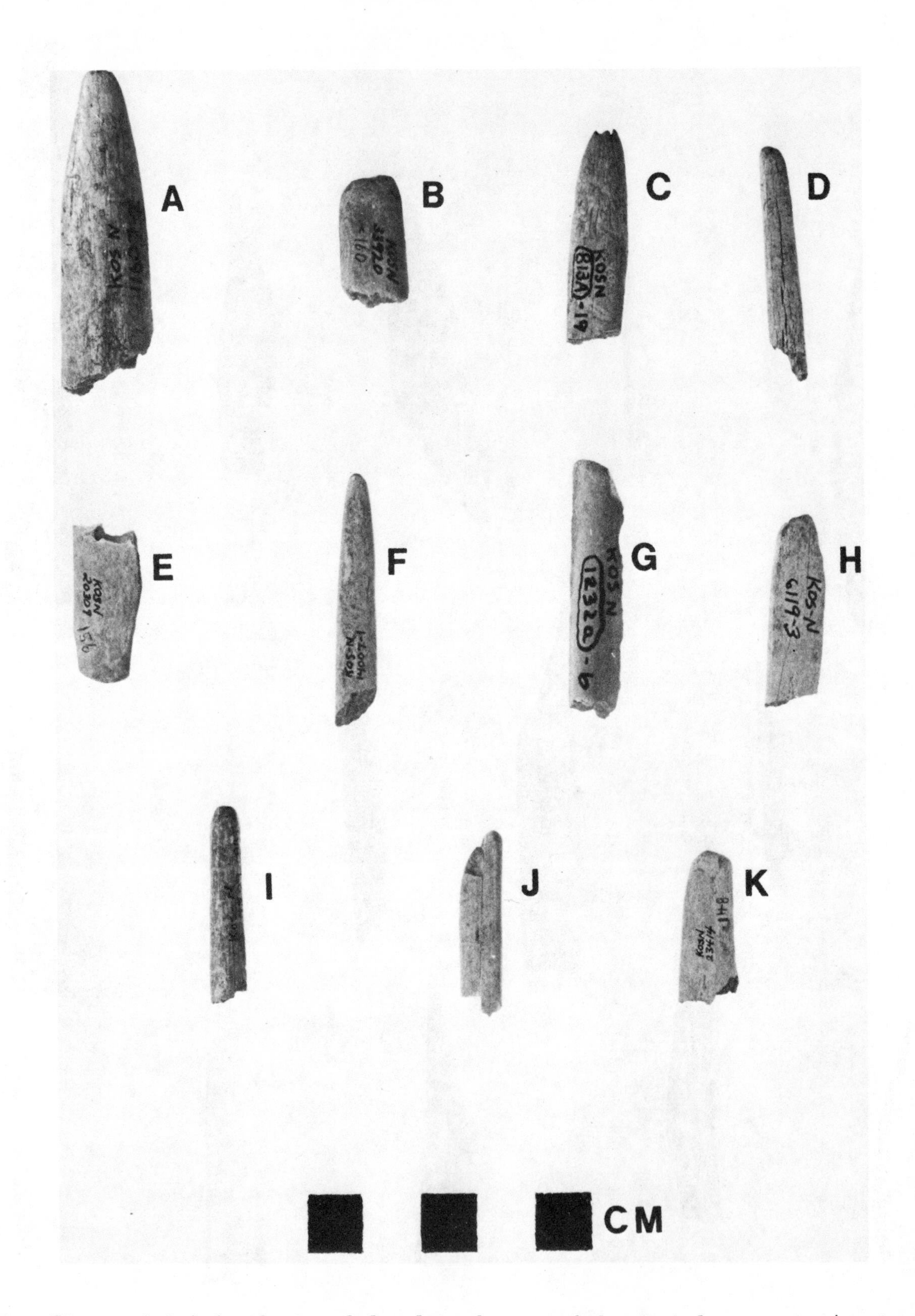

Figure 70. *a,d,f,i,j*, Blunt ended awls. *b,c,e,g,h,k*, Spatulae or weaving tools. (Helton phase.)

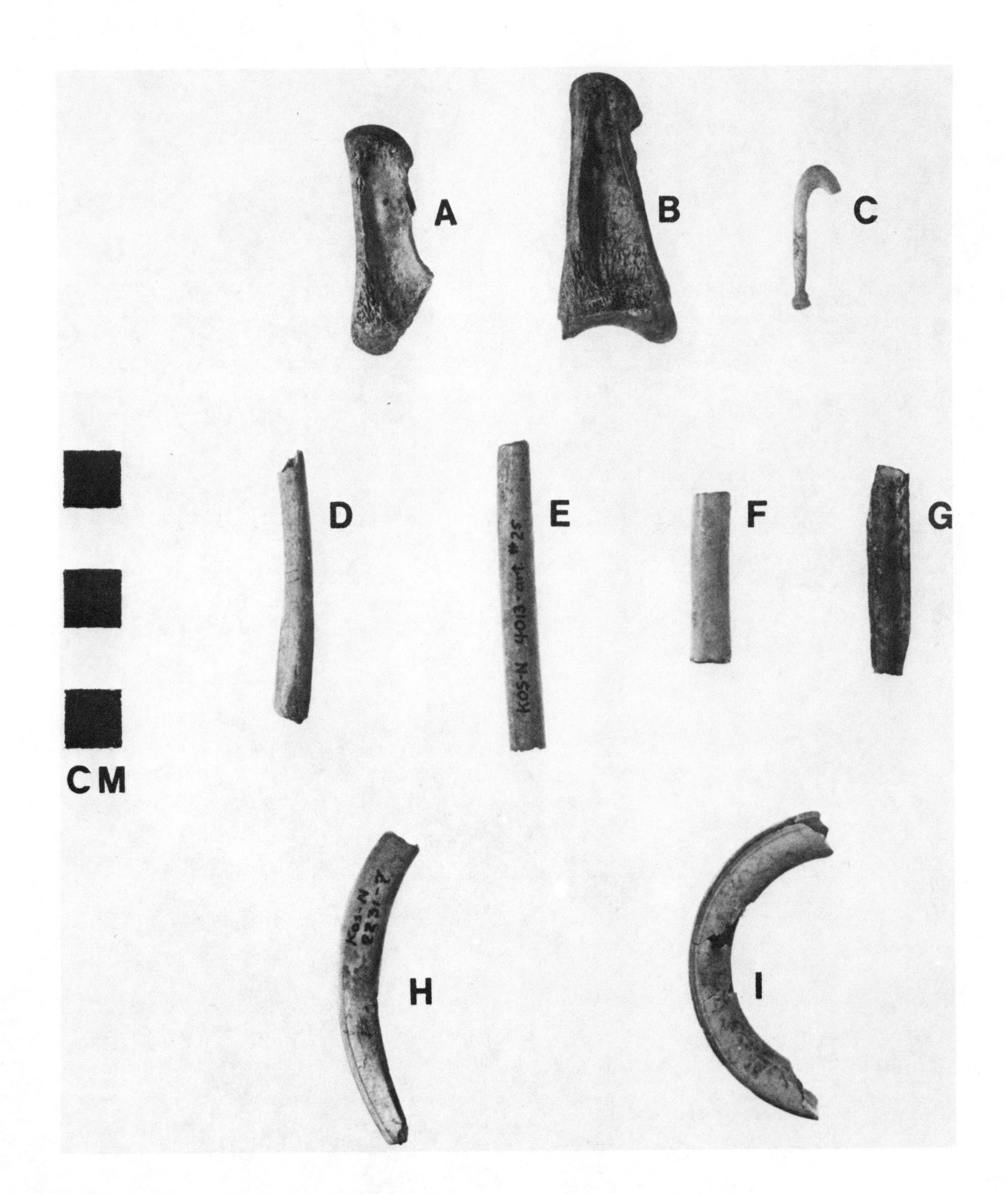

Figure 71. *a,b*, Split deer phalanges. *c*, Carved bone fishhook. *d,e*, Bone tubes. *f,g*, Bone beads. *h,i*, Worked beaver teeth. (Helton phase.)

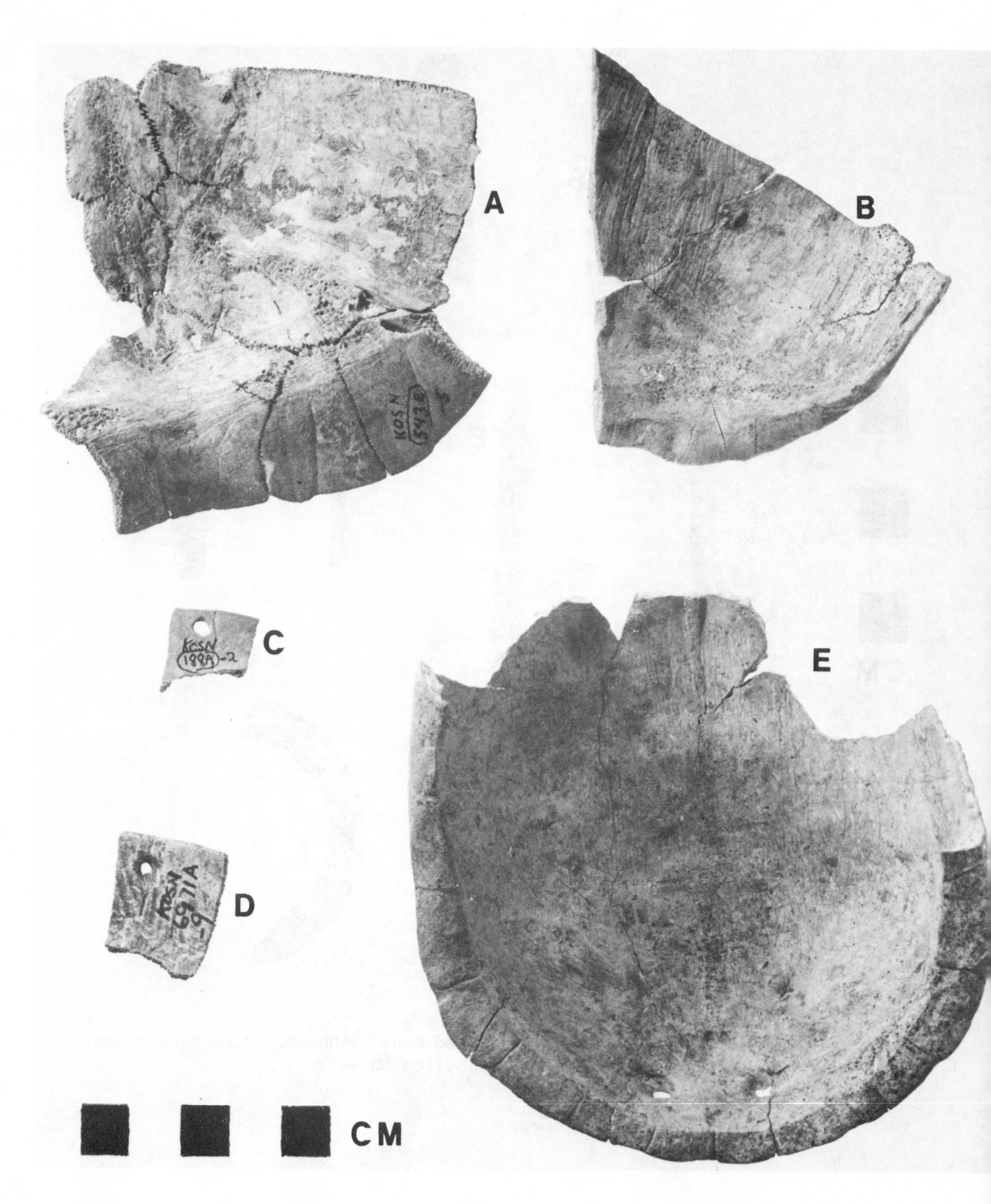

Figure 72. *a,b,e*, Turtle carapace cups. *c,d*, Drilled peripheral bones. (Helton phase.)

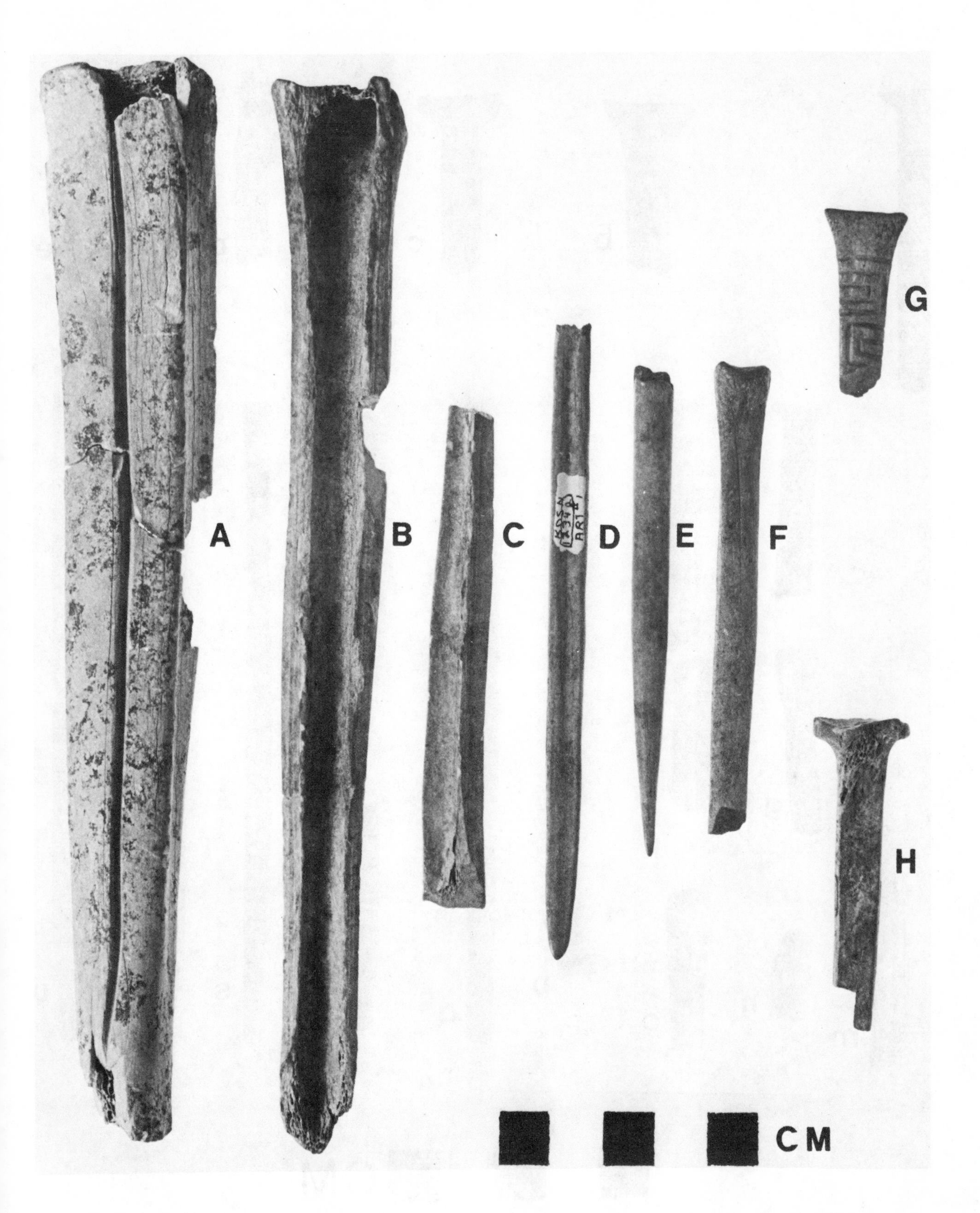

Figure 73. Manufacturing trajectory of bone pins made from deer metapodia. *a*, Incised metapodial. *b*, Split metapodial or beamer. *c*, Quartered metapodial. *d-f*, Ground and shaped pin shafts. *g,h*, Incised pin and carved pin shapes. (Helton phase.)

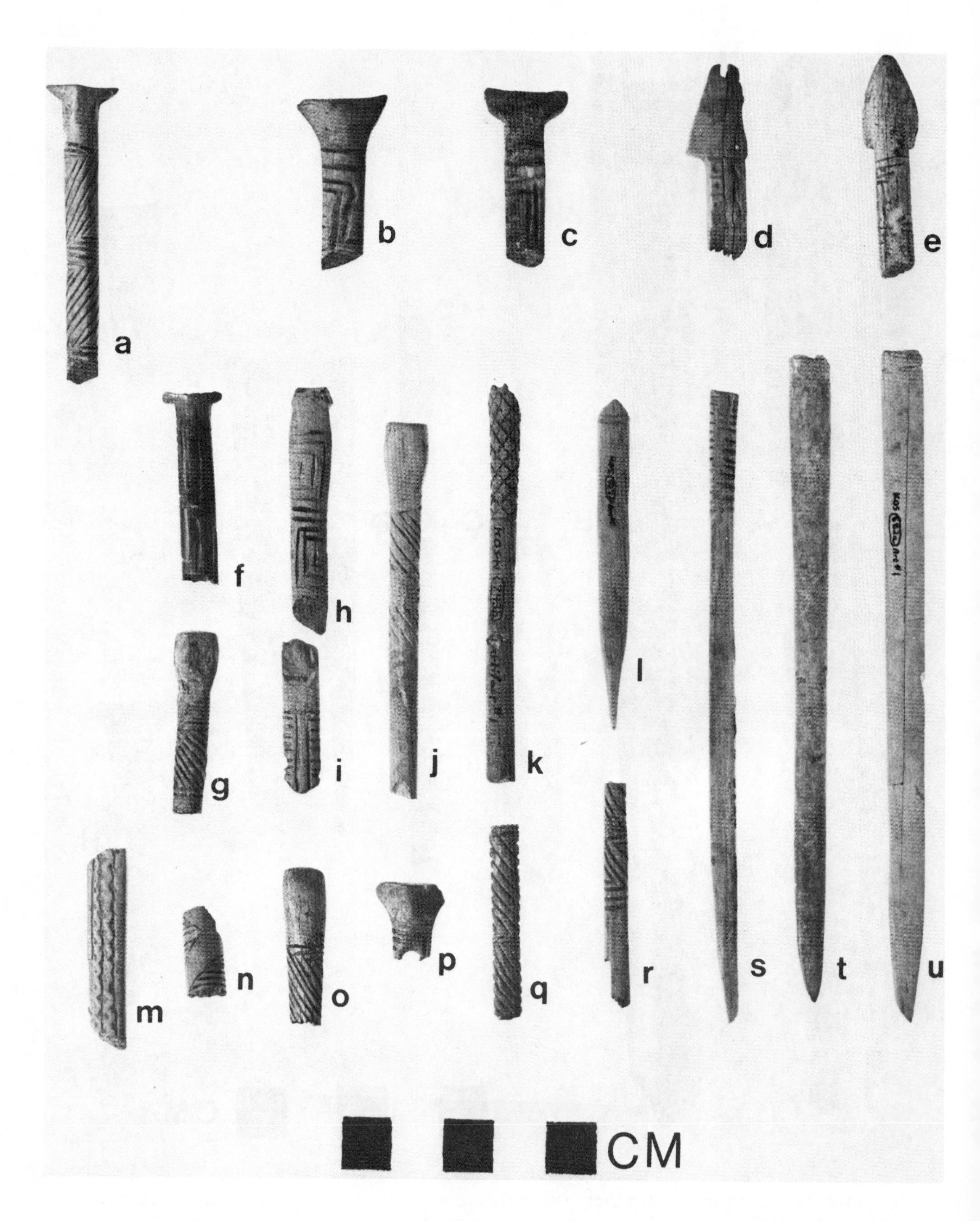

Figure 74. Geometrically incised and carved bone pins. (Helton phase.)

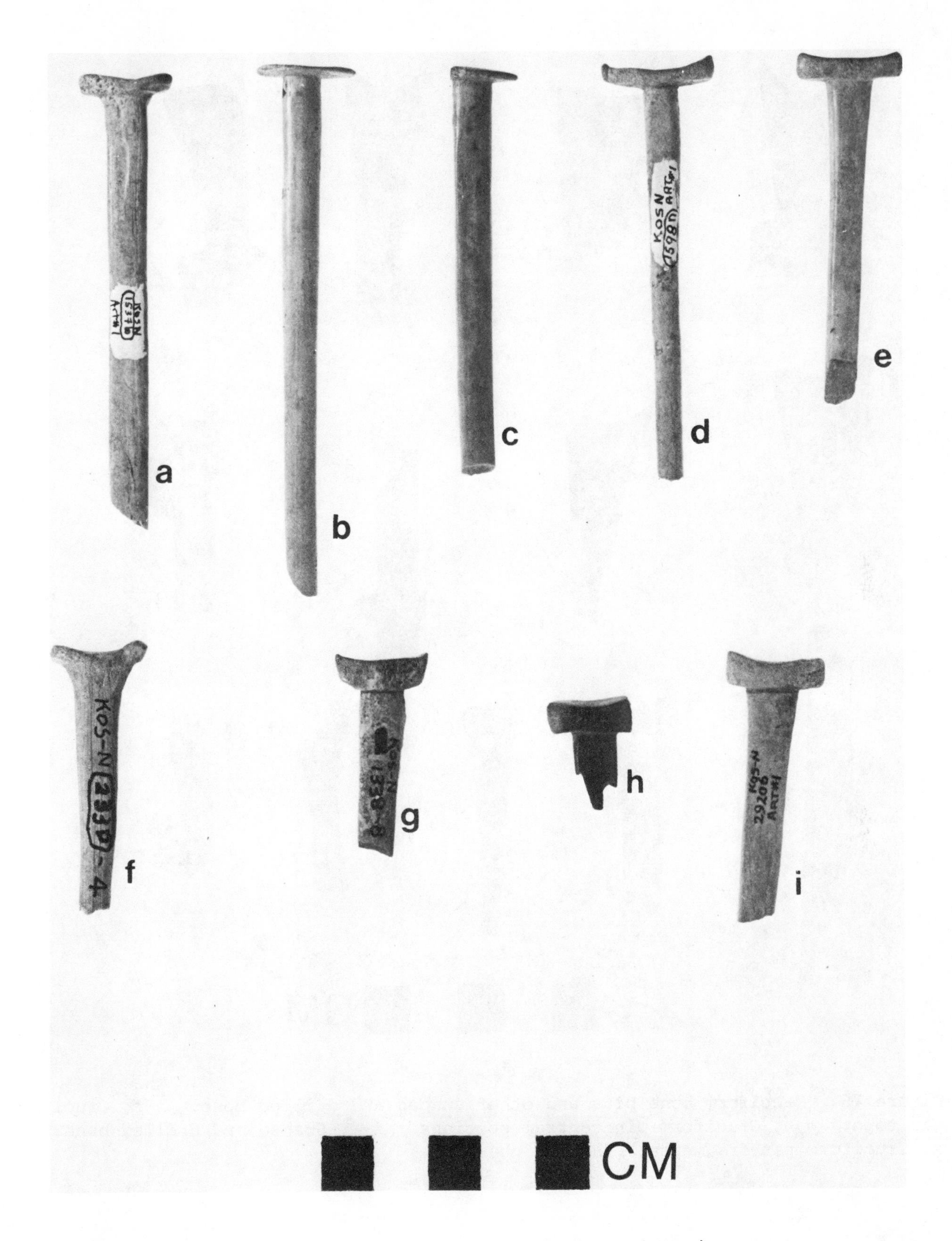

Figure 75. Crutch top carved bone pins. (Helton phase.)

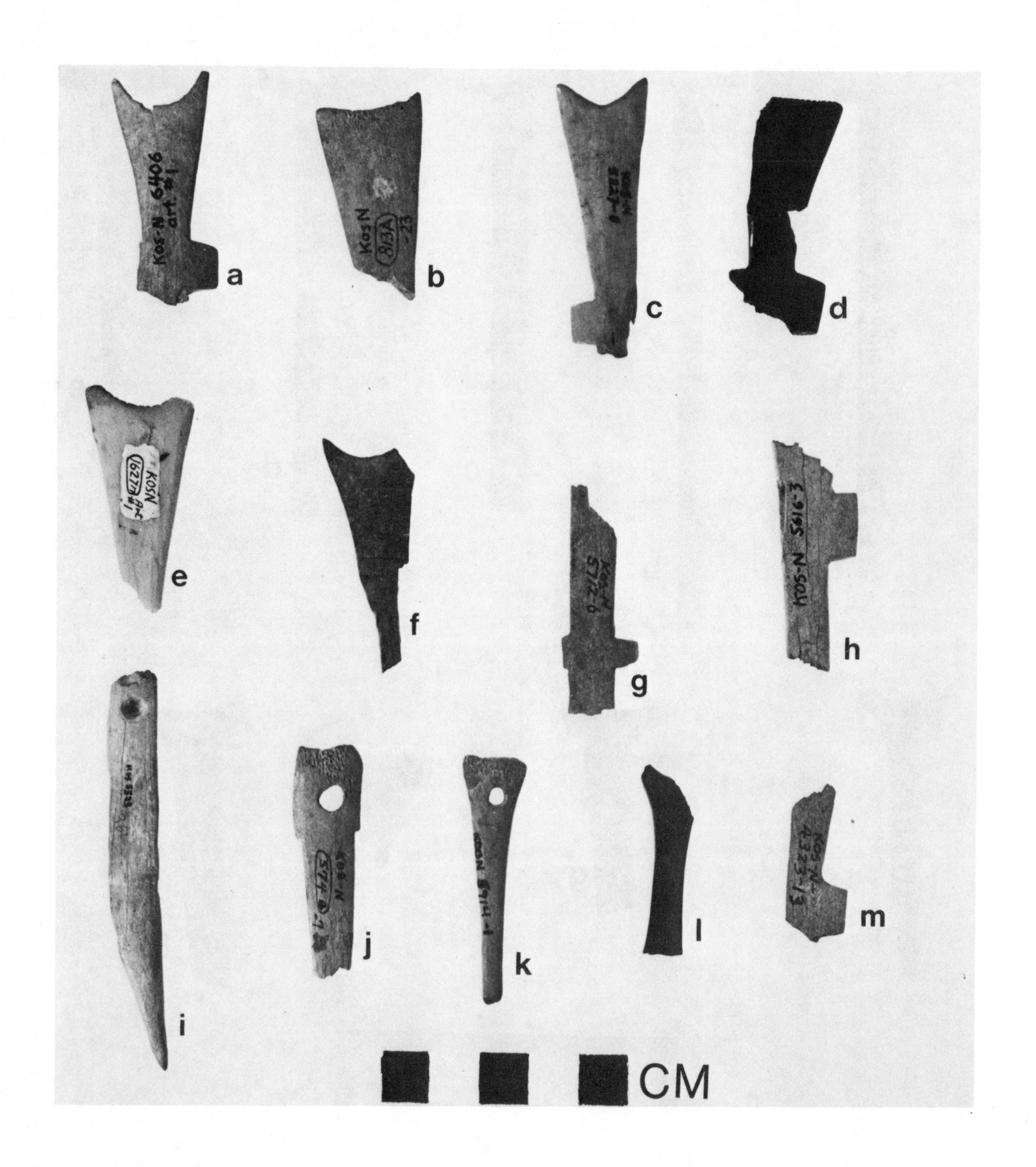

Figure 76. Cruciform bone pins and other shaped and drilled bone. *a-f*, Cruciform pin tops. *g,h*, Cruciform pin central sections. *i-k*, Shaped and drilled bone. *l*, *m*, Cruciform pin fragments. (Helton phase.)

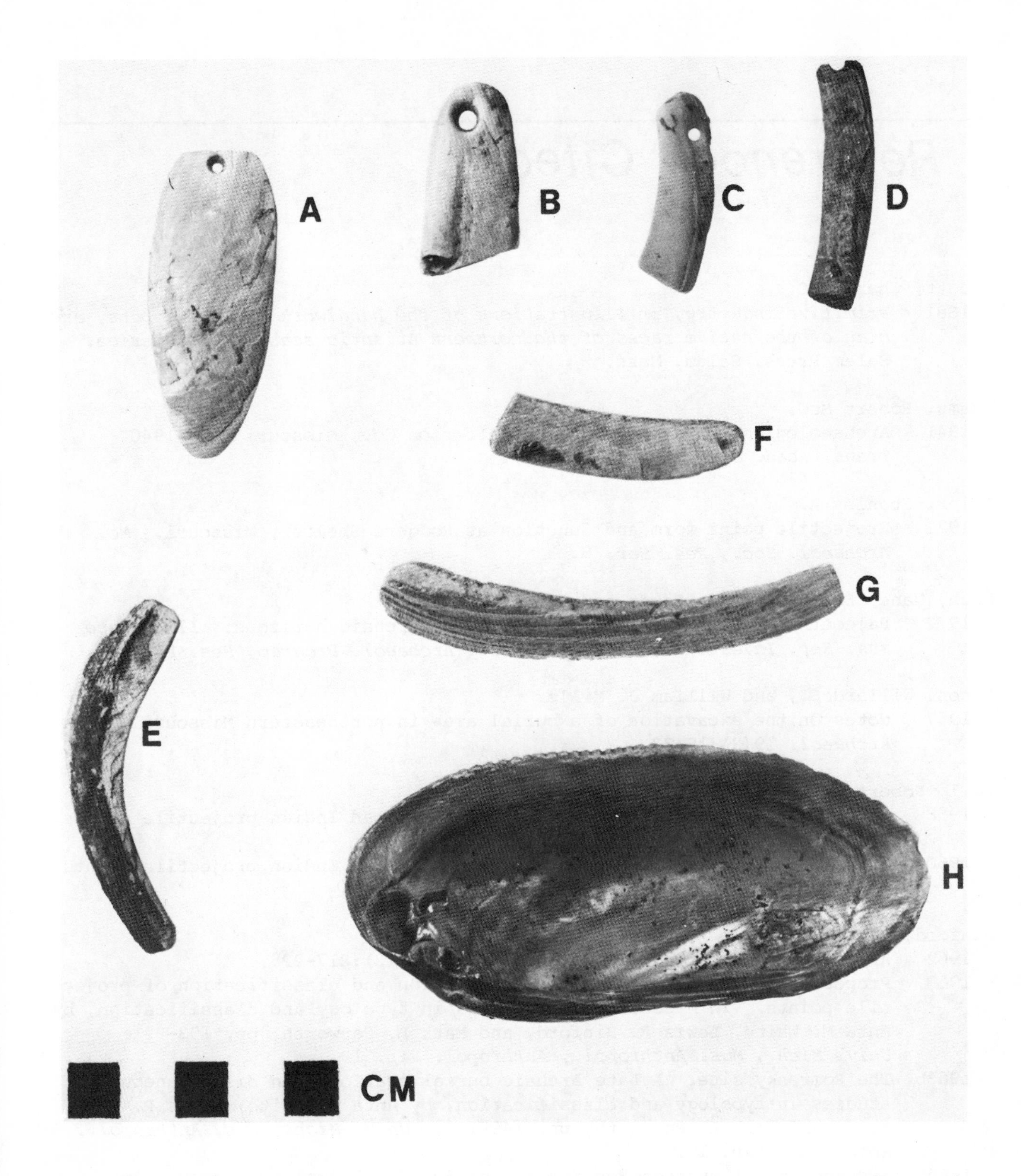

Figure 77. Shell artifacts. *a,b*, Shaped and drilled pendants. *c,d*, Drilled distal shell margins. *e,f*, Cut distal margins. *g*, Cut and ground distal margins. *h*, Serrated edge on shell (flenser?). (Helton phase.)

References Cited

Abbott, Charles C.
1881 *Primitive industry, or illustrations of the handiwork in stone, bone, and clay of the native races of the northern Atlantic seaboard of America.* Salem Press, Salem, Mass.

Adams, Robert McC.
1941 Archaeological investigations in Jefferson Co., Missouri 1939-1940. *Trans. Acad. Sci. St. Louis* 30(5).

Ahler, Stanley A.
1971 Projectile point form and function at Rodgers Shelter, Missouri. *Mo. Archaeol. Soc., Res. Ser.* 8.

Asch, Nancy B., Richard I. Ford, and David L. Asch
1972 Paleoethnobotany of the Koster site: the Archaic horizons. *Ill. State Mus. Rep. Invest.* 24, and *Ill. Valley Archaeol. Program, Res. Pap.* 6.

Bacon, Willard S., and William J. Miller
1957 Notes on the excavation of a burial area in northeastern Missouri. *Mo. Archaeol.* 19(3):19-33.

Bell, Robert E.
1958 Guide to the identification of certain American Indian projectile points. *Okla. Anthropol. Soc., Spec. Bull.* 1.
1960 Guide to the identification of certain American Indian projectile points. *Okla. Anthropol. Soc., Spec. Bull.* 2.

Binford, Lewis R.
1962 Archaeology as anthropology. *Am. Antiq.* 28(2):217-225.
1963 Proposed attribute list for the description and classification of projectile points. *In* Miscellaneous studies in typology and classification, by Anta M. White, Lewis R. Binford, and Mark L. Papworth, pp. 193-221. *Univ. Mich., Mus. Anthropol., Anthropol. Pap.* 19.
1963b The Pomranky site. A Late Archaic burial station. *In* Miscellaneous studies in typology and classification, by Anta M. White, Lewis R. Binford, and Mark L. Papworth, pp. 149-192. *Univ. Mich., Mus. Anthropol., Anthropol. Pap.* 19.
1965 Archaeological systematics and the study of cultural processes. *Am. Antiq.* 31(2):203-210.
1968 Archeological perspectives. In *New perspectives in archeology,* Sally R. Binford and Lewis R. Binford (eds.), pp. 5-32. Aldine, Chicago.
1972 *An archaeological perspective.* Seminar Press, New York.

Binford, Lewis R., and Sally R. Binford
1966 Preliminary analysis of functional variability in the Mousterian of Levallois facies. *Am. Anthropol.* 68(2 part 2):238-295.

Binford, Lewis R., and Mark L. Papworth
1963 The Eastport site, Antrim County, Michigan. *In* Miscellaneous studies in typology and classification, by Anta M. White, Lewis R. Binford, and Mark L. Papworth, pp. 71-123. *Univ. Mich., Mus. Anthropol., Anthropol. Pap.* 19.

Binford, Lewis R., and George I. Quimby
1963 Indian sites and chipped stone materials in the northern Lake Michigan area. *Fieldiana:Anthropol.* 36:277-307.

Blackwood, Beatrice
1950 Technology of a modern Stone Age people in New Guinea. *Pitt Rivers Mus., Univ. Oxford, Occas. Pap. Technol.* 3.

Bordaz, Jacques
1970 *Stone tools.* Natural History Press, Garden City, New York.

Bordes, Francois
1969 Reflections on typologies and techniques in Paleolithic assemblages. *Arctic* 6(1):1-29.

Bordes, Francois, and Denise de Sonneville-Bordes
1970 The significance of variability in Paleolithic assemblages. *World Archaeol.* 2(1):61-73.

Boserup, Ester
1965 *The conditions of agricultural growth.* Aldine, Chicago.

Brose, David S.
1975 Functional analysis of stone tools: a cautionary note on the role of animal fats. *Am. Antiq.* 40(1):86-94.

Brown, James A.
1971a Introduction. *In* Approaches to the social dimensions of mortuary practices, James A. Brown (ed.), pp. 1-5. *Mem. Soc. Am. Archaeol.* 25.
1971b Dimensions of status in the burials at Spiro. *In* Approaches to the social dimensions of mortuary practices, James A. Brown (ed.), pp. 92-112. *Mem. Soc. Am. Archaeol.* 25.

Brown, James A., and Gail Houart
1975 Application of an archeological site survey retrieval system in the Lower Illinois Valley Research Program. In *Personalized data systems,* Benjamin Mittman and Lorraine Borman (eds.), pp. 111-128. John Wiley, New York.

Brown, James A., and Stuart Struever
1973 The organization of archeological research: an Illinois example. In *Research and theory in current archeology,* Charles Redman (ed.), pp. 261-280. John Wiley and Sons, New York.

Bryan, Kirk
1950 Flint quarries--the source of tools and, at the same time, the factories of the American Indian. *Pap. Peabody Mus. Am. Archaeol. Ethnol.,* 17(3).

Buettner-Janusch, John
1954 Use of infrared photography in archaeological fieldwork. *Am. Antiq.* 20(1):84-87.

Butzer, Karl
1973 Preliminary review of the stratigraphy and sediments of the Koster site. Paper presented at 31st Plains Conference, Columbia, Mo.

Caldwell, Joseph R.
1958 Trend and tradition in the prehistory of the eastern United States. *Am. Anthropol. Assoc., Mem.* 88.

Chapman, Carl
1952 Recent excavations in Graham Cave. *In* Graham Cave, an Archaic site in Montgomery County, Missouri, by Wilfred D. Logan, pp. 87-101. *Mo. Archaeol. Soc. Mem.* 2.
1975 *Archaeology of Missouri, I.* University of Missouri Press, Columbia.

Childe, V. Gordon
1936 *Man makes himself.* Watts, London.

Clark, David L.
1968 *Analytical archaeology.* Methuen, London.

Cleland, Charles E.
1966 Prehistoric animal ecology and ethnozoology of the Upper Great Lakes Region. *Univ. Mich. Mus. Anthropol., Anthropol. Pap.* 29.

Coe, Joffre L.
1964 The formative cultures of the Carolina Piedmont. *Trans. Am. Philos. Soc.*, 54 (5).

Cole, Fay-Cooper, and Thorne Deuel
1937 *Rediscovering Illinois.* University of Chicago Press, Chicago.

Coleman, Dennis D.
1974 Illinois State Geological Survey Radiocarbon Dates V. *Radiocarbon* 16 (1):105-117.

Collins, Michael B., and Jason M. Fenwick
1974 Heat treatment of chert: methods of interpretation and their application. *Plains Anthropol.* 19(64):134-145.

Cowgill, G. L.
1968 Archaeological applications of factor, cluster, and proximity analysis. *Am. Antiq.* 33(3):367-375.

Crabtree, Don E.
1967a Notes on experiments in flintknapping: 3. Flintknapper's raw materials. *Tebiwa* 10:2-24. Pocatello.
1967b Notes on experiments in flintknapping: 4. Tools used for the making of flaked stone artifacts. *Tebiwa* 10:60-73.
1968 Mesoamerican polyhedral cores and prismatic blades. *Am. Antiq.* 33(4): 446-478.
1970 Flaking stone with wooden implements. *Science* 196:146-153.

Crabtree, Don E., and B. R. Butler
1964 Notes on experiments in flintknapping: 1. Heat treatment of silica materials. *Tebiwa,* 7:106.

Crane, H. R., and J. B. Griffin
1958 University of Michigan Radiocarbon Dates XII. *Radiocarbon,* 10(1):61-114.

Didier, Mary Ellen
1967 Distribution study of the Turkey Tail point. *Wis. Archaeol.* 48(1):3-73.

Downey, C. E., D. R. Grantham, and J. B. Fehrenbacher
1974 Soil survey of Greene County, Illinois. *Ill. Agr. Exp. Stn., Soil Rep.* 93.

Dragoo, Don W.
1958 Archaic hunters of the Upper Ohio Valley. *Ann. Carnegie Mus.* 35:139-246.

Dunnell, Robert C.
1971 *Systematics in prehistory.* Free Press, New York.

Eggan, Fred
1954 Social anthropology and the method of controlled comparisons. *Am. Anthropol.,* 56:743-763.

Ellis, H. H.
1940 Flint working techniques of the American Indian: an experimental study. *Ohio State Museum.* Columbus.

Farnsworth, Kenneth B.
1973 An archaeological survey of the Macoupin Valley. *Ill. State Mus. Rep. Invest.* 26 and *Ill. Valley Archeol. Program Res. Pap.* 7.

Fenenga, Franklin
1953 The weight of chipped stone points. A clue to their function. *Southwest. J. Anthropol.,* 9:309-323.

Fitting, James E.
1967 Camp of the careful Indian: an Upper Great Lakes chipping station. *Pap. Mich. Acad. Sci. Arts Lett.* 52:237-242.

Fitting, James E., Jerry DeVisscher, and Edward J. Wahla
1966 The Paleo-Indian occupation of Holcombe Beach. *Univ. Mich., Mus. Anthropol., Anthropol. Pap.* 27.

Flannery, Kent V.
1968 Archaeological systems theory and early Mesoamerica. In *Anthropological archaeology in the Americas* Betty J. Meggars (ed.), pp. 67-87. Anthropological Society of Washington.
1973 The origins of agriculture. *Ann. Rev. Anthropol.* 2:271-310.

Fogel, Ira L.
1963 Dispersal of copper artifacts in the Late Archaic period of prehistoric North America. *Wis. Archeol.* 44(3):129-179.

Ford, James A.
1962 *Quantitative methods in deriving cultural chronology.* Pan American Union, Washington.

Ford, James A., Philip Phillips, and William G. Haag
1955 Jaketown site in west-central Mississippi. *Am. Mus. Nat. Hist., Anthropol. Pap.* 45(1).

Ford, Richard I.
1974 Northwestern archeology: past and future directions. *Annu. Rev. Anthropol.* 3:385-413.

Forde, C. Daryell
1963 *Habitat, economy, and society* (5th ed.). Dutton, New York.

Fowke, Gerald
1894 Material for aboriginal stone implements. *Archaeologist* 2:238-335.
1928 Archaeological investigations - II. *Bur. Am. Ethnol., 44th Annu. Rep. (1926-1927)*, pp. 401-455.

Fowler, Melvin L.
1959a Modoc Rock Shelter: an Early Archaic site in southern Illinois. *Am. Antiq.* 24:257-270.
1959b Summary report of Modoc Rock Shelter 1952, 1953, 1955, 1956. *Ill. State Mus. Rep. Invest.* 8.

Fowler, Melvin L., and Howard Winters
1956 Modoc Rock Shelter preliminary report. *Ill. State Mus., Rep. Invest.* 4.

Freeman, Leslie G.
1968 A theoretical framework for interpreting archaeological materials. In *Man the hunter*, Richard B. Lee and Irven DeVore (eds.), pp. 262-267. Aldine, Chicago.

Frison, George C.
1967 Piney Creek sites, Wyoming. *Univ. Wyo., Publ.* 33.
1968 Functional analysis of certain chipped stone tools. *Am. Antiq.*, 33: 149-155.
1971 The buffalo pound in Northwestern Plains prehistory: Site 48CA302, Wyoming. *Am. Antiq.*, 36(1):77-91.

Funkhouser, W. D., and W. S. Webb
1930 Rock shelters of Wolfe and Powell counties, Kentucky. *Univ. Ky., Rep. Archaeol. Anthropol.* 4.

Geis, James W., and William R. Boggess
1968 The Prairie Peninsula: its origin and significance in the vegetational history of central Illinois. *In* The Quaternary of Illinois, Robert E. Bergstrom (ed.), pp. 89-95. *Univ. Ill. Coll. Agr., Spec. Publ.* 14.

Gibson, Jon L.
1974 Poverty Point: the first North American chiefdom. *Archaeology* 27(2): 97-105.

Goldstein, Lynne
n.d. Analysis of plummets in the lower Illinois River valley. Manuscript on file at Department of Anthropology, Northwestern University.

Griffin, James B.
1941 Additional Hopewell materials from Illinois. *Indiana Hist. Soc. Prehist. Res. Pap.* 2(3).
1952 Cultural periods in eastern United States archaeology. In *Archeology of eastern United States*, James B. Griffin (ed.), pp. 352-364. University of Chicago Press.
1968 Observations on Illinois prehistory in Late Pleistocene and early Recent times. *In* The Quaternary of Illinois, Robert E. Bergstrom (ed.), pp. 123-137. *Univ. Ill. Coll. Agr., Spec. Publ.* 14.

Griffin, James B. (ed.)
1952 *Archeology of eastern United States*. University of Chicago Press, Chicago.

Haggett, Peter
1966 *Locational analysis in human geography*. St. Martin's Press, New York.

Harn, Alan D.
1971 An archeological survey of the American Bottoms in Madison and St. Clair counties. *In* Archaeological surveys of the American Bottoms and adjacent bluffs, Illinois, pp. 19-39. *Ill. State Mus., Rep. Invest.* 21.

Henning, Dale R.
1961 Archaeological research in the proposed Joanna Reservoir, Missouri. *Mo. Archaeol.* 23:133-183.

Hester, Thomas Ray, Delbert Gilbow, and Alan D. Albee
1973 Functional analysis of "Clear Fork" artifacts from the Rio Grande Plains, Texas. *Am. Antiq.* 38:90-96.

Hester, T. R., and R. F. Heizer
1973 Problems in the functional analysis of artifacts: scraper planes from Mitla and Yugal, Oaxaca. *Univ. Calif. Archaeol. Res. Facility, Contrib.* 14:107-123.

Hill, Frederick C.
1972 *A Middle Archaic dog burial in Illinois*. Foundation for Illinois Archeology, Evanston.

Hodges, Henry
1964 *Artifacts: an introduction to primitive technologies*. A. Praeger, New York.

Holmes, W. H.
1919 Handbook of aboriginal American antiquities. Part 1: The lithic industries. *Bur. Am. Ethnol., Bull.* 60.

Houart, Gail L.
1971 Koster: a stratified Archaic site in the Illinois Valley. *Ill. State Mus. Rep. Invest.* 22 and *Ill. Valley Archeol. Program, Res. Pap.* 4.

Huntley, H. E.
1967 *Dimensional analysis*. Dover Publications, New York.

Jaehnig, Manfred
n.d. Archaeological malacology in the lower Illinois Valley: snails at Koster. Manuscript on file at Department of Anthropology, Northwestern University.
1974 Koster 1973. *Cent. States Archaeol. J.* 21(2)50-57.

Jelinek, Arthur J.
1966 Some distinctive flakes and flake tool types from the Llano Estacado. *Pap. Mich. Acad. Sci. Arts Lett.* 51:399-405.

Jolly, Fletcher, III, and Ralph G. Roberts
1974 Projectile point sequence at the Williams Shelter (23PH34) in the southern Ozarks of Missouri. *Cent. States Archaeol. J.* 21(2):58-78.

Judge, W. James
1971 Systems analysis and the Folsom-Midland question. *Southwest. J. Anthropol.* 26:40-51.

Kellar, James H.
1956 *Archaeological survey of Spencer County.* Indiana Historical Bureau, Indianapolis.

Kelley, H., and Robert F. Heizer
1962 Burins and bladelets in the Cessac collection from Santa Cruz Island, California. *Proc. Am. Philos. Soc.* 106:94-105.

Klippel, Walter E.
1969 Booth site: a Late Archaic campsite. *Mo. Archaeol. Soc. Res. Ser.* 6.
1970 Preliminary observations on heat-treated chert from Late Archaic and Woodland sites along the southern border of the Prairie Peninsula in Missouri. *Mo. Archaeol. Soc., Newsl.* 239:1-7.
1971 Graham Cave revisited: a reevaluation of its cultural position during the Archaic period. *Mo. Archaeol. Soc. Mem.* 9.
1972 An Early Woodland manifestation in the Prairie Peninsula. *J. Iowa Archaeol. Soc.* 19.

Knoblock, Byron W.
1939 *Bannerstones of the North American Indian.* Published by the author. LaGrange, Ill.

Kroeber, A. L., and S. A. Barnett
1960 Fishing among the Indians of northwestern California. *Univ. Calif., Anthropol. Rec.* 21(1).

Leroi-Gourhan, Andre
1943 Évolution et techniques. L'Homme et la matière. Éditions Albin Michel, Paris.
1945 Évolution et techniques. Milieu et techniques. Éditions Albin Michel, Paris.

Levins, Richard
1968 *Evolution in changing environments.* Princeton University Press, Princeton.

Lewis, Thomas M. N., and Madeline Kneberg
1959 The Archaic culture in the middle South. *Am. Antiq.* 25(2):161-183.
1961 *Eva: an Archaic site.* University of Tennessee Press, Knoxville.

Logan, Wilfred D.
1952 Graham Cave: an Archaic site in Montgomery County, Missouri. *Mo. Archaeol. Soc., Mem.* 2.

Luchterhand, Kubet
1970 Early Archaic projectile points and hunting patterns in the lower Illinois Valley. *Ill. State Mus., Rep. Invest.* 19 and *Ill. Valley Archaeol. Program, Res. Pap.* 3.

Luedtke, Barbara
n.d. Chipped stone tools: an experimental approach. Unpublished manuscript.

Martin, Paul S.
1971 The revolution in archaeology. *Am. Antiq.* 36(1):1-8.

McGregor, John C.
1954 Chrisman site, Illinois River valley Archaic culture. *Ill. State Archaeol. Soc. J.* 4(1):12-21.

McHugh, William P.
1973 "New archaeology" and the old copper complex. *Wis. Archaeol.* 54(2): 70-83.

MacNeish, Richard S.
1973 The scheduling factor in the development of effective food production in the Tehuacan Valley. In *Variation in Anthropology,* Donald W. Lathrap and Jody Douglas (eds.), pp. 75-90. Illinois Archaeological Survey, Urbana.

McQueen, H. S.
1929 Clay and coal resources of the Perry area (Missouri). *Mo., Bur. Geol. Mines, Bienn. Rep. State Geol., (1927-1928).*

Mellars, Paul
1970 Some comments on the notion of functional variability in stone tool assemblages. *World Archaeol.* 2(1):74-89.

Meyers, J. Thomas
1970 Chert resources of the lower Illinois Valley. *Ill. State Mus., Rep. Invest.* 18 and *Ill. Valley Archaeol. Program, Res. Pap.* 2.

Miller, James Andrew
1973 Quaternary history of the Sangamon River drainage system, Central Illinois. *Ill. State Mus., Rep. Invest.* 27.

Miller, Rex K.
1941 McCain site, Dubois County, Indiana. *Indiana Hist. Soc., Prehist. Res. Ser.* 2(1).

Montet-White, Anta
1968 Lithic industries of the Illinois Valley in the Early and Middle Woodland periods. *Univ. Mich., Mus. Anthropol., Anthropol. Pap.* 35.

Moorehead, Warren K.
1912 Hematite implements of the United States together with chemical analyses of various hematites. *Phillips Acad., Dep. Anthropol., Bull.* 6.

Morse, Dan F.
1971 The Hawkins Cache: a significant Dalton find in northeastern Arkansas. *Arkansas Archeol.* 12(1):9-20.

Munson, Patrick J.
1971 An archaeological survey of the Wood River terrace and adjacent bottoms and bluffs in Madison County, Illinois. *In* Archaeological surveys of the American Bottoms and adjacent bluffs, Illinois, pp. 1-17. *Ill. State Mus., Rep. Invest.* 21.

Munson, Patrick J. and Alan D. Harn
1966 Surface collections from three sites in the central Illinois River valley. *Wis. Archaeol.* 47(3):150-168.

Nance, J. D.
1971 Functional interpretations from microscopic examination. *Am. Antiq.* 36: 361-363.

Nero, Robert W.
1957 A "graver" site in Wisconsin. *Am. Antiq.* 22:300-304.

Newcomer, M. H.
1971 Some quantitative experiments in handaxe manufacture. *World Archaeol.* 3:85-93.

Oakley, Kenneth P.
1959 *Man the tool maker* (4th ed.). University of Chicago Press, Chicago.

Osgood, Cornelius
1940 Ingalik material culture. *Yale Univ., Publ. Anthropol.* 22.

Perino, Gregory
1954 The Titterington focus-Red Ochre. *Cent. States Archaeol. J.* 1(1):15-18.
1961 Tentative classification of plummets in the lower Illinois River valley. *Cent. States Archaeol. J.* 8(2):43-56.
1962 Review of Calhoun County, Illinois prehistory. *Wis. Archaeol.,* 43(2): 44-51.
1963 Tentative classification of two projectile points and one knife from west-central Illinois. *Cent. States Archaeol. J.* 10(3):95-100.
1968a Guide to the identification of certain American Indian projectile points. *Okla. Anthropol. Soc., Spec. Bull.* 3.
1968b The Pete Klunk mound group, Calhoun County, Illinois: the Archaic and Hopewell occupations. *In* Hopewell and Woodland site archaeology in Illinois, pp. 9-128. *Ill. Archaeol. Sur., Bull.* 6.
1971a Guide to the identification of certain American Indian projectile points. *Okla. Anthropol. Soc., Spec. Bull.* 4.
1971b The Mississippian component of the Schild site (No. 4), Greene County, Illinois. *In* Mississippian site archaeology I: site reports from the St. Louis and Chicago areas, pp. 1-148. *Ill. Archaeol. Surv., Bull.* 8.
1973a The Koster mounds, Greene County, Illinois. In Late Woodland site archaeology in Illinois: I., pp. 141-210. *Ill. Archaeol. Sur., Bull.* 9.

1973b Chipped flint celts. *Cent. States Archaeol. J.* 20(3):106-107.
1973c The Late Woodland component at the Pete Klunk site, Calhoun County, Illinois. *In* Late Woodland Site Archaeology in Illinois I, pp. 58-89. *Ill. Archaeol. Sur. Bull.* 9.

Pi-Sunyer, Oriol, John Edward Blank, and Robert Williams
1967 The Honey Run site (33Co-3): a Late Paleo-Indian locality in Coshocton County, Ohio. *In* Studies in Ohio archaeology, O. H. Prufer and D. H. McKenzie (eds.), pp. 230-251. Western Reserve University Press, Cleveland.

Pond, Alanzo William
1930 Primitive methods of working stone based on experiments of Halvor L. Skavlem. *Logan Mus. Bull.* 2(1).

Purdy, Barbara W., and H. K. Brooks
1971 Thermal alterations of silica materials: an archaeological approach. *Science* 173:322-325.

Reese, Don
1957 *Flint chipping.* Beedle, Carlsbad, New Mexico.

Ritchie, William A.
1932 Lamoka Lake site: type station of the Archaic Algonkin period in New York. *Res. Trans. N.Y. State Archaeol. Assoc.* 7(4).
1945 An early site in Cayuga County: type component of the Frontenac focus, Archaic pattern. *Res. Trans. N.Y. State Archaeol. Assoc.* 10(1).
1968 *Archaeology of New York State* (revised ed.). Natural History Press, Garden City, New York.

Ritzenthaler, Robert
1946 The Osceola site. *Wis. Archaeol.* 27(3):53-80.
1957 Reigh site report No. 3. *Wis. Archaeol.* 38(4):278-310.

Rogers, Edward S.
1967 Material culture of the Mistassini. *Nat. Mus. Can. Bull.* 218, and *Anthropol. Ser.* 80.

Roper, Donna C.
1974 The distribution of Middle Woodland sites within the environment of the lower Sangamon River, Illinois. *Ill. State Mus., Rep. Invest.* 30.

Rubey, William W.
1952 Geology and mineral resources of the Hardin and Brussels quandrangles (in Illinois). *U.S. Geol. Surv., Prof. Pap.* 218.

Sackett, James R.
1966 Quantitative analysis of Upper Paleolithic stone tools. *Am. Anthropol.* 68(2 of 2):356-394.

Saxe, Arthur Alan
1970 Social dimensions of mortuary practices. Unpublished Ph.D. thesis, University of Michigan. Ann Arbor.

Schiffer, Michael B.
1972 Archaeological context and systematic context. *Am. Antiq.* 37:156-165.

Schoenwetter, James
1972 Archaeological pollen studies in the lower Illinois River valley. Paper presented at annual meeting of the Society for American Archaeology.

Scully, Edward G.
1951 Some central Mississippi Valley projectile point types. *Univ. Mich., Mus. Anthropol.*

Seelan, R. M.
1961 Preliminary report of the Sedalia complex. *Mo. Archaeol. Soc., Newsl.* 153.

Selby, Samuel, and Leonard Sweet
1963 *Sets, relations, functions, an introduction.* McGraw-Hill, New York.

Semenov, S. S.
1964 *Prehistoric technology* (transl. by M. W. Thompson). Cory, Adams, and MacKay, London.

Shafer, H. J.
1970 Notes on unifacial retouch categories. *Am. Antiq.* 35:480-487.

Sheets, Payson D.
1973 Edge abrasion during biface manufacture. *Am. Antiq.* 38:215-218.

Shippee, J. M.
1948 Nebo Hill: a lithic complex in western Missouri. *Am. Antiq.* 14(1):29-32.
1966 Archaeology of Arnold Research Cave. *Mo. Archaeol.* 24(4).

Siegel, Sidney
1956 *Nonparametric statistics for the behavioral sciences.* McGraw-Hill, New York.

Simpson, G., A. Roe, and R. Lewontin
1960 *Quantitative zoology.* Harcourt, Brace, New York.

Smith, G. V.
1893 Use of flint blades to work pine wood. *Smithson. Inst. Annu. Rep. 1891*, pp. 601-605.

Smith, Philip E. L., and T. Cuyler Young, Jr.
1972 The evolution of early agriculture and culture in Greater Mesopotamia: a trial model. In *Population growth: anthropological implications*, Brian Spooner (ed.), pp. 1-59. MIT Press, Cambridge.

Smith, William A.
1971 A grooved axe typology. *Wis. Archaeol.* 52(1):20-41.

Snyder, John F.
1898 A group of Illinois mounds. *Am. Archaeol.* 2(1):16-23.

Spaulding, A.
1953 Statistical techniques for the discovery of artifact types. *Am. Antiq.* 18:305-313.

Speth, John D.
1972 Mechanical basis for percussion flaking. *Am. Antiq.* 37(1):34-60.

Struever, Stuart
1968a Flotation techniques for the recovery of small-scale archaeological remains. *Am. Antiq.* 33(3):353-362
1968b Problems, methods, and organization: a disparity in the growth of archeology. In *Anthropological archeology in the Americas*, Betty J. Meggars (ed.), pp. 131-151. Washington Anthropological Society, Washington.
1968c Woodland subsistence-settlement systems in the lower Illinois Valley. In *New perspectives in archeology*, Sally R. Binford and Lewis R. Binford (eds.), pp. 285-312. Aldine, Chicago.
1973 Chert utilization in lower Illinois Valley prehistory. In *Variation in anthropology*, D. W. Lathrap and J. Douglas (eds.), pp. 61-74. Illinois Archaeological Survey.

Struever, Stuart, and Gail L. Houart
1972 Analysis of the Hopewell interaction sphere. *In* Social exchange and interaction, Edwin N. Wilmsen (ed.), pp. 47-79. *Univ. Mich., Mus. Anthropol., Anthropol. Pap.* 46.

Swanton, John R.
1946 Indians of the southeastern United States. *Bur. Am. Ethnol., Bull.* 137.

Taylor, Walter W.
1948 A Study of archaeology. *Am. Anthropol. Assoc., Mem.* 69.

Titterington, Paul F.
1950 Some non-pottery sites in the St. Louis area. *J. Ill. State Archaeol. Soc.* 1(1):18-31.

Tuck, James A.
1971 An Archaic cemetery at Port au Choix, Newfoundland. *Am. Antiq.* 36(3): 343-358.

Turner, Richard
1965 Green Ridge: a Late Archaic site of the Sedalia complex in west-central Missouri. *Mo. Archaeol. Soc., Res. Ser.* 3.

White, Anta M.
1963 Analytical description of the chipped stone industry from Snyders site, Calhoun County, Illinois. *In* Miscellaneous studies in typology and classification, pp. 1-70, Anta M. White, Lewis R. Binford, and Mark L. Papworth (eds.), pp. 1-70, *Univ. Mich., Mus. Anthropol., Anthropol. Pap.* 19.

White, Leslie A.
1949 *The science of culture*. Farrar, Strauss, New York.

Willey, Gordon R., and Philip Phillips
1958 *Method and theory in American archaeology*. University of Chicago Press.

Wilmsen, Edwin N.
1970 Lithic analysis and cultural inference: a Paleo-Indian case. *Univ. Ariz., Anthropol. Pap.* 16.

Winters, Howard D.
1959 The Archaic period. *In* Illinois archaeology, pp. 9-16. *Ill. Archaeol. Sur., Bull.* 1.
1967 Archaeological survey of the Wabash Valley in Illinois. *Ill. State Mus., Rep. Invest.* 10.
1968 Value systems and trade cycles in the Late Archaic of the Midwest. In *New perspectives in archeology,* Sally R. Binford and Lewis R. Binford (eds.), pp. 175-221. Aldine, Chicago.
1969 The Riverton culture. *Ill. State Mus., Rep. Invest.* 13.

Witthoft, J.
1967 Glazed polish on flint tools. *Am. Antiq.* 33:383-389.

Wittry, Warren L.
1959 Raddatz Rockshelter: Sk5 Wisconsin. *Wis. Archaeol.* 40(2):33-69.

Wray, Donald E.
1952 Archeology of the Illinois Valley: 1950. In *Archeology of eastern United States,* James B. Griffin (ed.), pp. 152-164. University of Chicago Press, Chicago.

Wright, H. E., Jr.
1968 History of the Prairie Peninsula. *In* The Quaternary of Illinois, Robert E. Bergstrom (ed.), pp. 78-88. *Univ. Ill., Coll. Agr., Spec. Publ.* 14.
1974 The environment of early man in the Great Lakes region. *In* Aspects of Upper Great Lakes anthropology: Papers in honor of Lloyd A. Wilford, Elden Johnson (ed.), pp. 8-14. *Minnesota Hist. Soc., Prehist. Archaeol. Ser.* 12.

Yarnell, Richard Asa
1964 Aboriginal relationships between culture and plant life in the Upper Great Lakes region. *Univ. Mich., Mus. Anthropol., Anthropol. Pap.* 23.
1972 *Iva annua* var. *macrocarpa:* extinct american cultigen? *Am. Anthropol.* 74:335-341.

Zawacki, April Allison, and Glenn Hausfater
1969 Early vegetation of the lower Illinois Valley. *Ill. State Mus., Rep. Invest.* 17 and *Ill. Valley Archaeol. Program, Res. Pap.* 1.